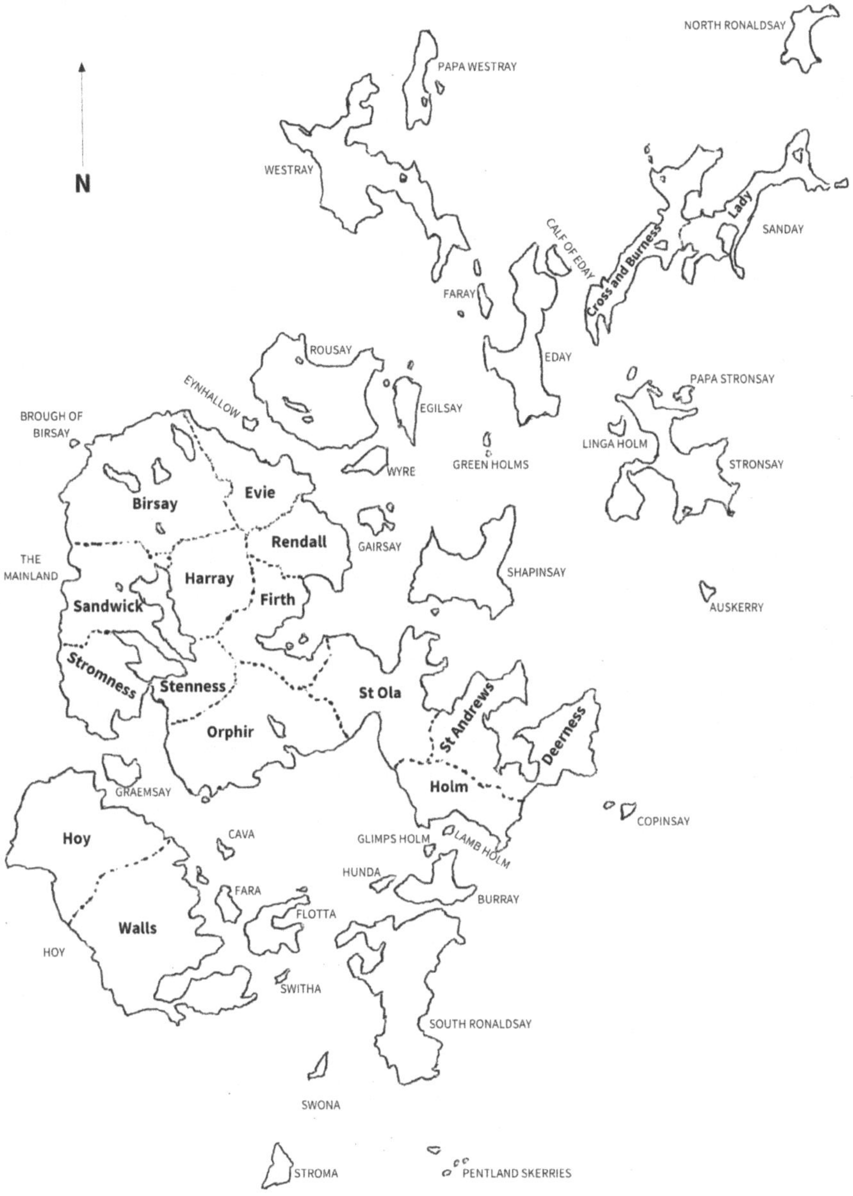
N
NORTH RONALDSAY
PAPA WESTRAY
WESTRAY
SANDAY
Lady
Cross and Burness
CALF OF EDAY
FARAY
EDAY
ROUSAY
EYNHALLOW
EGILSAY
PAPA STRONSAY
BROUGH OF
BIRSAY
LINGA HOLM
WYRE
GREEN HOLMS
STRONSAY
Birsay
Evie
Rendall
GAIRSAY
THE
MAINLAND
Harray
SHAPINSAY
Firth
Sandwick
AUSKERRY
Stromness
Stenness
St Ola
St Andrews
Deerness
Orphir
Holm
GRAEMSAY
COPINSAY
Hoy
CAVA
GLIMPS HOLM
LAMB HOLM
HUNDA
FARA
BURRAY
FLOTTA
Walls
HOY
SWITHA
SOUTH RONALDSAY
SWONA
STROMA
PENTLAND SKERRIES

A–Z of Orkney Placenames

Gregor Lamb

ORKNEYOLOGY
PRESS

Published by Orkneyology Press

Stromness, Orkney Islands

www.orkneyology.com

ISBNs:

978-1-915075-09-3 - hard cover
978-1-915075-10-9 - paperback
978-1-915075-11-6 - ebook

Book Sales:

https://shop.orkneyology.com/collections/orkneyology-press-books

Text © 2024 Gregor Lamb

Cover image © 2024 Britt Harcus

All rights reserved.

The contents of this book may not be reproduced in any form without written permission from the publishers, except for short extracts for quotations or review.

By the Same Author

Come Thee Wiz: Orkney Dialect Poems, Kirkwall Press, 1978

Nivver Spaek, Kirkwall Press, 1980

Orkney Surnames, Paul Harris Publishers, 1981

Hid Kam Intae Words: Orkney's Living Language, Byrgisey, 1986

Orkney Wordbook: a Dictionary of the Dialect of Orkney, Byrgisey, 1988

Sky Over Scapa, 1939–1945, Byrgisey, 1991

Aviation War Diary, 1939–1945, Byrgisey, 1991

Naggles O Piapittem: The Placenames of Sanday, Orkney, Byrgisey, 1992

Testimony of the Orkneyingar: The Placenames of Orkney, Byrgisey, 1993

The Orkney Dictionary, Orkney Language and Culture Group (with Margaret Flaws), 1996

Lamb's Tales: Gregor's Concert Stories, Byrgisey, 1997

Langskaill (novel), Byrgisey, 1998

Orkney Family Names, Bellavista Publications, 2003

Orcadiana: Pen Portraits of the Past, Bellavista Publications, 2004

Lamb's Tales: Another Wag, Kirkwall Press, 2004

Whit Like The Day?: Understanding Orkney Dialect, Bellavista Publications, 2005

Carnival of the Animals, Capall Bann Publishing, 2005

The Place-Names of South Ronaldsay & Burray, Bellavista Publications, 2006

Sky Over Scapa 1939–1945, expanded edition, Bellavista Publications, 2007

Willie's World, 1959 (based on his diary), Byrgisey, 2008

The Orkney Word Book, Byrgisey, 2012

The Amazing Journey of the Word Hogmanay, Byrgisey, 2013

Mary Ann O Linnabrake (novel), Byrgisey, 2020

Contents

Acknowledgements	1
Foreword	3
Introduction into the Origin of Orkney Placenames	5
The Placename 'Orkney'	9
Mysticism in the Placenames of Orkney	13
Notes on the Glossary of Placenames	17
A	21
B	29
C	73
D	107
E	119
F	129
G	143
H	171
I	211
J	217
K	219
L	239
M	263
N	287
O	301

P	311
Q	323
R	333
S	349
T	401
U	417
V	419
W	427
Y	443
Z	445
Appendix	447
References	453
About the Author	456

Acknowledgements

The cover is the work of Finstown artist Britt Harcus, who, on my advice, adapted a photograph the author had taken of a confusing signpost in southern Ireland. She cleverly catches the spirit of the photograph and sets the tone for a light hearted look at the diverse and sometimes amusing placenames in our islands.

Lastly, Tom Muir, the publisher of this book and a busy man, cannot be praised too highly for his enthusiasm about my undertaking and the enormous effort he made to get everything right. A number of entries in the glossary can be attributed to Tom himself. It has been a great pleasure to work with him and Rhonda.

Foreword

This book attempts to trace the origin of the placenames of Orkney — hills, coastal forms, farms, cottages and fields. No one has attempted anything similar before, with the exception of Dr. Hugh Marwick, Rector of Kirkwall Grammar School, who undertook studies in Rousay, North Ronaldsay and Stronsay. In the 1950s, he published the results of his outstanding research on the origin of Orkney farm names. Marwick's last foray into placenames was the study of the placenames of Birsay, ably assisted by a local man, William Sabiston of Scrutabreck, and Professor Wilhelm Nicolaisen, at that time, head of the School of Scottish Studies.

Thirty years ago, the University of Aberdeen made it possible for me, with the help of local folk, to make a thorough study of the placenames of the isle of Sanday. Alistair Cormack, Head of Sanday School, kindly organised the distribution of papers around the islands for local residents to record the names of fields and old houses which otherwise would have been lost. In this study, Karl Cooper was particularly helpful, allowing me to make use of detailed maps he had made of the island. The outcome was the publication of *Naggles o Piapittem, the Placenames of Sanday, Orkney*. Inspired by the interest in the placenames of South Ronaldsay and Burray shown by George Esson of St. Margaret's Hope, a very detailed study of South Ronaldsay and Burray was undertaken too, which led to the subsequent publication of *The Placenames of Burray and South Ronaldsay*.

Others who have added to our knowledge of Orkney placenames include Norwegian student Berit Sandnes, who undertook research into the placenames of Harray parish as part of her master's degree for the University of Trondheim and is now Professor of Placename Studies at the University of Bergen. All the placenames of Rendall were recorded and their origins tentatively explained by Robert Baikie of Rendall, who took his interest further by studying at the

University of the Highlands and Islands. The placenames of the district of Costa in Evie were noted and carefully mapped by Alistair Marwick, working in his own 'klogang'. Mary Bichan and Sheila Spence undertook a similar research project for the parish of Harray, mapping their location using the first Ordnance Survey sheets as a basis. The resulting booklet is indeed a treasure trove of old names. With the support of Shapinsay Community Council and Manpower Services Commission, Karen Wood named and mapped all the field names of the island of Shapinsay and she is to be congratulated on the superb work she did in this respect. Kirsty Sinclair was particularly helpful in solving problems relating to Westray placenames.

While I was studying the placenames of the islands, I was contacted by many individuals who wished to note a local placename which otherwise would have been lost. These included: Peter Leith and Johina Leith, Stenness; Len Wilson, Kirkwall; Frank Eunson, Stromness; Mrs Muir, Cornersquoy, Orphir; John Wood, Cruanbreck, Rendall; Ethel Young, Stromness; Ida Gorn, Holm; Mabel Eunson, Deerness; Magaret Flaws, Wyre; Margaret Horrie, Firth; Freda Brown, Firth; Nick Gould, Rousay; Ralph Groat, Birsay; and Ralph Faulkner, Eday. Without the work undertaken by all these contributors and researchers, many of whom, regretfully, have passed away, the compilation of this final list of placenames would have been much poorer.

Introduction into the Origin of Orkney Placenames

Thirteen thousand years ago, the islands were in the final stages of recovering from the Scandinavian Ice Sheet which, when it had completely melted, left widespread boulder clay, a sodden landscape and a few glacial erratics, the most striking of which is the Stone of Scar in Sanday — but it was the sodden landscape that made the real impression.

Many of the placenames in this glossary relate to when marshland reigned supreme in Orkney, very different to what we see today, and in fact very different from the landscape recorded by the Ordnance Survey in the 1880s. Our placenames are peppered with names relating to marshes and pools, many of which carry reference to 'smell' and 'stink', emphasising their stagnant nature. Several farms carry such names today, though mercifully disguised in the Norse language! 'Folster' in Birsay, 'Foubister' in Tankerness and 'Saither' in Dounby are examples. The Scots also made reference to foul smelling pools using the word 'kanker', which referred to the evil smell of decay, and crofts nearby adopted the word. As an example, there was a cottar house in Sellibister, Sanday, which carried the name 'Canker'. The 'Pows (pools) o Quoycanker', which lay on the side of 'Ravie Hill' in Birsay, show the association with water. A particularly interesting placename, 'Stumpo', is recorded in the Burness district of Sanday. It is a disguised form of 'Stinkpool'! The smell given off by these stagnant pools is caused by microbes digesting organic material and producing foul smelling hydrogen sulphide gas. A 'stinking' landscape was not unique to

Orkney. Before the English Fens were drained and turned over to agriculture, an early writer quoted by Annie Proulx in her book *Fen, Bog and Swamp*, described the Fens as a 'place of a thousand stinks'.

Gradually, vegetation cover re-established itself in Orkney after the ice retreated. When the vegetation died, deposits of peat, sometimes very deep, were formed. This was the landscape faced by Neolithic farmers who settled mainly on the coast, on the better soil and in areas where they could safely winter their delicate craft. They in turn were followed by a highly organised group of settlers in the Bronze Age and Iron Age who, in the absence of timber, found the horizontal beds of sandstone ideal for building their fortresses, or 'brochs' as they came to be named. In the 9th century A.D., a trickle of Scandinavian peoples who moved westward from their homelands heralded a much greater migration and settlement in Orkney. These settlers, like the Celts before them, spoke an Indo-European language and for the most part eliminated the Celtic names. It is for this reason that we have a fine collection of Norse names in the islands, but apparently few instances of Celtic, if we are to believe the work already undertaken on interpreting Orkney placenames. Researchers, blinded by the Norse elements in the placenames, gave scant attention to the Celtic. This was unfortunate, since there are many instances of placenames associated with water and marsh, which the accompanying glossary reveals.

After six hundred years of Norse occupation, the islands were transferred to Scotland and the Scots language began to replace Norse. As for the Norse language, the Scots interpreted the few extant charters that they did not understand, and many of these wrong interpretations appear on maps today. The best example is the change from Norse *Kirkjuvágr* to 'Kirkwall', in the belief that Norse *vágr*, which was pronounced 'wa', surely meant 'wall' instead of 'bay'. Eventually, the local Norse language, 'Norn', died out and the adjective 'nornaway' was applied to anyone who was old fashioned or cantankerous. Fortunately for us, hundreds of 'Norn' placenames were retained and appear on maps today.

With the demise of Scandinavian control of the islands, many Scots field names and house names were added to the list of placenames, but farm names and coastal names were largely retained, though in many cases so mangled that their interpretation is elusive. From the early 1800s onwards, a new type of placename appeared in the islands, brought back by those who had emigrated to foreign countries and returned, or who had visited them by nature of their occupation such as sailors or soldiers. 'Buxa' in Orphir is a good example of the latter. In the latter part of the 19th century, a variety of names, applied especially to crofts and often derogatory, were introduced. An example is 'Bucket' in Rousay and Evie, the name suggesting that an old bucket with the bottom removed made a good chimney. An interesting development was the use of Biblical names, many of which had no doubt been inspired by the local minister. For a long time, I was completely puzzled by the old house name 'Samaria' in South Ronaldsay; the solution can be found in the glossary. There are several examples of such Biblical names. An example is 'Jericho', not an entirely unsuitable name for a roughly built stone cottage where the walls were in danger of tumbling down!

The Placename 'Orkney'

Before our general introduction to the placenames of Orkney, we should consider the origin of the name 'Orkney' itself, perhaps the most difficult of all the names! The latter part of the name is easily explained. Norse *ey* is 'island' and the 'n' is said to be a Norse modification of the fundamental part 'ork'. In Norwegian, *erkn* was a big seal, dolphin or whale, in other words, a fat or plump animal. The word existed at one time in the dialect of North Ronaldsay, where it took the form 'erkny' and referred to a big seal. It is the root of this name 'orc/ork', which presents a huge problem.

The island group was first recorded by the Greek geographer Pytheas, who toured the coast of what became 'Britain' more than two thousand years ago, spending some time ashore in different locations. Pytheas called the isles 'Orcas', a name he must have been given by one of the natives. The name was later used by the Greek geographer, Strabo, writing at the time of the birth of Christ.

Several years ago, I wrote an article entitled 'What is an ork?' in my book *Orcadia, Pen-Portraits of the Past*. Although I discussed many possibilities for the origin of 'ork' — at the time of writing, I made no definite conclusion about its origin. In Gaelic, *uircean* is a pig. A similar word for pig, *orcán*, occurred in Middle Irish. 'Ork' was seemingly a pig, a fertility figure, a big, fat and powerful Earth Mother. There are very few instances of the name 'ork' in Orkney placenames. In the West Mainland, one of the runic inscriptions on the spectacular tomb of Maeshowe reads 'Orkahowe'. Why is it called 'Orkahowe'? This name must be highly significant, but the element 'howe' means only 'mound' and adds nothing to our understanding of 'ork'.

Of the other instances of 'ork', they are scattered in the east and south of the county only. In the 1653 Land Tax Register of Orkney, the 'Tumail of Orkeness' appears in North Ronaldsay in the 'Hollandstoun' district. There is no record of this placename today anywhere in 'Hollandstoun'. The word 'tumail' (Norse *tún-völlr*) is usually the best of land attached to a house name — but there is no trace of a house here today. Another instance of this root exists in the old farm name 'Ork' in Shapinsay. The farm has vanished but the name 'Ness of Ork' still exists in the extreme northeast of the island. Why should these ness promontories refer to a pig? In the East Mainland there is only one instance of an 'ork' placename and that is in the parish of Holm. It is 'Orkland quoy' which suggests an enclosure attached to a larger farm known as 'Orkland'. Like most of the other 'ork' placenames in Orkney, the location of 'Orkland' is unknown. On the island of Flotta, two distinctive reefs of solid rock called Big Ork and Little Ork protrude from the coast to create a peninsular form. There are two instances of 'ork' in Shetland. In his study of the placenames of Shetland, Jakob Jakobsen, the Faroese scholar, struggled with the 'ork' placenames which he found there. In Unst, he remarked on a steep rock promontory used as a landmark by fishermen and called 'Da Orka'. The placename 'Orka' in Shetland lies at the extreme southern end of 'Orka Voe'. To the west of 'Orka Voe' is a large peninsula called 'Caldback'. This name must have been substituted at one time for 'Orka(ness)'. Notice that most of these 'orks' are associated with promontories or nesses, just as some promontories are associated with Norse gods and goddesses, such as Thor, Odin, Inga and Freya.

We can go further with our connection between promontories and pigs if we consider the Norse word *göltr* 'pig'. There are several instances of peninsulas which carry this Norse name. There is 'The Golt' in South Ronaldsay at the right-hand entrance to St. Margaret's Bay and a very impressive peninsula called 'Golta' in Flotta, a site chosen by the oil industry. In Shapinsay 'The Galt' is a prominent peninsula in the northwest of the island and in North Ronaldsay 'Galtie Rock' is an outlying rock in Linklet Bay. Its position suggests that it was joined to the island at one time, in which case it would have made a very distinctive promontory. 'The Galt' is a ridge of rocks making a small headland in the Bay of Tresness, Sanday.

We can see from these examples that there is overwhelming evidence of an association between pigs and nesses. We find the same association between dedications to pagan gods and goddesses in peninsulas such as 'Thor' who gives his name to 'Torness' in Rendall, North Ronaldsay, Stronsay, Sanday and Walls. 'Odin' promontories are found in Sanday, Stronsay and Gairsay and the goddess 'Inga' in Sandwick, Westray and St. Ola. What is not understood, is the significance of peninsulas as dedication sites. The most significant peninsula of all — where neither 'ork', 'golt' nor a Norse god is named, is known simply as the 'Ness o Brogar', where 'Brogar' means 'bridge farm'. It cannot be an original name. The 'Ness of Brogar' is so significant that it must have had a special name. Perhaps the original was 'Orkaness'? Two thousand metres to the east as the crow flies, lies the pig-shaped 'Orkahowe' and there is little doubt that the two are closely connected spiritually.

One conclusion is that all these different landscape forms can be brought together by the meaning 'pagan sacred'. 'Orkahowe' (Maeshowe) is surely the supreme example of this. 'Orka' may have been a supreme goddess, the equivalent of the Old English goddess 'Erce', a word related to Gothic *airkns*, holy. The name of this goddess was frequently used in personal names, always along with another Anglo-Saxon element to give the idea of 'power' or 'eminence'. There are many examples to illustrate this, such as Eorcanbald which has come down to us as Archibald!

In Orkney, 'Ork' was adopted as a surname. The first instance noted is in Egilsay in 1695, where it takes the form 'Hork'. Like many medieval words and names, it collected an initial 'h' in transcription, just as 'ospital' in English became 'hospital', for example. The name (H)ork had appeared long before 1695. One of the runic inscriptions in Maeshowe mentions the patronymic name *'Orkasonr'*, someone who was 'son of Ork'. In 1449, there was a Walter Arcusson/Arcus, a Norse mercenary and one of the guards of the King of France. The 'Ork' surname must have initially carried the meaning 'holy', and everything associated with that word such as greatness, power and eminence. The Arcus families certainly lived up to these qualities, though they would have no idea of the origin of their surname. Robert, John and George Hercus fought in the Battle of Summerdale in 1529. William Arcas/Orcas, a bailie, was witness to a deed signed in Kirkwall in 1568 relating to lands in Sandwick, which suggests that he was bailie of Sandwick, a district official next in line to the Lawman, the supreme justice in Orkney. The names Arcus and Harcus became standard forms of the original 'Ork'. Harcus is by far the more common, concentrated particularly in Westray,

Papa Westray, Eday and at one time in North Fara. The written form 'Arcus', in the same area, is rare.

What are we to conclude about the origin of the placename 'Orkney'? In addition to what we have already said, it may be significant that, in the islands, during the most important fertility ceremony to take place — the wedding — the consumption of pork was taboo. On all other occasions, pork was consumed. It is a further pointer to suggest that Orka/Orca was one of that great pantheon of pre-Celtic/Celtic/Norse gods, whose roots lie deep in history and their association with peninsulas is unfathomable.

Mysticism in the Placenames of Orkney

Although Christianity took hold in Orkney, many of the mystical beings of the old religion remained and influenced the placenames and dialect of the islands. As an example, we begin with 'Cubbie Roo', first mentioned by Joe Ben in what was possibly the first quarter of the 16th century. He writes of the island of Wyre: 'Here there once lived a tall giant.' In Barry's *History of the Orkney Islands*, he quotes Joe Ben's belief that 'Cubbie Roo' is a form of the pronunciation of Kolbein Hrúga, a 12th century Norse chieftain who built a castle on the island of Wyre. It was this way that the fortification on the island came to be called 'Cubbie Roo's Castle'. Cubbie Roo has in fact, nothing to do with Kolbein Hrúga, who is an attested historical figure, so who or what is 'Cubbie Roo'?

'Koppierow', the original form of his name which appears in Ben's notes, gives us a clue. The 'row' element is Norse *rauðr* red and 'koppie' is related to German *Kopf* head. The name translates as 'Red Head', which places him alongside other sprites such as 'Redcap', an evil goblin who haunted the south of Scotland or, to give an English example, 'Rawhead', whose head was red with the blood of his victims. In Orkney, holes in wild rock cliffs are inhabited by a harmless sprite called Wattie Red (Norse *vaettr* spirit, *rauðr* red). A good example of such a hole can be found in the cliffs of the Brough of Birsay. Another example, the exact location of which is forgotten, was in the cliffs of Stromness parish. It appears that in a number of instances, only the word *rauðr* red, was applied to this spirit, the best example being the 'Hole o Row' in Sandwick. There is another 'Hole o Row' in Flotta and a 'Hole o Roe' in St. Andrews.

Cubbie Roo, like his Norse forebears, is a troll or a trow, associated with big rocks or stones and pools of water. 'Cubbie Roo's Lade' is a pier-like promontory in Stronsay. It is also referred to as the 'Danes Pier'. 'Dane' here refers to mythical beings as in Norse *berg-danir,* giants associated with rocks and stones. On the east coast of Shapinsay, the 'Burn o Trolldgoe' on the Galt peninsula has the alternative name 'Cubbie Roo's Burn'. There is an insignificant stream here and no ravine since 'goe', in this sense, is a 'marsh' (see Appendix).

These trolls loved throwing stones — at kirks or, in Orkney, at each other, and such stones can be found scattered throughout the islands. In Rousay, we have the 'Fingerstone', so called because it supposedly has the marks of Cubbie Roo's fingers on it. A fingerprint stone also lies in Eday, thrown by a troll on Rousay whom he must have offended! In Wyre, a boulder there is called 'Cubbie Roo's Rock', after a duel fought between Cubbie Roo and an adversary on Egilsay. There are other similar stones such as the one on Cruff Hill in Orphir which, according to legend, had been thrown from Hoy. There is yet another stone in Evie, though I'm unaware of its exact position. The 'Dwarfie Stone' in Hoy gets no mention of being a Cubbie Roo type stone, probably because it has lost its original name, but we can have a tentative attempt at establishing what it was.

The stone lies at the head of 'Trowie Glen', which suggests that the original name of the 'Dwarfie Stone' may have been the 'Trowie Stone' or 'Troll Stone'. Other uses of 'troll/trowie' in Orkney placenames are: 'Trolle Geo' in Evie; 'Trull', a small geo in Eday; 'Trolla Shun' (Norse *tjörn* pond) in Harray; 'Trollawatten' (Norse *vatn* lake) in North Ronaldsay; 'Trows Well' in Birsay and 'Trow's Buil' (*ból* resting place of the troll) in Sanday, which is part of an ancient earthwork wall, or 'Treb', which divided the island. Norse *jötunn* giant is used instead of a troll name, as in 'Yetnasteen' in Rousay and 'Yettna Geo' in Sandwick. In Burray, 'Echna Loch' is a corruption of Norse *jötunn,* so the name should read: 'Yettna Loch', which parallels 'Trolla Watten' in North Ronaldsay.

Some other names are recorded in Orkney for mystical beings. Take 'carlin', a troll woman, for example. The old name of 'Barrel o Butter', a small island in Scapa Flow, was 'Carlin Skerry'. Other instances of this name are in South Ronaldsay, 'Carlan Geo'; Stronsay, 'Carlin Geo' and in Sanday, 'Carlin Foot' or 'Giant's Foot'. 'Carlinghill', southwest of 'Brunt Hill' in Stromness, was the name given to a small cottage which at the time of the publication of the original Ordnance Survey map, was already abandoned.

In the Norse language, *gýgr* was an ogress but *gýgr* was also an abyss, a frightening depression in the landscape! In Orkney, this Norse word took the form 'gyre', sometimes with the modification 'gorie'. 'Gorie' was a sprite and appears as a cleft in the rocks east of 'Marwick Head' in Birsay, which was called 'Gories Bight'. 'Gories Saddle' is on the east coast of the Calf of Eday. 'Gorseness' in Rendall was originally 'Gorysness', which suggests that some point on the coast here, was favoured by Gorie. The word 'gyre' was also used in Scotland and sometimes took the form 'giral', a contraction of 'gyre-carlin'. A coastal point (presumably a cave) in Flotta was called 'The Giral's Hoose'. There are three other spirit names which appear in the placenames of the islands. Returning to the wild rocky cliffs of Birsay, a cave in a geo here is called 'Gunyasilya', the *hellir* (Norse 'cave') of 'Gunnie', another sprite. This Norse word is found only in Swedish today in the plural form *gonnar*, goblins. In Sanday, there is a field name 'Crue Maaron Deme'; '*Merran*' was a local spirit, her name being derived from Norse *marin* the ogress: 'Deme' = Scots 'Dame'. In the case of Sanday, the name really applied to a mound of burnt stones. 'Lucky Merran' was a Shetland witch and the witch/ogress name is also recorded in Westray in the saying: 'He's tin ap wi ither company like Merran Da's cat'. 'Merran' seems to be the equivalent of the Orkney witch 'Lucky Minni', whose name is recorded in Birsay and elsewhere, e.g., the local name for moorland cotton grass was 'Lucky Minni's oo' where 'oo' is Scots for 'wool'.

Glimps Holm in the South Isles has an intriguing name. It is a name which appears again on The Mainland in 'Glims Moss' near Dounby and in the 'Waal o Glumsgar' in Stenness. These locations are marshy damp places and it seems that the spirit haunting these places is a frightening 'Will o the Wisp' type figure. An interesting mythological figure recorded only once in Orkney is Norse *þurs*, a giant. He can be found in 'Trussens Geo' in Westray. Lastly some thought needs to be given to the well-known Rousay chambered cairn, 'Taverso Tuick'. 'Tooick' is a diminutive form of Norse *tó*, really a 'tuft' but also used in Orkney in the sense 'mound'. The Taver element is Norse *taufr*, enchantment or witchcraft but seems to be used here in the sense 'witch', since it appears in a genitive case, giving the meaning of this significant archaeological feature as 'the mound of the witch'.

Notes on the Glossary of Placenames

There are approximately ten thousand placenames in Orkney, and it was the writer's aim to interpret them all. However, after four years' research, it was decided to limit the study drastically to eight thousand. Many placenames quoted in this glossary have vanished for a variety of reasons, such as land use, but it is important nevertheless that they are included. The objective of this book is primarily to collect and interpret placenames but, in some instances, interesting little notes are added.

Where the word 'Norse' is used in the entries, 'Old Norse' should be substituted. Scots' 'loch' is used for 'lake' and coastal ravines are called 'geos', from Old Norse *gjá*.

A–Z of Orkney Placenames

from Aan to Zion

A

Aan Stenness: marked on the 1760 map of the Planking of Stenness, i.e., the Division of the Commonty [Norse *á-n* the stream: (see 'Waal o Aan')].

Aanie's Rig Rendall: Crook: personal name 'Annie' [formerly pronounced 'Aanie' in Rendall and Evie: Scots *rig* which in the old system of land holding was a strip of land (see 'Jaspert's Head Rig', Orphir)].

Aaways, The Sanday: a shoal off Newark [origin unknown].

Aber Loch Sanday: long since drained, it lay just northeast of 'Mires' in Cross: [Gaelic *eabar* mud, Irish *abar* marsh: Orkney dialect 'iper', midden ouse].

Aboon the Water Stronsay: above the 'Loch o Rothiesholm' [Scots *abune* above].

Aboondariggs Sanday: house name, Burness [Scots *abune* above, Scots *rig* strip of cultivated land].

Abune-Hoose Birsay: above 'Skelday' [Scots *abune* above, or higher up in this case: 'ap', or with the diminutive 'appie' was the normal word used on The Mainland of Orkney to describe a house in a higher position than its namesake].

Abytoon North Ronaldsay: position unknown [perhaps a form of the more common *Appietoon* the higher up field].

Ackalay Westray: [Norse *öxl* shoulder used metaphorically here of a hillside: the 'a' is a diminutive].

Ackerstoun Orphir: [Norse *akr* arable land].

Ackes Orphir: [probably *akr* as above (with English plural)].

Ackla Orphir: (see 'Ackalay' above).

Acklar, Slap o Rousay: [Norse *axlar* genitive of *öxl*, i.e., 'of the shoulder of the hill', Scots *slap* gate].

Addis Quarry (see below).

Addis's Sanday: alternative name for 'Otterswick' [a late 19th century owner had the nickname 'Addis' from his habit of agreeing to a statement by saying 'Ah, dis so' = 'It is so'].

Aiverso, Knowe o Papa Westray: (see 'Evars Knowe', Sanday).

Affall Flotta: [perhaps a form of dialect *tofall*, of a semi-detached building, 'falling or leaning to' but used here in the sense of 'detached field'].

Agla Bar Stromness: coastal name [suggests Norse *öxl* shoulder of a hill plus a diminutive 'a' and *boði* a shoal which usually takes the form 'baa' in Orkney placenames].

Aglath Stenness: (see below).

Aglath, Braes o Harray/Firth boundary: [Norse *öxl* shoulder but also the shoulder of a hill: notice that in Orkney *öxl* is neuter gender which explains the 'th' suffix].

Aiclstoun Stenness: [Norse *öxl* shoulder of a hill].

Aikerbister Holm; Evie; Westray: [Norse *akr* arable land, Norse *ból-staðr* normally a significant farm].

Aikers Orphir; St. Andrews; South Ronaldsay: [Norse *akr* arable land (with English plural)].

Aikerskaill Deerness: [Norse *akr* arable field, *skali* dwelling which can mean 'hut' or 'large residence'! In Orkney dialect, a 'forskal' was a protective porch which carried a similar meaning in Norse *forskali*. Since Aikerskaill had arable land, it probably fell into the category of 'a large residence'].

Air 1. Swona: the gravelly landing area in 'The Haven' [Norse *eyrr* gravel beach].

Air 2. Walls: [Norse *eyrr* gravel beach].

Airaby Sanday: vanished house/farm near 'Tresness' [Norse *eyrr* beach, *bær* farm settlement].

Airafea Sanday: (see 'Erafea').

Airafea/Erafea Stronsay: a farm [Gaelic *airigh* a hillside animal shelter; Norse *fjall* hill].

Airckebister Harray: 1637 [possible misspelling of 'Aikerbister', not otherwise recorded].

Aire of Burness Sanday: 'Whitemill' area [Norse *eyrr* beach].

Airon, Airan, Arion Sanday: [the farm lies at the end of a gravel bank: Norse *eyrr* gravel bank, *endi* end].

Airy Birsay; Stronsay; Westray; Sanday: [Gaelic *airigh* a shieling].

Ais Geo Stronsay: [suggests an inlet with a stream running into it: Norse *gjá* deep inlet, Gaelic *uisge* water or stream: the 'Burn of Ess' forms part of the boundary of the parishes of Sandwick and Birsay].

Aisdale St. Ola: [Gaelic *uisge* water (i.e., stream), Norse *dalr* dale].

Aith 1. Sandwick: [there is no isthmus here: probably the Norse personal name *Eiðr*, the farm name etc. being lost (see 'Ettit')].

Aith 2. Stronsay; Walls: [Norse *eið* isthmus].

Aithsdale Walls: (for 'Aith' see above) [Norse *dalr* shallow valley, in this case].

Aitkilith Harray: [see 'Aglath' above for explanation].

Aiverso, Knowe o Papa Westray: (see 'Evars Knowe', Sanday).

Alister's Geo Sanday: [Norse *gjá* sea inlet: personal names usually relate to favoured spots, for example for rock fishing].

Allegar Sanday: [Norse *ali-dýr* cattle, *garðr* farm].

Allibelli Geo South Ronaldsay: [Norse *ali* (as above), *boeli* animal enclosure, presumably there was such a pen in the close vicinity, Norse *gjá* ravine].

Alma South Ronaldsay: [after the battle fought in the Crimean War in 1854].

Almoney Rendall: recorded in the 1841 Census [origin unknown: perhaps after an occupant with the rare English surname 'Almoney'?].

Altar, The South Ronaldsay: [offshore rock, presumably like a pulpit].

Altars o Linay North Ronaldsay: (see above).

America Sandwick: field on Lyking [presumably there was a house here at one time: many foreign placenames were brought back to Orkney by returning Orkneymen (cf. 'Canada' in Birsay)].

Anchor Cottage Sanday: [fanciful name, 'at anchor' = retired].

Ancum/Anckhum North Ronaldsay: 1653 [Norse *eng* meadow, *hólm* a small island: the ancient settlement of the house is elevated and the low-lying surrounding land would have been water-logged, drying out in the summer to make wonderful water meadows, in fact, the area to the south of Ancum Loch is called 'Enyan', Norse *eng-in* 'the' meadow].

Ancum Loch North Ronaldsay: (see above).

Anderswick Stenness: 'Anderwirk' in 1653 [the latter form 'wirk' is probably correct: a rare use of Norse *virki* in the sense 'modest building': the only other examples in Orkney are 'Arwick' in Evie and 'Workwell' in Orphir: *virki* is normally used to describe forts such as 'The Work' in Rousay or the prehistoric structure at the 'Head of Work' in St. Ola, Norse *Andres* Andrew].

Andrew Davison's Quoy Birsay: [Norse *kví* enclosure: the Davi(d)sons were first recorded in Birsay in 1595: the position of the enclosure is unknown].

Andrew's Ebb Sanday: ['ebb' is used in Orkney in the sense 'foreshore': Andrew might have been entitled to collect ware, i.e., seaweed, from this part of the shore to use as manure].

Angerquoy/Quoyangry Westray, Broughton: [Norse *engjar* meadows, *kví* enclosure].

Anglybar South Ronaldsay: [Norse *berg* rock, 'angling' rock? All around the Orkney coast there were favoured fishing spots on rocks].

Angusquoy Holm: [the surname 'Angus' was first recorded in Orkney in the early 16th century, Norse *kví* enclosure].

Annabreck Sanday: [probably for 'Hangiebreck': Norse *hengi* slope, *brekka* slope: to the south of Annabreck is the 'Brae o Annabreck'].

Annabreck, Brae o (see above).

Annags South Ronaldsay: [a house occupied by 'Ann' with diminutive suffix 'ag', which usually takes the form 'ick' in the South Isles].

Annie Harpers Rendall: (see 'Quarryhole).

Annie o Airon's Creu Sanday: Inner Holm [(see 'Airon'): Gaelic *crò*/Norse *kró*, enclosure].

Annie's Geo Sanday: [Norse *gjá* ravine].

Annynsdeall Holm: [Scots surname 'Annand', which later took the form 'Annal', Norse *deild* division of land].

Antabreck/Antibreck North Ronaldsay: [Norse *önd* duck, *brekka* slope: (see below)].

Antashun Harray, Netherbrough: [Norse *önd* duck, *tjörn* pool i.e., (wild) duck pond!].

Ap-trow Birsay: Northside, 'Quoys o the Hill' [English 'up through', a nickname for an ale house! There were also 'Doontrow' placenames in Orkney: a '*trow-gjeung*', i.e., 'a through going', in Orkney dialect was a pathway].

Aphouse Orphir, Kirbister: ['ap' usually takes the form 'appie' as below; it means 'the upper house'].

Appiehoose Sanday; Stenness; Firth; Sandwick: (see above).

Appieteen Stromness: Garth [in this case 'teen' = Norse *tún*, a large enclosed piece of land which is often anglicised to 'town' in placenames].

Appietown Sandwick; Rendall; Evie: (see above).

Arch Land Sanday: Elsness, 18th century [perhaps 'Archdean's Land?' (see below)].

Archdeansquoy Shapinsay: [land which paid tributary to the Archdeanery of St. Magnus Cathedral in Kirkwall].

Are/Air Westray: probably refers to 'Airy' (above).

Arian Stromness: (see 'Ayrean').

Aribea/Erraby Stronsay: a field to the northwest of Holland [Norse *eyrr* beach ridge, *boer* farm: there is no evidence of such a farm today].

Ark 1. Birsay, Marwick: [Norse *örk* a large chest and formerly used in Orkney and Shetland dialect in this sense, e.g., 'butter ark' as in the 'Neuar Sang' sung at the end of the year in Orkney. In Norwegian dialects, *ark* can describe cottage features such as a garret and has an extended meaning in Orkney and Shetland dialect to 'cottage'. There are six 'Ark' cottages in Shetland, two in Orkney].

Ark 2. Westray, Rackwick: (see above).

Arneip South Ronaldsay: [Norse *örn* eagle, referring to the sea eagle which had favourite resting sites, *gnúpr* headland].

Arnesk Evie: [probably the same place as 'Askiday' (below): Norse *ár-inn* the streams, Gaelic *uisce* water or stream].

Arp Burray; Flotta: [origin unknown; there is a possibility that the placename is a corruption of 'Ark'].

Arquoy Evie: [Norse personal name *Ari*: *kví* enclosure].

Arraquoy Harray: (see above).

Arsdale Evie: [Norse personal name *Ari*, Norse *deild* division of land].

Arsgiddie Evie: [a corrupt form of 'Askiday' below].

Arstais, Arstas, Erstas Sanday: [Norse personal name *Ari*, Norse *staðr* farmstead but usually applied to a large stretch of land like an estate (see 'Costa')].

Arvoquoy Stronsay: [Norse *arfi* inherited, *kví* enclosure: (cf. 'Ervadale')].

Arwick Evie: [Norse personal name *Ari*: (see 'Anderswick' for further explanation)].

Askiday, The Midden o Evie: [a combination of Gaelic *uisce* water or stream and Norse *dý* bog, both seemingly referring to sludgy ground].

Atla South Ronaldsay: [see 'Ackla' and 'Ackalay' for explanation: the location would apply to 'Kirkie Hill' here].

Augmund Howe Sanday: Elsness, probably the remains of a chambered cairn [Norse *haugr* mound, on the land of *Ögmund* (see 'Avaldsay' below)].

Auks, The Eday: coastal feature northeast flank of Noup Hill [perhaps Norse *öxl* shoulder: used here metaphorically of the shoulder of a hill].

Aurabister Sanday: [Norse *aurr* clay, *ból-staðr* farmstead].

Auskerry An island [Norse *aust(r)-sker* east skerry (see 'Pentland Skerries'), Norse *sker* reef *was* rarely applied to large islands; five families lived on 'Pentland Skerries' in the early 19th century: one family has lived on Auskerry for over 30 years caring for a flock of North Ronaldsay sheep, in case the native North Ronaldsay animals are wiped out by disease].

Avaldsay Rousay: [Norse *Augvalds-haugr* a mound on the land of *Augvald*].

Aversque Evie: [Norse male personal name *Alvar* (see 'Evershowe', below), *kví* enclosure].

Avidale Rendall: [a farm lying in a slight valley above a stream on the side of 'Gorseness Hill': Norse *á* stream, *fjall* hill, *dý* marsh: (cf. 'Ravie Hill', Birsay)].

Axe, The South Walls: [small island in 'Axe Geo' (below)].

Axe Geo South Walls: [early Celtic as in Old Irish *easc* water which suggests that there is a spring in the cliff face here (see 'Axna' and 'Exna' forms below), Norse *gjá* ravine].

Axna Geo Eday: [as above but shows a Norse definite article suffix].

Axnaday Birsay, Gelderhouse: a powerful spring in low-lying ground [(for 'Axna' see above), Norse *dý* marsh].

Axness Geo Sanday: [Norse *haugs-nes* mound point, Norse *gjá* ravine].

Axni Geo 1. Rousay: (see 'Axna Geo', Eday).

Axni Geo 2. Sandwick: (see 'Axna Geo', Eday).

Ayran Sanday: (see 'Erran').

Ayre Sanday, Cross; Orphir; Holm: [Norse *eyrr* usually a gravel beach ridge].

Ayre/Barns of Ayre Deerness: on the shore facing Copinsay: because of the threat of flooding by the sea, it was rebuilt inland [see 'Ayre' Sanday, above, for explanation].

Ayre of Langamay Sanday: [Norse *eyrr* gravel spit, Norse *langr* long, *melr* gravel (bank)].

Ayre of Skaill Rousay: (see 'Ayre' above and 'Skaill').

Ayre o Leashun Stronsay: formed by a shingle bar across a bay (see 'Ayre' above: see also 'Leashun').

Ayre Sound Sanday: [(see 'Ayre' above), Norse *sund* a channel of water between two islands].

Ayrean Evie: [Gaelic *aerigh* summer hill pasture or the hut in such an area: the word was adopted in Norse but given a neuter gender: in Orkney it had a feminine/masculine gender: nearby are the 'Styes o Aikerness'].

B

Baa, The Sanday: a reef [Norse *boði*].

Baa Green o Rinnabreck/Runnabreck Sanday: (see 'Baa' above and 'Rinnabreck' below).

Baa o Strangquoy Sanday: (see 'Baa' above and 'Strangquoy' below).

Baa o Tanger Sanday: (see 'Baa' above and 'Tanger' below).

Baa (Bars) o Trevan/Baa o Thrave, Sanday: [Norse *boði* a reef, literally 'warner' (to boats): (see 'Trevan' and 'Thrave')].

Baa Taing Auskerry: [Norse *tangi* point of land (see above)].

Baabie Tait's Clive Birsay: ['clive' is usually written 'cliv' in Orkney placenames: Norse *klyfja* to split which in Orkney applies to a path in a cliff face giving access to the sea, in this case, probably to collect shell sand for poultry: there is no record whatever of such a person in Birsay: it is said she was a witch so the name may relate to a spirit: (see 'Walter Reid')].

Babbie's Sanday: Braeswick, Cross [a former occupant with the name 'Barbara' lived here].

Babbo's Rendall, Upper Cottiscarth: [a field name still retaining the name of the inhabitant of a house which once stood here: Barbara Wood?].

Back, The Orphir: [part of 'Hangaback'].

Back Castra Geo Birsay: (see 'Castra Geo').

Back Geo Sanday: in Burness [English 'at the back'].

Back Geo o Clett Evie: (see 'Geo o Clett').

Back Holm Sanday, Burness: island 'at the back' [Norse *hólmr* island].

Back Longaber Birsay: [a rock at the back of 'Longaber'].

Back o Mires Sanday: (see 'Mires').

Back o the Quoy North Ronaldsay: (see 'Backaquoy').

Back o the Treb Sanday: ['at the back of the Treb' (see 'Treb')].

Back Pund's Geo Sanday, Cross: (see 'Punds Geo').

Backakelday Holm, Westerbister: [Norse *bakki* slope, *kelda* well].

Backaland Eday: [Norse *bakki* slope].

Backalie Orphir: [both elements from Norse *bakki* slope, Norse *hlíð* slope].

Backans Birsay, Hayon: field name [Norse *bakki-nn* the slope or bank: there is a field on that farm called 'Banks'].

Backaquoy 1. North Ronaldsay: in the Westness area [Norse *bakki* slope (towards a beach in this case) *kví* enclosure].

Backaquoy 2. South Ronaldsay: [Norse *bakki* slope (towards a beach in this case), *kví* enclosure].

Backaquoy, Point o Firth: near the farm of 'Burness' (see below).

Backarass Westray, Dykeside: [possibly a transferred name from 'Batyeras/Backarass' near 'Saviskaill', Rousay, since the translated name does not fit its position in the landscape: (see 'Batyeras')].

Backaskaill 1. Papa Westray: (see 'Breckaskaill').

Backaskaill 2. Sanday: [Norse *bakki* slope but in Orkney was also used to describe a 'shore bank': the farm is at the edge of the shore: Norse *skáli* had two meanings, 'house' or 'hall': in this case it would have been 'hall' (see 'Sutherbie')].

Backaskaill, Bowman's Sanday: [Scots *bowman* tenant farmer but in Orkney it meant 'farm servant' so these were farm servants' cottages].

Backatown Firth: [John Firth in his *'Reminiscences of an Orkney Parish'* referred to this small district of Redland in Firth as 'Badyateun'].

Backber o Klett Birsay: (as above; see 'Klett').

Backber, Geo o Evie: [English 'back' in the sense 'to the rear', Norse *berg* rock, *gjá* ravine].

Backbighouse St. Ola: recorded once only in the 1492 Rental; it lay in the 'Saverock/Hatston' area [English 'at the back of the big house'].

Backhose Firth, Binscarth: [Norse *bakki* slope: 'hose' is difficult to interpret: there is a Hoswick in Shetland and Hosin/Hosen placenames in Shetland and Orkney: Norse *hauss* skull suggests 'lump' when applied to landscape features. 'Backhose' could be an old name for 'Harpers Howe', a mound on the hill slope above Binscarth farm].

Backness North Ronaldsay: on north side of 'Dennis Ness' [Norse *bakki* slope, *nes* point of land].

Backsaddles Hoy: no information [English 'saddle' in a hill].

Backsillers Rousay: part of the cliff on 'Scabrae Head' [suggests Scots *sellar* a kind of storeroom which could be a basement, hence 'caves at the back' used metaphorically here].

Backwargarie Sanday, Tresness: field name ['backwar' = backward in the sense of 'towards the back', Norse *geiri* a triangular strip of land].

Backwater North Ronaldsay: a burn flowing from 'Sandsheen Loch' to 'Hookin Loch' along Linklet [Norse *bakki* slope (of the 'Ayre')].

Badyateun Firth: called 'Back of Town' in 1851 Census and earlier 'Redland': afterwards it was referred to as 'Backatown' [John Firth in his *Reminiscences of an Orkney Parish* referred to this small district of the half tunship of Redland in Firth as Badyateun: this seems to be the correct name: it was here in the 15th century that we presume John Baddie lived: he was a kinsman of John Flett, the Lawman of Orkney at that time, who also lived in Redland: (see 'Backatown')].

Baikie Sheed Stronsay: fields to the west of 'Mount Pleasant' [Scots *shed* a piece of ground, Norse *bakki* slope].

Baikie Skerry Westray: just off 'Berst Ness' and south of 'Langskaill' [Norse *sker* a reef, *bakki* slope].

Bailie Fea Walls: [many hills in Orkney were named after the fires which were lit on the top to commemorate festival days, particularly St. Johnsmas Day, Norse *bál* fire, Scots *bale* beacon faggot, Norse *fjall* hill].

Bailies Knowe Birsay/Sandwick: (see 'Bellies Knowe').

Baillie Hill Firth; Evie: (see above).

Bailliequoy Firth: [(see above), Norse *kví* enclosure].

Baillieval/fiold Stenness/Firth border: north of 'Hill of Lyradale' [see 'Bailie Fea', above, for explanation].

Bain Sandwick: [Norse *boer* farm settlement with the Norse definite article *inn* suffixed (see 'The Bay', Stronsay)].

Baits, Point o the St. Ola: a name given to part of the coast south of 'Lingro' [Norse *beit* pastureland which usually takes the form 'Bett' in Orkney placenames: here it applies to the inland coastal area].

Baka/Bakka Westray, Fribo: [Norse *bakki* slope].

Bakegar Firth: position unknown [Norse *bakki* slope, *garðr* wall or farm].

Bakhow Sandwick, Wasbister: vanished [a Magnus Bakhow lived here at the end of the 16th century; perhaps this placename gave rise to the Orkney surname 'Baikie': Magnus Baikie is recorded in Isbister Sandwick before 1534: Norse *bakki* slope *haugr* mound].

Baki Ber Deerness: (cf. 'Back Ber o Klett').

Bakingstone Hill Walls: [Norse *bakki-inn* the slope (it has an exceptionally steep southern slope) and *stein* standing stone, is a suggestion: there is no recorded standing stone (which can be quite small) in that area (see 'Crustane')].

Bakkakelday Holm: [Norse *bakki* slope, *kelda* well].

Bakkakeldie North Ronaldsay: (see above).

Bakkan Swarto Firth, Redland: [Norse *bakk-inn* the slope, *svartr* black, referring to heather cover probably].

Balaclava Shapinsay, South Ronaldsay, Sanday, Flotta: [named after a battle of that name fought in the Crimean war: it is difficult to account for similar house names related to the Crimean War such as 'Alma', 'Inkerman', 'Sebastopol' etc.].

Balarat South Ronaldsay: [named by an emigrant to Australia who returned home from the goldfields there (see 'Bendigo')].

Bald Willie/Bold Willie Sanday: a smooth rounded rock below the water line in Cross [Norse *boði* reef, 'ba' in dialect, *vella* to boil: whirlpools in Orkney were sometimes called 'wells': (cf. 'Wells o Tiftaly', South Ronaldsay)].

Balfour's Brae Sanday: Cross parish (see below).

Balfour's Geo Sanday: [two Balfour brothers from 'Backaskaill' in Sanday got into difficulties at sea: one lost his life, the other took refuge in this ravine, Norse *gjá* ravine: 'Balfour' was not a common surname in Sanday].

Ball Hill South Ronaldsay: (see 'Bailie Fea' for explanation).

Ballarat Harray, Netherbrough: (see 'Balarat').

Ballasquoy/Bullersquoy Evie: [Norse *bolir* bulls (with additional English plural!), *kví* enclosure].

Ballgreen South Ronaldsay, Burwick: [a field set aside for playing the game of 'ba', this game is played today only on Christmas Day and New Year's Day in Orkney where the 'Uppies' in the higher part of the town of Kirkwall play the 'Doonies'. It is principally a game of rugby with no referee and no rules].

Banks 1. Holm: ['banks' placenames are almost always on slopes or near a beach: English form of Norse *bakki* slope: not surprisingly it gave rise to the Orkney surname 'Banks', first recorded in 1548 and widespread in Orkney but now confined principally to South Ronaldsay].

Banks 2. Flotta; Orphir; Rendall; Rousay; Birsay; Sanday; Stronsay; Westray: (see above).

Banks o Traddletown Shapinsay: (see 'Traddletown').

Banno Water/Bannawatten North Ronaldsay: a small boggy area on 'Dennis Hill', originally a small stretch of water [Norse *baen* prayer, a suggestion that this water had healing properties (see 'Loch o St. Tredwell')].

Banta Bay North Ronaldsay: the position, like the etymology, is unknown.

Bar, The Sanday: shoal running east from the beacon of 'The Riv' [Norse *boði* shoal].

Bar, The o Pool Sanday: a rock feature in Pool Bay [similar to the 'Danes Pier' in Stronsay: local people believed that these 'piers' had a supernatural origin].

Bar Root o Clarkshouse Sanday: 18th century field name [English 'baroot' a field in which the crop 'bere' (a primitive form of barley) is grown two years in succession (see 'Clarkshoose')].

Barameero Firth, Wasdale: a hillside shared with 'Barmira' Binscarth below [Norse *barð* edge of a hill and *mýrr* with a variety of meanings all relating to poor quality, usually wet soil; the suffix 'o' is a diminutive].

Barber's Tuo/Tower Sanday: a mound west of 'Backaskaill' ['barber' is a puzzling name, perhaps a corruption of the first name 'Barbara': 'tuo' is a corruption of Norse *Þúfa* mound, and 'tower' is the plural form *Þúfa*].

Barboss, Birboss Sanday: a shoal in the 'Bay of Lopness' [Norse *berg* Rock, *boði* shoal (with English plural)].

Bardieflaws South Ronaldsay: field name [Norse *barð* edge of a hill, *flá* strips of meadowland].

Barebraes Rousay: [English 'bare', Scots *brae* slope].

Barebreck Evie: [English 'bare', Scots *breck/s* poor land].

Barebrecks South Ronaldsay: (see above).

Barfie Stronsay: northeast of 'Whitehall' farm [Norse *barð* edge of a hill, *fjall* hill].

Barm Firth: [Norse *barmr* edge, e.g., of a loch/stream: unsure how the word is applied here].

Barmira Firth, Binscarth: part of the hillside to the west of 'Binscarth House'; this name is shared with the adjacent farm of 'Wasdale' where it is called 'Barameero': in this case 'a' is a diminutive].

Barn Wyre: vanished but still remembered by the 'Brae o Barn' (see 'Barron').

Barn, The Birsay: a rock (near The Stable!).

Barnettsdeal Holm: [Norse *deild* division of a piece of land, a 'Swyne (Sveinn) Barnet' was recorded in Holm in 1601. Several old Orkney records confirm that the surname Barnett is a corruption of the Norse personal name *Bjarni*].

Barnhouse Birsay, Southside: [as above, the barn of 'Vigga', a significant farm, which lay on this site].

Barni Taing South Ronaldsay: [Norse *bjarni* bear, animal names were sometimes given to coastal features: (cf. 'Honey Geo')].

Barnhouse Stenness: [the 'barn' of what was obviously the head house of the tunship of Stenness].

Barrel o Butter Orphir: a small island in Scapa Flow [so called because the owner offered the right to hunt seals here on the payment of a barrel of butter. The original name of this island was 'Carlin Skerry'].

Barrenha' North Ronaldsay: [English 'barren' which usually referred to poor land, 'ha' is Scots *hall* but is used here pejoratively in the sense 'small cottage'].

Barrets Deerness, South Keigar: field name (see 'Baroot o Chung').

Barron South Ronaldsay: a farm recorded in the 'Aikers' district in the 17th century [English 'barren'].

Barrot o Chung Sanday: [Scots *baroot* is the grain 'bere' grown in ground where it had been grown before, Norse *tjörn* pool].

Bars o Thrave/Trevan: Sanday: a shoal off 'The Riv' [Norse *boði* reef: The 'Riv', a long rocky peninsula, must be seen as a barrier, hence the name 'Thrave' applied to it: notice the definite article suffix].

Barswick South Ronaldsay: [Norse *barð* edge of a hill, *vík* bay].

Barth Head South Ronaldsay: (see above for etymology).

Basso Rendall: near 'Appieteen' [Norse *báss* cow house].

Batavia South Ronaldsay, Widewall: a vanished house [probably named by a seaman around the year 1800 when Napoleon renamed Holland as 'Batavia'. Batavia was formerly capital of the Dutch West Indies and approximates to what is now Jakarta].

Bathgate Birsay, Northside: pronounced Batyith, in the Ordnance Survey Name Book it is referred to as 'Bitgarth' [in Orkney, Norse *bati* improvement, developed the special meaning 'source of an improvement in health' as in Norse *batnaðr* convalescence, Norse *gata* is 'path' so the placename Bathgate means 'path to a place which offers the hope of better health', in this case it would have been St. Magnus Kirk where the sagas record miracle cures, Norse *garðr* enclosure].

Batquoy Harray: an enclosure [Norse *kví* enclosure, *bati* improvement, usually of health but more likely to be 'soil' here].

Batyaloan Harray: (see 'Batyerass', below).

Batyebreck Harray: (see 'Batquoy').

Batyeras/Backarass Rousay: beach feature near 'Saviskaill' [Norse *bakki* slope but in Orkney can also mean 'shore bank': (see 'Coldrass', Birsay, for possible explanation)].

Bawks Birsay, Greeny: [probably Norse *bálkr* the normal meaning of which is 'beam' as in dialect 'couple baak' a cross beam in a building; here it would mean an earthen wall (see 'Gerbo')].

Bay, The Stronsay: [Norse *boer* farm settlement with English definite article 'the' (compare 'Bu' forms and see 'Bain')].

Baywest Stronsay: originally 'Rothiesholm-Bewes't, i.e., 'West Rothiesholm': [Norse *boer* farm].

Bazlie Sanday, Elsness: field name, [Norse *báss* a cow house, Norse *hlíð* a slope].

Be o Barn Wyre: (see 'Barn').

Bea 1. Sanday: Cross parish, another name for Housegarth, now part of 'How', Kettletoft [Norse *boer* farm. There is another 'Bea' on 'Saville', Burness parish, but now only a field name].

Bea 2. Birsay; Sandwick; Stenness; Stromness; Harray: (see above).

Beafield Sanday: possibly an old house site because of its position on top of a mound: no archaeological investigation has been conducted here (see 'Bea' above).

Beaslie Sanday: West Brough, Cross parish (see 'Bazlie' above).

Beawly Sanday, Northwall: vanished house [Norse *boeli* farm].

Beboran Harray: [Norse *boer* farm: 'boran' suggests Norse *borg-in* 'the fortified tower', i.e., a broch: there is no such broch in the immediate vicinity though there are several close by which suggests that this is a name transferred from one of these sites].

Bee Skerries Stronsay: east of Dritness [probably one of the many variants of Norse *boði* reef].

Beeman, Taing of St. Andrews: [Norse *tangi* point of land: there was a 'Quoy-bewmont' in that area in 1492: a James Beamond lived in Holm in 1701].

Beeniesfield Firth: [a form of the personal nickname 'Bina'].

Beetho Rendall: a field name on 'Brettobreck' with an old well [Norse *bati* improvement which suggests that the well water had healing properties (see 'Bathgate')].

Beglo/Breckerhouse Birsay: [Norse *brekkur* slopes: according to the *Orkneyinga Saga* Richard farmed at *Brekkur* in Stronsay: 'Beglo' was the nickname of a former inhabitant].

Bell Dag South Ronaldsay, Windwick: a rock in the sea [Norse *böllr* ball-shaped, *dagr* day: at one time the rock must have been used as a so-called 'day mark' by a farming family, i.e., when the sun was above this rock, it was a certain time of day. Such 'day marks' were common in Iceland].

Bell Heum Harray: [a former very marshy area which suggests that 'heum' here means Norse *hólm* a small island elevation above a low-lying marsh (compare 'Ancum')].

Bell Kirk Sanday: alternative name for Cross Kirk [the only kirk on the island to have a bell tower. The bell came from the German emigrant ship *Johannas* which foundered on 'Howar Sand' in 1861 but which was successfully refloated].

Bellaquoy Firth: (see 'Bailliequoy').

Belle o Juip Orphir: [Norse *bál* fire, i.e., location of a Johnsmas fire festival; *djúp* deep, almost always referring to a marshy area (see 'Jubidee')].

Bellies Fiold Orphir: also called Burgir [Norse *bál* fire, *fjall* hill: a hill on which a fire festival was held].

Bellies Knowe Birsay, Marwick: [Oliver Bellie was recorded here in 1627].

Belltower Westray, Aikerness: [recorded as a small farm in the 1880s Ordnance Survey: an imported name].

Belyafiold Birsay: (see 'Bellies Fiold' above).

Belyegrate/Belyagrut North Ronaldsay: a ridge of loose stones sheltering the naust (boat shelter) of 'Stuan' [Norse *grjót* stones, the prefix suggests *böllr* round shaped].

A–Z OF ORKNEY PLACENAMES

Belyer Sanday: the west reef of 'The Riv' [Norse *böllr* round shaped (stones), *garðr* wall in a metaphorical sense].

Bendigo St. Ola: [named by an emigrant returning from Bendigo, the gold mining centre in Australia].

Bengie's Corner Sanday: Burness parish [named after Benjamin Drever who had a smithy here in the late 19th century (see 'Smithscott')].

Benistay Sanday: on the coast south of North Mire [Norse *boenar-staðr* place of (heathen) prayer in this case: the reason for the choice of such a place is unknown: perhaps water related, hence a pool?].

Benlaw Evie: near Mounthooly [a fanciful name apparently given by a Baikie family sometime before 1861].

Benni Kuml Stronsay: [Norse *beini* help, *kuml* a cairn: invoking the help of a spirit thought to be inside was forbidden even in heathen times because it smacked of sorcery].

Benston Hall Eday: [the Benstons were first recorded in Westray in 1595; long established in Eday: Scots *ha* cottage].

Bent Geo Burray: [English 'bent grass' growing near the ravine, Norse *gjá*].

Benzieclett Sandwick: [Norse *beini* help, *klettr* rock but inland the word was applied to some kind of stone-built structure, a cairn or even a broch (see 'Klett' in the Appendix)].

Benziecot Westray: [Norse *kot* small building, cottage etc. (see above)].

Benziecott Sanday: (see above) [one of these could be a transferred Name].

Benzieroth Firth: locally pronounced 'Binyaroo' [Norse *beina-hrúga* a cairn of stones, a 'helping cairn', i.e., where a traveller would have said a prayer: (see 'Benzie' forms above)].

Ber Log Hoy: [Norse *berg* rock, 'log' is a corruption of the more common 'lod' or 'lo' from Norse *hláð* load. In other words, this is a rock where cargo may be loaded (see 'Lober Rock', South Ronaldsay)].

Ber of Twitha Cava: a rocky point to the northeast of the island [Norse *berg* rock, *þváttr* washing but what the washing refers to here is uncertain, perhaps fulling cloth (see 'Well o Twitheday')].

Bergiben Wyre: [Norse *berg* landing place: 'giben' suggests family name Gibbon introduced to Orkney before 1821 in Stromness but unknown in Wyre or nearby Rousay].

Bergoodale/Guidall Rousay: a ruinous cottage in Sourin in 1947 when Hugh Marwick was collecting Rousay placenames [an intriguing placename: the Goodalls were first recorded in Orkney in 1577 when Michael Goodall was a burgess of Kirkwall; the name appears in several 16th century charters and was still apparently extant in Orkney until the 19th century: it must have existed in Rousay at one time: 'ber' is probably Norse *berg* referring to a large offshore rock where small boats could load or discharge cargo (see 'Lober Rock')].

Berridale Westray; Hoy, Rackwick: [Norse *berr* open, bare or perhaps *berg* hill, Scots *dale* a piece of land].

Berriedale South Ronaldsay: (see above).

Berry, The Walls: (see above).

Berry Head Rousay: [Norse *berg* hill].

Berry Hill St. Ola: [Norse *berg* hill].

Berry Moss Birsay, Dirkadale: (see above).

Berry, Glen of the Walls: [Gaelic *glean* valley (for 'Berry' see 'Berridale' above)].

Berrybank Evie: (see 'Berridale' above).

Berrybraes Evie: (see above).

Berryburn Evie: (see above).

Berstane Sanday: Cross parish, an old house now vanished stood here [probably a transferred name from Berston in South Ronaldsay].

Berston 1. South Ronaldsay: [Norse personal name *Bersi*, Norse *staðir* estate].

Berston 2. St. Ola: [Norse personal name *Bersi*, Norse *staðir* estate].

Beskyer Stronsay: a reef on 'Dritness' [Norse *boði* reef, *sker* reef].

Bessy Jenkin's Sanday: now vanished: it lay on Hermisgarth land [there were Jenkinsons in St. Ola in the 17th century but none have been recorded in Sanday].

Beten Longie Rousay, Wasbister: [Norse *beit* pasture land was neuter in Norse but here it is masculine/feminine, *langr* long].

Betts (The) Stromness, Garth: (see above).

Betts 1. Birsay, Cavan: (see above).

Betts 2. Birsay, Howe: (see above) [English plural].

Betty Anderson's Birsay, Northside: vanished: it stood near 'Cauldhame'.

Betty Omand's South Ronaldsay: field name, Kirkhouse [Betty Omand was born in 1807: it is remarkable that this field name, the site of her house, is still known].

Betty's Sanday: Cross parish [personal name: this house is still occupied].

Betyihoose, Sanday: coastal feature Ire, Burness [Norwegian *bedehus* chapel: there is no such chapel near here today, but the placename evidence suggests that such a prayer house existed].

Beuly Road Sanday: (see 'Boulie Road').

Bevan Sanday: rocks, the position of which is unknown: only referred to as such in relation to the shipwreck in this location of the *Margaretta* of Amsterdam in 1767 [possibly a corruption of 'Trevan'].

Bewan North Ronaldsay: [Norse *boe-inn* the farm].

Bewan Papa Westray: (see above).

Bewin Birsay, Northside: (see above).

Bias Knowe Birsay, Marwick: a burnt mound [named after the local owner in the late 1880s, James Bias of South Waird, Scots *knowe* knoll].

Biest Harray: recorded in 1771 [origin uncertain: perhaps 'bi-east', i.e., to the east?'].

Big Bushan Sandwich, Lyking: field name [Norse *boer* farm, *tjörn* stretch of water e.g., pond or pool (see 'The Bush')].

Big Howe St. Andrews: a mound in the parish [Norse *haugr* mound].

Big Less Papa Westray: (see 'Little Less').

Big Links Sanday: [Scots *links* sandy stretches near a shore].

Bigbreck Birsay, Twatt: [Norse *bygd* settlement, *brekka* slope].

Bigging Birsay, Twatt (now 'Twatt Farm'); Birsay, Greeny; Shapinsay; Westray, Rackwick: [Scots *bigging* a building].

Biggings St. Andrews; Stenness; South Ronaldsay; North Ronaldsay, Senness: (see above).

Bight o Hamnavoe Copinsay: lies to the west of 'Corn Holm' [Norse *hamn* a haven, *vágr* bay].

Bight o Lindy Evie: [Celtic *linne* pool, Norse *dý* marsh or poor quality soil].

Bight o Lotheran Sanday: [English *bight* = bay, Norse *hljóð* sound (of the sea): several words were used in Norse to describe such a sound (see 'Loth')].

Bight o Scessan Copinsay: lies to the south of 'Corn Holm' [a difficult name to interpret. It may be Norse *skessa*, an ogress: the rocky nature of this area would seem to add credence to this interpretation].

Bights Sanday, Ire: coastal feature [English *bight* little bay or indentation].

Bigland Rousay: [Norse *bygð* settlement].

Bigoo Harray: [English 'big': Norse *haugr* mound].

Bigore Head South Ronaldsay: a prominent headland [Norse *eyar* islands (see 'Owers o Stews')].

Bigswell Stenness: a district and a difficult name to interpret ['Big' may be a lost Norse personal name, several of which are found in Orkney, e.g., *Kjarrekr* who farmed Cairston and *Garékr* who gave his name to Gairsay: the personal name here could be the rare Norse *Bicci* and *völlr* field].

Bilinga, Brae o Harray: [Norse *boer* settlement, *langr* long].

Bill Rosies South Ronaldsay: personal name [field name to the west of Biggings/Cleat: William Rosie lived in Lower Bigging in 1851].

Billiescarth Eynhallow: mentioned in Ordnance Survey description of 'Eynhallow' [corruption of 'Helliascarth'].

Billy Geo Evie: [Norse *boeli* enclosure: presumably an animal pen existed near here at one time (see 'Allibelly' Geo, South Ronaldsay)].

Bimbister Harray: [Norse *boer-inn* the settlement, *ból-staðir* farm: the 'b' of *ból-staðir* changes the 'n' of *boer-inn* to 'm'].

Bing Well Eynhallow: [Norse *baen* prayer: position unknown; this may have been the original holy well which gave Eynhallow its name].

Binga Fea Walls: a significant 600-foot-high hill (compare 'Bingascarth', one of the earlier recorded names of 'Binscarth') [Norse *baen* prayer, *fjall* hill: the significance of the association with prayer is unknown: perhaps at one time playing the same role as 'Croagh Patrick' in Ireland].

Bingwall Evie: position unknown [may have the same origin as 'Bing Well' (above)].

Binkly Sanday, Newark: field name [origin uncertain: Old English *benk* bench, Ork. dialect 'bink' stone shelf, 'ly' may possibly be explained as *hlíð* slope].

Binna's Kirk Papa Westray: [Norse *baena-hús* chapel].

Binnaquoy Firth: [Norse *baen* prayer, *kví* enclosure: sometimes enclosures could be quite small (see 'Whilco')].

Binscarth Firth: [Norse *baen* prayer, *skarð* a pass through hills: probably the site of an old well in the hill saddle].

Binyaclaith Harray: [Norse *baen* prayer *klettr* cairn (see 'Benzieclett' and 'Klett' in the Appendix)].

Birboss Reef Sanday: (see 'Barboss').

Birran/Boren/Borrieness Sanday: field name between Stove and Warsetter [origin unknown].

Birs Labis Holm: a flattish rock on the coast to the east of 'The Gloup' [a very difficult name to interpret: the nature of the rock suggests that 'Labis' might be a contraction of hlað-*berg a* rock (with English plural). *hlað-berg* means 'loading rock', i.e., a rock which may be used as a pier: origin of 'Birs' unknown].

Birsay A parish in the northwest of the 'Mainland' (see 'Burray Taing' for explanation).

Birsi Geo South Walls: [probably Norse first name *Bersi*, *gjá* ravine].

Birtie's Quoy Stronsay: on Stebb Hill ['Birtie' = 'Bertie', Norse *kví* enclosure].

Bis Geos/Bisgoes Westray, Dykeside: [Norwegian *bust*, Orkney dialect 'biss' bristles, used here in the sense of 'coarse grass': quite often the surrounding vegetation gives a name to the ravine, Norse *gjá* (see Greenie 'Geo/Go' Orphir)].

Biscuit and Butter North Ronaldsay: [location and origin unknown].

Bisgarth Evie: [(see 'Bisgeos' above for 'bis' element), Norse *garðr* enclosure].

Bismira Firth, Binscarth: [see 'Bisgeos' above for 'bis' element and 'Baramira'].

Bitch Ha Firth: an uncomplimentary name for 'Croonofinya' (below).

Bitgarth Birsay: (see 'Bathgate').

Bizber, Point o St. Andrews: [origin unknown].

Black Chapel Firth: in the 'Thickbigging' area of Finstown ['black' suggests a supernatural association referring perhaps to the superstitious practice of going round such old sites on the knees in the hope of a cure or of good luck].

Black Craig Stromness: [Scots *craig* = *crag*].

Black Geo Orphir: [Norse *gjá* ravine].

Black Ha Birsay: near 'Lower Grindally' [Scots *ha* cottage, 'black' probably relates to the appearance of what originally was a heather-thatched cottage, the walls of which were made of turf: compare the 'black houses' of the Western Isles].

Black Hammers Rousay: rocky exposures on the hillside [Norse *hamarr* rock].

Black Holm Copinsay: [Norse *hólmr* island (for 'black' see 'Black Knowe')].

Black Holm Kiln Copinsay: [sea spray in a storm is compared here with smoke from the grain-drying kiln on Orkney farms: 'black' may refer to the grass blackened by the salt in the sea spray].

Black Knowe 1. Birsay, Greeny Hill: [Scots *knowe* = knoll, heather-covered in this instance].

Black Knowe 2. Rendall, Blubbersdale: field name [Scots *knowe* = knoll, 'black' in this instance probably relates to heather cover].

Black Moss o Evrigert Rendall: (see 'Evrigert').

Black Nev Hoy: [Norse *nef* nose used metaphorically applied to a high rock east of Rackwick].

Black Rock 1. Sanday: a rock on the shore of Otterswick Bay which marks the meeting point of the three parishes Burness, Cross and Lady (for 'black' see 'Black Chapel' above).

Black Rock 2. Sanday: near the 'Point o Nevin': it was from this rock that the passenger and mail boat to North Ronaldsay sailed: later a pier was built.

Blackawall Flotta: [this placename appeared in the 1871 census of Orkney; also referred to as 'Blackywall' and 'Bleckawell': origin uncertain].

Blackbraes Stenness; Stromness; Orphir: [Scots *brae* slope, English 'black' in the Scots sense 'heather-covered'].

Blackfield Stronsay: (see 'Bleachfield').

Blackhall St. Ola; Stronsay: (see 'Black Ha').

Blackpow/Bleakpow Stronsay: a dwelling house [probably originally named after a local pool, (Norse *pollr*); it was surrounded by three wells in the Ordnance Survey of 1879!].

Blackpows Walls: (see above).

Blaland Firth, Horraldshay: [Norse *blá* blue-black, probably relates to heather cover].

Blan Loch Stronsay: ['blan' has a Norse root with meanings related to 'blow' as for example in Shetland dialect *blan* wind, hence 'exposed': it lies on the isthmus connecting Rothiesholm to the rest of Stronsay and is in fact very exposed (see 'Blanster' below)].

Blans Firth, Ouraquoy: [probably an abridged form of 'Blanster' (below): this example from Firth is very exposed].

Blanster South Ronaldsay: also referred to as 'Blosetter' [Shetland dialect *blan* wind hence 'exposed' (see 'Blan Loch' above), Norse *setr* temporary summer hut].

Blaster Hole Deerness: [a natural rock bridge on the 'Horse of Copinsay' through which the sea 'blasts' in a storm].

Blaten Evie: a flat area at the mouth of the 'Burn of Whitemire' [Norse *blað* literally a leaf but used of anything flat, Norse *endi* end, applying to the stream: the Norse word *óss* was usually used for the mouth of a stream].

Blates o Northskaill Sanday: flat rocks on the sea coast (see 'Blaten' above for interpretation).

Bleach Knowe Stronsay: location unknown.

Bleachfield, Blackfield Sanday: a vanished house in Cross parish [a field where linen was bleached (see 'Bleach Knowe')].

Bleaching Green, The Sanday: (see 'Runnaclett').

Bleet South Ronaldsay: on 'East Masseter', field name [Norse *bleyta* mud].

Blemish Knowe Sanday: former name of 'The Knowe' [Scots *blemish* to destroy or damage].

Blett Eday: houses near the coast overlooking Carrick [probably Norse *blað* literally a leaf but used for anything flat].

Bletts 1. Birsay, Upper Fea: (see above).

Bletts 2. Sanday: rocks (see above).

Bletya-dieth Birsay: [Norse *bleyta* mud, *dý-it* the bog].

Bletyith Birsay: (see above).

Blindie Sanday: a skerry off the coast of Burness [Norse *blind-sker* 'blind' in the sense that it is normally under water and cannot be seen].

Blinkbonny Burray; St. Ola; Westray; Stronsay; South Ronaldsay; Rendall: the Rendall 'Blinkbonny' was usually called 'Blink' until the name was changed to 'Scottshall'; [a common Scots placename meaning 'lovely place'].

Blinkim Evie/Rendall: [possibly a form of 'blink' above].

Blitchen Slates South Ronaldsay: location uncertain [an old name for 'Liddell Loch'? (see 'Bludgeon Loch' Sanday for explanation): Norse *bleyta* mud, *tjörn* small lake, *sletter* smooth of stone etc.].

Bloie Geo South Ronaldsay: [English 'blow', Norse *gjá* ravine].

Blomer/muir Flotta: a house [English 'blow', Norse *mýrr* poor land].

Bloodo Firth, Coubister: [Norse *blautr* wet and muddy, *dý* bog].

Bloody Quoys Deerness: (see above) [Norse *kví* enclosure (with English Plural)].

Bloody Rock Sanday: near 'Helliehow', Burness parish [said to mark the site of a feud over seaweed division which may be true since the normal explanation of 'bloody' placenames in Orkney does not apply here].

Bloody Tuacks Westray: mounds on west side of Fitty Hill [(see 'Bloodo' above), Norse *þúfa* mound with dialect suffix 'ck' (with English plural): (see 'Dog Too')].

Bloomro Firth, Coubister: [probably a form of 'Blomer' (above)].

Blossan, The Rousay: an exposed ridge on eastern slope of 'Kearfea' [related in some way to Norse *blása* to blow].

Blotchniefiold Rousay: [Norse, probably related to *blotna* to become moist or soft, perhaps a reference to sphagnum moss here, *fjall* hill].

Blow Geo/Sinclair's Geo Birsay: an exposed ravine [the names of individuals often appear in the names of coastal features, frequently as a result of a tragedy, Norse *gjá* ravine].

Blow Harray: exposed area of poor land [English 'blow'].

Blow Hole o the Standard Evie: [a hole in the rock through which storm winds and waves blow (see 'Standard')].

Blowhigh Rousay, Westness: [name for an exposed cottage which is now ruinous].

Blowholes Rousay: (see above).

Blows Deerness: a house (see above): an 'Aim' family once lived here!

Blows Moss South Ronaldsay: [Norse *blása* to blow (see Blossan above)].

Blubbersdale Rendall: [Norse *blábers-dalr* blueberry valley].

Bludgeon, Loch of Sanday: [Norse *bleyta* mud, *tjörn* small lake].

Blue Clett North Ronaldsay: flat rock on the coast near Howar [Norse, probably in the sense blue/black often used for coastal rocks, *klettr* rock].

Blue Geos Rousay: (see above).

Blue Hole Evie; Sanday: a deep circular, ravine said to be bottomless! (see above).

Bluebraes Rendall: (see 'Blubbersdale').

Blut Shun Sandwick: [Norse *blautr* wet or miry, *tjörn* small lake].

Bluthamo Harray: [see *blautr* (above), *mór* moor].

Bluthers Geo Stronsay: [related perhaps to Norwegian *buldra* to make a Noise, Norse *gjá* ravine].

Blythemo Evie: (see 'Bluthamo').

Blythemor Rendall: (see above).

Bo, The Stronsay: a rock in Mill Bay [Norse *boði* reef].

Boar, The Papa Westray: a tidal race off the north end of the 'Mull o Papay' [Norse *bára* a wave or tidal race].

Boardhouse Birsay, Southside: apparently land and house set aside to provide sustenance for the Earl of Orkney when in residence in Birsay.

Boat Geo North Ronaldsay; Evie; Sanday: a ravine where it is possible to haul up a boat [Norse *gjá* ravine].

Boat Meadows Evie: [coastal area where boats may be safely hauled during winter].

Boats Hellia Evie: a flat rock where a boat may approach [Norse *hella* a flat rock].

Boats Myre Sanday: near 'Whitemill Point': [area of poor soil where boats may be hauled during winter, Norse *mýrr* poor soil].

Bockan Sandwick: formerly 'Brocken' [a local form of Norse *brekkan* the slope].

Bocky Birsay, Ingsay: field name [probably marks the site of a 'Bockyha'].

Bocky/Bockyha Birsay: a ruinous house east of Swannay Post Office [many old houses built in the 19th century had such nicknames, probably a house believed to be haunted by a 'bogle'].

Boden Papa Westray: flat rocks on east side of Papa Westray, south of 'The Boar' [Norse *boði* reef, the 'n' suffix represents the definite article, i.e., 'the reef'].

Boggie Burn Orphir: [English 'boggy'].

Bogie Evie: (see above).

Boglan Geo Papa Westray: on the east coast [Orkney dialect 'bogle' to make a loud noise like a bull, a variant of English 'bugle': nearby is 'Bull Flag'].

Bold Willie Sanday: (see 'Bald Willie').

Boloquoy Sanday, Cross parish [Norse *boli-kví* bull enclosure].

Bomasty Stronsay: a house [Norse *boli-mór* poor land where a bull is Kept, Norse *stía* animal enclosure, usually for pigs (see 'Steegolt')].

Bomo Hill of Eday: [Norse *boli-mó* poor land where a bull is kept].

Bonie-hole Rousay: on the west side of 'Mansmas Hill' [Norse *baena-hóll* prayer hill: the name 'Mansmas Hill' suggests that it was here where a fair was held annually on 16th April to mark the feast of St. Magnus (compare 'Georgemas' in Caithness): a large stone which formerly lay in this location may have marked the spot].

Bookan Sandwick: (see 'Brocken').

Boondamira Rendall: on Hall of Rendall land: poor land for crofters [Scots *abune* above, Norse *mýrr* poor land].

Boondatoon St. Andrews; Stronsay: [Scots 'abune (above) the toon'].

Boondland Sanday: land given over to crofters [Norse *bondi* worker on the land].

Boorin/Quoyburing Deerness: [Norse *borg-in* which suggests the site of a vanished 'broch'].

Boos Breck Sandwick: a ruin on a hill slope south of 'Doehouse' [Norse *bú* farmstead, *brekka* slope].

Booth South Walls: at the head of 'Kirk Hope' [Norse *bøð* is normally applied to a temporary shelter built of wood (see 'Nethabooth') but in this case it would have been far more substantial, built as a storehouse for those engaged in the fishing industry. 'Booth' is a very common placename in Shetland where many of these booths were built by Hanseatic merchants, principally Dutch, pre-19th century].

Booth, Kirn o Birsay: [Norse *bøð* temporary hut (for fishermen in this case), *kirna* a churn, a reference to the churning of the sea below].

Boothie Geo Flotta: (see 'Bothy Geo', Burray).

Bor Taing Hunda: island off Burray [Norse *bára* wave but used in Orkney in the sense 'tidal race' (see 'The Boar'), *tangi* a point of land].

Boray: island off Gairsay, Rendall: [relates possibly to the tidal race between Gairsay and the 'Holm of Boray', Norse *bára* wave, *ey* island (see 'Bor Taing')].

Bore, The Papa Westray: (see 'The Boar').

Borehammer Rousay: on Faraclett Head [Norse, *hamarr* rock face, *bára* 'waves' usually used in Orkney to describe a tidal race: perhaps it refers to the churning of the sea around the many reefs here].

Boreland Sanday: a vanished farm mentioned in Burness in the 1601 Rental: probably related to the choppy waters off 'The Riv' (see 'Well o Nesgar') [Norse *bára* wave].

Borrowland South Ronaldsay: [probably Norse *borg* in the sense of 'rounded hill', referring to the spur of 'Ward Hill'].

Borrowstone Hill St. Ola: [Norse *borg* rounded hill, English 'stone'. probably the location of a low stone marker].

Borwick Sandwick: [Norse *borg* defensive tower, *vík* bay].

Bosan Westray: [Norse *boði* reef, *sandr* sand].

Bosker, Rock of Birsay: [Norse *boði* reef, *sker* reef].

Bosquoy Harray: [Norse *bólis-kví* bull enclosure].

Bossack St. Andrews: [Norse *botns-vík* the bottom or end of a bay: Norse *botn* usually takes the form 'Button' in Orkney placenames and means 'end of a field' for example].

Botany Bay Sanday: original name of this house was 'Leaquoy' [probably renamed by an emigrant returned from Australia as in the case of 'Balarat' and 'Bendigo' for example].

Both Hellia Stronsay: [Norse *boði* reef, *hella* flat rock].

Bothabir, Gloup o Orphir: on the rocky coastline south of 'Twartquoy' [Norwegian (Nynorsk) *gloppa* a big hole in a cliff: Norse *boði* reef, *berg* rock].

Bothy Deerness: a small cottage (see 'Bothy' above).

Bothy Field Birsay, Howan: (see 'Bothy' above).

Bothy Geo Burray: [a sea inlet where a fisherman's hut would have Existed, Scots 'bothy' a booth, Norse *gjá* ravine].

Botquoy Deerness: mentioned in the 1502 Rental of Orkney: position unknown but probably near 'The Gloup' [suggests Norse *bót/baetr* a place of prayer for betterment of health etc. (see 'Helly Boot'), *kví* enclosure].

Botulfyord Sandwick: recorded in 1739 as part of the tunship of 'Skorwell', what is now the area around 'Stove' [Norse *Bótulfr* a personal name, *jörð* probably meaning 'extent of land' here].

Bought Stronsay: southwest of 'Rosebank' on the coast (see above).

Bought, The Deerness: [a form of English 'bight': here it refers to a small coastal indentation].

Boulie Sanday, Northwall: [Norse *boeli* farm (see 'Instabillie')].

Bountyfur Papa Stronsay: a beach name [Norse *fjara* beach which usually takes the form 'furrow' in dialect: the significance of 'bounty' is unknown unless it refers to free access to seaweed etc. granted by the proprietor, Colonel Balfour of Shapinsay].

Bousta Stronsay: same name as 'Busta' in North Ronaldsay [Norse *ból-staðir* a farm].

Boustay North Ronaldsay: (see 'Busta').

Bouts 1. Evie: (see above).

Bouts 2. Sanday: in 'Skitho Bay': small coastal indentations (see 'Bought' above).

Bow Birsay, Northside: does not appear in Orkney records before 1794: represented today by a field named 'The Bu Field' on the farm of Walkerhoose [Norse *bú* significant farmstead, usually preceded by the definite article].

Bow, The Rousay, Scockness: [used to describe the stretch of land between the farm of Scockness and the coast, originally the area enclosed by the 'Bow Dyke' (below)].

Bow Dyke, The Rousay, Scockness: [Norse *bálkr* a turf wall: compare 'Gerbo' the original form of which was 'Gerback', Scots *dyke* wall].

Bow Geo Birsay: [named after the 'Bow Rock' nearby].

Bow Head Westray: prominent headland in northeast coast of the island [Norse *boði* reef].

Bow o Hermaness Sanday: a shoal off the coast of the 'Ness o Brough' [Norse *boði* a shoal (see 'Hermaness')].

Bow Rock Birsay: one of two rocks off the north coast of the 'Brough o Birsay' [Norse *boði* reef].

Bowbreck Stromness: vanished: it lay in the 'Quholm' area [probably Norse *bálkr* turf wall (see 'The Bow Dyke' above), *brekka* slope].

Bowbustirland Stromness, Innertown: a stretch of land entered in the early Rentals, also referred to as 'Bowbusterland' [first element uncertain but probably same explanation as 'Bowbreck' (above), Norse *ból-staðir* a collection of farm buildings].

Bowcheek Eynhallow: headland in the northwest of the island [Norse *boði* reef: 'cheek' seems to be a corruption of Norse *djúp,* deep sea offshore (see 'Bring Deeps')].

Bowster-a-Choin Birsay: a field on Hammer, Greeny, [Norse *ból-staðir à tjörn,* farm buildings by a pond, pool or lake, in this case the 'Loch o Sabiston': there is no trace of any such building today].

Boyan/Boian Skerries North Ronaldsay: [Norse *boð-inn* the reef].

Boynda Harray: a field in Grimeston, southeast of Biggings [the final element 'da' is normally Norse *dý* boggy land, 'boyn' is difficult to interpret but does suggest Norse *bóndi* a worker on land, in this case, a crofter: in other words, this is a piece of land set aside for crofters].

Braas Geo Sanday: (see 'Braes Geo').

Brabnersquoy Westray: vanished, it lay in the 'Fribo' area [from the surname 'Brabner': in the 1881 Census there is a Benjamine Brabner recorded who is visiting the farm of 'Perth': the Census says he was born in Westray and is the last Brabner recorded in Westray].

Brabustir, Braebuster, Brabist Sanday: now an area in Burness parish [Norse *breiðr* broad, *ból-staðir* farm].

Brace Garth Sanday: (see Braesgarth).

Bradgarth Rendall, Skiddy: also recorded as 'Brarigar' [Norse *breiðr* Broad, *garðr* farm].

Brae Broch Hoy: a piece of rough ground surrounded by a rocky precipice south of St. John's Head [its shape looks like the foundation of a broch: 'brae' suggests Norse *breiðr* broad].

Brae-an-Finyan Rousay: a field to the southwest of the farm of 'Faraclett' [Scots *brae* refers to the steep hill to the west of the farm, Norse *fen-in* the marshes refers to the area to the south which was once marshland, as indicated by the farms of 'Pow' and 'Myres'].

Braebister/Braebuster Deerness: [Norse *breiði-ból-staðir* broad farm though 'broad' in what sense is not clear].

Braeland South Ronaldsay: formerly 'Borrowland'.

Braes Rousay: [abbreviation of 'Quarrybraes'].

Braes Geo Sanday: Cross parish [Norse *brestr* a fissure, *gjá* ravine].

Braes o Stron Rendall: on the land of 'Mill Farm' near 'Loch o Brocken': the 'brae' is nearer 'Skaill Farm' [Norse *strönd* beach].

Braes Wick Sanday: a bay in the south of Cross parish [Norse personal name *Brúsi*, *vík* bay: (compare 'Otterswick')].

Braesgarth Sanday: old house site north of 'Tafts', Lady parish [personal Norse name *Brúsi*, *garðr* farm].

Braeswick Sanday: area named after the adjacent bay [from Norse personal name *Brúsi*, Norse *vík* bay (compare 'Otterswick' Sanday)].

Braethus Firth, Smogarth: [suggests Norse *breið-hús* broad house (see 'Braebuster'): only a field name today].

Braga Stromness: an offshore reef separated from the coast by the 'Sound of Braga' [Norse *braka* to make a sound as if breaking].

Braid Geo Birsay: [Norse *breiðr* broad, *gjá* ravine].

Brain/Brae South Ronaldsay, Paplay: [a difficult name to interpret: perhaps Norse *breið-eng* broad meadow: now renamed 'Orkadee'].

Brance South Ronaldsay: (see 'Yorbrandis').

Brandies Westray, Swanson's: [Norse personal name *Brandr*].

Brandy Evie: only one recording in 1871: clearly a clipped form of 'Quoybrandy' [Norse personal name *Brandr*].

Brandyquoy Deerness; South Ronaldsay: (see above).

Bransquoy Firth: (see above).

Branstane Westray, Skelwick: [a difficult name to interpret: perhaps Norse *Brands-þúfin* Brand's mound].

Brarigar Rendall: (see 'Bradgarth').

Bratlee Ber Burray: a precipice on the southeast coast of the island [Norse *brattr* steep, *hlið* slope but also used of a sheer cliff, *berg* rock].

Brawel Shapinsay, Weland: [Norse *breiðr* broad, *völlr* field].

Bre Broch Hoy: (see 'Brae Broch').

Breaching Stronsay: just southwest of 'Whitehall Village' [unsure to what the name refers: perhaps the isthmus separating 'Mill Bay' and 'Papa Sound'].

Break of the Ayre Stronsay: sea off the 'Sand of Crook' [English 'breaking waves', Norse *eyrr* a gravelly beach].

Breakna, Hillock of Orphir: [Norse *brekkan* the slope].

Brebister Hoy: (see 'Braebister').

Brebuster Westray: (see above).

Breck Rousay; Orphir; Papa Westray; North Ronaldsay; Birsay; Rendall; Sanday; Stronsay: [Norse *brekka* slope].

Breckan Birsay; Firth; Harray; Sanday; North Ronaldsay; Rousay: [Norse *brekkan* the slope].

Breckan, Swarta Rousay: [Norse *svartr* black, referring in this instance to heather cover].

Breckan's Laytey Sanday: [Norse *hluti* share].

Breckannoy Birsay: [a field with a hillock, hence probably Norse *haugr* mound].

Breckanquoy Sanday: [Norse *kví* enclosure].

Breckaskaill 1. Papa Westray: close by is 'Backaskaill' which suggests that this is an old udal farm divided in two as in the case of 'Langskaill' and 'Netherskaill' in Marwick [Norse *skáli* hall].

Breckaskaill 2. Westray, Rapness: [Norse *skáli* hall].

Breckerhouse/Beglo Birsay: (see 'Beglo').

Breckin(s) South Ronaldsay: [Norse *brekka* slope (with English plural)].

Breckness 1. Birsay, Northside: a deserted croft now part of 'Fidgarth' [probably a transferred name from 'Breckness', Stromness].

Breckness 2. Firth: 1642 [Norse *brekka* slope, *nes* point: there are dwellings North Breck and South Breck in the vicinity].

Breckness 3. Stromness, Ootertoon: [the house takes its name from the breaking waves on 'Braga', an offshore skerry].

Breckney Orphir: [can only mean Norse *brekkan* in the Orkney form 'breckna' where the definite article 'na' assumes the form 'ney'].

Breckowall Westray: ['Breck' in the district of 'Wall': it was originally called 'Breck' (see 'Pier o Wall')].

Breckquoy Birsay; Holm: [Norse *brekka* slope, *kví* enclosure].

Brecks 1. Deerness; South Ronaldsay; Westray; Shapinsay; Stronsay: [Norse *brekkur* slopes: 'the placename 'Brecks' presents a problem in interpretation because it has two meanings: apart from Norse 'slopes' it can also mean Old English *bræc* ground broken up for cultivation similar to Orkney dialect 'brecks' poor quality heather-covered land with a thin soil as in 'Barebrecks', 'Crumbrecks', 'Harray Brecks' etc.].

Brecks 2. Stronsay: vanished [recorded in the *Orkneyinga Saga* as *brekkur* slopes, the Norse plural of *brekka* slope: Brecks lay near 'Whitehall'].

Brecks, The o Banks Rousay: low reddish banks below Banks in the Sourin district.

Brecks o Scarataing Evie: (see above).

Breckway Orphir: marked on 1813 map in northwest area of Swanbister Bay area [Norse *brekka* slope, significance of 'way' element uncertain: it appears also in 'Skethway', Burness, Firth].

Bredakirk/Bradakirk Eday: a house [suggests the former site of a chapel dedicated to St. Bride: no trace of such a chapel exists].

Breek Rousay, Frotoft: named after a house in 'Quandal' which has vanished [probably a form of Norse *brekka* slope].

Breeks o Betyihoose Sanday: northwest point of the 'Inner Holm o Ire' [English 'breech' referring to the narrow tideway between the 'Inner Holm' and the Outer Holm].

Breeran Evie/Birsay: in the peat hill on the boundary between the two parishes [origin uncertain].

Bregaday Rousay: north of the 'Loch o Saviskaill' [an unusual form of Norse *brekka* slope, Norse *dý* marshy ground].

Brekisyord Sandwick: old name for land in what is now the 'Stove' area [Icelandic personal name *Breki*, Norse *jörð* land or estate].

Brekkur Stronsay: (see 'Brecks', Stronsay).

Brenaniar Harray: a field in Harray but the name originally related to stepping stones in the 'Burn of Netherbrough': Norse pedestrian bridges were stepping stones similar to the ancient bridge in Somerset called Tarr Stepps: there is a lovely stepping stone causeway known as the 'Brig o Brue' near Quivals farm Burness, Sanday [Norse *bruarinn nyar* the new bridge].

Brench, The Sanday: (see 'Warsetter Branch').

Brencherhoose Birsay, Northside: [Norse *bringur* slopes, *hús* house].

Brenches, The Swona: [Norse *bringa* chest applied to a variety of slopes, cliffs etc.].

Brenchicott Sanday: a vanished cottage [dialect 'brench' branch of a road etc.].

Brenda 1. Birsay, Bea: [Norse *brenna* fire, *dý* marsh: marshland where 'Will o the Wisp' may be seen].

Brenda 2. Evie: (see 'Brenda', Birsay, above).

Brenda, Knowe o Birsay, Twatt: [Norse first name 'Brandr': a mound on the land of 'Brandr].

Brendale Rousay: (probably a form of 'Brenda' above) [*dalr* valley].

Brendo Firth: field name (see 'Brenda', Birsay, above).

Brescoe Westray, Midbea: [Norse personal name *Brúsi*, 'co/coe' is one of the rarer spellings of Norse *kví* enclosure (see 'Whilco')].

Bressigarth Sanday: earlier 'Brusgarth' [Norse personal name *Brúsi*, Norse *garðr* farm].

Bretaness Rousay: small peninsula jutting into the 'Loch of Wasbister' [believed to be the site of a small chapel: possible dedication to St. Bride (compare 'Bredakirk' in Eday), Norse *nes* point of land].

Brettabreck Stromness: [Norse *bratta-brekka* steep slope].

Brettavale Harray: [Norse *brattr* steep, *fjall* hill].

Brettimes Geo Rousay: [Norse *brattr* steep, *nes* point of land].

Brettobreck/Brattobreck Rendall: (see 'Brettabreck' above).

Breval Rousay: [an old croft which takes its name from the hill where it stands, Norse *breiðr* broad *fjall* hill].

Briabeth Harray: a field in Netherbrough [Norse *breiðr* broad, *beit-it* the pasture land: the final Norse neuter 'it' usually takes the form 'th' in Orkney placenames].

Bride's Kirk North Ronaldsay: ['Bride's' in this instance and below refers to the Irish/or pagan saint of that name].

Bride's Loch North Ronaldsay: (see above).

Bride's Ness North Ronaldsay: (see above).

Bride's Pund North Ronaldsay: [Scots *pund* English 'pound' enclosure for animals, in this case, sheep].

Bridesnoust North Ronaldsay: [Norse *naustr* a safe haven where boats may be drawn up in the wintertime].

Bridles Sanday, Rue: field name [St. Bride 'lees'?: the fieldname to the south is 'Kurkister' which suggests an ancient chapel site: Scots *leys* arable land left untilled].

Brig Rousay: tidal islets, Sourin: rocks which look like stepping stones [same origin as Orkney dialect 'brig stones', stepping stones, (usually flagstones) placed around old Orkney houses to prevent muddy footpaths forming].

Brig o Brue Sanday: stepping stones near 'Quivals' farm, Burness [Scots *brig* bridge, Norse *brú* bridge].

Brig o the Euce Sanday: (see 'Brig o Tofts' above).

Brig o Tofts Sanday, Elsness: field name, early 18th century: 'brig' must have referred to stepping stones which once existed from 'Ouse Point' to Elsness: it may be the same placename as 'Brig o the Oyce' (see below): just north of 'Ouse Point' is 'Bridgend' [Norse *topt* site of a house (with English plural)].

Brigafea St. Andrews: formerly in a marshy area [dialect 'brig' refers to stepping stones which existed at one time across part of this marsh (see above)].

Brigg North Ronaldsay: there is little evidence of marsh here today, but 'Brigg' formerly lay between 'Langmire' and 'Kuters Mire' ['kuters' is an English plural of Norwegian *køytar* marshes and 'brig' is an Orkney dialect word for a stepping stone over a stream or wet, muddy soil as in dialect 'brigstones', i.e., flagstones placed near the door of old Orkney houses to prevent mud being brought into the house].

Brim Birsay, Abune-the-Hill: vanished cottage which lay above 'Queena': perhaps a name transferred from 'Brim' in Evie.

Brim/s Evie: [lies at the edge of the 'Woodwick Burn' and suggest an origin from the rare Scots word *brim* a stream].

Brim-noven Rousay: (see 'Kilns o Brim-Noven').

Brimquoy/Broomquoy Birsay Village: [Scots *brim* stream: it lies beside the stream which drains the 'Loch o Boardhoose'].

Brims/Brimness Walls: [Norse *brim* surf].

Bring Deeps Hoy/Orphir: the expanse of sea in the northwest of 'Scapa Flow' [(see 'Bring Head' below), Norse *djúp* deep].

Bring Head Hoy: [Norse *bringa* chest, used metaphorically to describe a headland. To the south of Bring Head another cliff is called 'White Breast'].

Bring Head Rousay: steep cliffs to the northwest of the island (see above).

Brings Rousay: a general name for the area around 'Bring Head'.

Brinhyan Evie: a name applied to the top of 'Burgar Hill' [Norse *brún* Slope, Norse *haugr-inn* the mound which relates to 'Howan Greenie' here].

Brinkie's Brae Stromness: [Norse *bringa* chest, used metaphorically of anything protruding and steep, Scots *brae* is tautological].

Brinkwall Papa Westray: [Norse *bringa* chest, referring to the rocky shore beneath a stretch of 30 feet cliffs in the northeast of the island: 'wall' in this instance suggests Norse *vella* 'boiling' whirlpool (see 'Well o Swona')].

Brinnigar Stromness: [Norse *brún* slope, *garðr* farm].

Brinnyan/Brinian, The Rousay: refers to the area between 'Trumland' and 'Avelsay' [Norse *bring-in* the chest referring to a spur of 'Knitchen Hill'].

Brinyaquoy Harray, Overbrough: [probably Norse *brún* slope, *kví* enclosure].

Briogrunye Sanday: shoal near 'Newark' [Norse *breiðr* broad, Norse *grunn* shoal].

Briskar Deerness: original name of what became the old Established Church Manse [a form of 'Bisgarth'?].

Brisniebrayo Sanday, Brabustir: field name, Burness parish [Norse *breiðr* broad: origin of 'brisnie' unknown].

Britain Birsay, Marwick: [Norse *bratta-brekkan* the steep slope].

Brittny Rousay: vanished cottage, Sourin [same origin as above].

Broad Geo Sanday:(see 'Geo' in Appendix).

Broad Taing Evie: [Norse *tangi* a point of land].

Broadi Face Hoy: a steep hill in Rackwick [Norse *brú* stepping stone bridge across the 'Rackwick Burn', Norse *dý* poor quality marshy ground, English 'face' commonly used in Orkney for something steep or sloping (see 'Face o the Toon')].

Broar Evie: (see 'Bruar').

Broch o Runnaclett Sanday: Burness parish, tradition has it that there was a mound/circular feature in this field at 'Westove': the placename suggests that the tradition is based on fact [Norse *borg* fort, *klettr* which in an inland setting suggests a stone structure (often a broch as in 'Noltklett/Netlater' Harray), Norse *hrun* ruin].

Brockan Rendall, Grind: Birsay, Marwick: [a variation of the more common 'Breckan'; 'Brockan' in Rendall is now called 'Grind', formerly 'Grindmira', Norse *brekkan* the slope].

Brockan Sandwick, Wasbister: it seems that this farm was subdivided and the divisions took the names 'Bockan' and 'Bookan' [all variants of Norse *brekkan* the slope].

Brockan Stromness: (see above).

Brogar Stenness: locally pronounced 'Brodyir' [Norse *brú* bridge, *garðr* farm].

Brokisland Rousay, Wasbister: [from local surname 'Brock' a form of 'Breck'].

Broland Rousay: a farm in Sourin [probably Norse *brú* stepping stone bridge over the 'Suso Burn'].

Broland South Ronaldsay: (see 'Braeland').

Broll South Ronaldsay: in Linklater district: earlier 'Burrowell' [difficult name to interpret: suggests Norse *borg* with the simple meaning 'walled area', *völlr* field (see 'Burrowstone' and 'Burroughstone Hill')].

Brook, The Swona: [Norse *brúk* rotten piles of seaweed on a beach].

Broon Deer Pow Evie: on the 'Burn o Whitemire' [Norse *brú-in* the stepping stone bridge over the *dýar* marshes, Scots *pow* pool].

Broonalanga, Moss o Firth: along the 'Burn o Cruan', Rendall [Norse *brú-in* the stepping stone bridge, *langr* long: marked by a 'ford' on the Ordnance Survey map].

Broti Ber Pentland Skerries: [Norse *brjóta* to break, *berg* rock: the 'breaking' element probably relates to the surf].

Brotmer Stronsay: beach name southwest of 'Rosebank' [Norse *brjóta* as above relating to the surf: origin of 'mer' here unknown].

Brough o Birsay island off the northwest coast of the 'Mainland' [Norse *byrgi* enclosure, referring to the earlier Celtic settlement on the island].

Brough Sanday; Gairsay; Rousay; Rendall; Evie; Westray; South Ronaldsay: [Norse *borg* fort].

Brough Slap Westray, Broughton [Scots *slap* gate].

Brough Soonds Birsay: the channel between 'The Brough o Birsay' and the coast [Norse *sund* channel].

Brown Hill Rousay: [Norse *brún* slope].

Browsky, Knowe o Harray: [Norse *bró* a path of stepping stones through (which was formerly) a marshy area, Norse *skjá* a rough, temporary shed].

Bruar Evie: small dwelling on the bank of the 'Burn of Woodwick' [Norse *brúar* stepping stone bridges, perhaps refers to old and new].

Bruces Loch Stronsay, Whitehall: [the surname 'Bruce' is recorded in Sanday at the beginning of the 18th century but does not appear in any Stronsay record].

Brue/Broo North Ronaldsay: part of 'Hoe Skerries' [Norse *brú* probably stepping stones along the rocks here].

Bruillie Sanday; Rousay: (see 'Brawel', Shapinsay).

Bruna Fea Stromness: [Norse *brún* slope, *fjall* hill].

Brunt Hill Stromness: [Scots *brunt* burnt, referring to heather burning at some time].

Bruntbigging Burray: [(see 'brunt' above), Scots *bigging* usually referring to a stone-built dwelling or farm building: the buildings must have burnt down at one time].

Brunthouse Flotta: (see above).

Bruntland Burray: (see 'Brunt Hill' above)

Bruntquina Harray: [Scots *brunt* burnt, Norse *kví-in* the enclosure but here referring to a house by that name].

Brusgarth (see 'Bressigarth').

Brya Evie: a shoal: one of a number of adjectives used to describe shoals: the word for shoal is missing [Norse *breiðr* broad].

Bryabist Sanday: in Burness and Lady (see 'Braebister' for explanation).

Bryameadow Sandwick: [Norse *breiðr* broad, 'meadow' suggests a corruption of Norse *mið-haugr* the middle mound: there were several mounds here, in fact 'Bryameadow' is built extremely close to the 'Knowe o Queena'].

Bryascow Stenness: [Norse *breiðr* broad, Norse *skjá* hut/shelter made of rough boards, stones etc.].

Bryland Birsay, Kirbister: [Norse *breiðr* broad].

Brymer St. Andrews: [Norse *breiðr* broad, *mýrr* moor or marsh].

Bu, The Norse *bú* estate, normally having a head house: it was this house which was referred to as 'The Bu' and which always carried a definite article, hence, e.g., 'The Bu of Orphir'. Below is a list of Orkney instances. Several of these were not original estates but combined farms which assumed the name 'The Bu'.

Bu, The Birsay, Northside: [Norse *bú* farm or estate: not an original 'bu'].

Bu, The o Aith Walls: [head house of the tunship of Aith].

Bu, The o Brough Sanday: [old name for 'West Brough'].

Bu, The o Burray Burray: a fine mansion house occupied by the Stewarts stood here in the 17th century.

Bu, The o Cairston Stromness.

Bu, The o Flotta Flotta: [earlier known as 'The Mains'].

Bu, The o Graemsay Graemsay: [not an original 'Bu'].

Bu, The o Halkisness/ness Sanday: Cross parish [head house of the estate].

Bu, The o Holm Holm: [formerly 'The Bu o Skaill': head house of the district of 'Paplay'].

Bu, The o Hoxa South Ronaldsay.

Bu, The o Hoy Hoy: northeast of the island.

Bu, The o Linkletter South Ronaldsay.

Bu, The o Lopness Sanday: Lady parish [old name for 'Lopness Farm'].

Bu, The o Orphir Orphir: [the best known 'Bu' in Orkney: formerly the seat of Earl Paul].

Bu, The o Rapness: Westray.

Bu, The o Rendall: [the old 'Bu o Gorseness' also known as 'Upper Inkster'].

Bu, The o Sandwick South Ronaldsay.

Bu, The o Tofts Sanday: Lady parish, Northwall.

Bu, The o Tresness Sanday: Lady parish.

Bu, The o Wa/Waas/Walls Sanday, Northwall.

Bu, The o Wyre [believed to be the head house of the estate of Kolbein Hrúga, alias Cubbie Roo].

Bu-house Shapinsay: south of 'Weland' [perhaps the head house of the tunship of 'Weland'].

Buan Stromness: [Norse *baen* the farm].

Buckakeeth North Ronaldsay: [Norse *bukk-kið* young male goat: the word for 'enclosure' is missing (see 'Buckquoy', Harray, below)].

Buckelsberry Westray, Aikerness: [a name transferred name from Bucklesberry, North Carolina, USA: comparatively few Orkney men emigrated to USA but two unnamed from Westray fought in the American Civil War].

Bucket 1. Evie: pejorative name [probably refers to a bottomless tin 'bucket' being used as a chimney!].

Bucket 2. Rousay: (see above).

Buckquoy 1. Evie: [Norse *bukkr* male goat, *kví* enclosure].

Buckquoy 2. Harray: (see above).

Buckquoy/Bikquoy/Biggaquoy Birsay: [difficult placename to explain: possibly original 'Buckquoy' was corrupted to Norse *bygð* a place already built on, Norse *kví* enclosure (see 'Bigland', Rousay)].

Buggery, Kirk o Evie: [origin doubtful: perhaps a derogatory name applied to a former Roman Catholic chapel: compare the 'Black Chapel': the Shetland placename 'Bugger' is explained as Norse *bú-garðr* farm but 'bu' would be inappropriate here].

Bught Orphir; Rendall: [English *bight* bay].

Bught Geo Stronsay: (see above).

Buldrie Birsay: a skerry [Norwegian *buldre* to roar, the noise of the sea breaking on this reef].

Buldro Birsay: a cleft in the cliff face (see above).

Bull Flag Papa Westray: a stretch of flat rock on the east coast of the island [nearby is 'Boglan Geo': both relate to the sound of the waves breaking here i.e., bellowing like a bull].

Bum 1. Evie: a dwelling shaped like a 'bum(mo)' a turned wooden bowl: it was probably made of turf [Norwegian *bomme* a round wooden box].

Bum 2. Birsay: west of Kirbister (see above).

Bunda Ridges Sanday: [probably strips of land allotted to the *bóndi* i.e., crofters in this instance].

Buoy o the Red Sanday: [a buoy marking the end of the shoal extending from 'The Foulan' ['red' = 'redware'= seaweed].

Burandi Hoy: a steep hillside to the east of the 'Red Glen' [Norse *borg-in* a dome shaped hill, Norse *dý* marshland/moorland].

Burgar Evie: [Norse *borg*, a fort *garðr* farm].

Burgar Hill Evie: [Norse *borgar* hills, relating to the many hills in this part of the parish].

Burgars Slap Birsay: field name, Nisthouse, Hundland [Scots *slap* gateway: 'Burgar's' can only relate to the Orkney surname 'Burgar': there is no record of Burgar in Birsay today, but it was the earliest recorded surname in Birsay when Magnus Burgar lived in 'Langskaill', Marwick, in 1492].

Burgir Orphir: (see 'Burgar Hill' above).

Burgis Pow North Ronaldsay: coastal pool in the Summer Ayre district [Scots *pow* pool, surname 'Burgess'].

Burke's Sanday, How: field name, Cross parish [probably originally a turf cottage: from the nickname 'Bill o Burke': the Burkes were Irish peddlers who were associated with Kirkwall and Stronsay in the mid 19th century: they are not recorded in Sanday though they must have lived here too].

Burlee/Burralee Orphir: the name is related to a small hollow in the west of the parish from which the 'Burn o Burlee' flows, crossing the Stenness boundary

[Norse *bur* (as above) but probably meaning 'temporary summer hut' here, Norse *hlíð* slope].

Burlie Shapinsay: a field name in the southeast of the island [(see 'Burrland' above), Norse *hlíð* slope].

Burly Rock Sanday: lobster set, Northwall [English *burly*].

Burn o Burlee (see 'Burlee' above).

Burn o Cheors Westray: (see 'Cheors').

Burn o Ease Orphir: to the east of Houton Bay (see 'Ease').

Burn o Jolmasey Orphir: runs parallel to the Burn o Burlee above [origin of 'Jolmasey' unknown].

Burn o Myres Orphir: (see 'Myres').

Burn o Russadale Orphir: north of Mid Hill (see 'Russadale').

Burn o Trolldgeo Shapinsay: [the alternative name of which is 'Cubbie Roo's Burn' (see 'Trolldgeo')].

Burness 1. Birsay: there were two cottages with this name in the parish, one in 'Hundland' and the other in the 'Hillside' area.

Burness 2. Firth: takes its name from an old broch mound nearby [Norse *borgar-nes* a point on which the fort lay].

Burness 3. Rousay: a small cottage which lay above 'Langskaill' in Wasbister district [a transferred placename from one of several such placenames in Orkney].

Burness 4. Sanday: a former parish now joined with Cross [Norse *bára* a tidal race, *nes* point of land, in this case in the 'The Riv/Whitemill' area].

Burness 5. Westray: a mile south of 'Noltland' on the edge of the 'Loch of Burness' [perhaps a transferred name?].

Burra Pool Evie: a small ravine near the 'Broch o Burgar' [Norse *borg* fort].

Burra Sound the stretch of water which separates the islands of Hoy and Graemsay [the name relates to the former broch at 'Quoyness', Hoy].

Burra Taing Birsay: a point on the south side of 'The Brough' [Norse *byrgi* an enclosure, referring to the earlier walled Celtic settlement, *tangi* point of land].

Burray Island in the south connected to The Mainland by the Churchill Barriers [Norse *borgar* fortifications, *ey* island: there were originally two brochs on this island: the population in 2021 was 409].

Burray North Ronaldsay: in the north of the island [a transferred name].

Burray Haas/Burray Ness Burray: coastal feature in the east of Burray [Norse *hals* neck, used metaphorically as 'ridge of land'].

Burrey Brae the boundaries of the parishes of Firth, St. Ola and Orphir meet at this point [Norse *borg* a dome shaped hill].

Burrian Firth: [Norse *borgin* the hill].

Burrian Broch North Ronaldsay: [Norse *borgin* the fort].

Burrian Knowe Harray: a broch site on the northeast shore of the Harray Loch [Norse *borgin* the fort].

Burrian Rousay: 1. The name of a small island in Saviskaill Loch, the site of a former broch; 2. Frotoft: both can be interpreted as Norse *borgin* a defensive site.

Burrian Sanday: a mound in Lady parish and a house nearby [Norse *borgin* a fort/broch].

Burriger North Ronaldsay: an old house which lay near the beach southeast of 'Howar' and not far from 'Burrian' above from which it takes its name [Norse *borgin* the fort, *garðr* farm].

Burristae Westray, Kirbist: [Norse *byrgis* (genitive of *byrgi*, an enclosed area), Norse *teigr* strip of land: i.e., strip of land attached to the *byrgi*, a rare Norse word applied to the nearby broch].

Burrland Papa Westray: [suggests Norwegian *bur* a former storehouse from which the bay takes its name].

Burro Birsay, Whitecleat: field name [Orkney dialect 'burro' applied to a type of rush].

Burrodys Hill Holm: [Norse *borg* rounded hill, *dys* a cairn].

Burrogarth Westray: Wasbister [location unknown today].

Burrowgate Stronsay: a small croft on Rothiesholm [Norse *gata* path: origin of 'Borrow' here uncertain].

Burrowland South Ronaldsay: (see' Braeland').

Burrowstone Shapinsay: near the site of an old Iron Age fort or broch [Norse *byrgi* fort, *tún* enclosure].

Burry Brae Firth: south of Rennibister [see above for explanation].

Burry Meadow Firth: on the southwest shore of 'Wasdale Loch' [Orkney dialect 'burro' applied to a type of rush].

Burwick South Ronaldsay: [Norse *borg* fort, *vík* bay].

Bus Taing South Ronaldsay: [Scots *buss* seaweed exposed at low tide especially eel grass, Norse *tangi* point of land].

Bush, The Stromness/Stenness: the name given to the area south of the 'Brig o Waithe' (see 'Bus' above).

Bushan Harray: islands in the Harray Loch [Scots *buss* seaweed, Norse *eyinni* the island].

Busta 1. Flotta: a vanished farm on 'Pan Hope' (see below).

Busta 2. North Ronaldsay: originally the name given to a district: truncated form of 'Kirbest' [Norse *kirkju-ból-staðr* farm with church attached].

Busy, Taing o The Shapinsay: [Scots *buss* seaweed exposed at low tide, Norse *tangi* point of land].

Butnaquean Harray: a field at the edge of the 'Harray Loch' in the Netherbrough region [Norse *botn*, in this case 'end of a field' and usually takes the form 'Button' in Orkney placenames, *kvín* the enclosure].

Buts North Ronaldsay: small pieces of land [Norse *bót* patches].

Butterland Birsay, Northside: (see 'Mirbister', Harray).

Butters Knowe Sanday, Garbo: [Scots surname *Butter* found in Orkney in the 17th century but not recorded afterwards (see Cutter's Knowe, Stronsay)].

Button Stenness; South Ronaldsay; Holm: (see 'Buttnaquean' above).

Butts Walls: (see Buts).

Buxa Orphir: [a name from Bengal, India imported by a serving soldier and first recorded on a map of Orphir in 1813].

Byasteen Rousay: a large stone known as the 'Finger Stone' (because of marks on it believed to be marks of fingers) said to be one of the stones thrown by the troll 'Cubbie Roo' at one of his adversaries, formerly used as a wayside prayer stone [Norse *beiða* to pray].

C

Caddies' Kil South Ronaldsay, Grimness: ['Kil(n)' refers in this case to a cliff where spume blowing over a cliff resembles smoke from a drain-drying kiln, Scots *caddie* a pet lamb suggests that lambs were penned nearby].

Caddlesbrae Westray: on the southeast corner of 'Pierowall Bay' [origin of 'caddle' unknown].

Caesar o Haan (Hawin) Skerry Birsay, Northside: [Norse *sker* reef, the Caesar referred to is probably Caesar Moar of Garthsetter; it is said he took refuge on the skerry when pursued by the Press Gang but it is more likely that he ran into difficulty while fishing near this small skerry, 'Haan' is probably the same place as 'Hayon'].

Cairn o Skartan: Sanday: ('Knowe o Skartan', see 'Skartan').

Cairns o Fea Orphir: (see 'Fea', Orphir).

Cairns o Queenagreenie Sanday: (see 'Queenagreenie').

Cairston Stromness: [Norse personal name *Kjarrekkr* not otherwise Recorded, Norse *staðr* estate].

Caither Lea Rendall, Upper Cottiscarth: field name [it lies on a very steep slope: Norse *hlíð* slope, formerly a marshy area before it was drained hence probably Norse *keyta* foul water (see 'Catherness')].

Cakie South Ronaldsay: a sharp pointed flat rock under the water mark near 'Harrabrough Head' [Norse *keikr* 'bending backwards' but it is not clear what this refers to here].

Calabar Deerness: vanished [an old house nicknamed after a lady who took great interest in missionary work in Africa!].

Caldale St. Ola: [Norse *kald-dalr* cold valley: west and east winds sweep through this saddle in the hills].

Caldkeengale St. Ola: [location and origin unknown].

Calf of Eday North Isles: uninhabited island [Norse *kálfr* calf].

Calgair/Cogar Rousay: [Norse *kald-garðr* cold farm (see 'Caldale' above)].

Calgarth Deerness: [Norse *kald-garðr* cold farm: the use of 'cold' and 'warm' in Scandinavian placenames is not always easily explained (compare 'Varmadale')].

Callos South Ronaldsay: [vanished: location unknown].

Calset St. Andrews: [Norse *kald-setr* cold (summer) enclosure].

Camberbosk South Ronaldsay: coastal feature [Norse *kambr* ridge, *bust* bristle extended metaphorically to a steep rocky face: *bust* was used in Shetland in the same way, for example 'Sinnabust' in Sandwick, Shetland, where it means 'spume flying over a steep cliff' (see 'Sinians o Cutclaws' Rousay)].

Cameral Joy Flotta: [a puzzling name for a cottage: it probably has some religious association — perhaps Mount Carmel (c.f. Mount Pleasant, Jericho, Babylon etc.) Mountjoy is a village in County Tyrone, Northern Ireland].

Camp o Jupiter Fring, The Rousay: [a completely corrupted Norse placename: Norse *kambr* (as above), Norse *djúpa-dý* deep marsh, Norse *hringr* circle, probably referring originally to a circular area e.g. a seasonal pool: the use of *kringla* to describe such round features is common in Orkney placenames (see placename entries beginning 'Crin' and 'Kring')].

Campie Rowa Firth: a hillside [Norse *kambr* ridge, Norse *rauðr* red, referring here to the colour of the vegetation].

Campie Rowo Rousay: (see above).

Camps, The Rousay: [hill ridges: Norse *kambar* (with English plural)].

Campston St. Andrews: [Norse personal name *Kampi*, Norse *staðr* estate: there were a number of these great estates in Orkney, all with a personal name attached, the majority being around the Stenness and Harray Lochs; they were rarer elsewhere].

Canada South Ronaldsay: (see 'Candle o Birsie Geo').

Canada West: Birsay, Hillside: (earlier 'Reekie Braes') [such names were given by Orkneymen who had emigrated and who had returned with enough money to build their own house].

Candle o Birsie Geo South Walls: a prominent conical rock in the geo (see 'Birsie Geo').

Candle o the Sale Hoy: southeast of 'The Bring': a large rock at the mouth of the 'Burn o Sel' [the origin of the word 'candle' for a large rock cannot be ascertained: perhaps 'candle shaped: origin of 'sale' unknown].

Candle o the Sneuk Hoy: a large and prominent rock on the west coast forming the western end of the boundary between Hoy and Walls: ['sneuk' seems to be a dialect word for headland and is probably related to the word 'nose' (see 'Nose o the Bring')].

Canker Deerness; Birsay; Sanday; Deerness: (Quoycanker): ['canker' is a fungal disease which affects animal and vegetable matter, sometimes giving off a foul smell and it seems that here it applies to rotting vegetation in a mire (compare 'Foulmire')].

Cannamisurdy Rousay: a well on the beach below the house of 'Cott' in Frotoft [Norse *saurr* marsh, *dý* marsh, Gaelic *canach* cotton grass?].

Canniesile Skerries Deerness: [Norse *sker* reef, Gaelic *ceann* headland, the reefs form a projecting point of land, 'sile' may be Norse *selr* seal].

Cannigal St. Ola: [named after a subdivision of an Australian aboriginal tribal area in the Sydney region: the nearest farm to Cannigal is Bendigo!].

Cannymire Deerness: [Gaelic *canach* cotton grass?, Norse *mýrr* poor heather-covered land].

Canquoy, Geo of Rousay: [origin and location of 'Canquoy' not known].

Cantack Swona: [Norwegian *kant* projecting part, plus local diminutive 'ack'].

Cantick Walls: a farm near Cantick Head [Norwegian *kant* projecting part, plus local diminutive 'ick': earlier 'Cantop', Gaelic *càin* tax (see 'Tollop')].

Caperhouse Harray: [Norse *koppari* a wood turner, Scots *caupar* a maker of wooden bowls: these shallow wooden bowls were originally imported from Norway but were certainly made in Orkney too where they were called 'bummies'].

Cara South Ronaldsay: same place as 'Garay' [Norse *gerði* an enclosed piece of land].

Cara Ber/Ben Orphir: coastal feature west of 'Clestrain' [origin unknown].

Carabrek St. Andrews: [Norwegian *kjerr* boggy land, Norse *brekka* slope].

Carapitten Birsay, Farafield: [Norwegian *kjerr* boggy land, Norse *pytt-inn* the pool].

Caraquoy Rousay: [Norwegian *kjerr* boggy land, Norse *kví* enclosure].

Carlan Geo South Ronaldsay: ravines were often considered the realm of evil spirits [Norse *kerling* old woman, Orkney dialect *carlin* a troll woman: (see 'Carlin Skerry' below)].

Carlin Foot/Giant's Foot Sanday: a shore feature, Cross parish (see above).

Carlin Geo Stronsay: on 'Burgh Head' and on 'Muckle Green Holm', Eday: (see above).

Carlin Hill Stromness: (see below).

Carlin Skerry, Scapa Flow: former name of 'Barrel o Butter' [Norse *kerling* old woman, in particular an evil old woman, i.e., witch or troll].

Carlquoy Holm, Banks: first recorded in 1492 [the only instance of the first name 'Karl' in Orkney placenames: vanished].

Carness St. Ola: [uncertain origin; perhaps Norwegian *kjerr* boggy land as in 'Carapitten' (above), Norse *nes* point of land].

Carpaquoy Eday: [Norse *kreppa* narrow, *kví* enclosure].

Carrick Eday: [a name transferred from 'Carrick' in Ayrshire].

Carse o Henzie Hunt Sanday: an old chapel site [Scots *carse* flat land (usually beside a river), Norse *hegna* to enclose: (for 'hunt' see 'Huant')].

Caskald Shapinsay: [a derogatory name for a house: Norse *köss* a heap of stones, *kaldr* cold (see 'Skeeticauld')].

Cassels Sanday: lobster set, Northwall [adjacent to two cairns or 'castles' on the coast].

Castal Rousay: field name, Wasbister [said in local lore to be the site of an ancient building but there is no archaeological proof].

Castall Harray: [location unknown].

Castal-hill(s) Rousay: an old cottage high up in the hill in Wasbister [the name 'Castle' or 'Castal' was often applied in jest to these cottar house in much the same way as 'hall' or 'ha'' were used].

Castel Birsay: coastal feature ['Castle' was often used to describe rock pillars in the sea, the best example in Orkney being the 'Castle o Yesnaby'].

Caster Stronsay: field name north of 'Yearnsetter' [Norse *köstr* a pile, hence a mound: (see 'Castra Geo' below)].

Casterbreck/Castlebreck Wyre: a field below 'Cubbie Roo's Castle' [Norse *brekka* slope, (for 'caster' see above)].

Castle 1. Evie: rock pillar on the coast.

Castle 2. Gairsay: (see 'Sweyn's Castle').

Castle 3. Rendall: [a neighbour allegedly asked: 'Whit kind o a castle are thoo buildan beuy?' and the name stuck!].

Castle, The South Ronaldsay: an ancient building, locally known by this name was built in the 17th century by Sir James Stewart of Burray for his illegitimate daughter but was never finished.

Castle Boundas Birsay: rock pillar on the coast [Scots *boundis* boundary marker in this case: it is not possible to establish today to what boundary this refers].

Castle Dearie Wyre: on Stromness Taing: a small rock stack at the shore, blown down in a gale in the late 1990s [origin of 'dearie' unknown].

Castle Field Rendall, Lower Ellibister: [said to be the site of a castle: no evidence left today].

Castle Geo Sanday: [Norse *gjá* ravine so called from the adjacent cairns known as 'Castle'].

Castle Hill Sanday: in Cross parish [the name 'castle' is given in jest].

Castle Hoan Wyre: [Norse *haug-inn* the mound: location uncertain].

Castle o Bothikan Papa Westray: on the 'Links o Moclett': a good example to show that 'castle' can be used to apply to any elevated area where it is assumed that an ancient structure lies underneath: there is some doubt about whether it was originally an Iron Age fort. [Scots *bothy* a booth, probably a fisherman's hut shows that the site was later used for another purpose, 'kan' is probably a diminutive suffix like 'kin'].

Castle o Burrian Sanday: a mound in the 'Park' district (see 'Burrian' place-names).

Castle o Burrian Westray, Rapness.

Castle o Oyce Birsay: a rock pillar near the outlet of the 'Burn o Swannay' (see 'Oyce')].

Castlehill Birsay, Northside and Twatt; Rousay; Stronsay; Sanday; Evie; Eday: [fanciful names].

Castles, The Birsay, Northside: rock pillars.

Castlewell/wall Flotta: a small cottage [Norse *völlr* field].

Castni Geo South Ronaldsay: nearby is 'Cumla Geo' [Norse *kuml* mound: 'Castni' derives from Norse *köst-inn* a heap such as a cairn].

Castra Geo Birsay: near the 'Point o Buckquoy' [Norse *köstr* pile i.e., a cairn: no record of such a cairn exists].

Cat Hill Rousay: [for 'Cot Hill'? (c.f. Cot-on-Hill, Shapinsay)].

Cata Sand Sanday: [Norse *keyta* foul water].

Catagoe Birsay: (see 'Dog Geo').

Catagreen Rousay: near the 'Loch o Loomachun' [Norse *keyta* foul Water, *groen* green, referring perhaps to algae filled pools].

Catherness Harray: the old name of 'Nistaben' farm [Norse *keyta* foul water (see 'Caither'), Norse *nes* a narrow point of land: (c.f. 'Nessbreck')].

Cathole Rousay: [must be a name given in jest to a miserable hovel].

Cattaby Deerness: part of 'Skea' tunship: vanished [Norse personal name *Kati*, Norse *boer* farm].

Cattiquoy/Cataquoy Stronsay, Whitehall: field name [Norse *kví* Enclosure, *keyta* foul water = mire?].

Cattispells/Katespells Sanday: field name, Burness (see above for possible explanation) [Norwegian dialect *spjell* a strip of ground].

Catty Maggie's Quarry St. Ola [a flooded quarry by the side of the road at the Heathery Loan, where a local traveller woman used to pitch her tent. She fed all the stary cats in the area, hence her nickname].

Cauldhame North Ronaldsay; Stronsay; Birsay: [refers to a poorly built draughty house].

Cava An island in 'Scapa Flow: inhabited until 1993 [Norse *kálfr* calf, *ey* island: 'calf' is often used to describe small islands lying off larger (c.f. 'Calf of Man')].

Cavan Sanday; North Ronaldsay; Birsay, Twatt, Eastabist (in 'The Hillside'): [a remnant of the Celtic language and one of the most difficult Orkney placenames to explain; Irish *cabhan* is a convex or concave feature in the landscape so it can mean a 'hollow' or a 'mound'! In the case of 'How-Cavan' in 'Leaquoy', Marwick, it can only mean 'mound' since Norse *haugr* is a mound. There are three instances of the related form 'Cuvan' in Sanday, one of which in 'Cleat', Lady parish, contains a large burnt mound: 'Stein-Cavan' in 'Farafield', Birsay, suggests a mound of stones. It can be assumed that most of the Orkney 'Cavan' placenames relate originally to mounds many of which have been levelled].

Cavelton South Ronaldsay: [Scots *cavel* in this case ownership of a piece of land decided by casting lots].

Cavit Wyre: [Norse *kúfóttr* a heaped, convex shape referring most probably to a turf dwelling like a 'black house' in the Western Isles].

Cellar Sanday: the beach at 'Nouster', Burness [Norse *hellur* slabs of rock].

Cellar o Hamargeo North Ronaldsay: [Norse *gjá* ravine which ends in a cave, *hamarr* projecting rock, *hellur* slabs of rock].

Cellardyke Burray; South Ronaldsay; Deerness: [Scots 'cellar' = 'silver': when shoals of herring were frequent on the east coast, the 'silver darlings' were split and placed on stone walls: there is a 'Cellardyke' in Fife on the Scottish Mainland].

Chair of Lyde Firth/Harray: [Norse *kjarr* low scrubland, *hlið* a trackway].

Chair Soond Birsay: entrance to 'Big Ramla Geo' [Norse *sund* a channel: origin of 'chair' here uncertain].

Chaldro Rock Sanday: a rock favoured by the oystercatcher [Norse *tjaldr* oystercatcher].

Chalmersquoy Westray, Dykeside: [originally occupied by a Chalmers family].

Charlie's Hole Stromness: the name given to a cave at the foot of the 'Black Craig' [Charlie was the only survivor of the sailing ship, *Star of Dundee*, which was wrecked there in 1834. He survived for four days in the cave before climbing the cliffs once the storm had abated.].

Cheese/Keys Geo Rousay: rocky inlet in 'Quandal' [Norse *gjá* ravine, Norse *kaesa* to ferment, in this case probably meaning 'foaming sea'].

Chenziebreck Holm: [Norse *tjörn* pool, *brekka* slope].

Cherra Taing (see 'Gerra Taing').

Chin-chinnet Rousay: [Norse *tjörn* pool, the second part of the placename suggests the female personal name 'Janet', but it would be unusual to have a personal name attached to such a feature: a good example of a rhyming placename (c.f. Meery-Mawry)].

Ching/Chung Sanday: field name, 17th century [Norse *tjörn* pool].

Chinglabreck Flotta: [Norse *tjörn* pool, *brekka* slope (see 'Chinglo' forms below)].

Chinglo Firth; Evie/Rendall; Birsay, Northside, Marwick, Kirbister: [Norse *tjörn* pool, Ny/Norse *lo/lôn* water, marsh (see 'Choinamo' below)].

Chingloo Stromness, Garth; Harray; Stenness: (see above).

Chinigar Orphir: in the Swanbister/Smoogro area [Norse *tjörn* pool, *garðr* farm].

Choin 1. Birsay, Marwick, Leaquoy: field name, in wintertime a pool forms in the middle of this field [Norse *tjörn* pool].

Choin 2. Birsay: near 'Folsetter' [Norse *tjörn* pool].

Choin, The Birsay, Marwick Bay: part of the bay blocked off by rocks which has created a sea pool [Norse *tjörn* pool].

Choinamo Birsay: between 'Marwick House' and 'Leabreck': also called 'Chingloo' [Norse *tjörn* pool, *mór* moor/marsh].

Choldertoo Skerry Birsay: [Norse *tjaldr* oystercatcher, *púfa* mound. A rocky eminence favoured by oystercatchers].

Choon Harray: (see Ching).

Choor-house Rousay, Westside: vanished [Norse *kjarr* low scrubland (as in 'Chair o the Lyde')].

Chuccaby Walls: [Norse *þykkvi-boer* 'thick' farm, probably in the sense of 'a number of buildings' as one would describe a 'thick' forest in English (see 'Thickbigging')].

Chuivity North Ronaldsay: [see 'Jubidee' forms for explanation].

Chun Stromness: (see 'Ching').

Citadale Stromness, Innertoon: [a farm first recorded in the 17th century. Therefore, the name is probably a corruption of some Norse forms: 'dale' is often a Scots orthographic form of Norse *dý* marshland: origin of 'Cita' unknown: there is however a placename 'Cripple Seety' recorded on the farm of 'Biggings' in Stenness].

Citadel St. Ola, Kirkwall: a small cottage: [name transferred perhaps from 'Citadale' in Stromness (above)].

City Birsay: a vanished cottage, Twatt [name given in jest for some reason or other].

Claisbreck Hoy: vanished [Norse *brekka* slope: origin of 'clais' unknown].

Clamer/Claymire/Klaimer Sanday, Hellihowe: field name [English 'clay mire'].

Clams North Ronaldsay: location and origin unknown [perhaps a field, from Scots *clamse* damp or moist].

Clankvengeance Rendall: (also called 'Pulaland') an old cottage which lay on the land of the 'Hall o Rendall' [Orkney dialect form of Scots *clatter-vengeance* a gossip: the name must have originally applied to an inhabitant and was then transferred to the cottage: there are several instances of such transfers in Orkney: (see 'Clatterha' below)].

Clarko Evie: a mound [a mound on the land of a person with the surname Clark/Clerk: there were Clark families in Orphir in the 18th century: Norse *haugr* mound: mounds often took the name of the owner of the land at a particular time].

Classiquoy Rousay: small, hilltop cottages above 'Avaldsay' [Norse *Klas* diminutive of first name 'Nikulas', *kví* enclosure].

Clatterha North Ronaldsay: [named from a woman (or man) who 'clatters' or 'gossips' (see Clankvengeance above)].

Clava Clivvy South Ronaldsay: ['clivvy' is the Orkney dialect form of Norse *klif* a cleft in a rock face, and also in the sense 'path down a cliff face': 'Clava' seems to be a duplicated form: several such duplicated forms are found in Orkney placenames e.g., 'Meery-Mawry', a former marshy area west of 'Leabreck' in Marwick (see 'Chingloo')].

Clavan (see 'Clevan').

Clay Toumels Stronsay: a field southwest of Clestran [Norse *tún-völlr* home field].

Claypows North Ronaldsay: [Scots *pow* pool].

Clayquoy Stronsay: east of 'Holin' [Norse *kví* enclosure].

Claysheed Birsay, Eastabist; Wyre: [Scots *sheed* a field].

Clead Knowes o Birsay: mounds on the top of the hill near 'Ruebreck' (see 'Klett' in the Appendix).

Cleat Stronsay; Sanday; South Ronaldsay; Westray; St. Ola: (see 'Klett' in the Appendix).

Cleatfurrows Birsay, Northside: a farm on the coast adjacent to St. Magnus Kirk but believed to originally have been further east [(for 'Cleat', see the Appendix), Norse *for-vað* 'shallow water between cliffs and tidal reach of the sea].

Cleftors South Ronaldsay, Herston: vanished [Norse *gljúfr* a gully: a 't' is inserted in the Orkney dialect forms e.g., 'Glifters o Pegal' on Hoy].

Clerkshoose Sanday, Elsness: [Norse *klerkr* scribe (see 'Quoyclerks')].

Clerksquoy Shapinsay: (see above).

Clestran Stronsay: [Norse *klettr* a sacred place: nearby is 'St. Margaret's Chapel'].

Clestran/Clestron Orphir: it takes its name from the tall prehistoric standing stone (2.6 metres high) near the beach, now removed and leaning on a field dyke [(see Klett in the Appendix), Norse *strönd* beach].

Cletig Sanday: (see 'Clett Geo' below).

Clett 1. Harray: field name to east of 'Mill o Russland' [Norse *klettr* suggests location of some pagan relic of which there is no trace (see Klett in the Appendix)].

Clett 2. North Ronaldsay: on the coast [Norse *klettr* rock].

Clett Geo North Ronaldsay: [Norse *klettr* rock, *gjá* ravine: the placename suggests a ravine with a prominent rock or rock stack in it].

Clett Roos North Ronaldsay: [a big rocky islet in Gue, the ravine mentioned below: 'roos' suggests Orkney dialect 'roos', heaps of stones/rocks from Norse *hrúga*, heap].

Clett Sweyns North Ronaldsay: an outlying rock near 'Burrian' [Norse *klettr* rock: several offshore rocks have personal names attached which usually indicate a stranding: this must be an early incidence of this since the name 'Sweyn' would pre-date the 19th century].

Clettack Skerry one of the 'Pentland Skerries' [Norse *klettr* rock with local diminutive 'ack'].

Clettaly Firth: (see 'Lettaly').

Clettkins Stenness: on the land of Biggings [Norse *klettr* rock: origin of 'kins' uncertain].

Cletton, Kirk o Harray: on shore of 'Harray Loch' [Norse *klett-inn* with its Orkney meaning 'the place of sacred significance': in this case the kirk has been built on pagan land (see 'Klett' in the Appendix)].

Cletts Graemsay: in the north of the island, near 'Fillets'. Seems to have originally covered a sizeable area because of the distribution of 'Clett' related names (see below).

Cletts South Ronaldsay: [Norse *klettar* plural of *klettr* rock: significantly they lie in the 'Paplay' district (see Klett in the Appendix)].

Cletts Walls: (see 'Cletts', South Ronaldsay, for an explanation).

Cletts, Pool o South Ronaldsay: a sandy bay lying off Cletts (above) [Norse *pollr* pool but sometimes used in Orkney to describe a small bay].

Cletts, Skerry of Graemsay: (see 'Cletts', Graemsay, above).

Clevan Sanday: a former small cottage: now a field name [Norse *klef-inn* the room].

Clevies, The South Walls: [Norse *klif* path in cliffs giving access to the beach (see Clava Clivvy)].

Clibberwick Rendall: [Norse *kleppr* a lump, *vík* bay].

Clickfart Wyre: a small field [origin of 'click' unknown unless it is a form of 'clink' (see 'Clinkhammer' below): English slang 'fart' used in the sense 'worthless': e.g., coarse dialect 'No worth a fart', useless].

Clickimin Sanday; Evie/Rendall; South Ronaldsay; Stenness; St. Ola, Kirkwall; Firth: [the placename became popular as the name of an inn after Scott published his novel 'Ronan's Well'. The Firth example was in the 'Grimbister' area].

Clicknafea Hoy: an exceptionally steep sided spur of 'Moor Fea' in Rackwick [Norse *klett-inn* the rock but used in the sense 'cliff' here, Norse *fjall* hill].

Cliff/Clifts Sanday: [origin uncertain: at the time of the Ordnance Survey in the 1880s Cliff/Clifts lay on a very distinct path, so the placename may be Norse *klifit* the path, but this word is normally reserved for paths down a cliff leading to the shore (see 'Clivvith')].

Clifftrall Stronsay: a field west southwest of Cleat [(for 'clifft' element see above): 'rall' suffix cannot be explained].

Climmer Sand Sanday: a shoal in the sandy area of 'Lamaness' (see 'Clamer' for origin of the name).

Climpers, The Rendall, Crook: field name [probably a form of Norse *kleppr* lump].

Clink Geos Rousay: ['clink' = Norse *klettr* rock, which suggests that there is or was an isolated rock in this ravine which explains the name].

Clinkhammer Sanday; Rousay; Westray: ['clink' is a variation of Norse *klettr* rock and appears in north English placenames as 'clint': Danish *klint* is a rock: the placename is therefore 'rock rock': Norse *hamarr-klettr* is 'rock' (see 'Hammarcleat', Sandwick)].

Clipperbreck Rendall: same house as 'West Shore'? [Norse *kleppr* a lump, *brekka* slope (compare 'Clibberwick')].

Cliva Stronsay: beach feature in northeast corner of 'Holland' near 'Lower Dishes' [Norse *klif* path down a cliff to the shore (see 'The Clevies')].

Clivgoe/Kliv Geo Birsay: coastal feature (see above) [Norse *gjá* ravine].

Clivie Bay St. Andrews: near 'Stembister' (see above).

Clivvith/Klivvith Birsay: [Norse *klifit* the path down a cliff to the shore].

Cloack Sanday: (see 'Clouk', Stromness).

Cloddy Hall South Ronaldsay; Burray: [English 'clod': probably refers to a primitive dwelling made of turf].

Cloen Sanday: field name, mentioned in Fea's 17th century diary [Norse *klauf* cattle, *eng* field (see 'Clowally' below)].

Clogg, The Sanday, Tresness: a narrow coastal channel [a form of Scots *cleuch*, English 'clough' a ravine: the name must pre-date the invasion of the sea here (see 'Clouk', Stromness)].

Cloke Birsay, Beaquoyside: (see 'Clouk', Stromness).

Clook Rendall: (see 'Clouk', Stromness).

Clouck Orphir: (see 'Clouk', Stromness).

Cloudy Westray, Cleatown: [= cloddy? (c.f. 'Cloddy Hall' above)].

Clouk 1. Evie: (see below).

Clouk 2. Stromness: [a form of English 'clough' ravine: in Orkney the word is used in the sense 'long depression' which sometimes has a stream in it: by far the best example of the use of this word is 'Clouk' in Stromness which has a stream passing by].

Clouster 1. Stromness: (see below).

Clouster 2. Westray, Aikerness: vanished [it is tempting to think that this was land bequeathed to a cloister, most likely in this case the Munkeliv Kloster in Bergen, which was long associated with Orkney, but it really means 'an enclosed place', the original meaning of 'cloister'].

Clouston Stenness: one of a number of important Norse estates which, surrounded the Stenness and Harray Lochs [all are prefaced with the name of the owner at a certain time: along with the Norse word *staðr* meaning 'estate' it became fossilised as a placename but changed by the Scots to 'ston': Norse personal name in this case is *Kló*: to the west of this estate is 'Onston', the property of a man *Örn* (the 'r' is lost in Orkney Norn)].

Clova St. Ola: now part of 'Fea' [Norse *klauf* cattle: part of this placename is lost (see 'Clowally' and 'Cloen' for comparison)].

Cloventots South Ronaldsay, Herston: a coastal feature [Norse *klofinn* cleft, *tota* protuberance].

Clovigar Stromness: [Norse *klauf* cattle, *garðr* farm].

Clowally Orphir: east of Houton Bay [Norse *klauf* a cloven-footed animal, usually cattle, *hlíð* slope (see 'Klogang')].

Clu Ber Deerness: a stretch of precipitous cliffs near 'The Brough' [Norse *berg* elevated rocky ground: origin of 'clu' unknown].

Cluik Rousay: vanished: lay near Banks in 'Frotoft' possibly on the banks of the nearby stream (see 'Clouk' Stromness).

Clumlie Sandwick: [Norse *kuml* mound, related to the 'Stones of Via', *hlíð* slope].

Clump o Backber Eday: a small headland on 'War Ness' [English 'clump' (see 'Backber Geo')].

Clumps, The Westray: two high-water rocks connected at low tide [English 'clump'].

Clumpy Rousay: croft in the 'Sourin' district [name must refer to 'clumps' in the landscape].

Clyar, Geo of Papa Westray: a small ravine on the west coast of the island [origin uncertain: perhaps Norse *kliðr* din or murmur: several ravines in Orkney have 'noisy' explanations which relate to breaking surf].

Clysper Evie: near 'Neigarth' [possibly a field name: no other information available].

Clyver Rousay: an old cottage which lay at the base of the 'Sinian Hammers' [plural form of Norse *kleif* hillside track (c.f. 'Cliva')].

Coal Hill Orphir: a small hill south of 'Greeniegoe' [it was said that the peat here was of such good quality that it resembled coal].

Coawin Orphir: [Norse *kví-in* the enclosure (c.f. 'Quean' in Sandwick)].

Cobrance St. Andrews: [originally 'Cockburnsquoy': Norse *kví* enclosure, 'Cockburn' is a Scots surname, in this case dating from an early period in Orkney].

Cockburnsquoy St. Andrews: (see 'Cobrance' above).

Cockle Hall St. Andrews: [named after the number of shells in the surrounding field: to the west is 'Cockle Bay'].

Cockle House/Cocklefist Westray, Fribo: (see references to 'cockle' above).

Cockleha' Sanday: Cross parish, near 'Odinsgarth', vanished [so called from the large number of shells in the area].

Cockmurra Holm: [Norse *mýrr* poor marshy or unproductive ground: origin of 'cock' in this context unknown].

Cockpen Rendall: [no doubt applied derisorily to an inhabitant, based on the ballad 'The Laird o Cockpen' in Midlothian who lived in a grand style].

Codling Stronsay: field name northwest of 'Midgarth' [metaphorical use of 'small cod' applied to a small field].

Cogar Rousay: (see 'Calgarth').

Cogar/Calgair Rousay: (see 'Calgair').

Cograne Harray, Grimeston: a small promontory on the 'Harray Loch' [Norse *kví* enclosure, *graen* green].

Coldamo Stenness: a farm [Norse *kaldr* cold, *mór* moor].

Coldras Birsay: part of a hill above 'Itherigeo' [Norse *kaldr* cold, 'ras' seems to be a local Norn word for a 'raising up' in the sense 'steep', related to Norse *hreysi* a cairn].

Coldras Sandwick: a headland on the coast (see above).

Coldras, Knee o Rousay, Tarraclett: [Norse *kné* knee, the cliff face having the shape of a bended knee (see also 'Coldras' above)].

Cole Pit Mire North Ronaldsay: [location unknown but name related to hard, coal-like peat found in a marshy area].

Colligan Sandwick, Lyking: field name [(for 'colli' see below) origin of 'gan' unknown].

Colligarth Sanday: [Norse *garðr* farm (see 'Colliness' below)].

Colliness Sanday: Lady parish [a coastal feature with a huge mound and a chapel site, etymology of 'Colli' (pronounced 'collya') uncertain but must be related to Norse *kollr* head in the sense 'heap' (see also 'Cuthilgarth')].

Colster Deerness: [Norse *saetr* seasonally used hut once animals were released on to the common, Norse personal name *Kollr*].

Colston Stenness: [(for 'col' see above): Norse *staðr* estate: it lay in the area of 'Moa' farm].

Comely St. Andrews: [Norse *kuml* a cairn: (c.f. 'Cumlaquoy)'].

Comely Stronsay: (see 'Cumley').

Coneyhole/Conninghole Stronsay: [English 'rabbit hole': a house name given in jest].

Congesquoy Stromness: (earlier 'Conquesquoy') [Norse *kví* enclosure, Scots *conquest* property acquired by the Earl, the Bishop or major landholder].

Congie Sanday: a coastal feature in east Burness [North Isles dialect *kungle* a boulder, a word related to German *Kugel* a ball shape].

Conglibanks North Ronaldsay: a beach name (see above).

Conglibist North Ronaldsay, Senness: (see above) [Norse *ból-staðr* farm].

Conningham (see 'Cunningham').

Conquoy Rousay: a field, probably originally a house which gave its name to a nearby ravine, 'Geo o Conquoy' [Scots *conzie* corner, Norse *kví* enclosure].

Consgar Sandwick: now Flotterstone (see 'Conyer' below).

Cony Geo Orphir: a small indentation in the rocky coast [Sots *coney* rabbit].

Conyer Harray: earlier 'Quoyconzie': suggests a form 'Quoycongie' [Norse *garðr* farm, Scots *conzie* a corner].

Conygue Orphir: [English dialect 'coney' rabbit, Norse *gjá* ravine].

Conziebreck Sandwick: [Norse *brekka* slope: (see 'Conyer' above)].

Coo Sanday, Cross parish: [Norse *kví* enclosure: (see below for 'coo')].

Coo's Belly South Ronaldsay: a depression in the cliffs near 'The Golt' [Scots *coo* cow, Norse *boeli* enclosure (c.f. 'Allibelly Geo')].

Cooan Westray: [Norse *kví* enclosure is often written 'co' in Orkney placenames as in above: here it has the definite article attached to give the form *kví-in* (c.f. 'Quean', a farm in 'Newgarth,' Sandwick)].

Coomire North Ronaldsay: [Norse *kví* enclosure, *mýrr* poor quality, generally wet land].

Coopalash Shapinsay: a rocky point on the east coast of the island [Norse *kobba* a seal, Norwegian *fles* a skerry: there are several skerries in Orkney named 'Less', 'Lesh' or 'Lashy', all of which lose the initial 'f'].

Cooperhall Sanday: [from the surname 'Cooper': 'ha' = hall, but in this case, a small cottage].

Cooperhouse Birsay, Marwick: [earlier 'Couphous' and 'Couperhouse' which suggests that this house name has a different explanation: perhaps Norse *kaup* to trade, hence *kaup-hús* a shop].

Cooperhouse Birsay, Northside: [from the surname 'Cooper': the Coopers came from Sanday to this area of Birsay].

Coorsa, The Stronsay: a rocky beach area (see 'Coursan' below).

Coorsan Harray: a field name Netherbrough, just to the west of 'Curcabreck' (see above).

Coorsan/Coursan Eday: a rocky stretch of shore to the west of Fersness Hill [Orkney dialect 'coorse' rough, seems only possible explanation].

Coorse North Ronaldsay: a rough, rocky stretch of beach in the northwest of the island.

Coos Moo Sanday: field name [Norse *kví* enclosure, *smár* small].

Copenageo St. Andrews: a farm in Yinstay [Norse *gjá* in this sense used of a stream (see 'Millgoe' and Appendix), Norse *kobbana* genitive plural of Norse *kobbi* a seal: it would seem that the mouth of this stream was a favoured place for seals to lie].

Copinsay An island off the coast of Deerness: inhabited until the 1970s: [Norse *Kolbeinsey* Kolbein's island].

Coplands Clevie Orphir, Veness: ['Copland', a rarely recorded surname in Orphir: (see 'Cliva' for explanation of 'Clivie')].

Coppa Stronsay: shore feature northwest of 'Blan Loch' [Norse *koppa* a convex/concave shape, most probably the latter, hence a cup shape in the rocks].

Corbie Ness Eday: [Scots *corbie* raven, Norse *nes* point of land].

Corkaquina Birsay, Marwick: [Norse *korki* oats (from Gaelic *coirce*), Norse *kví-in* the enclosure].

Corkatae (see 'Curcaday').

Corn Goe/goe Sanday; Orphir: [Norse *korn* corn, *gjá* ravine, i.e., an inlet from where corn was imported/exported].

Corn Graand Papa Stronsay: [Norse *korn* corn, *grandi* beach, which suggests that 'corn' was exported/imported from this location].

Corn Holm Copinsay [Norse *korn* corn, *hólmr* island].

Cornquoy Holm: [Norse *kví* enclosure, Norse *korn* corn i.e., 'bere'].

Corrigill Graemsay: (same placename origin as above) there is no stream here today, only a drainage ditch which opens on to the shore at 'Burra Sound'. It must be one of many hundreds of little streams in Orkney which have vanished due to drainage. When the Graemsay 'Corrigill' placename was first recorded in the 15th century, bairns could still probably float their little boats in it.

Corrigill/Corrigall Harray: ['Corri' is an extremely rare early Celtic stream name found only in Dorset 'Cory' and the Somerset River 'Cary', Norse *gil* a ravine but with the sense 'stream': the change from Norse *gil* to Norse *gall* (English 'gall'), describes the poor quality of the land here, 'as bitter as gall' (see 'Geo' in Appendix)].

Corse Rousay: a farm in 'Frotoft' [probably takes its name from the rough shoreline (see 'Coorsan')].

Corse St. Ola: [probable site of a former cross, Norse *kross*].

Corsegate/Costgate North Ronaldsay: [Norse *kross* a cross, *gata* path i.e., path to, or past, a cross].

Corsey's Pin Sanday: a wooden post marking the limit of 'Northskaill's' land [a previous inhabitant had the surname 'Corsie'].

Corsquoy Sanday: [Norse *kross*, kví enclosure].

Corston Harray: [one of several Norse estates in the West Mainland, all being named after the proprietor at the time, in this case probably *Kári*: (see 'Cairston')].

Corwin Orphir: in the 'Swanbister' area: no other information.

Coss/Cause Swona: [Norse *köss* a heap (of rocks in this case)].

Costa Evie: [Norse *staðr* estate, Norse personal name, perhaps *Kollr*].

Cot Birsay, Southside: there are dozens of 'Cot' placenames in Orkney: only a few significant ones are mentioned below [English 'cot', Norse *kot*: most cot names would have an English origin].

Cot o Rusness Sanday: former name of 'Hogsha'.

Cot-on-Hill Shapinsay: this name explains 'Cottonhill' (below).

Cottiscarth Rendall: [Norse *kot í skarði*, Norse *skarð* a hill saddle].

Cottonhill Evie: (see 'Cot-on-Hill' above.)

Cottorochan Westray, Rapness: [Rochan is an extremely rare form of the Orkney surname 'Richan'].

Coubister Orphir; Firth: [Norse *kví* enclosure, *ból-staðr* farm].

Coubister Skerry Orphir: lies off the coast of 'Petertown'.

Coulls South Ronaldsay: [Norse *kular* hillocks (c.f. 'Earny Coulags')].

Couls Geo North Ronaldsay: a large ravine on the east coast (see above for possible derivation).

Coupersquoy Westray: [the surname 'Cooper', Norse *kví* enclosure].

Coursan Eday: (see 'Coorsan').

Couse Point Holm: [perhaps Norse *köss* a heap (of stones?)].

Couters Hill Westray: [Norwegian (Nynorsk) *køyte* marsh, used here in the plural form (see Kuter's Mire', North Ronaldsay)].

Cove's Hole Birsay: a large cave on 'The Brough' [figurative use of Norse *kofi* a room].

Cowbister (see 'Coubister' above).

Cowquoy Sanday: mentioned in Goodfellow's *'Church History of Sanday'*, it was situated on the 'Plain of Fidge' [Norse *kýr* cow (the 'r' is not pronounced), *kví* enclosure].

Cox Field Stronsay: northwest of 'Midgarth' [there is no official record of a 'Cox' family in Stronsay].

Cra Pow, The Rendall: a pool on top of 'Land Hill' [Norse *kró*, pen, Scots *pow* pool].

Cra Pen Rendall: an old house and land, the remains can still be seen [carries the same meaning as 'Craco'].

Cra's Nest Sanday: a coastal feature, Burness parish [a small rock stack broad at the top and tapering to the base similar to the 'crow's nest' of a ship].

Craa Heid Sanday: a mound near 'Backaskaill' [origin uncertain; probably Norse *kró* pen, corrupted to dialect *craa* crow, dialect *heid* head, used metaphorically].

Crabtoe Sanday: near 'Whistlebrae', now a field name: [a nickname referring perhaps to the shape of the field].

Crack Sanday, Northwall: also recorded in Shetland [Norse *kraki* a pole, perhaps originally a boundary marker (compare 'Corsey's Pin')].

Cracka Longi Evie: the upper reaches of the 'Burn of Savegarth' [Norse *krókr* anything crooked, in this case a stream, *langr* long].

Craco Westray, Dykeside: [Norse *kró* pen, *kví* enclosure: 'Craco' is also the name of an abandoned mountain town in 'Basilicata', Italy!].

Craffin Stromness, Ootertoon: [Norse *kró* enclosure, *fen* marsh].

Crafty there are several small fields in Orkney called 'Crafty' e.g., at 'Walliwall', St. Ola and in 'Kirkwall', just off Junction Road, where it was the traditional site of the 'Lammas Market' [Scots *craft* a small piece of land, plus diminutive ie/y].

Craie, Knowe o Rousay: [Scots *knowe* knoll, Norse *krá*, Orkney dialect *kreu* small enclosure].

Craig o Nevs Stronsay: cliff below 'Odness' (see 'Nevs').

Craig o Rittin Evie: (see 'Rittin').

Craig o the O Sanday: a coastal feature near 'Gresmay', Burness parish [Scots *craig* cliff, Norse *á* stream].

Craiglands Birsay, Southside: [near the 'craig' or cliff].

Craigs o Scarataing Evie: ('see Scarrataing').

Crairie St. Andrews: name given to a hilltop which forms the boundary of St. Andrews and Holm [Norse *kraer* plural of *krá* corner, used here in the sense of 'animal pen' for summer use: usually on hilltops or hillsides].

Crantit St. Ola: earlier 'Crannystoft' [Norse personal name *Grani*, Norse *topt* a house site].

Cranybar Eynhallow: northeast coast [Norse *grandi* beach, *berg* rock].

Crapygoe Burray: [Norse *krappr* narrow, *gjá* ravine].

Craw Stane o Gue North Ronaldsay: a prominent rock feature on the west coast of the island [suggests 'crow stone', Norse *gjá* ravine].

Craw's Nest Westray, Kirkbrae: ['crow's nest', a name given in jest to an old cottage here].

Crawfords Rendall, Upper Cottiscarth: field name, site of an old house [no one by the name 'Crawford' is recorded in Rendall but in the 1850s there was a pedlar with this name living in' Dowaker' in Firth, the site of which is unknown — perhaps just across the parish boundary: it is presumed that the pedlar lived in this cottage at one time and his name became linked with it].

Craya Evie; Stromness, Innertoon, Kirbister: [animal pen (see 'Creya' below)].

Creara Head South Ronaldsay: [Norse *krókar* plural of *krókr* nook or corner but used here in the sense animal pen].

Crearhowe Holm: (see 'Creara' above) [Norse *haugr* mound].

Creekland Hoy: a rocky and sandy stretch to the north of 'Moness Pier' [Norse *kriki* a crack, referring to the nature of the rocks here].

Creels, The Copinsay: (see below).

Creels of Banks Holm: refers to the rocky shore to the south of 'Banks' [a place where 'creels' may be set].

Creeso Sanday, Taftsness: beach name [dialect *kreu* enclosure (with English plural), possibly Norse *haugr* mound].

Cressy Geo Evie: there is no ravine here [(see 'Geo' in the Appendix), origin of 'Cressy' uncertain].

Creu Rendall, 'Quoyhenry': field name [Gaelic *crò*, Norse *kró* enclosure].

Crewgather North Ronaldsay: beach name in northwest of the island [Norse *krókr* nook but used in Orkney in the sense 'animal pen', *garðar* walls].

Creya (earlier Gregay) Deerness; Orphir; Rousay; Stromness: [Norse *krókr* nook or corner but used here in the sense animal pen].

Creyabreck Holm: (see above).

Cribbaquoy Harray: a dwelling house [Norse *kreppa* narrow, which may apply to the land, *kví* enclosure: (see 'Crubban')].

Cringamaya (see 'Kringlamaya').

Cringlafiold Stromness, Kirbister: [Norse *kringla* circle, *fjall* hill: refers to the rounded shape of the hill].

Cringlags Deerness: beach feature: [Norse *kringla* a circle, *lág* a deep hollow: this word applies to a small lake/pool in Shetland: the etymology would be 'deep circular pool'].

Cringlaquoy, Hammers o Rousay: possibly a round enclosure several of which were found in some parts of Orkney [Norse *kringla* circle, *kví* enclosure].

Cringlefield St. Andrews: (see above and below).

Cringlejean Sanday, Rue: field name [Norse *kringla* a circle, *tjörn* a small pool: (compare 'Klingresjon', a pool in Shetland)].

Cringleringer Holm: a well in the field next to the old kirk [Norse *kringla* a circle, *hringar* circles: the duplication is not understood].

Cringley Geo Sanday, Tresness: [Norse *kringla* a circle used in the sense 'bent' or 'twisted' here (compare 'Crinky Geo')].

Cringlimire Geo North Ronaldsay: (see 'Kringlamaya').

Cringlin Firth: a feature near or in 'North Gue' [Norse *kringl-in* the circle].

Cringlo Dounby: near Hyval [Norse *kringla* circle, Norwegian (Nynorsk) *lo/ló* a marshy moor].

Cringloo Stenness; Harray: (see above).

Crinilag South Ronaldsay, Windwick: precise location uncertain but near 'Ossi Taing' [origin as above].

Crinky Geo Evie: (see 'Cringley Geo' above).

Cripple Seety Stenness: on the site of 'Biggings' farm [origin unknown (compare 'Citadel')].

Crismo Evie/Birsay: a farm [personal name *Kristin*, Norse *mýrr* poor quality land].

Cro Taing Orphir; Stronsay: [Norse *kró* nook/animal pen, *tangi* point of land].

Croan Evie: [Norse *kró-in* the enclosure].

Croannie Quoy Evie: (see above).

Crobist Harray: field name Grimeston, southeast of 'Biggings': ancient farm site [Norse *kró* nook/animal pen, *ból-staðr* farm].

Crock Ness Walls: (see above).

Crock Orphir: [Norse *krókr* nook or corner but used here in the sense animal 'pen'].

Crofty St. Andrews: (see 'Crafty').

Cronstad South Ronaldsay, Hoxa: field name 'Roeberry Farm' (see below).

Cronstadt/Kronstadt South Ronaldsay, Grimness: vanished: remains still visible in the year 2000: [named by a naval man: 'Kronstadt' was the commercial seaport of St. Petersburg before the 1880s: the relationship with the above is unknown].

Crontatt Rendall: 1642: location unknown [a form of 'Kronstad' — from Baltic trading days].

Croo Evie: (see 'Creu').

Croo Stone South Ronaldsay: (see 'Crustane' for possible explanation).

Croo Taing Graemsay; South Ronaldsay: (see 'Creu' above).

Crook 1. Rendall; Birsay, Swannay, Kirbister, Marwick; Eday, Russness; Wyre; Westray; South Ronaldsay: [Norse *krókr* nook but used in the sense 'small enclosure' in Orkney].

Crook 2. Sanday: near 'Pool' [Norse *krókr* a bend, in a field in this case].

Crook, The Sanday, Tresness: a beach name [Norse *krókr* in this sense, a nook].

Crooks Nest/Ness Stronsay: northwest corner of Mill Bay [Norse *krókr nes* a point of land with an enclosure on it].

Crooly Rousay: old houses in Quandale [Norse *kró* enclosure *hlíð* slope].

Croonofinya Firth, Glebe: [Norse *kró-in* the enclosure, *fen-it* the marsh: the suffix 't' of a neuter Norse noun is pronounced 'th'].

Croos Sanday: beach feature [dialect 'creus' (compare 'Craa Heid')].

Croostane Orphir: location unknown.

Croosteeths /Cronsteethes Orphir: [Norse *kró* 'animal pen', Icelandic *stoeði* position or site].

Cross parish Sanday: [named from the Holy Cross Kirk 3 kilometres northwest of 'Kettletoft' village and built on a prehistoric site].

Crossgate 1. Sanday: two houses in Sanday had this name; they would have been built near to, or past, a cross (see above).

Crossgate 2. Westray: location uncertain (see above for possible explanation).

Crossgate Shapinsay: a farm: originally a path to, or past, a cross [Norse *gata* path].

Crossgate/Corsegate North Ronaldsay: a path leading from the 'Senness' area past a cross: (see above).

Crossiecrown St. Ola: farm of 11 acres in 1851, situated on the shore northwest of 'Quanterness' farm [origin of name unknown].

Crotaing Orphir: [Norse *kró* enclosure, *tangi* point of land].

Crotrive Sanday: [Norse *kró* pen, (for 'trive' see 'Treb')].

Croval Sandwick; Orphir; Stromness: [Norse *kró* enclosure, *völlr* field].

Crow Taing Sanday: coastal feature, 'Tafts' [Norse *kró* enclosure, *tangi*, a tongue of land].

Crow Tuo Westray, Rapness: probable burial mound [Norse *kró* enclosure, *þúfa* a mound].

Crowald Westray: [Norse *kró* enclosure, *völlr* field].

Crowanna Stronsay: east of 'Little Water' [Norse *kró-in* the enclosure].

Crowar (see 'Cruar' Rendall).

Crowber Eday: a small cottage on the west coast of the island [Norse *kró* Enclosure, *berg* rock which must relate to the nearby coast].

Crowdue Birsay, Northside: [Norse *kró* enclosure, (for 'due' see Geo in the Appendix)].

Croweoura Orphir: [Norse *króar* enclosures, *efri* upper or higher].

Crowland Westray: [Norse *kró* enclosure].

Crowness St. Ola: [Norse *kró* enclosure, *nes* point of land].

Crownest Flotta: (see 'Crowsnest').

Crowra Rendall: (see also 'Cruar').

Crowrabreck Birsay, Whitecleat: [Norse *króar* enclosures, *brekka* slope].

Crowsnest Hoy: [name given in jest to two other old Orkney houses e.g. Flotta (Crowness) and Kirkbrae, Westray (Craa's Nest)].

Croy Hill Orphir: [Norse *kró* enclosure (see 'Cru Hill' below): no connection with the surname 'Croy'].

Croy's Park Sanday: field name, now the site of the Council Houses [from the Scots surname 'Croy'].

Cru Hill St. Andrews: [Norse *kró* enclosure].

Cruaday Sandwick: [Norse *kró* enclosure, *dý* marshland (compare 'Cruddy' and 'Crudy' below)].

Cruan Rendall; Firth: [Norse *kró-in* the enclosure].

Cruanna Stronsay: [Norse *kró-in* the enclosure: often a meaningless 'a/ie/o' suffix appears in Orkney placenames, the best example being *kvín*, enclosure which frequently takes the form 'Queena'].

Cruannie Rousay: (see above).

Cruar Rousay; Rendall: the Rendall placename is now known as 'Crowrar' [Norse *króar* enclosures].

Cruargeo Westray, Skelwick: a farm near the shore (see above).

Crub o Causn Flotta: sheltered noust inside 'Point o Hasbin/Heyspan' [(see 'Cruban' below), Norse *kös-in* the heap (of e.g., stones)].

Cruban Sandwick: a narrow inlet on the west coast of Sandwick [related to many Germanic words meaning narrow or confined e.g., Shetland dialect 'krobb' a small enclosure (compare 'Crapygeo' above): the 'an' suffix suggests a definite article].

Cruddy Sanday, Garbo: field name (see 'Cruaday' above).

Crudy/Cruddy (see 'Cruaday').

Crue Maaron Deme/Kromerandeem Sanday: field name with a burnt mound, Northwall [Norse *kró* enclosure, Merran was a local female spirit derived from Norse *marin* an ogress, 'Deme' = Scots 'Dame'].

Crue Taing Sanday: coastal feature, Tresness [Norse *kró* enclosure, *tangi* tongue of land].

Crues o Ire Sanday: enclosures on the 'Holms o Ire' [Norse *kró* pen (see 'Ire')].

Cruesbreck North Ronaldsay: [Norse *kró* pen, *brekka* slope].

Cruff Hill Orphir: [a clip*ped* form of Norse *kró* pen, *fjall* hill].

Cruiko Sanday: an old mill at Boloquoy, also known as the 'Mill o Stousater' [Norse *krókr* a bend, *á* stream].

Cruis Taing Sanday: [Norse *kró* (with English plural), *tangi* point of land].

Cruland Sandwick: (see 'Crowland').

Crumbrecks Orphir: ['crum' represents 'Cruan': the 'b' of 'brecks' changes the 'n' to 'm'].

Crumlay Deerness: should read 'Cumlay' (see 'Cumlay/lie' forms below).

Crusday Rousay: [Norse *kró* (with English plural), *dý* marshland].

Crusgate Harray: [Norse *kró* (with English plural), *gata* pathway to or past a cross].

Crustan Birsay, Northside: [Norse *kró* enclosure, *steinn* stone: the suggestion is that there was a standing stone at the enclosure].

Crustan, Knowe o Birsay: [Scots *knowe* knoll, Norse *kró* enclosure].

Cruyertus North Ronaldsay: [Norse *króar* enclosures, 'tus' suggests *þúfa* mound (with English plural) meaning 'remains of enclosures'].

Cubbidy Rousay: (compare 'Cupoday' in Deerness).

Cubbie Geo Sanday: [Norse *kobbi* a seal].

Cubbie Geo Westray; Shapinsay: [Norse *kobbi* a seal, *gjá* ravine: a place where seals lie].

Cubbie Roo's Burden Rousay: apparently a mound south/southeast of 'Shingly Hill'.

Cubbie Roo's Lade Stronsay: a pier naturally made of large rocks but ascribed in folklore to the work of the spirit 'Cubbie Roo': it is also recorded as the 'Danes Pier' [Norse *hlaða* to build (see 'Cubbie Roo' below)].

Cubbie Roo's Rock Wyre: he threw it at a troll on Egilsay: Cubbie Roo was a local troll whose speciality was throwing boulders at adversaries: there are several such rocks or boulders throughout Orkney some of which show the finger marks of the troll! [Norse *koppr* head, *rauðr* red: many European spirits had heads reddened by the blood of their victims!].

Cubbie Roo's Stone Evie: applies to a big stone (just north of 'Ayrean') with several holes in it, thrown from Rousay to a giant in Hoy but fell short, dropping in Evie (see 'Cubbie Roo's Rock').

Cubbie Roo's Stone Orphir: Cruff Hill: referred to as 'Giant's Stone' on the 1813 Map of the Division of the Commonty: the compiler of the map, James Johnston of Coubister states that it shows a thumb mark and was thrown from Hoy.

Cudanna Geo Stronsay: east side of Odness [Norse *kóð-in* (the) immature fish, Orkney dialect 'cuithes'].

Cuean Birsay, Beaquoy: [Norse *kví-n* the enclosure: (compare 'Kewing' Rendall and 'Quean' Sandwich)].

Cufter Evie: a small farm now part of Bisgarth [difficult name to interpret: perhaps Norse *kurfr* a piece (of land) cut off: alternately a corruption of 'Tufter'].

Cuiffie Hill Firth: [Norse *kví* enclosure, *fjall* hill (compare 'Quoyfea', Deerness)].

Cuilags Hoy: at 435 metres, the Cuilags is the second highest hill in Orkney [Norse *kollr* summit with dialect diminutive 'ag'].

Cuin Geo Westray: [Norse *kví-in* the enclosure, *gjá* ravine].

Cuivnahay Birsay: a vanished house in the Northside of Birsay [Norse *kví-n* the enclosure, *hagi* pastureland].

Culdigeo Eday; Egilsay; Orphir; Westray: [Norse *kuldi* cold: the use of 'cold' and 'warm' in Scandinavian placenames is not understood (see 'Varmady' in Rendall): they are usually associated with water or marsh. In these examples Norse *gjá* can mean 'ravine' or 'marshy land' (see Geo in Appendix)].

Culdykes Evie/Rendall: must be a misspelling of 'Puldykes'— c.f. 'Powdykes', Westray, and 'Pow o Puldeek', Sanday: Rendall/Evie position unknown [it is difficult to explain the origin of this placename since 'dyke' can be translated as Norse *dík* ditch or Scots *dyke* wall: in these examples probably Norse *dík* ditch].

Cullavelt Sanday: an area of land, Northwall [Norse *kúla* a knob, Faroese *velta* field: compare 'Veltigar' in Tankerness].

Cultisgeo Shapinsay: [Norse *kuldi* cold (see Geo in Appendix)].

Cumany Howe Stenness: a prominent mound near the farm of 'Cumminess'.

Cumla Geo South Ronaldsay: [Norse *kuml* a mound, *gjá* ravine].

Cumlaquoy Birsay, Marwick: [Norse *kuml* mound, *kví* enclosure].

Cumley/Comely Stronsay; Sandwich: [Norse *kuml* mound].

Cumlins of Maovi Shapinsay: [Norse *kuml* mound (the definite article suffix 'in' is feminine/masculine with English plural: in Old Norse, the gender was neuter but there are several instances of gender change in Orkney Norse placenames: Norse *mór* moor, *fjall* hill)].

Cumlofeels Birsay, Leaquoy: [Norse *kuml* mound, English 'fields'].

Cumlos Birsay, Yeldabreck: [Norse *kuml* mound (with English plural)].

Cumminess Stenness: [Norse *kuml-in* the mound, *nes* point of land (see reference to gender change at 'Cumlins o Maovi')].

Cumminsquoy South Ronaldsay: [from the surname 'Cumming', Norse *kví* enclosure].

Cunnan Gairsty, The Papa Westray: a so-called 'Treb' dyke [Scots *coney* Rabbit, *garð-staðr* wall position].

Cunnie's Deerness: [it's said that a 'cunning woman' lived here!].

Cunningham/Conningham Sanday: it lay to the west of 'Newark' [Scots *coney* rabbit, *hame* home].

Cunninghole (see 'Conninghole').

Cup Evie: [Norse *koppr* a cup-shaped hollow: a common Orkney placename].

Cup Steven Evie: [Norse *koppr* (as above), Norse *stúfr* a bit cut off, *fen* marsh].

Cupablack Harray: a hollow between 'Hindera Field' and 'Ernie Tower' [Norse *koppr* (as above), 'black' usually refers to 'heather-covered', a direct translation from the common Norse word *svartr* black (see 'Swartland')].

Cupoday Deerness: renamed 'Diamonds' after 'Cupoday' was turned into a byre [Norse *koppr* (as above), *dý* marsh].

Cuppa Sanday: coastal feature [Norse *koppr* (as above)].

Cupper Evie: [Norse *koppar* cup-shaped hollows].

Cuppers o Vacquoy Rousay: [Norse *koppar* (as above), (with English plural), (see 'Vacquoy')].

Cuppie Kerr Harray: [Norse *koppr* (as above), *kjerr* scrubland].

Cuppin Evie; Firth; Harray; Papa Westray; Birsay, Skelday; Stenness: [Norse *koppr-inn* the hollow].

Cuppingua Firth, Wasdale: [Norse *koppr-inn* the hollow (for 'gua' element see 'Geo' in the Appendix)].

Cuppo Firth, Horraldshay: [Norse *koppr* a hollow].

Cupster Nelster Firth, Redland: a good example of a rhyming placename (see 'Meery-Mawry'): [Norse *koppr* a hollow, Norse *stíar* pens for sheep etc.: origin of 'Nelster' uncertain].

Curcabister Sanday: mentioned in *Fea's Diary* [Norse *kirkja* chapel, *ból-staðr* farm].

Curcabreck Stronsay, Whitehall; Stenness; Rendall; Harray: [Norse *kirkja* chapel, *brekka* slope].

Curcaday/Curcatae Sanday, Elsness: [Norse *kirkja* chapel, *teigr* a strip of land].

Curcasetter (see 'Kurkister').

Curcum Birsay: [Norse *kirkja* chapel, *hólm* literally an island but here it seems to refer to an elevated piece of land probably above a marshy area (see 'Ancum')].

Curly Geo Rousay: [origin uncertain].

Curquoy Westray; Evie; Rousay; Birsay: [Norse *kýr* cow, *kví* enclosure].

Curries Flotta: [a Scots surname from the placename 'Currie' in Midlothian: recorded in Orkney at the beginning of the 17th century].

Cursetter North Ronaldsay: [Norse *kýr* cow, *saetr* summer enclosure].

Cursiter Firth: (as above).

Cusvie/Cusbay Eday a district and bay in Eday [Norse *vágr* bay: origin of 'cus' element unknown].

Cutclaws Rousay: [Norse *kot* small house, *Klas* familiar Norse form of personal name *Nikulas*].

Cuthilgarth Sanday: old name of 'Colligarth' [perhaps Celtic (Welsh) *cuddle* a cell, a reference to the chapel located here (see 'Colligarth')].

Cutkelday Stronsay: a house [Norse *kot* small house, *kelda* a well or spring].

Cutlass Röst between 'Isles Skerry' and 'Eynhallow' [(see 'Cutclaws' above), Norse *röst* rough tideway].

Cutpool Deerness: [Norse *kot* cottage, *pollr* pool].

Cutters Tooer Stronsay: a mound on Griceness [probably a reference to the North Isles surname 'Cutt', Norse *þúfa* mound (plural form)].

Cuvan 1. Sanday: near 'Sandback' (see 'Covan').

Cuvan 2. Sanday, Cleat: field name: this field encloses a prominent burnt mound (see 'Covan').

Cuvan 3. Sanday, Scar: field name (see 'Covan').

Cuween Hill Firth: [Norse *kví-n* the enclosure].

D

Dale Stronsay, Aith; Eday; Rousay; Rendall, on Breck; Stromness; Hoy; Birsay, on Loons, Helzie; Deerness; Redland, Firth: [a difficult name to interpret: sometimes it means 'valley' from Norse *dalr* valley, at other times 'marsh' from Norse *dý* marsh. The latter is a mistake by map-makers who assumed that the local pronunciation of *dý* as 'day', meant that it should be 'dale'. The best example of this is from Firth, where 'Syraday' became 'Syradale'].

Dale, The Orphir: west of 'Bellie's Field' (see above).

Dam Stronsay; Evie; Flotta: [some are English 'dam' but the earlier could be Norse *dammr* (see 'Dams' below)].

Daman Harray, Mirbister: [this must be a Norse example since it carries a masculine definite article suffix, hence Norse *damm(r)-inn*: because of its location, as a marshy area to the north of a small pool called 'Padachun' (Norse *padda-tjörn* toad pool), it could not have been a 'dam' but rather a 'pool'].

Damaquoy Westray, Garthstown: it lies on a coast which has been severely eroded and the 'dam' element may refer to a large sea pool which has disappeared [Norse *dammr* dam, *kví* enclosure].

Damaschool, Upper/Lower Evie: recorded as crofters' houses in the earliest Ordnance Survey [one was a simple private school for young girls, called a 'Dame's School' hence the name 'Damaschool': no reference can be found to this building as a school. 'Dame Schools' are recorded only in Stromness and Kirkwall but they were never called by that name in Orkney, merely 'private schools for young girls'].

Dams Stenness: ['dams' here must refer to 'pools' rather than 'dams'].

Damsay Island Firth parish: one of two islands in the 'Bay o Firth': uninhabited [Norse personal name *Dagmund*, Norse *ey* island].

Damsay Westray: [like 'Gairsay', probably a transferred name from the island of Damsay].

Damsheet Evie, Costa: a field close to the 'Burn o Pow' [Orkney dialect 'sheed/sheet' a small piece of land cut off from a larger piece: the burn must have been dammed here at one time].

Damsquare Firth, Burness: [origin unknown].

Danes' Pier Stronsay: (see 'Cubbie Roo's Lade') a natural rock 'pier' made of huge stones, now much eroded, the form suggesting the work of supernatural origin ['Dane' here refers to mythical beings as in Norse *berg-danir*, giants associated with rocks and stones].

Dangerfield Firth: field name, 'Lettaly', Lyde [at first sight appears to be from the rare English surname 'Dangerfield': Rev. John Dangerfield was minister of Lady Church in Sanday for almost 30 years: it is more likely that this was the site of a gallows, since nearby lay a gateway called the 'Gallow's Slap' and not far away the house of 'Purgatory'! (see 'Purgatory' Birsay where a nearby house was called Hell!)].

Dardle Stronsay: a croft on 'Rothiesholm' [origin uncertain: seems to have been a boggy area at the time of naming, hence Norwegian *darra* to shake, dale = Norse *dý* shaking bog (see 'Dale')].

Dave in the Drain Sanday: a lobster set, the maithe (sea mark) being 'Howbell' in line with the drain at 'Hucklinsower'.

David's Holm Sanday: coastal feature [refers to David Muir of Howbell, Norse *hólmi* a small island].

David's Shead Sanday, Elsness: field name (see 'Damsheet' above).

Daystar Deerness: formerly 'Quoycanker'.

Dead Man's Knowe Birsay, Hundland: [said to have been the location of a cist burial].

Deall, The Sanday, Elsness: field name, early 18th century [c.f. Rousay dialect 'deel' a wet boggy place].

Dealt, Well o Firth, Redland: [many Orkney placenames carried an unexplained 't' suffix: c.f. 'Huant' in Birsay = 'Howan', Norse *haug-inn* the mound (see origin above)].

Dealy (Upper and Nether) Sanday, Elsness: field names, early 18th century (see 'The Deal' above).

Deasman Stromness, Innertown: a small farm in 1739 [Norse *dý* marsh (with English plural), (for 'man' element see Appendix)].

Dee, The Birsay, Dirkadale: field name [Norse *dý* marsh].

Deealt Birsay, Marwick: (see 'Deall, The').

Deedman's Snore Sanday: a blow hole near 'Whalgeo' ['dead man's snore'].

Deekeldy Harray: [Norse *dý* marsh, *kelda* a well].

Deepdale Stromness: [Norse *djúp* deep, the 'dale' element is a corrupt form of *dý* marsh: there are many examples in the index of such corruptions].

Deerness a parish [Norse *dýr* animal, *nes* point of land].

Dees 1. Evie: also known as 'Whitehouse' [Norse *dý* marsh (with English plural)].

Dees 2. Harray: (see above).

Dees 3. Sanday, Airon: field name (see above).

Dees 4. Sanday, Clickimin: field name (see above).

Dees, The 1. Birsay/Harray border: (see above).

Dees, The 2. Sanday: coastal feature (see above).

Deesaldo, Grip o Birsay: [Norse *dý* marsh, for origin of 'saldo' (see 'Sultigo'), suffix 'o' may represent Norse *á* water or stream (see 'Woo')].

Deesbreck Birsay, Dirkadale: [Norse *dý* marsh (with English plural), *brekka* slope].

Deesgate Sandwick: path from St. Peters Kirk to the coast [Norse *dý* marsh, or moorland in this case (with English plural), *gata* pathway].

Deith Rousay: recorded Quoydie in 1601 [Norse *dý* marsh with definite article 'it' suffixed: this definite article was always sounded 'th' hence the spelt form: the placename means 'the marsh'].

Deldale/Delday Deerness: [a good example to show how the Norse placename *dý* a marsh in Orkney placenames, alternated between 'dale' and 'day' (see 'Syradale')].

Dello Harray: (see 'Deall' above).

Den Longie Rousay; Egilsay: [Norse *dýna* a marsh, *langr* long].

Denni Geo South Ronaldsay: [Norse *dýna* a marsh].

Dennis Ness North Ronaldsay: (see 'Dennis Skerry' below).

Dennis Röst North Ronaldsay: [Norse *röst* rough tideway].

Dennis Skerry Sanday: a reef off Dennisness [Norse *dynr*, roar (of the sea), *nes* point].

Dennis Taing North Ronaldsay: [Norse *tangi* point of land (see above for 'Dennis')].

Denwick Deerness: [Norwegian *dynn* a marsh, *vík* a bay].

Deolan Birsay: a ravine [Norse *gjá* a ravine was normally pronounced 'geo' in Orkney but in Birsay the initial 'g' of this word was sometimes pronounced 'd', Norse *hlið-inn* the steep cliff face: (see 'Deolie Trunnie' below)].

Desso Burn o Evie, Aikerness: [the suffix 'o' of 'Desso' represents Norse *á* stream: the first element is Norse *des* a hayrick and is applied in Orkney dialect in the same way where it takes the form 'diss': it is also applied to several mounds: in Orkney the low eminence near the mouth of the stream is now called the 'Knowe o Desso' but its original name would have been merely 'Desso' (see 'Disses o the Holm' below)].

Devil's Causeway South Ronaldsay: flat rocks on the beach at 'Grimness' where their unusual form gives the impression of a wide road: such features are usually attributed to some supernatural agency, compare 'The Giant's Causeway' in Northern Ireland: [notice that this area was called Grimness and 'Grim' was a byname of Odin!].

Diamonds Deerness: (see 'Cupoday').

Dicksquoy Stenness; Rendall: a field name [English personal name 'Dick', Norse *kví* enclosure].

Dieth Rousay; Harray: (see 'Deith' above).

Dieth-Hellya, Burn o Birsay: [Norse *dý-t* the marsh, *hellur* slabs of rock].

Digger Rousay: part of the beach and the inland area near 'Quoynalonga Ness', Quandal (a form of 'Digro').

Digro Rousay: on the east slope of 'Kierfea' [Norse *dý* marsh, Norse *gróf* a stream which has carved out a deep trench: used in the general sense of 'stream' in Orkney (see 'Digger')].

Dill Skerry Evie: [a wrong usage of English 'dill' which is a herb: it ought to be 'dulse', Gaelic/Irish *duileasg*, an edible red seaweed which was gathered on the reef there at low tide, Norse *sker* reef].

Dingieshowe Deerness: [Norse *þing-haugr* parliament mound: mounds were often used in Viking times for their assemblies].

Dinnatoon Stronsay, Rothisholm: ['below the tunship': long since vanished (compare 'Aboondatoon')].

Dinnies Rendall: a field on 'Hogarth' [probably an old house/fields occupied by a Dennison; there were Dennisons living in Gairsay at that time, so it is quite likely that they had a foothold on 'The Mainland'].

Diolie Trunnie Birsay: coastal formation [Norse *gjá* ravine, *hlíð* steep or sheer, *þröngr* narrow].

Dirkadale Birsay: [English 'dark'(?), Norse *á* water, *dalr* valley]. 'Durka' is certainly not Norse so it must be a Celtic stream name. As in the case of the 'Corri', the nearest namesake of the 'Durka' lies right at the other end of Britain in the placename 'Dorking' in Surrey. Today the river which runs through Dorking is the 'Mole', but it is believed that its original name was the River Dorce, an ancient Celtic word for 'brightness'.

Dirlings Evie: [origin unknown].

Dishan Holm: on the coast of 'Rose Ness' taking its name from a nearby cairn [Norse *dýs-in* the cairn].

Dishans Firth, Lyde: [from the Orkney family name 'Dishan' originating most probably from 'Dishan' (see above)].

Disher North Ronaldsay: [Norse *dysjar* mounds].

Dishero, Knowe o Rendall, Queenamuckle: [Scots *knowe* knoll, Norse *dysjar* mounds, *haugr* mound].

Dishes Stronsay: [Norse *dysjar* mounds (with English plural)].

Disses o the Holm, The Papa Westray, Holm o Papa: chambered cairn (see 'Dishes' above).

Divalts Rendall, Hackland: field name [probably 'lumpy' from Scots 'divot', a lump of earth: the word 'devo' was used in Shapinsay for a large stone on which clothes could be dried].

Doehouse Sandwick: [without an earlier recording in 1595, it would be impossible to explain the origin of this farm name: the revenue of the produce of this land was provided by one of the Sinclair Earls to the St. Duthus Chapel in St. Magnus Cathedral: St. Duthus was a highly venerated saint in Scotland and was buried in Tain, Rosshire].

Dog Geo Evie; North Ronaldsay: [probably a translation from Norse of *hundr* dog: on the Birsay coast there is also a Hunda Geo as well as a Cata Geo: animal names were often used for coastal features in Norse].

Dog Too/Dogtoo Birsay, Swannay; Westray, Midbea, former name of 'Myrtle-lane' [Sanday dialect *dog too*, a tuft of grass favoured by Dogs, a pejorative name for a poor (probably turf-covered) dwelling, Norse *púfa* mound].

Dogtoos Burray: [English plural of 'Dog Too' above].

Dog Tuag South Ronaldsay: [same as above with diminutive suffix typical of South Isles].

Dog's Geo South Ronaldsay, Pentland Skerries: (see 'Dog Geo' above).

Dogger Beach Stronsay: Whitehall district [so named because of the frequency of Dutch dogger boats visiting/based here as early as the 16th century during the herring fishing season: the name is now Forgotten].

Doggerboat North Faray: a small farm [a 'doggerboat' was a broad-beamed fishing boat which operated in the North Sea from the 14th century onwards: the origin of the application of this placename is unknown: perhaps it was an old upturned boat used as a house: there is an old rhyme about this placename and others on Faray]:

Quoy, Cott, Doggerboat

Hammer on the Hess,

Leaquoy, Windywa,

Holland on the Ness

Dogtuin Westray; Papa Westray: same as above ['tuin' represents Norse *fan*, the 'tuft' of grass in this case].

Don Stromness: recorded as 'Done' in 17th century [*dýna* boggy ground, soft like eiderdown].

Donald's Plate/Stripe North Ronaldsay: [a narrow strip of land cultivated by Donald Tulloch of 'Cruesbreck'].

Dond Birsay: Kirbister area (see 'Don' above).

Donkey's Hole Birsay: a cave near 'Skippy Geo' [origin unknown].

Doo Geo Evie; North Ronaldsay; Sanday, Warsetter: [Scots *doo* dove].

Dooaa Harray, Corston: field name beside the 'Burn o Corrigall' [origin of 'dooaa' here uncertain: there is a field in 'Westersands', Deerness, called 'How-dooa' which has the same element in it: perhaps it is a corruption of *Þúfa* a small mound].

Doocot Westray, Cleat; Rendall; Evie; Sanday, Lopness Farm and near Warsetter: [Scots *doocot* = English 'dovecot'].

Doomaday Sanday: a house in Northwall [Norse *dómr* judgement, Norse *deild* division; perhaps the site of a former gallows].

Doonabrya Geo Birsay: [Norse *gjá-n* the ravine, *breiðr* broad].

Doonagua Geo Birsay: a tautological placename [Norse *gjá-n* the ravine, *gjá* ravine].

Doonaminya Geo Birsay: [Norse *gjá-n minna* the smaller geo, smaller in relation to the others: it was possible for boats to land fish here].

Doonatoon Birsay, Twatt: [the lower part of the toonship: it may have been an old ale house (see examples below)].

Doon-Hads, The Rousay, Scockness: [Scots *doon* down, Ork. and Shet. dialect *had* a cave].

Doonitherla Geo Birsay: also referred to as 'Fiddle Hume' [Norse *gjá-n* the ravine, *aeðr* duck, *hlað (berg)* a loading/unloading place, in this case, of fish].

Doonthroo/Downatown North Walls: a small farm [bought by a Stroma man who was nominally a farmer but who preferred brewing ale. Doonatoon became an ale house with the alternative nickname 'Doon-throo'].

Doon-Trow Birsay: Kirbister area [literally 'down through', a strange name: in fact, it was a nickname for an ale house because it was very likely that most men-folk would go through it rather than pass it (see 'Ap-Trow')].

Doors o Dounhelzie Sanday: a coastal feature [Norse *dynr* sound, Norse *hellir* cave, English 'doors' large holes in cliffs].

Dorno/Dornock Sanday, Elsness: field name, recorded in the 17th century ['dorn' or 'dornick' was a linen fabric made in Doornick (now Tournai), Flanders: its use here is not understood unless it was a name given in jest to a 'sheet' of land: Orkney dial. 'sheet' a distinctive piece of land].

Douglas Clog Swona: coastal feature [Scots surname 'Douglas', Scots *cleuch* a cleft].

Dounby Birsay, 'Upper Fea', Greeny: field name [a field 'doon by' i.e., further down].

Dounby is a village at the junction of the parishes of Birsay, Harray and Sandwick and has a convoluted history. It takes its name from a house known locally as 'Doon-by Farm' (pronounced 'Doomby') so called in relation to 'Appiehouse' (the upper house), now vanished, which stood approximately on the site of the present house of 'Kelton': (see 'Smithfield' and 'Hourston Farm').

Doverhouse/Flecketsquoy Birsay, Northside: two very difficult names to interpret since the name 'Doverhouse' was given to this dwelling in the 1841 Census but it was called 'Flecketsquoy' by the Ordnance Survey 40 years later. Both seem associated with the supernatural ['Flecketsquoy' suggests Norse *flagð-it* the troll and 'Doverhouse', Norse *taufr* sorcery (see 'Taiverso')].

Dowasand Stronsay: a fishing bank [Norse *sandr* sand: origin of 'dowa' element unknown].

Downies Deerness: near 'The Gloup' [Downie families have been recorded in Orkney since the 17th century and though there are records of them in St. Andrews and Holm, there is no official record of them in Deerness].

Dowscarth/Dowsgar Stenness: ['Dow' suggests a Norse personal name such as *Tófi* or a clipped form of *Dagfinnr*, Norse *garðr* farm].

Draughts, Upper and Nether Sanday, Elsness: field names, early 18th. century [English: (compare 'Chequerboard')].

Drawen Teinds North Ronaldsay: 1653 [a field from which a tenth part of the produce was 'withdrawn/drawn' to support the church].

Dreggs, The Rousay: low-lying, flat, wet ground on 'Scockness' [suggests muddy, wet ground akin to English 'dregs'].

Dridda Stromness, Garth: field name [Norse *drit* excrement, especially of Birds, *dý* wet and marshy (see 'Puldrite')].

Dritness Stronsay: a rocky stretch of beach south of 'Odin Ness' [Norse *drit* excrement of birds, *nes* point of land].

Drowins Brae Firth, Northbreck: (perhaps related to 'Drawen Teinds' above).

Drubba Skerry Birsay: coastal name: a good place to gather dulse [Norse *boði* a reef, the first element is a clipped form of Norse *drit* bird excrement].

Drummond's Sanday, Hermisgarth: now a field name; earlier known as 'Hillhoose' [named after a Drummond family who lived here].

Drummondfield Sanday, Schoolhouse: (field named after the same Drummond family above).

Drumy, Burn of Orphir: flows into the 'Kirbister Loch' [origin of 'Drumy' uncertain: the only related form of this placename is the vanished house of 'Langadrum' which lay near 'Newbigging' in Birsay: probably Gaelic *druim*, Welsh *drum* a ridge (see 'Burn o Russa')].

Druntan Harray: field name near 'Beboran' [Orkney folk referred to 'Trondheim' in Norway as 'Druntin' and after the conversion to Presbyterianism, it was used as a curse meaning '(Go to) Hell'. The field must have been 'hellish' to work. The name 'Trondheim' dates only from the middle of the 16th century: before that it was called 'Nidaros'].

Dubhall North Ronaldsay: [Scots *dub* mud, English 'hall' used in jest to refer to a small miserable cottage].

Ducrow Holm: a farm in a former marshy area dating from the 15th century or earler [Norse *dý* marsh, Norse *kró* an animal pen].

Duetoe Birsay: a deep hole in a field called 'Runalieth' in 'Queena', Abune-the-Hill, Birsay [probably a corruption of Duepoe: Norse *djúp* deep, *pollr* pool].

Dulse Skerry Burray: directly opposite 'Glimps Holm' [English 'dulse' edible seaweed, *sker* a reef].

Dulytrongy Birsay: coastal feature (see *'Deolie Trunnie'*, Sanday).

Duncan's Breck/Duncan's Sanday, How: [no known association with a Duncan, Norse *brekka* slope].

Duncans Deerness: a ruin; abandoned after inhabitants contracted tuberculosis.

Dungeon, The Sanday: coastal feature, 'Skitho Bay' [Norse *dýna* soft, muddy ground, *tjörn* pool].

Dunkirk Kirkwall: there was a building near the pier-head in Kirkwall at one time and it was also called 'Dunkirk'. It is said to be named after Earl Patrick Stewart's finest ship, which must have been anchored nearby.

Dunkirk St. Margaret's Hope: [in the 1821 Census of South Ronaldsay there was an ale house called 'Dunkirk.' In English, a 'Dunkirk' was a French privateer, and the allusion was that if one entered the 'Dunkirk' one would be robbed just as one would be on the high seas].

Durrisdale) Upper and Lower Evie: small crofts and according to the Ordnance Survey of 1882 they were built in the late 19th century [Norse *deild* division (of land): probably named by one of the many Scots farmers who took over poor land: a name transferred from 'Durris' in Aberdeenshire].

Dusty, Kiln of Rousay: [Norse *dust*, English '(corn drying) kiln': the reference to 'dust' here is sea spray blown over the cliff which reminded one of the smoke from such a working kiln].

Dwarfie Hammars Hoy: projecting rocks from which the so-called 'Dwarfie Stone' was believed to have originated (see below) [Norse *hamarr* projecting rock(s) on a hillside].

Dwarfie Stone Hoy: [so called because of the small misshapen 'doorway' carved into it: this name was used by early antiquarians, probably as early as the 17th century, replacing an original 'Troll Stane' or 'Trowie Stane': in Scott's *'The Pirate'*, Norna told of the legend of a famous demon called 'Troll(d)' who lived in it: such stones are usually called 'Cubbie Roo's Stones': immediately to the south of the Dwarfie Stane is 'Trowie Glen': (see 'Burn o Trolldgeo', Shapinsay)].

Dwarmo, Hill o Evie: a spur of 'Vishall Hill' containing the 'Grunshall Burn', interpreted by Hugh Marwick as Norse *dvergr-mál* an echo, literally 'dwarf talk' but dwarves play no part in Orkney folklore [Norse *Þverr* across, but what the hill lies across, is uncertain (see 'Twartquoy', Orphir), *mór* moorland (as in 'Bluthamo', 'Choinamo' etc.)].

Dyke North Ronaldsay; Evie; Rendall (2): [Scots *dyke* wall].

Dyke o Sean Stenness/Sandwick: [Scots 'dyke' (a boundary wall in this case) a tortuous turf wall separating the parishes of Stenness and Sandwick, Norse *tjörn* small lake which lay near this boundary (see 'Sane Sheet', Sanday)].

Dykend Orphir; Burray: where a boundary wall reaches the sea [Scots *dyke* wall].

Dykesend, Geo o Evie: [Norse *gjá* ravine: boundary walls often ended at the coast].

Dykeside Evie; Westray; Walls; Stromness: [Scots *dyke* wall: beside the boundary wall].

E

Earl's Knowe Papa Stronsay: a small mound in the southeast of the island and to the west of the site of 'St Nicholas Chapel' [Scots *knowe* knoll: the association with an Earl is said to be part of local folklore].

Earny Coulags South Ronaldsay: recorded in 'Windwick' by Low in his tour of Orkney and Shetland in 1774 [Norse *örn* sea eagle in this case, Norse *kúla* lump, plus dialect diminutive (c.f. 'Ernes Tower')].

Ease, Burn o Orphir: [Gaelic *uisge* stream or water, 'burn' is a duplication].

Ease, Well o Rousay: [Gaelic *uisge* water, 'well' is a duplication].

East Ayre Sanday, Northwall: coastal feature [Norse *eyrr* gravel ridge].

East Banks Sanday: the sandy shore which extends from 'Tresness' to 'Newark'.

East Bow Sanday, Ire: coastal feature [English 'bow' bend].

East Brough Sanday: renamed 'Newark' by the Stewarts to distinguish it from 'West Brough'.

East Corny Quoy Papa Westray: [Norse *korn-it* the corn, *kví* enclosure].

East Cott Sanday: [Norse *kot* cottage].

East Howar Sanday: vanished, also known as 'Howar Links' (see 'Howar').

East Langamay Sanday: (see 'Langamay').

East Langapool Orphir: coastal pool good for fishing coalfish and 'sillocks', Norse *síld* herring, is the nearest equivalent word.

East Lanties Sanday, Brabuster: field name (see 'Lanties').

East Lettan Sanday: Lettan district (see 'Lettan').

East Mire Sanday: (see 'Mire').

East Pow Sanday: coastal feature, 'The Riv' [Scots *pow* pool].

East Quoy Birsay, Eastabist: field name [Norse *kví* enclosure].

East Side Beneath the Gate Sanday, Elsness: field name, early 18th century ['beneath the gate' meant 'below the path to the common'].

East Thrave Sanday: (see 'Treb' for origin of the name).

East Tumall o Clerkshoose Sanday, Elsness: field name, early 18th century [Norse *tún-völlr*, home field (see 'Clerkshoose')].

Eastabist Birsay, Hillside: [Norse *austr* east, *ból-staðr* farm].

Eastafea Rousay: an old farm in the 1595 Rental in the 'Faraclett' area [Norse *austr* east, *fjall* hill: immediately to the west was 'Mithvie' 'mid hill'].

Eastaquoy Harray; Rousay: [Norse *austr* east, *kví* enclosure].

Eastbister Walls: (same as 'Eastabist' above).

Eastbreed/East North Ronaldsay: an eddy formed by the tide east of 'Seal Skerry' [origin of name of the eddy unknown].

Eastigarth Stronsay: east southeast of 'Cleat': small farm, ruinous in the 1890s [Norse *aust* east, *garðr* farm].

Eastin North Ronaldsay: (see below).

Eastin, The Sanday, Northwall: a district composed of a row of houses [Scots *eastin* on the east side, Norse *(fyrir) austan*].

Ebb o Airon Sanday: coastal feature (see 'Airon').

Ebb o Gresmay Sanday: coastal feature (see 'Gresmay').

Ebb o Hucklinsower Sanday: coastal feature [Scots 'ebb' that part of the shore between high and low water (see 'Hucklinsower')].

Ebb o Rusness Sanday: (see 'Rusness').

Ebb o Scottie Sanday: (see 'Scottie').

Ebb o Seatter Sanday: coastal feature, 'Boloquoy', close to the old house of 'Seatter'.

Ebb o the Riv Sanday: coastal feature, Sanday (see 'Riv, The').

Ebb o Woo Sanday: (see 'Woo').

Ebback South Ronaldsay, Windwick: [Scots 'ebb' foreshore, Norse *bakki* slope or bank].

Ebbgate Birsay, Boardhouse: [seemingly an old path: Norse *gata* path, which led to the shore].

Echna Loch Burray: [possibly a corruption of 'etna' = Norse *jötunn* giant: compare 'Yettna Geo' Sandwick and 'Yetnasteen' Rousay: folklore says it is the footprint of a giant].

Eday one of the North Isles of Orkney and a parish [originally recorded 'Ethay' i.e., Norse *eið* isthmus, *ey* island referring to the narrow 'waist' in the middle of the island, the location of the island airport at 'London': the population in 2011 was 160].

Edditoon Sanday: a well beside the 'North Loch' [origin uncertain perhaps Norse *iða* a whirlpool, Norse *tún* enclosure].

Edmonstone Shapinsay: [transferred name from 'Edmonstone' near Edinburgh].

Ednarhouse Stromness: [origin unknown].

Eefie Hill Birsay: [perhaps an eclipsed form of 'East Fea Hill', i.e., east of 'The Barony', the 'fie' element, normally spelt 'fea' in hill names is Norse *fjall* hill].

Eengly/Englie Sanday, Stove: field name [Norse *eng* meadow *hlið* slope].

Efaday Rendall: mentioned in the witch trial of Janet Rendall in the 17th century (a form of 'Avidale', Rendall).

Eferadale Orphir: on the southeast slope of 'Mid Hill' [Norse *yfir* upper, *dalr* valley].

Egger's Grund Sanday, Elsness: a field, early 18th century [although the farm name Aikers is not recorded in Elsness this is possibly a corruption of that name: 'grund' is dialect pronunciation of 'ground'].

Eggleton Sanday, Northwall: [English 'eagle', Norse *þúfa-n* the mound: 'eagle' is clearly, in this case, a translation of Scots *erne* sea eagle (see 'Ernie Tooin' and 'Ernie Tooer')].

Eggletoor Sanday: old name of 'Mills', 'Hermisgarth' [English 'eagle', Norse *þúfar* mounds].

Egilsay An island: scene of the murder of Earl Magnus and famous for its round towered church dedicated to St. Magnus [Norse personal name *Egill*, Norse *ey* island].

Eldocrue Sanday, Ire: coastal feature [Norse *eldr* fire Norse, *kró* Enclosure: related to kelp burning as in obsolete Orkney dialect 'to elt tang' (seaweed)].

Elicant Rendall: high in the Rendall hills north of 'Blubbersdale' [Norse *ali* Cattle, Middle English *kant* slope].

Ellenbreck Rendall: to the west of 'Layburn' [a crofter's house probably no older than mid 19th century (personal name 'Ellen'), *brekka* slope].

Elliar Holm Shapinsay: [Norse *hellar* genitive of *hella* flag stone i.e., a beach of flagstones].

Ellibister Rendall: [recorded in the 16th century as 'Alibustar': Norse *ali* cattle, *ból-staðr* farm (see 'Allibelly Geo')].

Elsinore Sanday: old name for 'Hammerbrake' [a fanciful name; 'Elsinore' was the name of Hamlet's castle in Denmark].

Elsness Sanday: first recorded 'Hellisnes' [the initial 'h' is likely to be intrusive: possibly named after the large number of burnt mounds in the area, hence Norse *eldr* fire, *nes* a point of land].

Elwick Shapinsay: 'Balfour Village' [it was called *Elliðarvík* in the *Hakon Saga* which tells of Hakon's Fleet lying there in 1263: there is a River *Elliðar* placename in Iceland near *Reykjavík* but so far it has not been possible to discover its origin].

Emess Hooses Stronsay: west of 'Whitehall' [corruption of 'eastmost houses' (see 'Uimest Hooses')].

Enegars Hoy: a steep cliff in the northwest of the island, southwest of 'Lounders Fea': the reference must relate to the top of the cliff [Scots *erne* sea eagle (with the loss of 'r'), Norse *gras* grass, often pronounced 'girs' or 'gars' in Orkney: sea eagles preferred such sites (see 'Yeulgars')].

England South Ronaldsay: [Norse *eng* meadow].

Englie (see 'Eengly').

Enisgeo Evie: location uncertain [Scots *erne* eagle, Norse *gjá* ravine].

Ennalias, Burn o Evie: [Norse *á-n* the stream, *hlíðar* slopes (with English plural)].

Enyamuir Stronsay: a field in 'Aith' [Norse *örn* sea eagle, *mýrr* moorland].

Enyan North Ronaldsay: [Norse *eng-in* the meadow].

Enzie Hill Rendall: [Norse *eng* meadow].

Eolies, Well o Birsay, Beaquoy: [difficult name to explain, perhaps originally Norse *skýlis-(hús)* shelter as in Orkney dialect 'skeeo', a temporary shelter for animals].

Erafea Sanday: a ridge of high ground near 'Warsetter' [Gaelic *airigh* shieling, Norse *fjall* mountain but in Orkney, 'hill'].

Erens Geo Sandwick: [Scots *erne* sea eagle, Norse *gjá* ravine].

Ericlett Egilsay: in the northeast of the island: small, round high-water rock [probably a clipped form of 'Erniclett', i.e., a rock favoured by an *erne,* Scots 'sea eagle', Norse *klettr* rock].

Eriksyord /Erixland Sandwich: [one of a group of six extensive areas in the 'Stove' region, some of which carry the unusual word *yord*, Norse *jörð* earth: origin of these units is unknown and the placenames are obsolete].

Ernatwick St. Andrews: [Scots *erne* sea eagle, Norse *púfa* mound, Ork. dialect diminutive 'ick'].

Ernie Tooer Evie/Birsay; Rousay: [Scots *erne* sea eagle, Norse *púfar* mounds].

Ernie Tooin Rendall; Harray: [Scots *erne* sea eagle, Norse *púfna* the mounds].

Erraby Shapinsay: it exists only in the form 'Noust o Erraby' [Norse *naust* boat shelter: *eyrr-boer* farm by a beach ridge].

Erraby, The Sand o Sanday: [Norse *eyrr* beach ridge, *boer* farm: there is no record of this farm today].

Erraby/Airaby Stronsay: field name: the original farm has vanished [Norse *eyrr-boer* farm by a beach ridge].

Erran Sanday: Seatter, Sellibister [Norse *eyrr* gravel ridge, *endi* end (compare 'Airon')].

Errigarth Stronsay: vanished farm: it lay on the east coast of 'St. Catherine's Bay' [Norse *eyrr* gravel ridge on a beach, *garðr* farm].

Erstas (see 'Arstais').

Ervadale Rousay, Sourin: earlier 'Overdale' [Norse *efra* upper: since 'Ervadale' is on the side of 'Kearfea' it cannot be Norse *dalr* valley but rather *deild* allotted piece of land].

Esgar Birsay, Dounby: [Celtic as in Old Irish *easc* water/stream, Norse *garðr* farm].

Esgro Stronsay: field in 'Clestran' [Celtic, as in Old Irish *easc* water/stream: Norse *gröf* a stream which has carved out a deep trench: used in the general sense of 'stream' in Orkney (see 'Digger')].

Eskishold Stromness: hill flank to the southeast of 'Mousland' [Celtic as in Old Irish *easc* water/stream: 'hold' is probably Norse *hol* depression: in other words, the placename means 'water hole': 'd/t' are sometimes added to Norse words ending in 'l' and 'd' and is sometimes removed from Norse words ending in 'ld'].

Esnaphy Deerness: now 'Little Colster' [Old Irish *easc* water/stream, Norse *fjall* hill].

Ess, Burn o Birsay/Sandwick: forms part of the border [Celtic as in Old Irish *easc* water/stream (see 'Ease, Burn o')].

Essaquoy Rousay: north of 'Housebay' in the 'Sourin' district [Celtic as in Old Irish *easc* water/stream, in this case referring to the 'Leeng Burn'].

Essness Harray: a promontory extending into the 'Harray Loch' [there is no stream or well here that is recorded: origin doubtful unless it is Norse *esja* a type of clay].

Esson/Essenquoy Eday: a small farm as described by the Ordnance Surveyors at the end of the 19th century: vanished: it faced the 'Calf of Eday' [most likely a transferred placename from the above].

Essonquoy St. Andrews: first recorded in 1550 [it is extremely unlikely that the first name 'Esson', a pet form of Alexander, explains the origin of this placename. Like 'Sutherquoy' in Sandwick it was an old and extensive area, both suggesting that *kví* (quoy) initially referred to something much bigger than an enclosure, which is the normal explanation: that aside, the derivation seems to be Celtic *iska* water or stream which became 'esk' or 'eax' and sometimes had the suffix 'an'. For example, an old name of Exeter in England was 'Eskanceaster': the stream in the Essonquoy case refers to the 'Burn of Wideford' and its tributary, the 'Gill Burn' which ran slightly to the west of the area].

Estaben Firth; Stenness: [Norse *austr* east, *boer-inn* the farm].

Estaquoy Orphir: it lay in the Houton area [English 'east', Norse *kví* enclosure].

Este Taing Orphir: coastal point in the 'Greenigoe' area [English 'east', Norse *tangi* point of land].

Estiber Rousay: rock(s) east of 'Sacquoy Head' [English 'east', Norse *berg* rock].

Estigar Stronsay: vanished house [English 'east', Norse *garðr* farm].

Ether Geo Evie: [Norse *aeðr* eider duck, *gjá* ravine].

Ether Grass Firth: south of 'Rossmyre' [Norse *aeðr* eider duck, *gras* grass: it seems that formerly eider ducks in Orkney sometimes nested some distance from the shore].

Ethergras Orphir: location unknown (see above).

Ettit Rendall: [Norse *topt* old house site; many such sites retained the first name of the original owner: Ettit was also recorded as 'Aithtit' which suggests the Norse personal name *Eiðr* (compare 'Kettletoft')].

Etyalith Birsay: spur on 'Ravie Hill' (see 'Aikilith' and 'Aglath' for meaning).

Euro, Knowes o Rendall: a group of cist burials in Gorseness, near 'Puldrite' [Scots *knowe* mound (for 'euro' see 'Point o Houro')].

Evars Knowe 1. Sanday: a mound west of 'How' [Norse *álfar* fairy, Scots *knowe* mound].

Evars Knowe 2. Sanday: a mound west of 'Boloquoy' (see above).

Evars Knowe/Ivars Knowe Sanday: a mound on the land of 'Garbo' (see above).

Everbist Sanday: vanished, now a district name [Norse *efri* upper, *ból-staðr* farm].

Everby Stronsay: [Norse *efri* upper, *boer* farm].

Everhand Rousay: applied to a mound on a field on 'Langskaill' [Norse *álfar* fairies, *haug(r)-inn* the mound].

Eversty, Burn o Birsay: [Norse *efri* upper, *stía* a sty].

Eves Howe Deerness: [Norse *álfar* fairies (with English plural), *haugr* mound (see 'Everhand' above)].

Evrabist Birsay: [Norse *efri* upper, *ból-staðr* farm].

Evribust Rousay: (see above).

Evrigert Rendall: (see below).

Evrigert, Knowe o Rendall: [Scots knowe = knoll: Norse *efri* upper or 'the higher', *garðr* enclosure].

Exna Geo Stronsay: [Celtic *iska* water with suffix '*an*' probably a reference to a stream issuing from the rock face of the 'geo', Norse *gjá* ravine].

Eynhallow An island [Norse *ey-in* the island, *helga* holy].

F

Faald Rendall: field on the land of 'Crook' [English 'fold'].

Faar Quoy Orphir: [location and meaning unknown].

Face o the Toon Firth, Binscarth: sloping field immediately to the west of 'Binscarth House' [English 'face' in the sense 'vertical wall' etc. also used in Orkney dialect with the meaning 'slope'].

Faegie Rendall, Hall o Rendall: field name [Icelandic *feygja* to let decay; perhaps a reference to marsh or midden ouse?].

Fairasippy/Farasibby North Ronaldsay: beach of the small bay which is sheltered by the 'Green Skerry' [origin unknown].

Fairisle Stronsay: house in 'Grobister' [many Fair Isle folk settled in the North Isles of Orkney and in this case named the house after the homeland].

Fairy Deerness: a ruin [a small cottage probably built in the 19th century: some unknown association with fairies: fairy ring? (see below)].

Fairy Brae North Ronaldsay: [a slope favoured by fairies!].

Fairy Gate Evie: [path along 'Rummerdale' and between 'Howe' and 'Georth', said to be used by fairies].

Fairy Knowe Firth, Wald: [Scots *knowe* mound: many mounds in Orkney were said to be inhabited by spirits].

Fairy Knowes Harray, Russland; Firth: (see above).

Fala Evie: a small stretch of stony beach near 'Scarra Taing' [perhaps relating to scree from a rock fall here: Norse *fall* a fall, as in *jarð-fall* an earth slip: the excrescent 'a' suffix is found in many Orkney placenames, the best example being found in 'Queena' forms where the original Norse would be *kví-n*, the enclosure].

Fald Birsay, Northside: [Scots *fald* fold].

Faldaral's Hole Harray, Russland: [a partially excavated mound where the pedlar/tramp 'Faldaral' used to sleep. At the beginning of the 20th century, he used to travel around the West Mainland selling crockery from a two wheeled barrow and relied on local people to provide him with free lodging].

Fall o Warness Eday: the channel between Eday and 'Muckle Green Holm' [Norse *fall* a rush of water, e.g., *að-fall* flood tide].

Falldown Rousay, Sourin: [name given in jest by neighbours because of poor standard of building: there are many instances in Orkney of such names, e.g., 'Pinap' in Swannay, Birsay].

Falquoy Rousay: [Norse *fjall* hill, *kví* enclosure].

Fan Knowe Sandwick: [Norse *fönn* a heap of snow, Orkney dialect 'fan': a transferred meaning from 'heap of snow' to 'heap of earth'].

Fananoo Rousay, Essonquoy: a field beside the 'Leeng Burn' (see 'Finyan') [Norse *á* stream].

Fancy Shapinsay, Gorn: field name [the name suggests that a cottage with this unusual name had stood here at some time: (compare 'Orem's Fancy', Stronsay)].

Fara, North An island: inhabited until the 1940s [Norse *fjár* sheep, *ey* island].

Fara, South An island: inhabited until the 1960s (origin as above).

Faraclett Rousay: ['clett' when used inland is often applied to a built stone structure: perhaps applied originally to the old Iron Age fort or 'broch' to the north of the 'Loch o Scockness': when ruinous it would have been used to pen sheep during 'retting' time or used merely as a sheep shelter, Norse *fjár* sheep:

(compare 'Noltclett', a broch in Harray, latterly used as a shelter for cattle), Norse *naut* cattle (see Klett in Appendix)].

Farafield: Birsay; Firth, Horraldsay: [Norse *fjár* sheep, *völlr* field].

Farahouse Eday: [unlikely to be Norse *fjár-hús* sheep shed since these houses face the island of Faray: probably introduced by those who moved from 'Faray'].

Faraval(d)/Farrivald/Faraval Westray: 'Dykeside' (see above).

Faravill Firth: (same name as 'Farafield', above).

Farewell South Ronaldsay: [Norse *fjár* sheep, *völlr* field].

Faro/Quoyfaras: Rousay, Sourin: [Norse *fjár-hús* sheep shed].

Fast Lang Sanday: [no information].

Fauld Rousay: (see below)

Fauld Green Sanday, Thrave: field name, Northwall [Scots *fauld* fold: it was here where cattle were penned in the summer after being tethered all day].

Fauld Hill Sanday, Elsness: field name, it cannot be said that there is a 'hill' on Elsness, rather an elevation! [Scots *fauld* fold].

Faulmire Stenness: [Norse *fúll* stinking, *mýrr* marshy ground].

Fay Geo Birsay: (see below).

Fay Pool Sanday: beach name, Park district, [Norse *fuí* rottenness, relating to rotting seaweed (compare 'Fue Geo' Rousay and 'The Dungeon')].

Fea 1. a very common Orkney placename deriving from Norse *fjall* hill: below are recorded instances: it is believed that the original pronunciation was 'fay', hence the pronunciation of the Orkney surname 'Fea' which is derived from one of these placenames].

Fea 2. Sanday: near 'Hobbister': a small ruin in 1877 when it was called 'Fell', Norse *fjall*, hill; Deerness (originally 'Quoyfea'); Birsay; Burray; Orphir; St. Ola; Holm; St. Andrews; Rendall; Sandwick; Sanday; Eday; Hoy; Stenness; Stromness; Walls: (see above).

Fea Hill St. Andrews: [Norse *fjall* hill, English 'hill'!].

Fea Hill/Fea Brae Sanday: [Norse *fjall* hill, a good example of a tautological placename (compare 'Erafea')].

Fealquoy Harray; Rousay; Stromness: [Norse *fjall* hill, *kví* enclosure].

Feaquoy Holm: (see above).

Feastown 1. Shapinsay: [a name transferred from 'Feastown' in Stronsay].

Feastown 2. Stronsay: [after the Orkney surname 'Fea'].

Feastown 3. Stronsay: a house east of Whitehall Pier [called after the surname 'Fea'].

Feaval 1. Birsay, Northside: [Norse *fjall* hill, *völlr* field].

Feaval 2. Sandwick, Tenston; Westray: (see above).

Feawell Stromness, Cairston: (see above).

Fed Geo o Arsdale Evie: [Icelandic *feygja* to let decay, a reference to rotting seaweed in the *gjá* or ravine].

Fed Geo o the Leeans Evie: northwest of 'Burgar' (for 'fed' element see above) [Norse *gjá* ravine, *hlíd-n* the slope, or cliff in this instance, (with English plural), (see 'Lee o Copinsay')].

Fedi Geo South Ronaldsay: (see above).

Feelie-ha Egilsay; Rousay: [Scots *feal* turf, Scots '*ha*' = 'hall' used in jest to describe a very simple dwelling, in this case one built of turf].

Feerless/Firaless North Ronaldsay: an outlying rock at the 'Noust o Howar' [Norse *fjara* beach, *fles* skerry: the initial 'f' of *fless* is almost always lost in Orkney placenames and is replaced by 'less' or 'lash'].

Feet o Howar Sanday, Newark: field name ['Howar' is an adjacent field, hence 'at the foot of Howar'].

Fell (see Sanday, 'Hobbister').

Fellsquoy Stronsay: a farm [a variant of 'Fealquoy' above].

Fenziehouse Orphir; Holm, 'Fenzieland', Swartaquoy: [Norse *fen* boggy land].

Feold Firth: near the top of the 'Lyde Road' [Norse *fjall* hill].

Feolquoy Evie; Stromness: (see 'Fealquoy' above).

Ferry Geo Shapinsay: on the 'Ness o Ork' [Norse *gjá* ravine: travellers from Stronsay would beach their boats here].

Ferry Point Firth: travellers from Rendall and Evie shortened the journey to Kirkwall by taking a boat from 'Burness' in Firth].

Fersness Eday: [Norse *ferja* ferry, *nes* point of land used by boats to and from Faray].

Fesber Rousay, Saviskaill: [origin unknown].

Festigarth Birsay: near 'Doonatoon', Twatt [origin unknown: this farm was requisitioned during World War II, so that the Naval airfield HMS *Heron* could be constructed].

Festrel Orphir: [origin unknown].

Feuld Westray, Rackwick: [Norse *fjall* hill].

Fewgan Stromness: [Norse *fúi* rottenness, referring to trapped seaweed, *gjá-n* the ravine].

Fiblia Fiold Rendall: [Norse *fifl* fool but with the original meaning 'spirit', as in Old English *fifal*: in the folklore of Shetland, 'Fivla' was such a spirit, Norse *fjall* hill].

Fiddle Hume Birsay, Northside: [origin unknown (see 'Doonithera Geo')].

Fiddlerhouse Sandwick: near 'Easter Voy', earliest recording 1739 ['the house of a fiddler': some of these occupational names go back to the 16th century].

Fidgarth Birsay, Northside: near the farm of 'Wattle' [Norse *fit* meadow flat, *garðr* farm].

Fidge Meadow Rousay: (see above).

Fidge o Piggar Orphir: (see above and 'Piggar').

Fidge 1. Sanday: a large area of links land used as a decoy airfield during World War II [Norse *fit* meadow flat].

Fidge 2. Sandwick: (see above).

Fidgeon, Sands o Firth, Grimbister: [Norse *fit-in* the meadow flat].

Fidges Stronsay: southwest of 'Oyce of Huip' [Norse *fit* meadow flat (with English plural)].

Fieldquoy Sanday: formerly 'Botany Bay'; now called 'Leaquoy', which was probably the original name.

Fila Sandwick: [location and origin unknown].

Filiber Skerries South Ronaldsay: [Norse *fúll* stinking (referring to bird dung), *berg* rock].

Fillets Graemsay: [a very puzzling farm name: a suggestion is that the name is derived from an unusual pronunciation of the Orkney surname 'Flett' (see 'Flett's', Stromness Parish)].

Filliberry Swona: (see above).

Filparhouse Birsay, Northside: [Icelandic *vilpa* a cesspool probably with the meaning 'mire' here: the plural of *vilpa* is *vilpar*].

Fin(y)anteens Evie: on the right bank of the 'Burn of Millhouse', across the road from the mill [Norse *fen* marsh, *tún* field in this instance, (with English plural), (see 'Appieteen'): adjacent is the house known as 'Wateries'].

Fingeo Stronsay: immediately east of 'Meikle Water' [Norse *fen* boggy land: (for 'geo' see Appendix)].

Finger Steen Rousay: marks on this stone are said to be the fingermarks of a troll (see 'Byasteen' and 'Cubbie Roo's Rock').

Fingerow St. Ola: 'Fingerow' = Fingro: location is unknown [Norse *fen* marsh, *gröf* a pit but in Orkney refers to an incised stream as in Norse *grafar-laekr* a stream which has dug itself a deep bed].

Finnian Geo Rousay: [Norse *gjá* ravine, Norse *fen-in* the boggy land, which must refer originally to the ground at the head of the geo: in Norse *fen* had neuter gender as in 'Queenafinnieth' in Harray but it frequently took feminine gender too, as in the examples below (for another example of fluid gender see 'Aglath, Braes o')].

Finning/Feenin Geo North Ronaldsay: a narrow sea inlet near 'Sholtisquoy' [Norse *gjá* ravine, *fen-in* the marsh referring to the area at the head of the inlet (see 'Finnian Geo' below)].

Finnio Rousay: south of the 'Point of Breck' (see 'Fingeo' above).

Finstown Firth: [a village named after the inn there (now 'Pomona Inn') which was established by an Irish soldier named 'Phin': the Post Office changed the placename to 'Fin', Norse *tún* in this case is the area around the inn].

Fint Rousay: [Scots *fint* the Devil (related in some way to 'Finties', below)].

Finties Birsay: old, abandoned houses, the site of one being unknown [Scots *fint* the Devil but the reason for the application of the name can only be guessed].

Finty Evie/Rendall: (see above).

Finyar Hoose North Ronaldsay: vanished [Norse *fenar* marshes (see 'Finnian Geo' for change of gender)].

Finyew Evie: field with an old well (see above).

Finyew Rendall: a field with a well in it: location unknown [see above for origin of name].

Finyo Stronsay; Rousay, Sourin: vanished [Norse *fen* swamp: (for *gjá* see Appendix)].

Finziehouse Orphir: (see 'Finyo' above).

Fiold Westray, Rackwick: (see 'Feold' above).

Firribar Stronsay: coastal feature north of 'Lamb Head' [Norse *fjara* beach, *berg* rock].

Firth a parish [Norse *fjörðr* a bay: in the Icelandic Sagas it was called *Aurriða-fjörðr* where *aurriða* is 'sea trout'].

Fishhoose North Ronaldsay: location uncertain (see below for possible explanation of meaning)

Fishoose Sanday: Park district, right on the coast of the 'Bay o Wheevie' [probably a type of fishing booth where cod could be prepared for drying in the wind].

Fisk Hellyia Evie: [Norse *fisk* fish, *hella* a flat beach stone, used as a fishing spot in this instance].

Fisligar North Ronaldsay: location uncertain [Norse *veslugr* poor, probably in the sense 'poorly stocked' i.e., with a miserable cow, *garðr* farm: compare Grim, a 'poor' farmer from Swona who, according to the *Orkneyinga Saga* happened to be a friend of Sweyn Asleifsson and was given a gold ring for ferrying him across the Pentland Firth: 'poor' here meant that he had no cattle].

Fitty Hill Westray: [Norse *viti* a fire beacon used in communication when danger was present].

Flag Evie: the herring boats were hauled here (see above).

Flag o Baikie Westray, Fribo: [English 'flag' (stone), Norse *bakki* slope or bank in this case].

Flaga Hoy: on a steep hillside to the west of 'Hoy Lodge' [Norse *flaga* flagstone].

Flagstaff/Flagstick Sanday: now 'Telegraph Cottage' [a flag was hoisted here when coals or kelp were handled in former times].

Flashes Hoy: rocky shore in the extreme north of the island [Norse *fles* a reef: normally in the case of such a feature the initial 'f' is lost: (see 'Feerless' above)].

Flaughton Hill Eday: described by the Ordnance Survey in their initial survey of the island as a 'hill much used for turf cutting' [Norse *flag* a place where turf has been cut].

Flaws Evie; Birsay, Marwick, Northside, plus fields in Linnabrake and Beaquoy; Holm; South Ronaldsay; Harray: always found in a plural form [Norse *flá* strips of meadowland].

Flaws o Holm Evie: on the right bank, downstream from 'Spithersquoy': in the second half of the 19th century this was still a very wet, marshy area unsuitable for peat cutting [Norse *flá* (see above), 'holm' has many meanings, Icelandic *hólmr* meadow flat, fitting best].

Flawsquoy Walls: [(see 'Flaws' above), Norse *kví* enclosure].

Flebister Sanday: [doctor's house and surgery: it sounds a genuine name, but no such placename has been known to exist anywhere in Orkney or Shetland].

Fleck Orphir: 'Houton' area: two houses in bad repair in the 1890s [Norse *flekkr* a spot].

Fleckitsquoy Birsay: [origin unknown].

Fleece, The Swona: [Norse *fles* reef].

Flenstaith/Sands Deerness: the name 'Flenstaith' appears only in old records [Norse personal name *Fleinn*, *staðr* estate].

Flesh House Stronsay: a field, formerly a building, southwest of 'Clestran': (see below).

Flesh-hoose Sanday, Elsness: [this building was used for the receipt of 'skat flesh', i.e., meat given in tax payment].

Flett North Ronaldsay: [Norse *flot* a flat piece of land, usually marshy (see 'Flotty' form below)].

Flettie's Toomal North Ronaldsay: ['flettie' is possibly a diminutive of the Orkney surname 'Flett' though there are no records of early Flett landowners/occupiers in North Ronaldsay, Norse *tún-völlr* home field].

Fletts Stromness: [from the Orkney surname 'Flett'].

Flingi Geo Hoy: a small indentation in the coast near 'Rora Head' [origin unknown].

Flinterquoy Rousay: vanished [Norwegian dialect *flindra* a piece broken off, in other words a small, detached piece of land, Norse *kví* enclosure].

Flitabout Birsay, Northside: [the base of a gadabout! (see 'Rinabout')].

Floss o Gill Westray, Rackwick: [Norse *fles* a reef, Norse *gil* incised stream].

Floss Westray, Rackwick: (see below).

Flossy Groups Walls: [Norse *fles* reef, English 'groups'?].

Flotta island: because of its position in Scapa Flow, it played an enormous part in two World Wars: population in 2021 was 80 [Norse *flat-ey* flat island as distinct from *há-ey* Hoy, the high island].

Flottahall Rousay: [Norse *flatr* flat (land), Scots *hall* used in the sense of 'simple cottage'].

Flotterston Sandwick: a name transferred from Midlothian (see 'Consgar', Sandwick).

Flotty Rousay; Birsay: the area between Eastquoys and the 'Loch o Banks', usually referred to as 'The Flotty' [Norse *flatr* (of land)].

Floura/Flourha Sanday: the Ordnance Surveyor was told that the name of this house was 'something tae deu wi' a flooer' (flower)!

Flúduness Firth: (see below).

Flyðruness Firth: this and the above are alternative spellings of the residence of Thorstein who is mentioned in the *Orkneyinga Saga*: across the water, his son Blann lived on 'Damsay' and they could communicate at one time along a reef, now broken, which is today known as the 'Skerries o Coubister' [Norse *flúd* reefs flooded by the sea or Norse *flaeði-sker* which has the same meaning].

Fokkers Gill Orphir: [(see 'Fokkers' above), Norse *gil* incised stream].

Fokkers Orphir: [land belonging to someone with the surname 'Farquhar', a common name in Orphir at one time].

Folly, The Deerness: near the 'Barns o Ayre': the Orkney poet Edwin Muir was born here [the name suggests that some unusual house (English 'folly') was erected here at some time: (compare 'Orem's Fancy' in Stronsay and 'Fancy' a field on 'Gorn' in Shapinsay)].

Folsetter Birsay: [Norse *fúll* stinking, *setr* seasonal pastureland with a shelter of some sort].

Foolputs Birsay, Curcum: [Norse *fúll* stinking, *pyttr* a water hole (with English plural)].

Forbus Stenness: location unknown [origin of name cannot be explained: it was referred to only in the 1760 planking (division) of the parish].

Forces, The Harray: [Norse *fors* waterfall (with English plural) but usually in Orkney was used in the sense 'rapid', i.e., a restriction in the stream].

Foreberry Hoy: according to the early Ordnance Survey, a projecting point in the northwest of the island but more likely applies to a rock off the point [probably English 'fore' in the sense 'to the fore', Norse *berg* rock].

Foreland St. Ola: recorded as early as 1492 and almost two hundred years later: vanished: ('fore' can be interpreted as above).

Forroway Sanday: John Forroway in Forroway, Commissariot Record 1642: location unknown [possibly Norse *forvað* beach where there is an element of danger in that one might be caught by the incoming tide].

Forse Stromness; Holm: (see 'Forces' above).

Forse, Burn of Walls: (see above).

Forstine Stromness: location unknown, perhaps near one of the streams in 'Ootertoon' [*fors* (explained above), *tún* field as in 'Appietoon', locally pronounced 'Appieteen'].

Forswell Sandwick: [Norse *fors* (see above), *völlr* field].

Fort Sanday, Colligarth: field name [a former gun emplacement in Old Volunteer days].

Fortifield Evie: a field on a former croft site just north of 'Cottonhill' [origin unknown: perhaps the number 'forty' and related to the planking (division) of the land in the late 18th century].

Fosky Reef Sanday: coastal feature off Elsness [Norwegian *fosse* to foam].

Foubister St. Andrews: [Norse *fúll* stinking, probably relating to rotting seaweed in the 'Bay of Suckquoy', *ból-staðr* farm].

Foulan, The Sanday: alternative name for 'Whitemill Point' [Norse *fúll* stinking (close to 'The Foulan' is a placename 'Puldrite'), Norse *pollr*, pool, *drit* dung of birds): the meaning of the suffix 'an' is not understood: the same problem arises with 'Trevan'].

Foulmire Stenness: [Norse fúll stinking, *mýrr* marshy land].

Fraasa Skerry Birsay: [Norwegian *frøse* 'to stream with a roaring sound': many Norse 'sound' words are used to describe 'roaring' reefs, Norse *sker* reef].

Fraasa, Bow o Birsay: coast [Norse *bugr* a bend in the cliffs: caves in the cliffs were used by young men to hide from the Press Gang (see 'Fraasa' above)].

Franks Stronsay: an unusal surname applied to a house/farm and recorded some time before 1841. It must have been a very important surname since it seems to have displaced the original Norse name of the nearby bay (see 'Bay of Franks').

Frey Geo, Soond o Birsay: [Norse *Freyr* a god associated with positive values such as good harvests, peace etc.: the names of Norse gods and goddesses as well as Norse spirits are frequently used for wild coastal features (see Introduction), *gjá* ravine].

Freya Geo, Point o Stronsay: [Norse *Freja* a goddess of love, *gjá* ravine].

Fribo Westray: [originally 'Furbo': Norse *boer* farm, *fjara* beach which usually takes the form 'furrow' in Orkney placenames: it seems that the original 'Fribo' was built on the edge of the coast then moved inland perhaps because of drifting sand].

Fromager Stenness: [location and meaning unknown].

Front o Mires Sanday, Beafield: field name, nearby is the house of 'Mires'.

Frotoft Rousay: originally a farm, now a district name [Norse personal name *Froði* and *topt* house site].

Frow and Wattin Sanday: (see Frow).

Frow Sanday: part of Stove, in the 16th century [origin uncertain, perhaps a clipped form of *Froði* and *garðr*].

Frowantown Sanday: [perhaps a compression of 'Frow' and 'Wattin'].

Frowney Birsay: this name changed from 'Wascra', 'Abune-the-Hill' [both placenames are not easily understood].

Fuag Field Shapinsay: west of the 'Bay of Linton', site of the old farm of 'Fuag' [a strange Orkney placename which is difficult to explain: possibly containing the Norse element *fúi* rotteness as in 'Fue Geo' (below) and would usually be used to describe a stagnant marsh: the suffix 'ag' suggests that this may be correct, Norse *agi* wet ground around a pool].

Fudgescoan Harray: [Norse *fit* meadow flat (see 'Fidge'), Norwegian *skaa* wooden shed used for drying meat/fish etc.: very common placename in Orkney taking a variety of forms in dialect such as 'skyo', 'skeeo' etc.: the form 'Scoan' has a definite article suffixed and normally appears in placenames as 'Scuan'].

Fue Geo Rousay; North Fara: [Norse *fúi* rotteness, referring to trapped seaweed, Norse *gjá* ravine].

Fuffy Evie: low tide rock [origin unknown].

Fuldan Birsay, Howe: [Norse *fúll* stinking, *dýna* soft boggy ground].

Fulgeon Harray: [Norse *fúll* stinking, *tjörn* small sheet of water].

Fulkya, Moss o Dounby, Hyval: [formerly a very marshy area liable to floods: a nearby farm was called 'Waterhall': Norse *fúll* stinking, *kví* enclosure].

Furrawallend Stronsay: [Norse *fjara* beach, 'wall end' i.e., where a wall reaches the beach and extends into the lower part of the ebb to prevent animals passing].

Furrigar Westray, Dykeside: [Norse *fjara* beach, *garðr* wall: (for interpretation see above)].

Furrigeo, Point o Westray: [Norse *forað* dangerous, *gjá* ravine].

Furrow of Grukelty/Grikalty Shapinsay: [Norse *fjara* beach: the name relates to a dividing wall which reaches the beach here (see 'Grukelty')].

Furrow of Traddleton Shapinsay: [Norse *fjara* beach: (see 'Traddleton')].

Furrowall Stronsay: house in Rothiesholm (see 'Furrawallend' above).

Furrowend Stronsay; Eday; Shapinsay; Sanday, Rooswick: [Norse *fjara* Beach, Norse *endi* end].

Fursan Evie: [Norse *fors-inn* the waterfall: in Orkney it meant merely 'rippling water' caused by some obstruction in the stream or perhaps a change in the rock strata].

Furse Rousay: [Norse *fors* waterfall but used in the sense 'rapid' in Orkney].

Furso Harray: [Norse *fors* waterfall (see above): the suffix 'o' is a common diminutive in this case].

Futte Sanday, Elsness: field name, early 18th century ['at the foot' (compare 'Hatt, The')].

G

Ga Gates Stronsay: cliff paths in Rothiesholm [Norse *gjá* ravine, *gata* path: such paths were used by people rock fishing or collecting shell sand for poultry: the normal dialect word for such a path was a 'clivvy'].

Gabray Shapinsay: [location and origin unknown].

Gaerstae Sanday: [Norse *garð-staðr* position of a wall: the house must have been sited near an old dividing wall].

Gafra Stromness: position unknown [see 'Gaifers' below for derivation].

Gaifers Firth: [Norse *gjá* literally ravine but often used for inland features such as an incised stream which in this case is the 'Burn of Redland', Norse *fors* waterfall but in Orkney often means 'rapid in a stream'].

Gaira/Gairy South Ronaldsay: [probably a form of Norse *garðr* farm].

Gairalily Sanday: coastal feature, Tresness [Norse *geir* an odd piece of land: (for 'lily' see 'Lily Skerry')].

Gairbacks Westray: [Norse *garðr* dividing wall(s), *bálkr* important dividing wall, sometimes prehistoric: the use of English plural here is not understood].

Gairbolls Papa Westray: (derivation as above).

Gaird Westray, Broughton: [a form of Norse *garðr* farm: (see 'Gert')].

Gairsay island: [the home of *Sigurd Asleifsson* and recorded in the *Orkneyinga Saga* as 'Gareksey', originally the possession of a man '*Garékr*'].

Gairsay Rendall: marshy land near 'Castle' [where Gairsay folk used to cut peat].

Gairsay Westray: [an imported name from the island of Gairsay].

Gairsay Park Sanday, Bellevue: field name (see above).

Gairsna Geo North Ronaldsay: [Norse *gjá* ravine: such ravines were often used to mark the seaward end of a dividing wall, Norse *garðs-endi* end of a wall].

Gairstay, The Green Rousay: [(see Gairsty above), English 'green' by virtue of the different vegetation which distinguishes disturbed earth].

Gairsts/Gairsty Orphir; Birsay, Northside, Southside; Sandwick; Shapinsay: [Norse *garðs-staðr* position, generally of a prehistoric wall: (see 'Muckle Gairsty')].

Gairsty o Hoo Papa Westray: remains of an old earthwork, (see 'Gairsty' above) [Norse *haugr* mound].

Gairy Westray: Oot o Toon [Norse *geiri* a triangular piece of land].

Gairy Hill South Ronaldsay: [Norse *geiri* a strip, often applied as in this case to a prominent green grassy strip caused by a spring in a heather-covered hill].

Gaitnip Birsay, Northside: [transferred name from St. Ola: (compare 'Lingro')].

Gaitnip 1. St. Ola: [the name appears in the *Orkneyinga Saga* as *Geitabergi*, 'goat headland': its later form is *gnípa* a headland (as in 'Noup Head', Westray)].

Gaitnip 2. Harray: [as above, transferred name from St. Ola].

Gaizger Stronsay: field northwest of Rothiesholm [origin unknown].

Galaha Wyre, Helziegitha: a field, site of a former house (see 'Gallowhall' below).

Galdry/The Galdry Sanday: [Shetland dialect *galder*, a high roaring wind, hence a 'draughty house'].

Galeed Stenness: [one of many Bible related names for 19th century houses in Orkney: in the Bible, 'a pile of stones erected by Jacob and Laban to mark a pact of friendship'].

Galilee Sanday: Lettan [many old houses in Orkney, crofter houses in Particular, had Biblical names (e.g., 'Jericho' in Dounby, 'Babylon' in Stenness etc.)].

Gallow Hill Westray, Broughton: [the presumed site of gallows].

Galloway Dyke Sanday: [a wall built on 'Stove' land by Mackenzie and masons in Galloway style, i.e., with stones upright instead of horizontal].

Gallowha Evie; Burray: [a form of 'Gallowhall'].

Gallowhall Evie; Sanday: (it stood near 'Purgatory'!).

Gallowhill, Sanday, Cross parish: also known as Stewart's [the presumed site of gallows].

Gallows Slap, The Rendall: a field on Lettaly [Scots *slap* gate (presumably on the path to the gallows): nearby field names are 'Purgatory' and 'Dangerfield'].

Gallows, The Rousay: a spot on the banks of the 'Sourin Burn' [perhaps the location of a gallows at one time].

Galpo Stronsay: small bay east of Rothiesholm [the name suggests Norse *göltr* boar (see below) and *pollr* pool].

Galt Sanday: coastal feature, Tresness [Norse *göltr* boar, a name usually applied to rocky coastal areas].

Galt Skerry Shapinsay: (see above).

Galt, The Shapinsay: (see above).

Galtie Rock North Ronaldsay: (see above).

Galtyha Eday: [Scots *ha/hall* small cottage, Norse *göltr* boar: the name suggests that the cottage was associated with pigs in some way or other: perhaps in jest].

Gamla 1. Harray: field name [Norse *gamla* old: in this instance there is no indication what is 'old' in this field].

Gamla 2. Rousay: fishing mark [the Norse word *miðr* middle, used as a fishing mark, is missing, Norse *gamla* old].

Gamon Park South Ronaldsay: [Norse *gaman-leikr* sport: older residents recall ball games being played here].

Gangsti Pier Graemsay: [Norse *gangr-stigr* a foot passage (to the pier)].

Gany o Gersty Shapinsay: [Norse *gjá-n* the ravine, *garð-staðr* wall].

Gap, The Sanday: a drain between 'Neigarth' and 'Thrave' [Norse *gap* space, in this case a water channel].

Gara/Gerra Orphir: Swanbister area [Norse *geiri* a triangular shape (or strip) of land].

Garaber Rousay: fishing rock, it lies just off the end of the 'Green Gairsty' [Norse *berg* rock, *garðr* wall].

Garalanga St. Andrews [Norse *geiri* a strip of land or vegetation, *langr* long].

Garay Sanday, position unknown; Orphir; South Ronaldsay: (see 'Gara' above).

Garbo Sanday, Sellibister: recorded in 1624 as 'Gairbak' [Norse *garðr-bálkr* a dividing wall 'Garbo' lies on a 'treb dyke': (see 'The Treb')].

Gardemeles Sanday: a farm on the land of 'Stove' [Norse *garðr* farm, *mels* genitive of *melr* sand (bank)].

Gardinian Evie: field name [Norse *garðr* farm, *eng-in* the meadow].

Gariel Hole, The South Ronaldsay: [Norse *grýla* an ogress: there are several instances of such spirits living in ravines and caves on the Orkney coast].

Garoondi Firth, Bridgend: this word is similar in meaning to 'Roundadee' in Sandwick [Norse *geiri* a patch or stripe, Norwegian *rund* round or circular, *dý* a wet marshy piece of land: 'circle' type words were often used to describe marshy wet spots since they were frequently circular: the normal 'circle' word used was *kringla* (e.g. 'The Waal o Kringlaquoy' in Marwick, Birsay)].

Garr Stronsay: southeast of Cleat [Norse *garðr* farm].

Garriecot Sandwick; Birsay, Southside: probably on the site of present 'Newbigging' [Norse *garðr* wall, *kot* a cottage].

Garsna Geo North Ronaldsay: [Norse *garðs-endi* the end of a wall, *gjá* ravine].

Garsni Geo Rousay: (see above).

Garsnya Geo Swona: (see above).

Garso North Ronaldsay: a small farm at the edge of the sea which gave its name to a loch ('Loch o Garso') and a bay ('Garsowick') the suggestion here is that the final 'n' of this placename is lost [Norse *garðs-endi* wall end].

Garson Birsay; Flotta; Graemsay; Walls; Stromness; Hoy; Sandwick; Rendall; Rousay: [Norse *garðs-endi* wall end (usually touching the shore)].

Garson Meadow Harray: [Norse *garðs-endi* wall end].

Garsons Pier Sanday: also known as 'Rousay's Pier', a tunship wall reaches the coast here [Norse *garðs-endi* wall end].

Garsowick North Ronaldsay: (see 'Garso' above) [Norse *vík* bay].

Gart Banks Stronsay: on south side of 'Mill Bay' [Norse *garðr* farm/enclosure near the beach].

Gart 1. Stronsay: field northwest of Rothiesholm: there are three 'gart' placenames in Stronsay [Norse *garðr* farm/enclosure].

Gart 2. St. Andrews (see above).

Garth Sanday, Warsetter; Westray; South Ronaldsay; St. Ola; Shapinsay; Stromness; Hoy; Deerness; Eday: [Norse *garðr* farm/enclosure].

Garthna Geo Hoy: [Norse *garð-inn* the wall, *gjá* ravine].

Garthsetter Birsay, Northside: pronounced 'Gesta' [Norse *garðr* wall rather than farm since it would be unusual to have a farm and a temporary summer pasture hut in such close proximity: Norse *setr* temporary dwelling].

Gasander South Ronaldsay: [Norse *garðs-endir* the end of a wall, usually where it reaches the shore/cliff].

Gate of Bull Rendall: on Gorseness Hill [Norse *gata* path, Scots 'bull' = 'Bu'].

Gateside North Ronaldsay; Sanday: [Norse *gata* path].

Gaudie's Hole Evie: a large cave [from the surname 'Gaudie': surnames were applied to caves for a variety of reasons e.g., hiding from the Press Gang, hiding contraband, getting stuck in a cave because of water level rising etc.].

Gayro o the Wart Firth: a strip of grass on the hillside [Norse *geiri* patch of green grass on hillside (see 'Wart')].

Gear Walls: [Norse *geiri* a triangular-shaped piece of land].

Gears St. Andrews: ('Gear' in English plural form).

Gearsan Deerness: (see 'Garson').

Gebro Shapinsay; Stronsay: [a metathesis of Gerbo? if so the derivation is Norse *garð-bálkr* a significant dividing wall].

Geddesta South Ronaldsay: [from Scots surname 'Geddes' a merchant family established in Kirkwall since the 17th century and possibly earlier. 'Geddesta' lay near Garth and is not on record after 1750: the suffix 'sta' is Norse *staðr* place or abode].

Geediesta/Giddysta Rousay; Wyre: [Norse *geitar* goat's, *staða* place or position, in other words a pen].

Geedista Rousay, Wasbister: (see 'Geediesta').

Geerons Firth: [Norse *geir-inn* the triangular-shaped piece of land (with English plural)].

Geitaberg St. Ola: [Norse *geitar* goat's, *berg* hill or cliff (see 'Gaitnip')].

Gelderhouse/Quoygelding Birsay, Northside, Sabiston; Dounby: [Norse *geldinga-hús* a shelter for wethers (castrated rams)].

Geldibist, Point o Westray: [Norse *geldr* barren specially of animals but also of fields, *ból-staðr* farm: in Orkney placenames *geldr* usually takes the form 'yelda' or 'yelya': (see 'Yeldabreck')].

Gemuglo, Waal o Firth, Redland: [Norse *gjá* ravine but when used inland has a different meaning (see general remarks on 'Geo' in Appendix), *mykill* large].

Genie Fea Walls: [Norse *tjörn* small lake, *fjall* hill].

Gentlemen's Ha Westray: a cave [by tradition, a refuge for North Isles lairds who supported the Jacobites and who would use the cave as a refuge].

Geo, The Rendall: a field on Gitterpitten (see 'Geo' in Appendix).

Geo Dannemarck North Ronaldsay: [presumed site of a vessel with this name, stranded or wrecked here].

Geo Dykend Rousay: [ravines were often used as terminations of boundary walls].

Geo Ginnis Stronsay, Linga Holm: this must be an insignificant ravine which gets no mention in the first OS survey though it is mentioned by Hugh Marwick in *Antiquarian Notes* [origin unknown].

Geo Luan Eday: [Norse *hljóðan* sound (of the sea) in the ravine (see 'Loth')].

Geo Nicol Shapinsay: [personal name or surname 'Nichol': many coastal places include personal names, no doubt associated with tragedy or near disaster].

Geo o Banks Birsay: a stream in 'Greeny' (see 'Geo' in Appendix).

Geo o Gessan Stronsay: [Norse *garðs-endi* wall end].

Geo o Graverend Stronsay: [*grafar-endi* from Norse *gröf* hole, pit or entrenched stream].

Geo o Jibidi Shapinsay: a small geo east of east of 'Castle Bloody' (see 'Jubidee').

Geo o Ootspay Stronsay: north of 'Burgh Head' (see 'Ootspay').

Geo o Shell Evie: [origin unknown].

Geo o Sourin Rousay: a valley: (see 'Geo' in the Appendix).

Geo o Steinsa Shapinsay: on the east coast but not connected with the 'geo' above [(see 'Geo' in the Appendix), 'a' in this placename can be interpreted as Norse *á* stream].

Geo o Stinniger Stromness: [this ravine divides 'Innertoon' and 'Ootertoon': (see 'Stinniger')].

Geo o the Coorsa Stronsay: at the south end of 'Rothiesholm' (see 'Coorsa').

Geo o the Lame Hoy: slightly to the west of 'Mel Fea' [Norse *hlamma* to thud, i.e., the sound of the sea in the ravine: (see 'Lampal')].

Geo o the Swans Birsay: a fishing geo [swans do not normally frequent ravines: origin unknown].

Geo o the Toe Copinsay: in the extreme north of the island [Norse *gjá* ravine, *tó* a grassy spot among rocks].

Geo Oden/Eden Stronsay: [an example of the name of a Norse god to describe a coastal feature, in this case 'Odin': this placename is also found in the spelt form 'Guiddin'].

Geo Ritch South Ronaldsay: [Norse *hrytr* snoring i.e., the sound of the sea in the ravine].

Geona Gui North Ronaldsay: [Norse *gjá-n* the ravine: 'gui' is not easily understood ('Googan' might offer an explanation)].

Geona Skoor Birsay: [Norse *gjá-n* the ravine, *skor* cleft].

Geona Trangie North Ronaldsay: [Norse *gjá-n* the ravine, *þröngr* narrow].

Geord Birsay: field name, 'Banks' and 'Bigging (Greeny)' [Norse *gjorde* meadow].

Geordie Reid Sanday, Ire: lobster set ['Reid' is a surname, hence the place where 'Geordie' set his creels: (compare 'Tammy Reid's Swarf')].

Geordie Ross South Ronaldsay: field name to the north of 'Braeland' [no doubt the site of an old house: it was common for cottar houses to be named after their owner: (c.f. 'Maggie Broon's')].

Geordie's Swarf Sanday: rocks southeast of 'Inner Ire' [probably the same 'Geordie Reid' mentioned above, Norse *svarf* tumult, of the sea].

Georth Evie: a farm (see above).

Georth Rendall: fields on Upper Bigging, Lower Bigging, Gitterpitten and Hogarth [Norse *gjorde* meadow].

Geos o Hangie North Ronaldsay: (see 'Hangie').

Geostane Shapinsay: a small ravine on the east coast of the island which encloses a rocky pillar [Norse *gjá* ravine, *steinn* stone].

Gera Orphir; Rousay: (see 'Gara/Gerra').

Geramont Rousay: also known as 'Cathole' [a transferred name from Sanday (above)].

Geramont Sanday: [the name was first recorded in 1601: rebuilt for John Trail Urquhart in 1835: the nearby Geramont Lodge was occupied until 1887].

Gerbo/Gerback North Ronaldsay: [Norse *garð-bálkr* a dividing wall: it lies adjacent to the 'Muckle Gairsty'].

Germiston Stenness: [an early tunship name, Norse *Geirmundar-staðr* the estate of *Geirmund*].

Gernoon, Cott o Orphir: originally part of the estate of James Johnston of Coubister in Orphir [Norse *geir-inn* a triangular-shaped piece of land, the suffix 'oon' suggests Norse *á-n* the stream: (see 'Waal o Aan')].

Gernori Orphir: [Norse *geirr-inn* (as above), *ár* genitive of *á* stream, hence 'of the stream'].

Geroin Harray: [Norse *geirr-inn* (as above)].

Geroyne Rousay: (see above).

Gerra/Gara Orphir: (see 'Gara').

Gerraquoy Birsay, Marwick: [a variant of Norse *garðr* normally interpreted as 'farm' but in this case it is 'wall': the wall of the tunship of Marwick passes close by: a nearby farm is called 'Gairsty', Norse *garðr* wall, *staða* position: (see 'Muckle Gairsty')].

Gerraquoy South Ronaldsay, Grimness: [earlier it was called 'Garrickquoy' from the family name 'Garrick' i.e., 'Garrioch', Norse *kví* enclosure].

Gerrascow/Garisco Stronsay: old house site, location uncertain [final element suggests Norse *kví* enclosure, first element may be *garðr* wall or enclosure].

Gerrataing/Cherra Taing Sanday: coastal feature, Lopness [Norse *garðr* wall, *tangi* point: promontories were often used for corralling sheep: sometimes they had walls to prevent them getting out].

Gerry Westray: [Norse *garðr* farm].

Gersmeera Stromness, Garth: [Norse *garðr* farm, *mýrr* poor, sometimes marshy land].

Gerson Auskerry: (see 'Garson').

Gersteith /Gersty Birsay, Southside: [Norse *garðr* wall, *staða* position].

Gersteven Birsay, Netherskaill: [Norse *garðr* enclosure, Norse *stúfr* a bit (of land) cut off, *fen* marsh: (see 'Cup Steven')].

Gersty Deerness: now 'Tiffyha' (see 'Gairsty' forms above).

Gervie Stone Birsay, Barony: also known as 'Stane Randa' [Norse *steinn* stone: origin of 'Gervie' uncertain].

Gerwin Orphir: (see 'Geroin').

Geyro North Ronaldsay: in 'Linklett toon' and 'Eastin' [Norse *geiri* an odd-shaped piece of land].

Giant's Foot Sanday: coastal feature, Spurness, also known as 'Carlin Foot' [the wild rocky shores of Orkney are frequently associated with mythical beings: (see Introduction)].

Giddista Wyre: field name [suggests a placename transferred from Rousay].

Giesbir Stronsay: a field southeast of 'Kelsbir' [origin unknown].

Gilbroch Burray: vanished [Norse *gil* a stream running in a narrow Channel, *byrgja* an enclosure].

Gill South Ronaldsay, Hoxa: (see above).

Gill Westray: a farm [Norse *gil* a stream running in a narrow channel].

Gill of Gart St. Ola: (see 'Gill' above and 'Garth').

Gillie's Toon Rendall: field on 'Breck' [Gilbert's portion of land: 'Gilbert' has not been identified].

Gillieselly South Ronaldsay: [Norse *gil* stream, *selr* seal].

Gillietrang Burray: [Norse *gil* a stream running in a deep, narrow channel, *þröngr* narrow].

Gilstrang Sanday: (see 'Gillietrang').

Gimleson Harray: [Norse *gamla* old, *tjörn* pond: 'old pond' does not make sense: probably from an original *gamla-kerling* ogress, hence *gamla-kerling tjörn*: close to 'Gimleson' is 'Trolla Shun', 'troll's pond'].

Gimps South Ronaldsay, Grimness: derelict house [probably a dialect form of Norwegian *gympa* mud or mire].

Gin, Loch o Harray: [Norse *tjörn* a small loch].

Gingerin Harray: [Norse *gin/ginn* wide, *geir-inn* triangular-shaped piece of land].

Ginn Guan, Geo o Westray: [Norse *gin/ginn* wide, *gjá-n* the ravine].

Ginnagairn Birsay: [Norse *gjá-in* the ravine, *garð-inn* the wall, referring to an old boundary wall which ends at the ravine].

Ginnis Skerry Stronsay: northwest of 'Linga Holm' [perhaps 'Gunni' (the spirit)].

Gion Evie, Costa: a flat stretch of rocky beach below 'Upper Midhouse' [the name may actually refer to a beach pond, hence Norse *tjörn* pond].

Girals Hoose, The Flotta: coastal feature (presumably a cave) [Norse a variant of *gýgr* an ogress, sometimes referred to in Scots as a 'gyre-carlin' (see 'Carlin'), a good example of spirits lurking among the rocks!].

Girndish Sanday, Tresness: coastal feature, named after the adjacent mound [Norse *dýs* mound, Orkney dialect 'girn' a metathesis of Norse *groenn* green' (see 'Knap o Girndish')].

Girnear Birsay, 'Nisthouse', 'Hundland': field name [Norse *groena* green: suffix cannot be explained].

Girnear/Cowgate Birsay, Abune-the-Hill: a deserted house (see above).

Girnigeo Sanday: coastal feature [Norse *groenn* green, *gjá* ravine].

Girnigo Shapinsay: (see above).

Girnillay Sanday: a small field below 'Warsetter Farm' [Norse *grind-hlið* lattice gate].

Girsay Schottis Burray: one of the earliest recorded Burray placenames [from the surname 'Scotty' recorded in Burray: 'Girsay' suggests a corruption of Scots first name 'Kirsy': (see 'Quoykirsay' in Harray)].

Girso Wasses Sanday: a mound at Taftsness, also known as 'Shelly Knowe' [Scots *girs* grass, Norse *haugr* mound: 'Wasses' = 'Wa's', local pronunciation of surname 'Walls': the interpretation of this placename seems to be 'a grassy mound on the land of someone by the surname Walls'].

Girth House Orphir: [an alternative name for the 'Round Kirk' at 'The Bu': Scots *girth* sanctuary].

Gitterpitten/Gutterpitten Rendall: [Norse *pyttr* hole in the ground with definite masculine article, hence *pytt-inn*, the hole, Norse *gytjer* mud: 'Gitterpitten' originally lay in a marshy area].

Glaesbro Sanday, Northwall: house and land area [Norse *glaesa* to make shining: the sense describes a piece of land distinctive from the surrounding area, *byrgja* an enclosure].

Glaitness St. Ola: [probably a variation of Norwegian *glette* an opening in the clouds: used metaphorically here of a grassy patch in what would otherwise be moorland, Norse *nes* a pointed piece of land].

Glasquoy Harray: (see 'Glaesbro' above).

Gleat Sanday, Northwall: (see 'Glaitness').

Glebe, The Orphir; Rousay; Evie; Firth; Birsay; Harray; St. Andrews etc.: [commonly used throughout Britain to describe land which provided extra income for the local minister/vicar].

Gleebna/Gliberness Skerry Birsay: coast [variant of Norse *gloppa* a big hole, a reference to the steep ravine nearby (see 'Langagleeb'), Norse *sker* reef].

Glen Westray, Broughton: [unusual to have a Celtic name in Westray; perhaps transferred: if original it would be Gaelic *gleann* a narrow valley].

Glens o Kinnaird Hoy: [Gaelic *gleann* valley (see 'Kinnaird')].

Glett, The Birsay: a green strip on the hillside, to the east of 'Dirkadale' [Norwegian *glette* an opening, bright in relation to its background].

Glifter Rousay: [Norse *gljúfr* a chasm with dialect suffix 'ter' as in 'sester' a dialect word for a channel to take away urine in old Orkney cowsheds].

Glifters o Lyrawa Hoy: (see above).

Glifters o Pegal Hoy: (see above).

Glims/Glimps Holm South Ronaldsay: ['Glim' seems to have been seen as some kind of evil spirit, probably along the lines of 'Will o the Wisp': they favoured wild marshy places].

Glims Moss Birsay, Beaquoy: it lay near Dounby village (see above).

Gloup Birsay, Northside: [Norse *gloppa* a deep hole in a rocky coast: in this case the roof of the tunnel which had been caused by sea erosion and has collapsed, and a ravine called 'Langagleeb' has been formed].

Gloup, The 1. Deerness: a deep and dangerous hole near the cliff top formed by the collapse of a cave roof [Norse *gloppa* hole: this 'gloup' is the most impressive of all the Orkney 'gloups'].

Gloup, The 2. Holm, Roseness: an impressive 'gloup' recorded by the Ordnance Survey in the 1880s since it was so far from the coast (see above).

Gloup, The 3. Swona: (see above).

Gloup o Bothabir Orphir: (see 'Gloup' above) [Norse *boði* skerry, *berg* rock].

Gloup o Halcro, The South Ronaldsay: [alternative name for 'Gloup o Root'].

Gloup o Root, The South Ronaldsay: alternative name for 'The Gloup o Halcro' [Norse *rjóta* to roar].

Gloupquoy Deerness: vanished: [it lay near 'The Gloup', Norse *kví* enclosure].

Glower Birsay: on the top of 'Ravie Hill' [Scots *glower* to stare but in Orkney its meaning seems to be merely 'look', i.e., a viewing point in this case].

Glower-ower Stromness, Innertoon: [no further information (see above)].

Glower-ower-him Flotta: [on a slightly elevated position: the same origin as above: the use of English 'him' here is not understood].

Glumsgar, Waal o Stenness: a well: position unknown: (see 'Glims Moss') ['gar' suggests Norse *garðr* meaning 'enclosure' here: it would seem that some kind of 'fence' had been erected to prevent damage to the well by livestock].

Goar Stronsay: field east of 'Whitehall' (see 'The Goard' below).

Goard, The Rousay: there are four examples of this in the island [Norse *gjorde* a meadow].

Goarhouse Rousay: [a variant of Norse *gjorde* meadow (see above)].

Goe Rendall: an old farm near 'Appieteen' (see Geo in Appendix).

Goe Backs Evie: they lie along the 'Burn o Pow' [Norwegian (Nynorsk) *bakki* bank, of a stream (with English plural): (for 'goe' see Appendix)].

Goe o the Swans Birsay: near 'Doonabrya' [Norse *gjá* ravine: origin of 'swans' uncertain: swans are not normally associated with ravines, preferring as they do calm water].

Gogarth Sanday: named after a house in Llandudno, North Wales!

Goir Sanday: a tumal in the 1595 Rental; position unknown but see 'Gray's Tumal' [Norse *gjorde* pasture].

Golback Firth, Breckan: (see 'Goldmeadows' below).

Goldero/Golderhall Evie: an old house near 'Jubidee' [Orkney dialect 'golder' a gust of wind: in this sense the word probably describes the exposed situation of the house].

Goldhall Flotta: [a fanciful name for a simple cottar house: Scots *hall* humble cottage].

Goldiger Sandwick: [(for 'go' element see Appendix), *dý* marsh, *garðr* farm].

Golmeadows Firth, Horraldshay: (see 'go' in Appendix to explain 'gol').

Golt, The South Ronaldsay: [Norse *göltr* boar but usually referring to 'pig' in Orkney dialect: a name applied frequently to prominent rocks and promontories in Orkney (e.g., 'Golta', Flotta, below)].

Golta Flotta: (see above).

Goltalea Sandwick: a field on Ness, [Norse *göltr* Orkney dialect pig, *hlíð* slope].

Goltequoy Westray: [Norse *göltr* pig (see 'The Golt' above), *kví* enclosure].

Goltsquoy Rendall: a small croft: it is now called 'Layburn' (see above).

Goodwalter Rendall: [named after a former inhabitant: the surname 'Goodwalter' is extremely rare: there is no written record of it in Orkney].

Googan Sanday: beach feature [Norse *gjá* ravine, Norse *gjá-n* the ravine, a good example of a tautological placename].

Goosanoris Birsay, Boardhouse: a small goose enclosure [Norse *gás* goose: owned by Norris? (see below)].

Goosie Krue Birsay, Dirkadale: [Norse *kró* in this case a small enclosure for geese].

Gooskerry Birsay: coastal feature [a skerry (reef) favoured by wild geese?].

Goras Sanday: [location and meaning unknown].

Gord of Banks Rousay: [Norse *gjorde* meadow].

Gorey's Saddle Calf of Eday: a point on the rocky coast of the Calf of Eday: presumably a saddle shaped rock where 'Gorey' sat: she was an ogress usually associated with wild rocky coasts: in Shetland placenames the spirit took the form 'geyr' and was applied to detached rocks in the sea such as 'The Geyr' in Delting and the 'Stack o Geyrasten' in Fetlar [Norse *gýgr* ogress].

Gories Stronsay: a house in Evirby [from the Orkney surname 'Goar'].

Gories Bight Birsay: (see 'Gorey's Saddle' above).

Gorn Birsay; Holm; Graemsay; Shapinsay; Sandwick; Sanday; Rendall; Harray; Wyre, (vanished); Westray: [Norse *garð-inn* the farm].

Gorn Sanday, Scar: field name [site of a former farm].

Gorn Sanday: a mound northwest of 'Neigarth' [Norse *garðr-inn* the farm].

Gornside Sanday, Stove: field name (see 'Gorn' forms above).

Gorsady Birsay, Howan: [Norse *gjorde* water meadow: *dý* marshland].

Gorseness Rendall: a large tunship, first recorded in 1492 as 'Goryssness' [taking its name from some point on the shore haunted by the ogress 'Gorey': (see 'Gorey's Saddle' above)].

Gorsippan Harray: [origin uncertain: (compare 'Fairasippy', North Ronaldsay)].

Gort o Orquil Rendall: [Norse *gjorde* water meadow (see 'Orquil')].

Gossaday Harray: [Norse *gás* goose, *dý* marsh].

Gossafer Birsay, Skelday: [Norse *gás* goose: origin of suffix 'fer' cannot be explained].

Gossaquoy Orphir; Westray: [Norse *gás* goose, *kví* enclosure].

Gossatte Sanday, Stove: field name (see 'Gossaday' above).

Gossely/Gosalie Sanday: on Hermisgarth land [Norse *gás* goose, Norse *hlíð* slope].

Gossigar South Ronaldsay: [Norse *gás* goose, *garðr* enclosure].

Goward Westray, Fribo: [Norse *gjorde* water meadow].

Gowers Dyke Birsay, Southside: an old boundary wall which reaches the coast at 'Garson' [Norse *garðs-endi*].

Gowkha Eday: [Scots 'gowk' fool: not a very complimentary name for the inhabitant or the house!].

Gowkheads Rousay: boggy and tussocky land east of 'Little Water' [probably relates to some type of plant e.g., Scots *gauks cheese* wood sorrel].

Gowrie Birsay: [Norse *geir* a triangular-shaped piece of land].

Gowrie, Brae of Westray: (see above).

Gowsday Rousay: (see 'Gossaday').

Graand, The Eday; Egilsay; Eynhallow: [Norse *grandi* a stretch of beach above the water at ebb tide].

Graemsay An island midway between The Mainland and Hoy: famed for its two lighthouses, Hoy Sound High and Hoy Sound Low: population in 2011 was 20: [originally Norse *Grímsey* but the spelling became confused with surname Graeme].

Graemshall Holm: built by Bishop Graeme in 1626 [originally 'Meall' before the change].

Graemshall Rendall: [a transferred name from Holm].

Graemston South Ronaldsay: [from the surname 'Graeme', Norse *tún* enclosure].

Grain 1. St. Ola: [Norse *geir-inn* the triangular-shaped piece of land (see 'Green', Marwick)].

Grain 2. Rousay: (see above).

Grainbank St. Ola: earliest recording 1841: developed by Andrew Gold, Newburn, Fife, later Chamberlain to the Earl of Orkney [probably an imported name].

Grainha Evie: [Norse *graen* green, Scots 'ha' = 'hall', used in the sense 'small cottage'].

Granabu Birsay, Beaquoy: [Norse *Grani* a personal name, Norse *bú* farm or estate].

Grandon Firth: [Norse *grandinn* the beach, referring to the beach of 'The Ouse' (see the 'Graand')].

Grange Eynhallow: [the barn of the former monastery].

Grannay Evie: [a corruption of 'Grainha' (above), part of 'Ploverha'].

Granooan Harray: (see 'Gernoon', Orphir).

Grass Holm Shapinsay: [Norse *gras* grass, *hólmr* island].

Grassquoy Birsay, Fea, Abune-the-Hill; Westray; Shapinsay: [Norse *gras* grass, *kví* enclosure].

Grassy Cletts Walls: [English 'grassy', Norse *klettar* rocks].

Grassy Geos Calf of Eday: [Norse *gras* grass, *gjá* ravine (with English plural)].

Graves Eday; Flotta; Holm; Orphir: [Norse *gröf* pit or hollow, i.e., water hole (with English plural)].

Graveshill Sanday: a small piece of land near 'Rock' [said to be a former burial ground but more likely to be Norse *gróf* pit or hole (as above)].

Gravin/Graven Rendall: field name; croft on 'Breck' [Norse *grófin* the hollow].

Gravity North Ronaldsay: [Norse *gróf* hollow, *dý* marsh].

Gray Ewe Swona: a sheep-like rock [compare French *roches moutonnés*, round boulders left at the end of the Ice Age].

Gray's Inn Orphir: [this name was given to an old coaching inn in Orphir in the 1860s and was revived some years ago].

Grays Toomal Sanday: mentioned in 1601 Rental; position unknown: [Norse *tún-völlr* home field].

Graysgate/Greasgate Sanday, Rue: field name [named after the adjacent 'Greasgate Road'].

Grear, Glen of Hoy: [Norse *geir* a triangular piece of land].

Greasgate Road Sanday: a farm road between 'Nouster' and 'Scar' [Norse *gata* path, *grið* sanctuary, usually a chapel].

Great Stead o Volyar Sanday, Stove: field name, also known as 'Volyar'; Hugh Marwick suggested that this was the site of 'Volunes' mentioned in the *Orkneying Saga* [Norse *vellir* fields, *nes* point of land].

Green 1. Birsay, Marwick: [originally 'Gyren' (see 'Gyren')].

Green 2. Walls; Eday; Rendall: (see above).

Green Gates Birsay: old peat road east of 'Sibbies', Hundland [Norse *gata* path].

Green Geyro Birsay, Greeny Hill: [Norse *geiri* an odd-shaped piece of Land, Norse *groena* green].

Green Klavey South Faray: gullies in the south of the island [Norse *klif* a path in cliffs giving access to the beach: (see 'Clava Clivvy')].

Green Knowe Birsay, Greeny: [Scots *knowe* mound].

Green o Risdae Evie: grassy slope in cliff [Norse *groen* green, *hrís* brushwood, *dý* moorland].

Greenakilda Stronsay: a well [Norse *groena* green, *kelda* a well: the reference must be to the grassy area around the well].

Greenan Nev Eday: [Norse *grundin* a green are, *nef* nose, in other words, a point of land].

Greengears Walls: [Norse *groen* green, *geir* a triangular piece of land (with English plural)].

Greenha Evie: [possibly relates to a green turf-covered roof].

Greenhill Birsay: [probably religious in origin, 'There is a green hill far away', etc.].

Greenigeo Holm: (see 'Greenigoe' below).

Greenigoe/geo Orphir: [Norse *groena* green, *gjá* ravine].

Greenli Stronsay, Ness: [Norse *groena* green, *hlíð* slope].

Greenlie Birsay, Skelday: (see above).

Greenquoy 1. Sanday: mound near 'Newark' [Norse *groena* green, *kví* enclosure].

Greenquoy 2. Walls: (see above).

Greenquoy's Laytey Sanday: field name [Norse *hluti* share: (see 'Breckan's Laytey')].

Greens St. Andrews: in the 1880s a farm near 'Vestlabanks' [origin uncertain].

Greenspot Sanday: [Norse *groena* green, *spottr* a small piece].

Greenspot/Greenyspot North Ronaldsay: (see above).

Greentoft Deerness; Eday; Birsay, Southside: [Norse *groena* green, *topt* old house site].

Greenvale South Ronaldsay: [Norse *graen* green, *völlr* field].

Greenwall Stronsay: a field east of 'Scoulters', Holm; North Ronaldsay; Westray, Greenwell: [Norse *groena* green, *völlr* field].

Greenwhystee, The Firth: [Norse *groena* green, *kví* enclosure, Icelandic *stoeði* position or site].

Greeny Birsay: earlier 'Grenying' (tunship) [from an assumed Norse *graeningr* a green place, a farm name, several of which are found in Norway].

Greeny Clavey South Fara: two gullies cut down the cliffs to the sea here: (see 'Clava Clivvy').

Greeny Grip Firth: [Norse *gröf* pit or hole: in Orkney it usually means 'small stream': in Norse *grafar-laekr* is a stream which has dug itself a deep bed].

Greeny Hill Birsay: [named from the tunship of 'Greeny'].

Greenya Ness Stronsay: [Norse *groena* green, *nes* point of land: Norse *nes* can also describe features on land as well as sea].

Grenigo Taing Deerness: [Norse *groena* green, *gjá* ravine, *tangi* point of land].

Gresmay Sanday: [Norse *gras* grass, *melr* sand].

Gressness Birsay, Newhall: ['gress' = grass: sometimes the word *nes* is used inland for points of land].

Gressy Geo Evie: ['gressy' = 'grassy', *gjá* ravine].

Gretness Westray: [Norse *grjót* gravel, *nes* point].

Grew Birsay, Southside: [Norse *gröf* pit or incised stream].

Grey Head Eday: to distinguish it from 'Red Head'.

Greystein Deerness: a field near 'Horries': nearly all of the following relate to boundary stones e.g. Graysteen, Rousay; Greystone, Sanday; Greystones, Evie; Greystones, Burray.

Grice Ness Stronsay: [Norse *gríss* pig, *nes* point: (compare 'Lamaness')].

Griceback South Ronaldsay: [Norse *gríss* pig (compare English 'hog's back'): these houses were probably built of turf and assumed a pig's back shape].

Gricey Water Stronsay: (see above).

Grid Birsay: beach feature [Norse *grjót* shingle].

Grid House Birsay, Dirkadale: [it lies on the 'Burn o Grid'].

Gridgar Orphir: [Norse *grjót* shingle, *garðr* farm].

Gridland Sanday: near Greenquoy [Norse *grjót* shingle].

Griffyelt Orphir: [Norse *gröf* stream, Orkney dialect 'yelt' = Norse *geldr* barren: (see 'Yeldabreck')].

Grigdar Birsay, Marwick: (see 'Gridgar').

Grihushen Graemsay: a gravelly beach on the south coast of the island [Norse *grjót* rocky ground, *hauss-inn* the skull, used figuratively to describe a round heap].

Grimbist Westray, Rapness: (see below).

Grimbister Firth: originally 'Grinbister' [both this placename and the above are identical. Both were farms adjacent to a *grind*, Norse for a 'gateway' leading from the arable settlements to the common land: Norse *ból-staðr*, farm: the 'bist' of Grimbist is a curtailed form of *ból-staðr*].

Grimbust Papa Westray: (see above).

Grimeston Stenness: [Norse *Grím-staðr* the estate of *Grím*. These estates were found primarily in the West Mainland of Orkney, several such as 'Onston', Clouston etc., being in the parish of Stenness. Most can be recognised by the ending 'ston' which has the definite article suffixed to give the form *stað-inn* the abode].

Grimisdale Rendall: [Norse *Grímr* a byname of Odin: many wild, exposed places carried the names of mythical beings and Old Norse gods (e.g., 'Grimness', South Ronaldsay; 'Odin Ness', Gairsay: etc.)].

Grimness South Ronaldsay: (see above).

Grimsetter St. Ola: [Norse personal name *Grím*, Norse *saetr*, originally a temporary summer grazing hut outside the tunship wall: later, a farm name].

Grimsquoy St. Ola [Norse *kví* enclosure, attached to 'Grimsetter' above].

Grinaby/Grinnavey, Westray: a slightly puzzling name: the Ordnance Survey describes 'Grinnavey' as a 'farm' but it does not appear on the map: there is no reference to 'Grinaby' [Norse *grjót* stone, *nef* nose but used figuratively as a headland].

Grind North Ronaldsay; Rousay; St. Andrews; Stronsay; Deerness; Sandwick; Orphir; Rendall; South Ronaldsay; Sanday: [Norse *grind* gate].

Grindamira Rendall: [old name of 'Grind': Norse *mýrr* poor heathery land: (compare 'Baramira')].

Grindcheek Deerness: also known as 'Watermoss' [Norse *grind* gate, *keikr* leaning backwards].

Grindigar Deerness: [Norse *grind* gate, *garðr* wall].

Grindilla/Grindally South Ronaldsay; Sanday; Birsay, Northside; Westray; Rousay; Orphir; Stronsay; Sandwick: [Norse *grind-hlíð* gate with a lattice, *hlíð* slope].

Grinds Burray: [Norse *grunn* shoal (with English plural)].

Grindyha Sanday: former name of 'Sunnybank' [Norse *grind* gate, Scots *ha* cottage].

Grinlaysbreck Rousay: [Norse *grind-hlíð*, English *breck* poor land].

Grinnabreck Rousay: (see above).

Grip o Dieth Hellia Birsay: [Scots *grip* a ditch/stream, Norse *dý-it* the marsh/moorland, *hella* a tableland of rocks].

Grip o Loonan Evie: (see 'Loonan').

Grip o Sandgeo Sanday: between 'Cata Sand' and 'Fidge' (see above).

Gripps Rousay: [Norse *gröf* incised stream (in plural form)].

Grit Ness Evie: [Norse *grjót* stony, *nes* point].

Grith North Ronaldsay: [Norse *grjót-it* the shingly area: the definite article suffix of this neuter word is pronounced 'th' in Orkney dialect].

Grith, The Shapinsay: (see above).

Grithamay Dyke North Ronaldsay: a ridge of boulders protruding through the sand in 'Lindswick' [Norse *grjót* rocky ground, *melr* sandbank].

Grithies, The Sanday: beach name, Tresness: gravel ridges extending into the otherwise sandy 'Cata Sand' [Norse *grjót* stony or rocky ground].

Grithin Rousay: (see 'Grittin' below).

Gritho Rousay: a mound on top of 'Cat Hill' [Norse *grjót* stony, *haugr* mound].

Gritlay Deerness: (see 'Grutill/Grittle').

Grittin Sanday, Stove: field name [Norse *grýtingr* a stony stretch].

Groanies Sanday: lobster set on 'The Start' [Norse *grunn* shoal (with English plural)].

Grobister Stronsay: old tunship between 'Aith' and 'Dishes' [Norse personal name *Gróa*, Norse *ból-staðr* farm].

Grobust Westray: a stretch of beach today but must originally have been the name of a nearby farm [Norse *gröf* stream, *ból-staðr* farm].

Grochlie Geo Stronsay: [Norse *grjót* stony or rocky, *hlíð* used to describe a sheer cliff face, *gjá* ravine: (see 'Lee o Copinsay')].

Grory 1. Eynhallow: (see below).

Grory 2. Rousay, Scockness: a shingly area of beach on the west side of the 'Holm o Scockness' [shingly beaches are usually referred to as *grjót* which probably explains the element 'gro': Old Scots *ree* a sheep pen (see 'Point o Ree')].

Grotsetter St. Andrews: [probably the surname 'Groat', Norse *saetr*, originally a temporary summer grazing hut outside the tunship wall: later, a farm name (compare 'Seator' in 'Seattersquoy', Stenness)].

Grotties Boat Eday: near 'South House': a large boulder near the high-water mark [Norse, from the spirit Grottie (see the Appendix)].

Grotties Geo Eday: [Norse, from the spirit Grottie (see Appendix)].

Groundwater/Grindwatter Orphir: [Norse *grunn* shallow, *vatn* lake].

Groups Hoy: [Norse *gröf* stream (with English plural)].

Growalee Birsay: at the foot of 'Birsay Hill' [Norse *grófar-hlíð* stream slope].

Gru Sanday: beach name, between 'Boloquoy' and 'Pool' [Norse *grjót* stony ground].

Grudgar Evie: 'Gruager' in 1653, also Egilsay [Norse *grjót* shingle, *garðr* farm].

Grudwick Rousay: [Norse *grjót* stony, *vík* bay].

Gruff Hill Orphir: [Norse *gróf* stream].

Gruffiels Orphir: [Norse *gróf* stream, *völlr* field (with English plural): Norse plural is *vellir*].

Grugar Evie; Egilsay; Birsay: (see 'Grigdar').

Grugoo Firth: the road which goes westwards beginning slightly north of the farm of 'South Heddle' [Norse *grug* muddy with suffix 'oo' as in dialect 'binderoo', a snowstorm].

Grukalty Shapinsay: [Norse *gröf* stream, *kelda* well].

Grunavi Head Sanday: coastal feature [Norse *grunn* shoal, Norse *nef* the bone of the nose, frequently used for headlands in Orkney and Shetland].

Grundstane Birsay: a light-coloured patch in the face of the cliffs at 'Marwick Head' [origin unknown].

Grunka Howe Birsay: a large mound near 'Dounby' [Norse *haugr* mound, *graenka* to become green].

Grunka Howe, Grip o Birsay/Sandwick: (see 'Grip' forms above).

Grunshall Evie: a small mound on the northern flank of the 'Hill o Dwarmo' [Norse *graen* green, Norwegian *skalle* skull, used figuratively for an eminence: (compare 'Vishall Hill')].

Grutchen North Ronaldsay: [Norse *grjót* stony, *tjörn* small lake].

Grutfea Hoy: [Norse *grjót* stony, *fjall* hill].

Grutha, Old South Ronaldsay: a large and imposing house in its day estimated to date from the 17th century [Norse *grjót* stony: the name and location suggests that it takes its name from the shore].

Gruthy Harray: a field name [uncertain etymology: possibly a transferred name from 'Grutha' (above)].

Grutill/Grittle Sanday: house above Backaskaill, recorded in the 1595 Rental [Norse *grjót-hóll* stone mound].

Grutquoy St. Andrews: [Norse *grjót* stony, *kví* enclosure].

Gubber Geo Birsay: [Scots *gub* foam or lather (caused by the movement of the sea), Norse *berg* rock, *gjá* ravine].

Gue Rendall; Rousay; Firth; North Ronaldsay: (see 'Geo' in Appendix).

Guestiquoy Westray: [uncertain etymology].

Guidall Rousay: a cottage in the 'Sourin' district [named from the Guidalls, a family of merchants who came to Kirkwall in the 17th century. They obviously had trade connections with Rousay; a rock on the nearby shore called 'Berg Guidall' suggests that this was a landing place for goods: the cottage must refer to a poor branch of this family].

Guidmas Ayre Stronsay: on the 'Bay of Franks' [Norse *eyrr* gravel ridge, personal name *Guðmundr*, hence *Guðmundis eyrr*].

Guithe/Geoth Eday; Harray: (see 'Geo' in Appendix).

Gulleroo Harray: [Norse *hrúga* a heap, sometimes applied to mounds (see 'Geo' in Appendix)].

Gulliver Sanday: the beach below 'Runnaclett' [Scots *gully* an area with rock pools (in this instance), an extended meaning of English 'gully': there are many pools in this stretch of beach (e.g., 'Wast Pow'), Norse *ver* a good place for fishing].

Gullow, Knowe of Harray: considered an old 'broch' site [English 'knoll', mound: (for 'gull' element see Appendix)].**Gullslate** (see 'Gullslate, Castle o').

Gullslate, Castle o Birsay: an outlying rock pillar also known as the 'Standard' to the west of 'Costa Head' [Norse *gulr* yellow, *slettr* smooth: seems to relate to the smooth surface of the rock shining in the evening sun].

Gump o Spurness Sanday: the highest part of the hill to the west of Stove [Norse *gumpr* rump: (see 'Spurness')].

Gumpick St. Andrews: [the suffix seems to be the common Orkney diminutive 'ick': a small mound: here lies the 17th century remains of a Cromwell Fort (see 'Gump' above)].

Gunnie's Geo Rousay: ['Gunnie' was a spirit who sometimes lived in caves: (compare 'Wattie Red' and other spirits in the Introduction)].

Gunnigar Sanday, Leavisgarth: field name [Norse personal name *Gunni*, Norse *garðr* farm: (compare Shetland 'Gunnigert')].

Gunyasilya Birsay: [Norse *gján* the ravine, *sellr* seal].

Gurl, The Westray: near 'Tuquoy' [a variant of Norse *gýgr* an ogress, sometimes referred to in Scots as a 'gyre-carlin' (see 'Carlin')]. **Gurnadee/day** Rousay: a valley in the 'Frotoft' hill [Norse *groena* green, Norse *dý* marshy, damp area].

Gurness, Knowe o (see Gorseness).

Guthrie's Park Sanday: field name in the northeast of the island: [Guthrie is a local surname].

Guttar South Ronaldsay: [Scots and North English dialect 'gutter' mud, Norwegian *gytje* mud].

Gutter Sound Walls/Fara: [refers in this case to seaweed decaying in pools to give the impression of mud].

Gutterhole Stromness: a field on 'Creya' [a muddy hole (see above)].

Gutterpitten Rendall: pronounced 'Gitterpitten' [Norse *pyttr* hole in the ground but with definite masculine article becomes *pytt-inn*, Norwegian *gytje* mud: 'Gitterpitten' originally lay in a marshy area].

Gutterpool Holm: (see 'Guttar').

Gutterquoy 1. Birsay, Kirbister: (see below).

Gutterquoy 2. Harray: [Norse *kví* enclosure: the addition of 'quoy' suggests that this may be the Norwegian form *gytjer* mud].

Gutteryha Deerness: [unlikely to be the surname Guthrie: there was only one crofting family with this surname in 1861: (see 'Guttar'): 'ha' here is Scots 'hall'/'ha' cottage].

Gutteryhall South Ronaldsay: [from the surname 'Guthrie'].

Gyer Walls: (see 'Gyre' below).

Gyerpigger Orphir: (see 'Gyre' and 'Piggar').

Gylliosquoy/Schusan South Ronaldsay: [personal girl's name Gilius, a form of 'Giles', Norse *kví* enclosure: (see present name 'Schusan')].

Gyollath Birsay: a large ravine [Norse *gjá* ravine, *hláð* load i.e., a place where, in suitable weather, goods or fish may be offloaded].

Gyphon Evie, Costa: a flat rocky beach [seems to be a mispronunciation of 'Gion'].

Gyran/Gyren Sandwick: [Norse *geir-inn* the triangular piece of land].

Gyre Orphir: [Norse *geiri* a triangular-shaped piece of land].

Gyrehouse Stenness: (see above).

Gyron Harray: (see Gyran above).

H

Ha Breck Rendall: an old croft on the 'Hall o Rendall'.

Haabreck Westray: [Scots *ha* cottage, Norse *brekka* slope].

Haafs Hellia Evie: [Norse *haf* sea, *hella* flat rock].

Haagar Firth: Grimbister (see 'Haggar', Stronsay).

Haagate Rousay: an old house site above 'Skaill' in Westside, northwest of 'Ward Hill': referred to as 'Hallgate' on OS Survey map [Norse *gata* path, Scots *ha* cottage: perhaps the cottage stood near a path to the top of the 'Ward' where a beacon fire would have been lit in times of danger].

Haan 1. Rendall: situated in the 'Dale of Cottiscarth': a mound near 'Gue' (see 'Geo' in Appendix): exact position of 'Haan' unknown (see below).

Haan 2. Sanday: cottar house near Sellibister [Norse *haug-inn* the mound: this placename is also recorded in Birsay and Rendall (below)].

Haanhuan Harray, Mirbister: an old house above 'Holodyke' [the placename seems to be one of several in Orkney which take a double form, both carrying the same meaning (see 'Meery -Mawry' for a good example of this): Norse *haug-inn* the mound].

Haap, The Swona: [Norse *hóp* small bay].

Haas Geo Swona: [the name applies to a narrow ravine: Norse *gjá* ravine (see 'The Hass' above)].

Haas o Beck Harray: near the 'Kame o Corrigall': exact position no longer known [may be a rare use in Orkney of Norse *bekkr* stream: (see 'The Haas' above)].

Haas o Muir (see 'Howes o Muir')

Haas, The Birsay, Dirkadale: a deserted farm on the hillside of the valley [a metaphorical use of Norse *háls* throat, usually applying to a narrow sea channel or valley].

Habreck 1. Shapinsay: in the northeast of the island (see above).

Habreck 2. Stronsay, Rothiesholm: (see 'Haabreck').

Habreck 3. Wyre: (see above).

Hacco Rendall; Deerness: [a corruption of Norse *haugr* mound and *kví* enclosure (see 'Howacow')].

Hackabeen Harray: a field to the west of 'Upper Bigging' in Overbrough [Norse *haugr* mound, *bae-n* the farm].

Hackla/Ackla Orphir: (see 'Ackalay', Westray).

Hackland 1. Rendall: a district on a spur of 'Enzie Hill' [Norse *öxl* shoulder, used here metaphorically of the 'shoulder' of a hill].

Hackland 2. Sandwick: [Norse *hauk-land* an area given over to providing a tribute of poultry to a feudal lord (originally the Earl of Orkney and Shetland) to provide for the upkeep of his hawks].

Hackness 1. Sanday: a farm, formerly part of 'Stove'.

Hackness 2. South Walls: the northeast point of the parish: [origin uncertain: perhaps a place given over to hunting with hawks].

Hackra Rendall: near 'Hallbreck' [Norse *há* high, *kró* enclosure].

Hacksness Sanday: a peninsula in Cross parish: a prehistoric burial mound stands on the point [Norse *haugs-nes* point of the mound].

Haddieweel St. Ola: a coastal placename [Scots *had* a place of refuge: used in a Shetland tale, '*The Dänschman's Had*' to describe a cave used as a temporary refuge: 'weel' seems to represent English 'well' in the sense 'securely'].

Hadds, The Sanday, Northwall: [no information available but suggests a lobster set, Scots *had* an animal lair or overhanging bank of a stream where fish lie].

Hafdroo Orphir: position unknown: no details.

Hagar/Haggar Stronsay 1. a vanished house on 'Strynie', 2. on the east coast of Rothiesholm, Stronsay, inland from the 'Bight o Doonatoon' [Norse *há* high, *garðr* farm].

Haggis Brae 1. Stromness, Crook: field name [Scots *hag*, plural *haggeis*, rough, pitted land].

Haggis Brae 2. Rendall, Crook: field name (see above).

Haggisbreck Stromness, Garth: [Norse *brekka* slope (for 'haggis', see above)].

Haggishall Holm: in the vicinty of 'New Holland' (see 'Haggis Brae' above).

Haghquoy Stronsay: in 'Strynie' [Norse *há* high, Norse *kví* enclosure].

Hagock 1. Evie: coastal feature: described by the Ordnance Survey as 'a small indenture in the coast' [origin unknown].

Hagock 2. Westray, Broughton: described by the Ordnance Survey as 'a small house east of 'Caddlesbrae' and separated by a small drain' [origin unknown].

Hainger Howe Harray: a mound southeast of 'Beboran' near the 'Braes o Cheston' [related in some way to the 'Hanga' forms below meaning 'slope' from Norse *hengi* sloping: Norse *haugr* mound (see 'Hinger Stone' Copinsay)].

Haist Hoy: a prominent height at the east end of 'Ward Hill' [a contraction of English 'highest' (compare 'Uimist')].

Haista Sanday: farm mentioned in Commissariat Record, 1623 [possibly same as 'Housta'].

Haiyon Harray: (see 'Hayon').

Halaclave/Hellicliff/Hillicliff Evie: described by Ordnance Survey as a small-detached house with a thatched roof: the dwelling takes its name from its location [Norse *hella* flagstone, Norse *klif* a path: a path seems to go eastwards from here towards the sea coast].

Halcro South Ronaldsay: [Scots *ha'* cottage, Norse *kró* enclosure].

Halfynscoffis Orphir: an alternative name for 'Hobbister', in 1500 [Norse personal name Hall-*finn*: for 'coffis' read 'toftis': Norse *toftir* old house sites (with English plural)].

Halkhouse Stronsay: position unknown (see 'Hawksbrae').

Hall Eday: [Scots *ha'* cottage].

Hall Geo Swona: [Norse *hallr* ledge, Norse *gjá* ravine].

Hall o Rendall Rendall: [Scots '*hall*' grand house, often used in Orkney in the sense of 'small cottage' too when it is spelt *ha'*].

Hallan Westray: an indentation in the coast southwest of Gallow Hill [its use here is not understood: (see below)].

Hallans, The Firth, Settiscarth: [Scots *hallan* really 'partition' or 'cross-beams in an old house' but can also mean 'simple cottage', hence 'cottages'].

Hallans o Hell Birsay, Wattle: (see 'Hallans, The' below and 'Hell').

Hallay Hoy: in the 'Breibuster' district (see 'Halley' above).

Hallbreck Rendall; South Ronaldsay; Sandwick; Wyre: [Orkney dialect *ha'* small cottage, Norse *brekka* slope].

Halley Deerness: earlier 'Halla' [Norse *halla* a slope, the land lies on a steep slope].

Hallow, The Sanday: coastal feature, Taftsness [Norse *hallr* a boulder].

Hallows Sanday: mounds between 'Scar' and 'Woo' [Norse *hóll* hillock; 'Hólar' was the ancient seat of a bishop of Iceland].

Hallwhite Evie: in the 1890s this was a ruined croft house [origin uncertain: named after a sailing ship? (c.f. 'Layburn')].

Hallywell/Hellywell Flotta: a well, the site of which is unknown [there is a reputed holy well known as 'Winster's Well' on 'The Roan' which could be the 'Hallywell'].

Halvers Point Birsay, Dirkadale: a meeting of two streams [Scots *havers* dividing into two].

Ham 1. Papa Stronsay: field name [from a lost Norse word meaning 'enclosure'; this word is still retained in English and most Indo-Germanic names e.g., Old English *hamm*, Low German *hamm* enclosure].

Ham 2. Rousay: (see above).

Ham Geo South Ronaldsay: [Norse *hamn* harbour].

Hamar North Faray: [Norse *hamarr* (as above)].

Hamar/Himero Geo North Ronaldsay: west of 'Ancum Loch' [(see 'Hamar' above): Norse *gjá* ravine].

Hamar Hill Rendall: [Norse *hamarr* a jutting out rock].

Hamarfiold/Hammerfield Rousay: [Norse *hamarr* exposed rock, *fjall* hill].

Hamari Brae Westray: Rapness district, a name applied to a mound west of 'Benziecott' [Norse *hamarr* rock, adapted to be an English adjective, i.e., 'hammery'].

Hamars Shapinsay: a rocky point on the east coast of the island to the east of 'Hamars Brae' (see 'Hamar' above).

Hamars Westray: a high cliff on the east coast of 'Rapness' (see above).

Hamarsquoy Evie/Rendall: recorded only as 'Burn o Hamarsquoy', which flows down from 'Hamar Hill' to form part of the parish boundaries between Evie and Rendall [(see 'Hamar' above), Norse *kví* enclosure].

Hamigar Orphir: recorded in 1813 (see 'Hammiger', Garth, Evie).

Hamiger/Hammiger Stromness: [Norse *hamn* sheltered bay, Norse *garðr* farm].

Hamisquoy South Ronaldsay: (see 'Hammarsquoy' below).

Hamly Hill Holm: a low hill north of 'New Holland' (see 'Ham', Papa Stronsay).

Hammagir (see 'Hammigar's Pund').

Hammar Birsay, Greeny: [Norse *hamarr* a projecting rock on a hillside].

Hammar, The Rendall, Breck: field name (see 'Hammar' above).

Hammar/Hammer Westray, Swansons Park: (see above).

Hammaron Geo Birsay: [Norse *hamarr-inn* the rock: *gjá* ravine].

Hammars Westray: a high cliff on the east coast of Rapness [Norse *hamarr* as above (with English plural)].

Hammars, The Birsay: east of Costa Head (see 'Hammers' below).

Hammarshurie Swona: [Norse *hamarr* rock (with English plural): 'the hurie' element suggest Norse *haugar* mounds in the vicinity (see 'Howar' and 'Hoor' forms below)].

Hammarsquoy/Hamisquoy South Ronaldsay: ['Hammarsquoy' is a corruption of 'Hamisquoy'. 'Hami' is an abbreviated form of the Norse personal name *Hámundr*: a Magnus Hamie lived at Sebay in Tankerness in 1614].

Hammer 1. Sanday: coastal feature [Norse *hamarr* a projecting rock].

Hammer 2. Stromness: a dwelling house northeast of 'Citadel' (see 'Hammer' above).

Hammer 3. Rousay: a vanished house in the 'Westness' district (see 'Hammer' above).

Hammer 4. Sandwick: a vanished farm in the 'Aith' district (see 'Hammer' above).

Hammer 5. Eday: it lies inland from 'Mill Bay' (see below).

Hammer 6. North Faray: [Norse *hamarr* a projecting rock from a hillside (see 'Doggerboat')].

Hammer, The Rendall, Breck: field name (see above).

Hammer/Hammyir Rousay: an old 'Wasbister' name (see 'Hammer' above).

Hammer o Moa Evie: east of 'Peerie Water' [Norse *mór* moor (see 'Hammer' above)].

Hammer Chunky Rousay: in the 'Wasbister' district [Norse *hamarr* as above, *tjörn* small pool, *kví* enclosure].

Hammer Mugly Rousay: [Norse *hamarr* as above, Norse *mikli* large].

Hammer Nick Rousay: [projecting rocks above 'Midhowe' broch: (see 'Hammer' above): 'nick' element suggests a mound, a word related to Norse *knykill*].

Hammerbrake Sanday: earlier, a fanciful name 'Elsinore' was ascribed [perhaps an old field name: Norse *hamarr* a rock, *brekka* slope].

Hammercleat Sandwick: [both elements mean 'rock': there are several instances of such duplications in Orkney placenames].

Hammeron Cottage Rendal: (see 'Hammeron Geo' above).

Hammers 1. Shapinsay: rocks on the east coast, inland from 'Purtaquoy'.

Hammers 2. Westray, Midbea: southeast of 'Fitty Hill' [Norse *hamarr* protruding rocks (with English plural)].

Hammers o Knarston Rousay: a stretch of coastline below Knarston (see 'Hammers' above).

Hammers o Syraday/Syradale Firth: an elderly resident told the writer that it was always known locally as Syraday and was changed by the Ordnance Surveyors to 'Syradale' [Norse *hamarr* projecting rocks, in this case producing a magnificent waterfall after a period of heavy rain].

Hammerykeldo Wyre: a well on 'Testaquoy' [there was a well in a field on the 'Kitchen o Brecks' in Deerness called the 'Waal o Hammer', which stood in a field called 'Linklett' where *lin* is the Celtic word for a pool! 'Linklett Brae' was on 'Testaquoy' in Wyre].

Hammigar's Pund Sanday: Burness parish ['Hammigar' is probably a lost Sanday placename: 'pund' = pound in the sense of 'enclosure'].

Hammiger Evie, Garth: ['ham' is probably a lost Old Norse word related to Old English *hamm,* an enclosure, frequently appearing in English placenames, Norse *garðr* farm].

Hammiger Evie: [Norse *garðr* farm (see 'Ham' Papa Stronsay above)].

Hammiger Stromness: [an old land on the east side of 'Hamnavoe' (see above)].

Hamnavoe 1. Stromness: a sheltered bay in Stromness parish: [Norse *hamn* a haven, *vágr* bay].

Hamnavoe 2. Corn Holm, Copinsay: (see above).

Hamrifield/Hammerfiold Rousay: [Norse *hamarr* rock, *fjall* hill].

Handfingie/Handfingle Sanday: location uncertain [Norse *hengi* slope, *fen* marsh].

Handi-Midgathy Rousay: [Norse *hengi* steep, *mið* middle, (for 'gathy' see 'Guithe'). It is difficult to establish the meaning behind these different elements].

Handis Harray: ['hand' = Norse *hengi* steep, used in Orkney placenames in the sense 'sloping': 'ist' represents a truncated Norse *hús-it* the house: the placename means 'house on the slope'].

Handy Geo Evie: [Norse *hengi* precipitous or steep, Norse *gjá* a ravine].

Hang the Cow Rendall: 'Hamar Hill' [Norse *hengi* slope, 'cow' = quoy = Norse *kví* enclosure].

Hanga Holm: a coastal point southeast of 'Gangsta' [Norse *hengi* slope (steep, in this case)].

Hangaback Orphir: a coastal area west of 'Swanbister' [Norse *hengi* steep, *bakki* slope].

Hangie Bay St. Andrews: east of 'Skibbowick' [Norse *hengi* steep slope (leading to the bay)].

Hangie Head Sanday: coastal feature, Tresness (see 'Hangie').

Hangie Sanday: eastern slope of 'Gump of Spurness' [Norse *hengi* hanging as in *hengi-flug*, a precipice].

Hangie, Rock o North Ronaldsay: a small rocky isle on the west side of 'Garso Wick' [Norse *hengi* a sloping down, of the land in this case].

Hanging Stone Westray: near the 'Mirky Hole' to the west of the 'Bloody Tuacks' [a large boulder on the cliff edge: 'hanging' suggests 'about to fall', a likely fate].

Hannahs Birsay: an old cottage near South Waird, Marwick, only the foundation remains [personal name 'Hannah'].

Hannatoft Shapinsay: [suggests the female Norse name *Hanna*, Norse *toft* old house site (compare 'Kettletoft')].

Hannibale Orphir: [suggests Norse *hengi* slope, Norse *ból* a place where cattle are penned].

Hannipow South Ronaldsay: [a large rock pool which never ebbs: in the olden days folk used to full cloth by the sea: in this case the cloth would have been 'harn', made from flax or hemp which was grown for a short period in Orkney: since local folk could not pronounce 'r' in any word where it was followed by 'n', the 'r' was missed out, the outcome being that 'harn' became 'han', hence 'hanpow' where 'Sc. 'pow' is 'pool' (see 'Henpow')].

Hanover 1. Sanday: a farm in Burness parish, the name was changed to 'Hillhoose' then appears to have reverted to the original [the name must relate to the Napoleonic War when British soldiers worked closely with the Hanoverian Brigade].

Hanover 2. Rousay: in the Sourin district, one of these two Hanovers is most likely a transferred name (see above).

Hap Rousay: a small geo, obviously considered a small bay from time to time [Norse *hóp* bay].

Hap, The Graemsay: an old name for 'Sandside Bay' [Norse *hóp* bay].

Haquoy Shapinsay: = 'Hawkquoy': southwest of 'Sholtaquoy' [the farm seems to have provided poultry for the Earl's hawks].

Harabreck Orphir: [Norse *harðr* hard, referring to the soil, Norse *brekka* slope].

Harbasue a small island south of the 'Brig o Waithe': a puzzling name: [unknown origin].

Hard Head Sanday: extreme north of Ire ['hard' = stony, compare 'hardy', a Shetland term for the seabed].

Hardbreck Holm: (see 'Harabreck' above).

Hardhall Sanday: on 'Warsetter' land [English 'hard' referring to the nature of the ground, Scots *ha* cottage].

Hardhill Firth: (see above).

Hardie's Ha Stronsay: north of 'Hagar', inland from the 'Bight o Doonatoon' [there were Hardy families in Stromness in the early 1900s, but none recorded in Stronsay: Scots *ha* cottage].

Hargar/Harga North Ronaldsay: a vanished house: [Norse *hörgr* a place of heathen worship].

Hark Hill Orphir: ['hark' is probably a form of 'ark': it was common for words beginning with the vowels 'a' or 'e' to collect an initial 'h', a good example is the surname 'Harcus' which developed initially from Ork to the form Orc(as), to Horcas then 'Harcus': *ark* is Scots cottage (see 'Ark', Flotta)].

Hark Lone Westray: coastal stretch south of 'Ramni Geo' in the 'Noup' area [origin unknown].

Harn o Heum Sanday: a boulder and rock beach, in the northeast corner of 'Braeswick' [Norse *horn* corner, Norse *hvammr* grassy slope or hollow].

Harper's Sanday: alternative name for 'Thorness Hill' [from the surname 'Harper', a family who lived there in the 1850s].

Harpersquoy Evie: [from the surname 'Harper', most Harpers lived in Rendall, Evie and Birsay, Norse *kví* enclosure].

Harpsquoy Birsay, Southside [probably from the surname 'Harper', a surname which has been recorded in Orkney since the 16th century: this house stands at the top of a slope known as the 'Brae o Herpsa': the name 'Herpsa' suggests an original *Herps haugr* where Norse *haugr* is a mound: there is no mound at the top of the slope but there is a significant mound at the bottom called 'Saverough'. The likelihood is that 'Herp', like 'Harp', is a truncated form of 'Harper'].

Harpy Taing Rendall: [dialect *harpi/harpo* a scallop, Norse *hörpuskel*].

Harrabrough Head South Ronaldsay: [see 'harra' (below), 'brough' = Norse *berg* rock].

Harradale Stronsay: just west of 'Meikle Water' [Norse *harðr* hard, 'dale' = Norse *deild* an apportioned piece of land].

Harraebb Sandwick: [a stretch of the Sandwick coast where Harray folk were legally permitted to harvest the produce of the foreshore: an agreement was made between the parishes of Harray and Sandwick in which the folk of Harray (with no coastline) could gather shellfish, and the folk of Sandwick (with no peat moor) could cut peat].

Harray a parish [the origin of this parish name is difficult to explain. It was early associated with the parish of Birsay, the first recording of which was in the *Orkneyinga Saga* as *Byrgisheراð*, Norse *herað,* which developed into 'Harray', it has many meanings the most suitable of which is 'district' (see 'Ledya Brae')].

Harray Men's Graves Rendall: in the 'Blubbersdale' area, embedded stones mark the point where it is said that a number of Harray men lost their lives when, during a time of famine, they went from Harray to Rendall hoping to collect shellfish but perished in a snowstorm (see 'Harraebb')].

Harrigart/Harri Garth Papa Stronsay: sandy beach on a small bay northeast of the island [must takes its name from a small, vanished, inland enclosure: Norse *harðr* hard (of the soil), *garðr* enclosure].

Haskie Taing North Ronaldsay: on the east coast [Norse *háska-tunga* dangerous point].

Hass Evie: a ruin [Norse *háls* literally 'neck' but also used to describe a hill or the side of a valley which is a perfect description of this location].

Hass, The Birsay: Dirkadale district, a ruin (see 'Hass' above which lies in a similar situation).

Hass o Glifter, The Rousay: a hill saddle above 'Hullion' (see 'Hullion' and 'Glifter').

Hass o Gowsday, The Rousay: [a saddle on the hill ridge between 'Blotchniefield' and 'Knitchen' (see 'Hass' and 'Gowsday')].

Hass o Ramna Geo Birsay: a narrow ravine on the Birsay coast [Norse *háls* throat, *hramn* raven].

Hass o Savedale Stenness: on the side of an unnamed hill in the 'Clouston' area [Norse *háls* meaning no more than 'hillside' here (compare 'Hass', Evie)].

Hass o Watnaskar Rousay: a saddle in the hill ridge northwest of 'Muckle Water' [Norse *skarð* hill saddle, ('Hass' as above), *vatn* pool, in this case].

Hassacrow (see 'Housecrow').

Hassen Graemsay: [Norse *háls-inn* the neck or the throat].

Hassie, The narrow channel between 'Thieves' Holm' and 'Carness Point' [Norse *háls* neck or throat used figuratively].

Hatston St. Ola: one of several Norse *staðr*, estate, placenames in Orkney. They are invariably on the best of land with the owner's name attached which shows that they are very old settlements: most are in the West Mainland of Orkney. The Scots almost invariably changed the *staðr* form to 'ston', e.g., 'Onston' in Stenness [personal name *Höttr*, literally the 'hooded one'].

Hatt, The Sanday, Elsness: field name, early 18th century: 'hat' is a common placename in Norway where it refers to the top or highest field [Norse *hattr* hat or hood].

Hattamoa Rendall: on the western slope of 'Hackland Hill' [Norse *hattr* highest (see above), Norse *mór* moor (see 'Hittamoa')].

Hattie Man o Ree Graemsay: [a rock pillar about 3 metres high on the 'Point o Oxan', so called because its overhanging top suggests a hat or cap: (see 'Ree')].

Hattie's South Ronaldsay: [also known as 'Hillhouses': from the personal name 'Harriet'; before the introduction of postal services, old houses occupied by spinsters were often called after the occupant e.g. 'Hannah's in Birsay and 'Babbie's in Sanday].

Haughend St. Ola: near 'Smerquoy' [probably transferred from one of many Scots 'Haughend' places: Scots *haugh* a piece of level ground].

Hauses Hoy: ruinous dwellings in the 'Breibuster' district on the west side of 'The Witter', standing on the hillside of a narrow valley [Scots *haus* a variant of Norse *háls* hillside: the ruins take their name from their location].

Haven, The Swona: plus others in South Ronaldsay [Norse *hamn* harbour].

Havey, The Bay of Westray: a small rocky bay in the Skelwick area [suggests Norse *efja* ooze but does not seem appropriate here unless it relates to a slow running stream running through the rocks (see 'Evie')].

Hawell St. Andrews: [Norse *hag-völlr* pasture field].

Hawks Brae Stronsay: a hill west of Samson's Lane [perhaps a favourite hunt of kestrels which tend to hover on the updraft of hilltops].

Hawn/Hawin Birsay, Northside: (see 'Haan').

Hawn/Castlehall/Castle/hawn Wyre: (see 'Hawn' above).

Hayan Rendall: [Norse *haugr-inn* the mound].

Haybrake Walls; South Ronaldsay: [Norse *hey* hay, *brekka* slope].

Haygam Stronsay: a field near 'Midgarth' [Norse *hey* hay: origin of 'gam' unknown].

Hayon Birsay: [Norse *hey* hay, *brekka* slope].

Hayons Clett Sanday: coastal feature, Ire [Norse *klettr*, rock: origin of first element uncertain: perhaps an outlier of the 'Rocks o Smeargeo'].

He Hill Sanday: a 'tumal' or infield: location unknown: mentioned in the 1601 Udal Book [English 'hay' or Norse *hey*].

Headback North Ronaldsay: part of a field at the foot of the 'Brae o Breck' [Norse *bakki* ridge (see 'Breck', North Ronaldsay)].

Headbanks Sanday: in the 1890s a small farm a quarter of a mile north of 'Stove' [the name probably relates to its elevated position].

Headlabreck Evie: a field adjacent to 'Mounthooly' [English 'head', uppermost (of a field), Norse *brekka* slope: origin of 'Headla' unknown].

Headskifts Sanday: position unknown [English 'head' uppermost, Norse *skipti* division of a field etc.].

Hearsie Cru Sanday: steep land near 'Skedgibist' [English 'hearse', Norse *kró* a small enclosure, a resting place for a funeral party].

Hearsie Hoose Sanday, Northwall: [a building which housed the parish's pony-drawn hearse: it continues to be maintained by the Community Council].

Heathercowspunk Burray: [a 'heather cowe spunk' in local dialect is a spark which flies out of a burning fire of peat which still has some heather attached to it. The house would have taken its name from the inhabitant who used the phrase in some particular way].

Heathercrow Westray, Lochend; Papa Westray: [English 'heather', Norse *kró* enclosure].

Heathery Blate Evie: just to the east of the 'Wateries' [Norse *blað* literally 'leaf' but applied to anything flat (see 'Blates o North Skaill')].

Heathery Point Evie: (see 'Point o Spurran', Evie).

Heckle o Hestimuir Stronsay: area of beach southeast of 'Torness' [Norse *heggitill* a flint type rock, Shetland dialect 'hjegel' (see 'Hestmuir')].

Heckra, Grip o Birsay, Marwick: between 'Muce' and 'Gerraquoy' [Scots *grip* a ditch, Norse *hey* hay, *kró* enclosure].

Heddle Firth: a district [Norse *hey* hay, *dalr* dale].

Heed o Holemay Sanday: field name [English 'head', Norse *hóll* hillock, Norse *melr* sand: (compare 'Gresmay')].

Hegglie Ber Sanday: coastal feature [a ridge of breccia type rock jutting out into the sea, Norse *berg* rock (see 'Heckle o Hestimuir' above)].

Heights o Aboondariggs Sanday: [highest part of 'Aboondarigs'].

Heights o Abraham Sanday: alternative name for the 'Black Rock', Otterswick Bay [related to the scaling of a cliff by General Wolfe and his men in the Battle of Quebec, Canada in 1759: the connection is unknown].

Heimar Gorn Sanday, Breck: field name [Norse *heimri* nearer home (see 'Gorn')].

Heimar Toon Sanday: a field beside the house of 'Tresness' [Norse *heimri* nearer home, *tún* enclosure].

Heldale Walls: a dwelling house on the coast near a stream of the same name which flows through a dale [Norse *dalr* a valley, Norse *hella* a flat, rocky surface].

Helen's Toomal North Ronaldsay: [personal name 'Helen': Norse *tún-völlr* the home field].

Hell 1. Birsay, Northside: like all the other 'Hell' houses in Orkney, this was an ale house. Most of these names were changed by later inhabitants, a good example being 'Hell' in St. Mary's, South Ronaldsay. In 1871 the Census Enumerator named it 'Hell'. In 1841 it was called 'Hill': in 1851 'New Inn': in 1861 'Hillside': in 1871 'Hell': in 1881, 'Hill'!].

Hell 2. Sanday: near 'Purgatory', Hillhead ['Purgatory' and 'Hell' placenames often co-existed (see above)].

Hell Mouth Sandwick: a rocky inlet in the northern part of the 'Noust o Borwick' [probably Norse *hella* flat rock].

Hell's Mouth Stronsay: a rocky stretch of coast on 'Lamb Bay' (see above).

Hella Orphir: [no information].

Hellalove Harray: a vanished placename in Overbrough: according to the Land Tax Register, in the 1650s James Spence lived in Hellalove [origin unknown].

Helli Boot Damsay: island in the Bay of Firth: an old name for the island of Damsay which had a chapel dedicated to the Virgin Mary; as in the case of the chapel dedicated to 'St. Tredwell' in Papa Westray, folk resorted to it for a cure [Norse *heilagr* holy, *baeta* improvement (in health)].

Hellia Hoy: a common shore name in Orkney [Norse *hella* flat rock].

Hellia o Odin Ness Stronsay: (see above).

Helliack South Walls: [Norse *hella* flat rock with local diminutive].

Helliaclov Stromness: southwest of 'Cauldhame' ['clove' is usually written 'cliv' in Orkney placenames, Norse *klyfja* to split which in Orkney usually applies to a path down a cliff to give access to the shore but this is not applicable here. The word seems to apply to the valley in which the 'Burn o Helliaclov' runs, Norse *hella* flat rock].

Helliar Holm Sanday: a small reef off 'The Foulan' [Norse *hellur* rocks, *hólmr* island: *hellur* is found in Faroese placenames].

Helliar/Hellie South Ronaldsay: east of 'Ward Hill' [Norse *hellur* rocks].

Helliascarth Evie: [Norse *hellur* rocks, *skarðr* hill saddle].

Helliaspur Rousay: a portion of cliff west of 'Innister' [Norse *hella* flat rock, *spori* a spur: there is no marked 'spur' here today: the suggestion is that it has vanished through coastal erosion].

Hellicliff Evie: (see 'Helieklif' Rousay).

Hellie South Ronaldsay: a rocky stretch of coastline southeast of 'Ward Hill' [Norse *hella* flat rock].

Hellihow Sanday: [Norse *helgi-haugr* holy mound: it was said to be occupied by a '*hogboon*', a spirit of the mound].

Hells Geo (see 'Helzie Geo').

Hellya Hesta Geo Birsay: an area of flat rock sloping seawards [Norse *hella* flat rock (see 'Hesta Geo')].

Hellyalonga Skerry Birsay: a long sloping skerry [Norse *hella* flat rock, *langr* long].

Hellyan 1. Birsay: coastal feature [Norse *hellan* 'the' flat rock].

Hellyan 2. Sandwick: (see above).

Helyie/Helziegitha Wyre: [Norse *hella* flat rock: (see 'Guithe' for final element)].

Helyieklif Rousay: above 'Ward Hill', Westness [Norse *hella* flat rock: (for 'klif' element see 'Helliaclov')].

Helzie Geo/Hells Geo Sanday: Cross parish, a small inlet in the coast with one of the most impressive sea caves in Orkney [Norse *hellir* cave, *gjá* ravine].

Helzie/Hell Banks North Ronaldsay: [Norse *hellu-bakki* flat rocks on the shore].

Hemp Stack St. Ola: a rocky pillar southwest of 'Gaitnip' [origin unknown].

Hen o Gairsay Gairsay: Rendall parish [Norse *haena* hen: like 'calf', applied to small islands close to larger].

Hen o Ness Orphir: according to an 1813 map, a small island which lies/lay off what is now 'Midland Ness' (compare with the above).

Henatoft Rendall: [Norse personal name *Heðinn*, Norse *topt* old house site].

Hendry Holes Hoy: caves southwest of 'St. John's Head' [reason for personal name unknown].

Henley Evie: [Norse *hengi* slope, *hlíð* slope].

Henly Harray: (see above).

Henpow St. Ola, Kirkwall: = Hempow, a small pool into which the streams (now underground) flowing through the present town of Kirkwall drained [Scots *pow* pool. It seems that this pool was used for retting flax (hemp): when this crop was grown in Orkney].

Henry Birsay, Muce, Sabiston: [probably a curtailed form of 'Quoyhenry' (see 'Quoyhenry' Rendall)].

Hensbister Holm: [Norse personal name *Heðinn*, Norse *ból-staðr* farm].

Hermaness Sanday: refers to the 'Ness o Brough'; Shetland also has a Hermaness and a legendary giant called Herman [Norse personal name *Hardmundigar*].

Hermisgarth Sanday: recorded in 1595 as '*Hardmundigar*' [Norse personal name *Hermundr*, Norse *garðr* farm].

Herston South Ronaldsay: [Norse personal name *Hörðr*, Norse *staðr* estate].

Hesacrow Sanday: location unknown [Norse *hestr* horse or stallion, Norse *kró* enclosure as in *hesta-rétt* (see 'Rittquoy')].

Hescombe Stronsay: formerly 'Hescanby' [Norse *hestr* horse, Icelandic *skjá-n* the shed, *bae* farm (see 'Yesnaby')].

Heshiber Rousay: high cliffs west of the 'Knee o Faraclett' [Norse *esja* a kind of clay rock, *berg* rock].

Heshiklif Rousay: on the Quandal shore near 'Kuthiny Klett' [Norse *kleif* a track, down to the ebb in this case (see *esja* above)].

Hesper Birsay: a projecting cliff on the shoreline [perhaps a corruption of 'Hestberg': Norse *hestr* stallion, *berg* rock].

Hess North Fara: (see 'Hass' forms).

Hesta Burray: a small headland to the west of the old jetty at 'Westshore' [Norse *hestr* stallion: animal names such as pig, calf etc. were frequently used to describe coastal features].

Hesta Geo /Dog Geo North Ronaldsay: [Norse *gjá* ravine: (for 'Hesta' see above)].

Hesta Head South Ronaldsay: (see above).

Hestigeo St. Ola; South Walls: (see 'Hesta Geo' above).

Hestikelday Holm: [Norse *hestr* stallion/horse, *kelda* well].

Hestily South Ronaldsay: [Norse *hestr* stallion/horse, Norse *hlíf* shelter].

Hestimuir Holm; Stronsay: [Norse *hestr* horse, *mór* moor].

Hestival Rousay: [Norse *hestr* horse, Norse *völlr* field].

Hestivald Shapinsay: (same interpretation as above).

Hestivall Evie: (see 'Hestwall' below).

Hestor Graemsay: a shingly stretch of foreshore on the southwest coast [Norse *hestr* horse].

Hestwall Holm; Sandwick: [Norse *hestr* horse, *fjall* hill].

Het Orphir: high coastal banks half miles south of 'Hobbister Hill' [Norse *hettr* highest].

Hettal/Hettle Sanday: now a field name behind 'Whistlebrae' [origin unknown].

Heum, The Birsay, Swannay Loch: [old pronunciation of 'holm': Norse *hólmr* island].

Hewan Shapinsay: (see 'Hewing' forms below).

Hewin Evie: (see 'Hewing' forms below).

Hewin Brew Harray: [Norse *breiðr* broad (see 'Hewing' below)].

Hewin o Ruein Harray: [a mound: Norse *hrúgin* the heap, i.e., mound in this case (see 'Rue')].

Hewin Swarto Stenness: [Norse *svartr* black, probably referring to the soil colour, Norse *hrúgin* the heap i.e., mound].

Hewing Firth: [a form of 'Cuean': Norse *kví-in* the enclosure].

Heyland Sandwick: [Norse *hey* hay, English 'land'].

Heyspan Flotta: [local surname 'Hay', English 'pan' = salt pan. There were several successful salt pans in Flotta but this part of the coast was quite unsuitable].

Hiallay Sanday, Sellibister: field name [probably Norse *hjalli* a step in a hillside: 'Hallay' is recorded in Deerness and Hoy].

Hiesbreck Birsay, Southside: part of 'Stanger' [Norse *brekka* slope: the first element is difficult to translate: an earlier form 'Hydesbreck' suggests Norse *heið* valuable (land), but this is not convincing and is the only instance of its use in Orkney placenames].

High Fea Hoy: two miles north of Rackwick [Norse *fjall* hill].

Higha Sandwick: between 'Ness' and 'Appieteen' [English 'higher', *kví* enclosure].

Highaclett Eday: coastal stretch southeast of 'Ward Hill' [English 'higher' which applies to the steep rocky cliff face here, Norse *klettr* rock, must have applied originally to a distinctive rock on the coast].

Highbreck Rendall: a field name but the remains of a dwelling are still visible [Norse *brekka* slope].

Hildaval Westray, Dykeside: [Norse *huldu* fairies, *fjall* hill: (see 'Hill Trows')].

Hill o Howness Stronsay: on Odin Ness [Norse *haugr* mound but there is no trace of a mound here today, Norse *nes* headland].

Hill Quoys Stronsay: on 'Burgh Hill' [Norse *kvíar* enclosures (with English plural)].

Hilldoor Evie: coastal feature to the east of 'Costa Head' [Norse *hella* a stretch of flat rocks: the second element 'door' is possibly English 'door', a hole in a cliff face which suggests a cave entrance as in Dirdle Dor a famous Dorset landmark].

Hillhead Sanday, Sellibister: formerly 'Purgatory', the name was changed to 'Hillhead' by George Muir in 1844; only the farm buildings are left now.

Hillhoose 1. Rousay: former name of 'Hanover'.

Hillhoose 2. Sanday: [former name of 'Drummond's' after a Drummond family who lived there].

Hillhoose 3. Sanday: former name of 'Westbank' also called 'Needlo's' and 'The Hill'.

Hillock Stronsay: southeast of 'Huip' [English 'hill' plus diminutive 'ock'].

Hillock, The Firth: on extreme end of the 'Bay of Firth' [a former Iron Age 'broch' or fortification].

Hillstreet Sanday: bowman's (farm worker's) cottage, 'Stove' [so named since, along with the other five cottages, they form a 'street' of houses].

Hilltoft Holm: southeast of 'Wilderness' [Norse *topt* old house site].

Hilltrows Sanday: mounds, Cross parish: vanished [Norse *huldar-haugar*, mounds of the troll woman (cf. 'Trows' Buil')].

Hiltersharn Rousay, Scockness: a field in a deep valley [Norse *huldar* hidden, *skjárn* shelters/huts].

Himmon Hill Birsay/Evie: to the east of the 'Loch of Swannay' [origin unknown].

Hinchaquoy/Hussaquoy Birsay: [perhaps a corrupt form of 'Ingasquoy': Norse *kví* enclosure, of 'Inga': (for 'Hussaquoy' see 'Housequoy', Stenness)].

Hindatun Harray: [Scots *hinder* at the back, but it cannot be established today what it is at the back of].

Hinderafiold Hoy: [Scots *hinder* 'at the back', Norse *fjall* hill].

Hinderayre Rendall: farmhouse right on the beach, named after the local coastal feature [Norse *eyrr* gravel beach: significance of Scots *hinder* here not known].

Hindigar/Hundigar Birsay: oblong rock on coast which ebbs dry at low water [Norse *hundr* dog: animal names were frequently used for coastal features: the 'gar' element might be a corruption of Norse *sker*, skerry, therefore 'Hundiskar'].

Hindu Geo North Ronaldsay: (see 'Dog Geo' and 'Hindigar' above).

Hinegreenie 1. Evie: applied to an old stone circle on the side of 'Burgar Hill' (see above).

Hinegreenie 2. Sanday: coastal feature 'Lettan': possibly named after a vanished inland feature (see above).

Hinegreenie 3. Sanday: recorded as 'Howan Greinay' in 1633 [Norse *haugr-inn*, the mound, Norse *groen* green].

Hingan Hoose Sanday: near Galloway Dyke, 'Stove' [English 'hanging' in the sense of 'about to collapse' (compare 'Toultrie')].

Hinger Stone Copinsay: on the extreme south point of the island [Norse *hengi* steep slope].

Hinshabreck Westray: [origin unknown (see 'Hinchaquoy', Birsay, above)].

Hinyan Evie: coastal feature close to 'Fed Geo o Arsdale' [the name suggests a local Norse word related to *hengi* steep, of the cliff here].

Hirst o Dealt Stenness: [Scots *hirst*, a hard barren knoll, the only record of this word in Orkney placenames (see 'Dealt, Well o')].

Hisber, Point o Evie: (see 'Hesper').

Hittaft Sanday: a small knoll on 'Lopness', now called 'Whale Head' [Norse *topt* house site, Norse personal name '*Höttr*'].

Hittamoa Harray, Huntscarth: high up on 'Hinderafiold' [Norse *hattr* highest (see above), *mór* moor: (see 'Hattamoa' Rendall)].

Hiveland Firth, Binscarth: [location and origin unknown].

Hlaupandaness Deerness: [a farm mentioned in the *Orkneyinga Saga*: (see 'Lopness', Sanday)].

Hobbister 1. Orphir: [Norse *haugr* mound, *ból-staðr* farm (see 'Halfynscoffis')].

Hobbister 2. Sanday: 'Quoylealand' is preferred today [Norse *haugr* Mound, Norse *ból-staðr* farm].

Hobbister 3. Stenness: [so named after mounds in this area *hauga- ból-staðir*].

Hodgalee/Hogalee Westray: on the shore of the 'Bay o Tuquoy': believed to be the site of a 'broch' [Norse *haugr* mound, *hlíð* slope].

Hoe Skerries North Ronaldsay: (see below).

Hoe Skerry Birsay: [Norse *há* high, *sker* reef].

Hoeming Harray, Grimeston, Overbrough: [Norse *eng* meadow: origin of 'hoem' unknown].

Hog, The Harray: a small hill feature on the west side of the 'Kame o Corrigall' [Norse *haugr* mound].

Hogarth/Hogar Rendall, Hackland: [Norse *hó* high, *garðr* farm].

Hoggan Park Sanday: a field name [Norse *haugr-inn*, the mound: the adjacent field, 'Knowe Park', must be named from the same feature].

Hogges Head Sanday: a sea mark or maithe [Norse *haugs*, genitive case of *haugr* mound: the fishing ground was located by reference to the 'Red Head o Eday'].

Hoghouse South Ronaldsay: three of these were recorded in the island [Scots *hog* a yearling female sheep: the application of this name to 'house' is difficult to explain, Norse *hús* house can also be applied to animal shelters e.g. *fjár-hús* sheep shelters: it seems that the yearling female sheep were specially protected during the winter and the attached houses were called after such shelters].

Hoglinns Water Walls: west of 'Cairn Hill', a small loch [Norse *vatn* loch, represented here by 'water', Celtic *linn* water: the origin of 'hog' here is uncertain].

Hogsets o Catagreen Rousay: [(c.f. 'Hoghouse' above) Norse *setr* pasture or '*saetra*' shed].

Hogsha Rusness, Sanday: [named from the house of the occupier who kept Rusness and Northwall sheep separate when there was common grazing there].

Hoin, The North Ronaldsay: in the 1880s the Ordnance Survey described it as 'a piece of rough pasture' [Norse *haug-inn* the mound].

Hoisteramera Evie: also called 'Willie's Croo', coastal feature [Norse *há* high, *stíar* animal pens, *mór* moorland].

Hole o Airon Sanday: coastal feature [hole = pool (see 'Airon')].

Hole o Bosker Birsay: beach (see above).

Hole o Brue North Ronaldsay: (see above).

Hole o Roe St. Andrews: (see below).

Hole o Row Flotta: on 'Stanger Head', a dangerous 'gloup' which inspired terror in the soldiers who built billets here in World War I (see above).

Hole o Row Sandwick: [Norse *rauðr* red: an abbreviated form of 'Cubbie Roo' (see 'Cubbie Roo's Rock')].

Holes o Cupstermum Orphir: near the top of 'Ward Hill' [Norse *koppr* a hollow, *stíar* animal pens, the origin of the 'mum' element cannot be explained].

Holin Stronsay: near southern shore of 'Mill Bay' [Norse *höll-in* the hall: it is uncertain what kind of 'hall' this refers to, but it must have had some particular significance].

Holland Birsay, Marwick; St. Ola; St. Andrews; Deerness; North Ronaldsay; Eday; Papa Westray; Stronsay; Shapinsay; Firth; South Ronaldsay; North Faray: a common farm name [Norse *hó* high land].

Holland's Brae Sanday: a mound on Hillhead Farm, Sellibister.

Hollin Harray: Overbrough district [Norse *hol(a)-inn* the hole or depression near the 'Burn o Netherbrough'].

Hollocast South Ronaldsay, Blanster, St. Margaret's Hope: [English 'holocaust': in this location, it is probably an inn! It is the only instance of the use of this noun to describe a public house: normally they were called 'Hell' or 'Purgatory'].

Holm 1. a parish: pronounced 'ham' [Norse *hamn* harbour: at an early date a scribal error produced the written form 'holm'].

Holm 2. North Ronaldsay: a farm, slightly north of the 'Loch o Hookin': originally in a flooded area which has been drained, leaving a knoll here, hence the name [Norse *hólmr*].

Holm/Quholm Shapinsay: farmhouse: birthplace of Washington Irving's father, William: named from the adjacent small island to the east of 'Veantrow Bay' [Norse *hólmr*, island].

Holm o Boray Rendall: a small island to the south of the 'Ness o Boray', Gairsay (see 'Boray').

Holm o Elsness Sanday: island off Elsness [Norse *hólmr* island (see 'Elsness')].

Holm o Houton Orphir: a sizeable island lying off 'Houton Head' (see Orphir parish).

Holm o Huip Stronsay: formerly 'Sygle Holm'.

Holm o Inyesum Sanday: a small island in 'Park' district and seen only at low tide [Norse *hólmr* island (see 'Inyesum')].

Holm o Midgarth Stronsay: formerly 'Meikle Linga/Linga Meikle': (see 'Linga').

Holm o Papa Papa Westray: lies to the east of Papa Westray.

Holm o Rendall Rendall: lies to the east of the 'Hall of Rendall'.

Holm o the Riv Sanday: [Norse *hólmr* island (see 'Riv', The')].

Holm Park, The Rendall, Breck: nearest to the 'Holm o Gairsay'.

Holm Point Firth: a point of land in Firth which faces the 'Holm o Grimbister'.

Holm Sound Orphir: the channel between the 'Holm o Houton' and 'Houton Hea' [Norse *hólmr* island, *sund* a narrow channel].

Holm Sound Sanday: stretch of water between 'Holm of Elsness' and 'Elsness' [Norse *hólmr* island, *sund* channel].

Holm Sound Shapinsay: the channel which separates 'Helliar Holm' from Shapinsay (see above).

Holm Taing Shapinsay: (see 'Holmatanga' above). 'Veantrow Bay' [Norse *hólmr* island].

Holmatang Birsay: on the coast of Birsay Bay, ridge of protruding rocks with a small rocky island off 'Snushan': because of coastal erosion there is no trace of the island and the rocks are best seen at low tide: [Norse *hólmr* island, *tangi* point of land].

Holmes Holm: [Norse *hólmar* islands, but since there are no islands in this eastern part of Holm, the name may be used in the sense of small areas of ground different (in vegetation?) from the surrounding land].

Holmie St. Ola: a small rock in the 'Peedie Sea' before the 'oyce' i.e., 'pool', was drastically altered [a diminutive of Norse *hólmr* island].

Holms o Ire Sanday: small islands off the northwestern part of Burness parish (see 'Ire').

Holodyke Birsay; Harray; Firth: at first impression this seems to mean 'a hole in a dyke/wall' but there was never any wall at these places when the name came into use probably about the beginning of the 19th century: a 'holodyke' seems to be a lost word for 'tramp' [Scots *to holl* means 'to loaf about' and usually 'to have no fixed abode'. Tramps stayed in old houses, or in barns with permission of the owner and sometimes stayed permanently there. If no roofed places were available, they stayed in fields in the shelter of a wall if possible. Holodyke in Birsay is now called 'Slinghorn': Holodyke in Harray (now a fine house) lies just above Dounby School: Holodyke in Firth, now vanished, lay near 'Cuween Cairn'].

Holt Geo Evie: to the northwest of 'Clouk' in Costa [Norse *hol-t* the hollow].

Holy Cross Kirk Sanday: (see 'Cross Kirk').

Honeyar Stronsay: a small enclosure in Rothiesholm [Norse *hyrning* a nook or corner, Norse *garðr* which normally translates as farm or wall, which is inappropriate here, hence 'yard'].

Honeys Geo South Ronaldsay: [Norse *húnn* a young bear: the Norse frequently used familiar animal names for coastal features, but a 'bear' name is quite unusual (see however 'Birsi Geo')].

Hoo Back Sanday: beach feature, west of Spurness [Norse *haugr* mound, *bakki* slope].

Hooan 1. Stronsay, Huip: field name (see above).

Hooan 2. Westray: a derelict farm [Norse *haugr-inn* the mound].

Hoobacker Stronsay: banks on the shore south of 'Grice Ness' [Norse *haugr* mound, *bakkar* banks].

Hookaly Rousay: field name near 'Hullion' [the name seems to have formed in the same way as 'Crook' from Norse *krókr* nook or corner (an old phrase in dialect is 'huikety-kruikity', in a crooked way) hence 'a small enclosure', Norse *hlíð* a slope].

Hookin Papa Westray: [Norse *hauga-kvín* from Norse *haugr* mound and *kvín* the enclosure].

Hookin(g) North Ronaldsay: (see above).

Hookin Links Sanday: meadows near 'Newark' (see above).

Hookney Holm Sanday: [Norse *haugr-inn* the mound or *hauga-kvín* the enclosure with the mound, Norse *hólmr* island].

Hool 1. Sanday, Everbist: (see above).

Hool 2. Sanday: a ridge of land near the field of 'Tofts' on Stove [Norse *hóll* hill].

Hools South Ronaldsay: (see above).

Hooly 1. Birsay, Ingsay: vanished [Norse *hóll* hill].

Hooly 2. Sanday: a shoal near 'Torsker', Rusness [Norse *hóll*, hill].

Hooly 3. Sanday: rocky inshore shoal [Norse *hóll* hill].

Hooly 4. Sanday: small burnt mound, Park district [Norse *hóll* hill].

Hoonagar Westray: near 'Iphs' [the Ordnance Survey references to this placename are unclear so the origin cannot be determined].

Hoopath Harray: Brettavale, Knarston, location unknown [Norse *hóp-it* a hoop like shape and usually applied to a bay but here it would likely apply to a field shape (see 'Hubbet')].

Hoora Meenya Birsay, Beaquoyside: [(see 'Knowes o Euro'), Norse *haugar* mounds, *minni* smaller].

Hooro Nev Westray: [Norse *haugar* mounds, *nef* a rocky point: the location is uncertain].

Hoors Grip Birsay, Marwick: [(for 'hoors' see 'Howerhouse'), Scots *gruip* a ditch].

Hoorsland Birsay, Langskaill, Marwick: (for 'hoors' see 'Howerhouse').

Hoosay Sanday: cultivated mound south of 'Boloquoy' [probably the 'Housa' of the 1601 Rental].

Hoosbreck Harray, Netherbrough: [Norse *hús* house, *brekka* slope].

Hoosefield (see 'Howsfield').

Hooso Grund Sanday: a shoal near 'The Riv' [Norse *grunn* shoal: origin of 'Hooso' element here is uncertain].

Hoosta/Houstiebreck Sanday: a mound on the west side of 'Cata Sand' [Norse *hús-staðr* house site, *brekka* slope].

Hoover Evie: old croft 'Dykeside/Cottonhill' area [Norse *ofar* higher up].

Hooveth Sandwick: [Norse *hof-it* the farm, one of only two instances of the use of this word in Orkney placenames (see 'Hoveth')].

Hope, The 1. Burray, Hunda: a small bay [Norse *hóp* bay].

Hope, The 2. South Ronaldsay: 'St Margarets village' [is usually referred to in this way].

Hope o Myre Orphir: (see below).

Hope o Swanbister Orphir: (see below).

Hope o The Bu Orphir: (see below).

Horay Evie: (see 'Horraquoy').

Horn Graemsay: a farm [Norse *horn* an angle shaped field].

Horn Skerry North Ronaldsay: a conical outlying rock near 'Bride's Loch' (see 'Horn' above).

Horn, Glen of the Hoy: just west of the Hoy Community Centre: a deep scar in the landscape [Gaelic *glean* valley: (see 'Horn' above)].

Hornops Point Deerness: southeast of 'Mirkady Point' [Norse *horn* a point of land: origin of 'ops' element unknown].

Horns o the Standard Evie: two pillars of rock on 'The Standard' (see 'Standard').

Hornsha Shapinsay: local name for 'Haraldsgarth' [here an 'n' is substituted for an 'l' to make it Hornsgarth: later 'garth' was dropped and replaced by Scots 'hall' or 'ha', the latter meaning 'cottage' (see 'Haraldsgarth')].

Horo Sanday: (see 'Horay' above).

Horonsay Harray: field name, Netherbrough: it used to be called 'Quoy o Horonsay' [possibly a transferred name (see 'Horraldsay' below)].

Horraldsay Firth: earlier 'Thorwaldishow' [with the loss of the initial 'th': locally pronounced 'horranshee' with 'n' substituted for 'l': the earliest form of the name 'Thorwaldishow' shows that the final 'ay' represents 'how' = Norse *haugr* mound: (see 'Horansay' above)].

Horraquoy 1. Deerness; Holm: (see below).

Horraquoy 2. Harray: [Norse *horr* a nasal discharge, but here probably has the Old English meaning 'filthy' referring to wet marshy land].

Horrie St. Andrews: (see 'Horraquoy' above).

Horriequoy Holm: (see 'Horraquoy' above).

Horries Deerness: [named after a family called 'Horrie' who lived there].

Horse Evie: landing place of inshore fishermen ['horse' is frequently used for names of cliffs or rocky shores: almost always a translation of Norse *hestr*, horse or stallion (see 'Hesta Head' above)].

Horse Bools o the Riv Sanday: coastal feature, 'The Riv' [Norse *ból* place where animals are penned (see 'Riv, The')'].

Horse Flags Papa Westray: flat rocks on the southwest side of the island [Norse *flaga* flat rock or stone].

Horse Geo Sanday: coastal feature: it was from here that horses were embarked for peat working in Eday [Norse *gjá* ravine].

Horse Geo South Ronaldsay: 'Burwick Bay', horses were transported to 'The Mainland' from this point.

Horse o Copinsay Deerness: an outlying uninhabited sea stack to the northeast of Copinsay (see 'Horse' above and 'Copinsay').

Horse o Longaber Birsay: [Norse *langa-berg* long rock: (see 'Horse' forms above)].

Horsequoy Egilsay: position unknown: [Norse *hross* horse, *kví* enclosure].

Horsick St. Andrews: at the head of the 'Bay o Suckquoy': an offshoot of the farm of 'Horrie' [Norse *vík* bay].

Hosen Birsay, Dounby: pronounced 'Hozen' [Norse *hauss-inn* the skull, used metaphorically to describe a rounded skull shape, probably a prehistoric mound which has been levelled].

Hoston Head South Ronaldsay: to the west of 'Sandy Hill' [Norse *haesti-tún* highest enclosure].

Hottit South Ronaldsay, Grimness: [Norse *haugr* mound, *topt* old house site].

Hourston Sandwick: now 'Dounby Farm' [Norse personal name *Þórr*, Norse *staðr* estate: one of several large estates, particularly in the 'West Mainland', all with personal names attached (see 'Germiston')].

Housa (see 'Hoosay').

Houscrow Sanday: north of 'Grindally', later called 'Housnea' [Norse *haugs*, genitive of *haugr*, mound Norse *kró* pen, *hús-nyja*, new house].

House Geo 1. Flotta: a sea inlet on 'Kirk Bay' [probably the same origin as 'House Geo', Swona].

House Geo 2. Swona: a long narrow ravine [Norse *hús* house, where *hús* is used in the sense of 'shelter'].

Housebay 1. Birsay, Beaquoy: [Norse *húsa-baer* farm (buildings); (see 'Bea', Birsay)].

Housebay 2. Shapinsay: (see above).

Housebay 3. Stronsay: (see above).

Housebreak Burray: [Norse *hús* house, Norse *brekka* slope].

Housegarth 1. Sanday: east of the present farm of 'How': alternative names 'Bea', Nearhoose, and Netherhoose [Norse *haugs-garðr* mound farm: there is a large broch mound here].

Housegarth 2. Sandwick: [like the above, an important farm with probably the same derivation: we should remember that many of these mounds have been completely flattened].

Housenea Sandwick: usually shortened to 'Snea' [Norse *hús-nyja* new house (see 'Houscrow' above)].

Housequoy Stenness: [Norse *hús* house, Norse *kví* enclosure].

Housey Sanday: (see 'Hoosay').

Housily Sanday, Lopness: field name [Norse *húsa-hlíð* house slope].

Houso (see 'Howso').

Housta Sanday: a tunship in Everbist, today the name is applied to an area south of the 'Geramount' to 'Hool' road [Norse *haug-staðr* mound position].

Housteith Rousay: (the same origin as above).

Houton Orphir: [Norse *haugr* mound, Norse *tún* farm].

Hoversta Rendall: [Norse *ofar* upper, *staðr* position].

Hoveth Harray, Grimeston: [Norse *hof-it* the farm, one of only two instances of the use of this word in Orkney placenames (see 'Hooveth')].

How Westray; Hoy; Flotta; Sanday; Stromness; Sandwick; Shapinsay; Holm; South Ronaldsay: [Norse *haugr* mound].

Howa 1. Evie: a vanished farm in Costa [Norse *haugr* mound with diminutive 'a', the equivalent of Scots 'ie'].

Howa 2. Holm: (see above).

Howa Tuo Westray: remains of an ancient monument, position unknown [Norse *haugr* with diminutive 'a' mound, Norse *tó* mound (literally) a 'tuft'].

Howaback Dounby: [Norse *haugr* mound with diminutive 'a', Norse *bakki* slope].

Howabreck Birsay, Marwick: [(see above), Norse *brekka* slope].

Howacrow Rendall: [Norse *haugr* mound, Norse *kró* enclosure].

Howajib Rendall: tide race next to the shore opposite the 'Ness of Boray' [Norse *haugr-inn* the mound, *djúpr* deep (of water): (see 'Bring Deeps')].

Howally Birsay, Dirkadale: [Norse *haugr* mound with diminutive 'a', Norse *hlíð* slope].

Howan 1. Dounby: (see 'Howan' above).

Howan 2. Egilsay: (see above).

Howan/Hooan North Ronaldsay: in 'Noltland-Bewest' [Norse *haugr-inn* the mound].

Howan-Granna Birsay, Eastabist: [Norse *haug-inn* the mound, *groen* green].

Howan Lickan Deerness: a small point north of 'Lang Geo' [(see 'Howan' above): the 'lickan' element is a nonsense 'rhyming' addition (compare 'Cupster Nelster')].

Howan Oot o Toon Westray: there are two mounds in Westray called by this name [Norse *haugr-inn* the mound, 'Oot o Toon' = outside the tunship wall].

Howana Geo Sandwick: a narrow ravine west of 'Stockan' [Norse *haugr-inn* the mound with diminutive 'a', Norse *gjá* ravine].

Howana Gruna Evie: a mound on northwest flank of 'Burgar Hill', recorded as 'Howan Greinay' in 1633 [Norse *haugr-inn* the mound (see above), Norse *groen* green].

Howaquoy Birsay: near 'Grew' (see 'Hacco/Howaquoy', Rendall): [Norse *haugr* mound with diminutive 'a', *kví* enclosure].

Howar 1. Stronsay: just west of 'Hargar' [Norse *haugar* mounds].

Howar 2. North Ronaldsay: (see above).

Howar 3. Sanday: formerly 'South Howar', now the farm steading of 'North Howar' [Norse *haugar* mounds].

Howar 4. Sanday: near Newark (see above).

Howarhouse Birsay, Marwick: it lay very close to 'Kastal' [Norse *haugar* mounds].

Howatoft 1. North Ronaldsay: southwest of the 'Loch o Hooking' (see above).

Howatoft 2. Rousay: a vanished house in 'Wasbister' (see 'Howatoft/Howato').

Howatoft 3. South Ronaldsay: to the west of 'Manse Bay' (see above).

Howatoft/Howato Rousay, Wasbister: vanished [Norse *haugr* mound (see 'How' forms above), Norse *topt* an old house site].

Howatoft/Howtoa North Ronaldsay: [Norse *haugr* mound with diminutive 'a', Norse *púfa* a small mound].

Howban Birsay, Eastabist: [(see 'Haugr'): origin of 'ban' unknown].

Howbell Sanday: Burness parish [Norse *haugr* mound, *baeli* farm].

Howbenorth Sanday: listed in the 1500 Rental of the island; position unknown [Norse *haugr* mound, 'benorth' = to the north].

How-Benorth Sanday: vanished [Norse *haugr* mound].

Howbustirland Orphir: later 'Hobbister', there is a considerable mound nearby [Norse *haugr* mound, *ból-staðr* farm (see 'Halfynscoffis')].

Howcavan Birsay: 'Leaquoy' (see 'Cavan').

Howdis Knowe Rousay: a mound near 'Hurtiso' [Norse *haugr* mound, *dýs* cairn].

Howdooa Deeress, Holland: a field with a mound in it [Norse *haugr* mound (see 'Dooa', Corston, Harray)].

Howe 1. Birsay, Marwick: [Norse *haugr* mound].

Howe 2. Evie; Rousay; Egilsay, west of 'Steedie Point'.

Howe 3. Sanday: Westside, Northwall [Norse *haugr* mound].

Howe, The Stromness: 'Cairston', the site of a broch, removed during excavation 1978-82: [Norse *haugr* mound].

Howe Harper Firth: a distinctive mound to the west of 'Binscarth Farm' [origin unknown: there were no Harper families living in this area].

Howea Evie, Breck: [Norse *haugr* mound: the suffix 'a' is a diminutive].

Howequoy Holm: [Norse *haugr* mound, *kví* enclosure].

Howes o Muir/Haas o Muir Sanday: a cairn on the beach face 'Ruthie Taing' [a corrupt form of 'Hows o Myre' (see 'Myre')].

Howes o Quoyawa Hoy: (see 'Quoyawa').

Howes Wick Holm: [Norse *vík* bay].

Howesti, Point of Graemsay: [Norse *haugr* mound, *stía* enclosure].

Howie Sound Rousay; Egilsay: [Norse *sund* channel].

Howinalidna Harray: [Norse *haug-inn* the mound, Norse *hlýð-in* the shed/shelter].

Howinawheel Harray: [Norse *haug-inn* the mound, *hvílan* the resting place, in this case for those who transported a coffin].

Howland Sanday: [Norse *haugr* mound].

Howmae Brae North Ronaldsay: [Norse *haugr* mound, Norse *melr* a sand hill (usually covered with bent grass)].

Howness, Hill o Stronsay: [Norse *haugr* mound, *nes* a point of land].

Howsfield/Hoose Sanday: field name between 'Cleat' and the shore, the site of the 'Chapel of Cleat' [Norse *haugs*, genitive of *haugr* mound].

Howsgarth (see 'Housegarth').

Howsground Sanday: a vanished house [Norse *haugs*, genitive case of *haugr* mound].

Howso Myre Sanday: field name near 'Ortie', see 'Hoosay' for possible interpretation [Norse *mýrr* marsh].

Howso/Houso Sanday: field name (see 'Hoosay' for possible interpretation).

Howth Orphir: the old name for the area around the 'Bay of Houton' [Norse *höfuð* head (land), referring to 'Houton Head'].

Hoxa South Ronaldsay: [Norse *haugs*, genitive of *haugr* mound, Norse *eið* isthmus].

Hoxa South Ronaldsay: [Norse *haugs-ey* mound island].

Hoy: at 1454m. the highest island in Orkney and also one of the largest: population in 2001 was 272 [Norse *há-ey* high island].

Hrossey name given in the *Orkneyinga Saga* to what, today is 'The Mainland' [Norse *hross* horse, Norse *ey* island, possibly a reference to the number of native horses on the island].

Huan Sandwick: in the 'Northdike' area [Norse *haug-inn* the mound].

Huanan Harray: location uncertain [Norse *haug-inn* the mound: the suffix is puzzling].

Huant Birsay, Marwick: vanished [Norse *haug-inn* the mound: the extraneous suffix 't' is found in several parts of the parish of Birsay].

Hubbers Geo Rousay: a ravine in the 'Scokness' area [Norse *há-bergs gjá* high rock geo].

Hubbet, The Egilsay: a small bay on the west coast [Norse *hóp-it* the bay].

Hubbit, The Rousay: position uncertain (see above).

Hucklinsower Sanday: coastal feature, Burness parish [Norse *haugr* Mound, Norse *land* land, Norse *saurr* mud: (compare 'Saverday')].

Huckoo Rendall: (see 'Howaquoy').

Hugh Libby's Field Sandwick: a field to south of 'Feaval' farmhouse [a corrupted form of Norse which is difficult to interpret: there is a local folk explanation relating to a neutered animal or man! Scots *lib* to castrate].

Huip Stronsay: [Norse *hóp* bay].

Hulder Sanday: a mound near 'Newark' [Shetland dialect 'hulder' a heap of stones].

Hull Evie: [close by is 'Spurn' which suggests that these cottages were built by seafaring men with Yorkshire connections].

Hullderhow Flotta: [(see 'Hulder' above), Norse *haugr* mound].

Hullion Rousay: 'Frotoft' [Norse *hóll-inn* the mound].

Hulter Burn Rousay: 'Wasbister' [origin uncertain].

Humason Point Sandwick: the southern point of the 'Ness o Tenston' [origin unknown].

Hume Stromness: location unknown [Norse *hvamm* a rounded valley].

Humo Firth: south of 'Nabban' [Norse *há mor* high moorland (leading to 'Keelylang')].

Hunagrund Sanday: coastal feature off 'The Riv'; marked on an old Admiralty chart [Norse 'grunn' shallow water: meaning of 'huna' here uncertain].

Hunber Rousay: (same as 'Hubber' above).

Hunclett Holm: (see below).

Hunclett/Howklett Rousay: [Norse *haug-inn* the mound, Norse *klettr* rock but a rock with perhaps some special sacred significance: (see 'Cleat')].

Hunda Burray: no longer an island as the Norse name *ey* island suggests but linked to Burray by a military road built in World War II [Norse *hundr* dog: animal names were frequently used in Norse placenames].

Hunda Geo Birsay: [Norse *hundr* dog, *gjá* ravine].

Hunday Stronsay: an old house (see 'Park of Hunday').

Hundigar/Hindigar Birsay: an oblong rock visible at low tide [Norse *hundr* dog, *garðr* wall in the sense of 'protector' (of the cliff face?)].

Hundland 1. Birsay: a tunship name [Norse *hundr* dog, land = land].

Hundland 2. Birsay, Marwick: a cottage [a transferred name from the above].

Hune South Ronaldsay, Grimness: a coastal feature [Norse *haug-inn* the mound].

Hunger-him-in Flotta: [a name jokingly given in contrast to the one above: locally it was said in jest that this cottage and the one above were separated by another dwelling called 'Hunger-him-in-Atween'!].

Hunger-him-out Flotta: [a nickname applied to a house with poor land which cannot support the inhabitant].

Hungrabreck Birsay, Bigbreck: [Norse *brekka* slope: this and the three named below relate to poor agricultural soil].

Hungerabreck Rendall: (see above).

Hungryha Eday: (see above).

Hungryquoy Rousay: [English 'hunger' a reference to the poor quality Land, Norse *kví* enclosure].

Hunigarth Firth: Redland, exact position unknown [Norse *haug-inn* the mound, *garðr* farm].

Hunnalie Birsay, Fea: Abune-the-Hill [Norse *haug-inn* the mound, Norse *hlíð* slope].

Hunni Geo South Ronaldsay, Pentland Skerries: [Norse *hyrning* a corner].

Huntis Evie: ruins to the west of 'Jubidee' [origin uncertain].

Hunto Birsay, Northside: [Norse personal name *Hundr*, Norse *topt* old house site: (see 'Howatoft' North Ronaldsay)].

Hunton Stronsay: [Norse *Hundr* a personal name, Norse *tún* farm].

Huntscarth Harray: [Norse *Hundr* a personal name, *garðr* farm].

Hunyeston Sanday: old burial ground, Westside, Northwall [Norse personal name *Hunni*, Norse *tún* farm].

Hurbe Rock Orphir: [origin uncertain].

Hurges North Ronaldsay: vanished, location unknown (see below).

Hurgis Howe Stronsay: a house in the east of 'Rothiesholm' [Norse *hörgr* a place of heathen worship, *haugr* mound].

Hurkisgarth Sandwick: earlier 'Thurkingisgarth' [Norse personal name *Þorkell* (with common substitution of 'l' for 'n'), Norse *garðr* farm].

Hurlacliff Birsay: [Scots *hurl* a rush of stones down a steep slope (i.e., a scree), English 'cliff'].

Hurliness Walls: a district name: [Norse *nes* a point of land: the 'hurli' element here cannot be explained].

Huro Meenya Westray: [Norse *haugar* mounds, *minna* smaller (see 'Doona minya Geo')].

Hurtiso 1. Holm: [Norse personal name *Þorstain*, Norse *haugr* mound].

Hurtiso 2. Holm: (see above).

Hurtiso 3. Rousay: earlier 'Thurstainshow' [Norse personal name *Þorsteinn*, Norse *haugr* mound].

Hurtiso Rousay: Sourin (see above).

Husabae Rousay: (see 'Housebay').

Husen Rousay: (see 'Hozen').

Husenter Point South Ronaldsay: [Norse *haugs*, genitive case of *haugr* Mound, *endir* end].

Hushan Sandwick, Lyking: field name [Norse *hús* house, Norse *tjörn* pond or pool].

Hushasteeth Evie: [Norse *hús* house, with diminutive 'a': 's' was often pronounced 'sh', Norse *staðr* position].

Husmasay Rousay: a field near 'Sketquoy', Wasbister: [Norse *hús* house: the 'masay' element cannot be explained].

Husmire North Ronaldsay: marshy land to the north of 'Howar', site of a former house [Norse *hús* house, *mýrr* moorland].

Hussa Sanday: Cross parish, near 'Boloquoy', the site of a large mound now ploughed out: there is a local legend that it was inhabited by a spirit [Norse *haugr* mound is the basis of this entry: the first element could be Norse *hús* house].

Hutchum North Ronaldsay: [no information].

Hutter Stromness: an old name, possibly dating back to the 18th century: in the Ordnance Survey in the 1880s it was a farm near 'Weardith' [Norse *hattr* highest?].

Hyan/Hyan a Lay North Ronaldsay: an old house site [Norse *haug-inn* the mound, 'a lay' = *á hlíð* on the slope].

Hyapols Rousay: a stretch of swampy ground between 'Sourin Burn' and 'Breval' [Norse *pollr* pool: origin of 'hya' unknown].

Hybreck Harray: [Norse *hey* hay, *brekka* slope].

Hyma Birsay, Beaquoy: (see 'Humo' for derivation).

Hyndgreenie/Hynegreenie Papa Westray: (see 'Hynegreenie' below).

Hynegreenie Sanday: (see 'Howana Gruna').

Hyneover Sanday, Braeswick: [Norse *haugr-inn* the mound, Norse *ofarr* higher up].

Hyval 1. Sandwick: [Norse *hey* hay, *völlr* field].

Hyval 2. Birsay, Twatt: (see above).

I

Iber Sanday: Burness parish, a tilted shelf of rock and sawtooth feature [Norse *berg* rock: first element uncertain].

Icegarth (see 'Isgarth').

Iceland Rock off Sanday [origin uncertain; perhaps Norse *ysya* noise].

Iceland Skerry St. Ola: in Kirkwall Bay (see above).

Icevay Eday: a small shallow bay northeast of 'Caldhame' [Norse *vágr* Bay: (see 'Iceland Rock' for possible definition)].

Icy Geo Rousay: a small geo near the 'Quern o Grithen' (see 'Iceland Rock' for definition).

Inbust/Inbuster Sanday: Cross parish, a vanished farm [Norse *ból-staðr* farm, *ból-staðir* farm buildings, Norse *inn* in the sense of 'inner'].

Ingale Skerry Stronsay: [origin of 'ingale' unknown].

Ingamyre Orphir: position unknown today [Norse *eng* meadow, *mýrr* bog].

Inganess Sandwick: just south of 'Yesnaby' [*Inga* was a Scandinavian goddess revered in Orkney placenames and her name is used particularly for headlands, Norse *nes* headland].

Inganess St. Ola: probably an old name for the 'Taing o Berstane': it gave its name to 'Inganess Bay': it is now a district name in 'Kirkwall' (see above).

Inganess Westray: to the west of 'Skea Hill' (see above).

Inganoust Stronsay: a field on Holland [Norse *eng* meadow, *naustr* a place where boats may be drawn up, e.g., for the winter].

Ingashowe Firth: a mound near 'Rennibister' [Norse personal name *Inga/Ingi*, Norse *haugr* mound].

Ingasquoy Orphir: vanished: it lay just to the west of 'Swanbister' [Norse personal name *Inga*, Norse *kví* enclosure].

Ingatus, The Stronsay: to the east side of Rothiesholm [Norse *eng* meadow, *þúfa* mound].

Inglass Geo North Ronaldsay: [origin unknown: perhaps an error for '*Ingas*'].

Inglie Sanday: coastal feature, possibly taking its name from a former inland feature [Norse *eng* meadow, *hlíð* slope: (compare 'Eengly')].

Ingo o the Head Orphir, Houton: [Norse *inn-gang* an entrance, to a cave in this instance].

Ingsay Birsay: Abune-the-Hill district [Norse personal name *Ingi*, second element 'ay' suggests one of the many forms of Norse *haugr* mound: (see 'Horraldsay' in Firth)].

Ingsetter Orphir: (see 'Inksetter').

Inkerman Sanday: after the battle of that name fought in the Crimean War, 1854 (compare 'Alma Cottage' and 'Balaclava').

Inkerman Shapinsay; South Ronaldsay: (see above).

Inkster Rendall, Gorseness: [Norse *eng* meadow, *setr* dwelling].

Inkster/Inksetter/ Ingsetter Orphir: just to the west of 'Swanbister' [Norse personal name *Inga*, Norse *setr* a dwelling: 'Ingasquoy' lay close by].

Innan Neb Flotta: the extreme south point of the island [Norse *innan* inside/within etc. (*innan* has many meanings and it is difficult to interpret the placename correctly), Norse *nef* (used metaphorically) point of land].

Inner Ganges Swona: one of two channels on the rocky beach parallel to the coast [Norse *gangr-stigr* a foot passage (to the pier): (see 'Gansti Pier')].

Inner Scaws South Ronaldsay: [Norse *innri* the innermost, *skjár* a hut made of slats used as a drying storehouse: later, in Orkney, applied to any hut].

Inneraer Stenness: on the northwest flank of 'Mid Hill' [Norse *innri* farthest in, Norse *erg* a word derived from Gaelic *àirigh* summer hut].

Innernoust Stronsay: field name, south of the 'Point o Innernoust' [Norse *naustr* a place where boats may be drawn up e.g., for the winter].

Innertoon Stromness: that part of the parish of Stromness immediately to the west of the present town of Stromness [Norse *tún* a division of land which can be anything from a small field to a larger 'tunship'].

Innigan Sanday: coastal feature, Northwall [Norse *innr* innermost, *gjá-n*, the ravine].

Innister/Ingisgar Rousay: Wasbister district [Norse personal name *Ingi*, Norse *garðr* farm: the family name which originated from this farm became 'Inkster'].

Innsker Shapinsay: the innermost reef [Norse *innsti* innermost, *sker* reef].

Insabysetter Birsay: Abune-the-Hill district [Norse *innsti* innermost, *boer* farm settlement, *setr* pasture land, i.e., the nearest piece of pasture land to the nearby 'Bea' farm].

Inskift, The Rousay: Sourin district, field name, 'Hurtiso' [Norse *eignarskipti* a piece of land not shared with others].

Instabely South Ronaldsay: vanished, it lay in the 'Flaws' district (see below).

Instabillie 2. Sandwick: North Dyke area (see above).

Instabillie 1. St. Ola: vanished; apparently lay between 'Orquil' and 'Warbuster' [Norse *innsta* innermost, *boeli* a night time secure area for cattle].

Instabreck Harray: Knarston district, southeast of 'Hozen' [Norse *innsta* innermost, *brekka* slope, i.e., the beginning of the slope].

Inverollit South Ronaldsay, Widewall: [Norse *ofar* upper, the 'n' is intrusive: (for 'ollit' see 'Olad)'].

Inya Taing Stronsay: [Norse goddess *Inga* (see 'Inganess')].

Inyamehellya/Inyamahelly Birsay: a large ravine which pierces a steep 100 metre cliff to the west of 'The Standard', 'Costa Head' [Norse goddess *Inga*, Norse *hellir* cave: the medial element 'ma' cannot be explained (see 'Ingermas')].

Inyan Brig Sanday, Northwall: [Norse *eng* meadow with definite article suffix *in* = 'the': old Sanday dialect 'brig' = Norse *brekka* slope].

Inyan Noust Stronsay: field on Holland [Norse *eng-in* the meadow, *naustr* where boats were hauled up in winter].

Inyawhee Birsay, Gelderhouse, Sabiston: (see 'Inyequoy' and 'Quoyinga').

Inyequoy South Ronaldsay: (see 'Quoyinga').

Inyeria Harray: in the hill above 'Winksetter' [Norse *inn* innermost, Norse *erg* a word derived from Gaelic *àirigh* summer hut (see 'Inneraer')].

Inyes Holm Sanday, Northwall: [Gaelic *innis*, island, Norse *hólmr* island: a fine example of a tautological placename].

Inyesum Sanday: beach name, Park district, Northwall [variation of 'Inyes Holm' (see above)].

Inyeth Geo Evie: northeast of 'Arsdale', this geo must be adjacent to a meadow (see below).

Inyeth Stromness: location unknown [the suffix 'th' indicates the definite article of Norse *engi* meadow].

Iphs Westray, Dykeside: [Norse *ups* eves of a house used figuratively in Norway applying to a very steep hillside].

Iquiver Shapinsay: field name, position unknown [Norse *kví* enclosure: *efri* upper].

Ire Sanday: a peninsula [Norse *eyjar* islands].

Irefurse Birsay, Gelderhouse, Barony: [Norse *eyrr* gravel/sand/hardpan, Norse *for* drain or ditch (with English plural), both suggesting poor quality land].

Ireland Stenness: [Norse *eyrr* gravelly bank].

Ires Taing North Ronaldsay: [Norse *eyrr* gravel/sand/hardpan (with English plural), Norse *tangi* point of land].

Ireso Rousay: a mound above 'Nears' in 'Frotoft' [Norse *haugr* mound, explains the last element 'o', *eyrr* is gravel/coarse sand (with English plural)].

Iron Birsay, Boardhouse: field name (see above).

Iron Evie: coastal feature north of 'Mucklepow' [Norwegian (Nynorsk) *auren* gravelly].

Iron Geo Hoy: described by the Ordnance Survey as a sandy creek between 'Burnmouth' and 'Greenhill' (see above).

Iron Geo North Ronaldsay: small creek south of 'Dennis Head' (see above).

Iron Geo Sanday: Burness parish, a small inlet north of 'Airon' (see above).

Iron Hellia Deerness: near 'West Shore' [(see above) in this case very rocky gravel, Norse *hella* a table land of rocks].

Iron Ness Sandwick: extreme north of 'Loch o Harray', south of the farm of 'Kirkness' (see 'Iron', Evie, above).

Isbister Rendall: [Norse *óss-ból-staðr* from Norse *óss* the mouth of a stream].

Isbister South Ronaldsay: [Norse *yztr-ból-staðr* outermost farm. There were in fact three places with this name close together].

Isgarth/Isegarth/Icegarth Sanday: this farm was in existence at the end of the 19th century [Norse *óss*, river mouth, referring here to the nearby 'Ouse', Norse *garðr* farm].

Isle Rough/Rift Copinsay: a rocky isthmus which joins Copinsay to 'Corn Holm' [Norse *rifa* a rift].

Issie Gutchers South Ronaldsay: [Isobel Gutcher lived in 'Gerrackquoy' in 1821, a name which was abbreviated to 'Gaira' and, seemingly, later to 'Cara': it was temporarily named 'Alma' after the battle of that name in the Crimea: it is now called 'West Gara'].

Itherhellyie, The Ha's o Rousay: [Norse *hellar* caves favoured by *aeðar*, eider ducks: Scots *ha* = small dwelling but in the case of the high cliffs here refers to the same caves].

Itherie Dale Rousay: a valley on the farm of Scockness [Norse *dalr* valley, *aeðar* eider ducks].

Itherie Geo Rousay, (a geo on the Quandal coast); Egilsay; Evie: [Norse *aeðar* eider ducks, *gjá* ravine].

Itheriegeo, Burn o Birsay: [Norse *iðri* inner: (see *gjá* in Appendix)].

Iveratty South Ronaldsay: in the Sandwick area [Norse *efri* upper, Norse *öxl* shoulder, which is used figuratively as the shoulder of a hill (see 'Aglath')].

Ivors/Ivers Knowe (see 'Evars Knowe').

Ivrigar Evie: [Norse *efri* upper, *garðr* farm, or more likely, 'enclosure' here].

J

Jack's Reef Stronsay: reefs were often named after people who had difficulties on them, for example by running aground or by a rising tide.

Jacky Flett's Hole South Ronaldsay: a cave named after John Flett (from Newbigging, Holland?) who hid here from the Press Gang during the Napoleonic War. It is said that he was eventually captured, served his term, and on his release 'captured' the constable who caught him — and flogged him with cart chains!

Jaddvorstauðum St. Ola: a farm mentioned in the *Orkneyinga Saga* (see 'Gaitnip').

Jaspert's Head Rig Orphir: it lay near the top of 'Keelylang Hill' (in the early 19th century map of Division of the Commonty): the only instance of the use of this first name recorded in Orkney.

Jeanie Broon's South Ronaldsay: vanished, this cottage lay near 'Hottit' in Grimness.

Jeck's Waal Sanday: a well near 'Smithscott' [Scots *waal* well, dialect Jeck = Jack: Jack lived in 'Smithscott' in the early 19th century].

Jehusment, Grip o Birsay, Kirbister: [a puzzling name: perhaps a corruption of 'Jerusalem' (see 'Jerusalem' in Westray below), Scots *grip* stream or ditch].

Jenny Fiold Orphir /Firth boundary: [Norse *tjörn* small loch or pond, fjall hill].

Jericho 1. Birsay, Dounby: (for 'Jericho' see below) it is now called 'Verdun', after the battle fought between France and Germany in 1916 near 'Verdun' in France.

Jericho 2. Westray, Dykeside: named after the ancient city in the Jordan Valley, Palestine.

Jerusalem Westray, Rackwick: named after the city which stood east of the Mediterranean and west of the Dead Sea.

Jewaday Firth: a valley to the east of the Heddle Road, Finstown (see 'Jubaday').

Jib, The Rendall: fields on 'Orquil' and 'Lettaly' [these fields take their name from English 'jib', a three-cornered sail].

Jockasy Stenness: position unknown [from the first name 'Jock': the suffix 'asy' cannot be explained].

Jockey's Quoy Stronsay: on 'Burgh Hill' [Norse *kví* enclosure].

Joe's Hole North Ronaldsay: ['hole' = cave: no further information].

John's Boat Papa Westray: [Norse *boði* reef].

John's Hilla Stronsay: a mound near 'Midgarth' [a mound on which Johnsmas celebrations were held: (see 'St. John's Head')].

Jolmaesy, Burn o Orphir: east of Clestran, marked on Commonty of Orphir map 1813 [origin unknown].

Jubaday Birsay, Northside: this placename and the three other instance below can be explained as Norse *djúp* deep, *dý* marsh (see also 'Jewaday').

Jubadie Hoy: (see above).

Jubidee Evie; Harray: (see above).

Juip, Belle o a mound [(see 'Belle'), *djúp* deep].

Jukabout Evie/Rendall: [Scots *jouk* move about clandestinely: compare 'Seek-about' and 'Runabout', all three relate to cottages occupied by beggars who persistently went round the district].

K

Kaelan Helier Stromness: coastal feature [Norse *keld-in* the well or spring, *hellar* caves].

Kaisburn Rousay: Quandale, coastal area [Norse *keisa* to jut out (see 'Keys Geo')].

Kake Firth, Savil: a field name [origin uncertain, perhaps Norse *kökkr* lump, i.e., mound, final element is Norse *kví* enclosure].

Kalder Well Sanday: a well near 'Backaskaill' [Norse *kelda* well, often takes the plural form *keldur* in Orkney].

Kam, The Evie: fishermen's term for 'Vishall Hill'.

Kame o Camy Deerness: a small, elevated point on coast northwest of 'Denwick' [Norse *kambr* ridge, 'Kamy' seems a curtailed form of 'kame' applying in this case to 'The Ward'].

Kame o Corrigall Harray: part of the West Mainland hill ridge, 176 metres high (see 'Corrigall').

Kame o Hoy Hoy: the extreme northwestern part of the Hoy Hills [Norse *kambr* ridge].

Kame o Stews South Ronaldsay: [Norse *kambr* ridge (see 'Stews')].

Kame South Ronaldsay: coastal placename [Norse *kambr* ridge].

Kames Geo Copinsay: in the northeast of the island [Norse *kambr* ridge but must relate to ridges of rock on the shore here].

Kanabeen (see 'Keengabeen' below).

Karapitten, Waal o Birsay, Farafield: a well in a field of the same name [Norse *kjarr* brushwood, *pytt-inn* the marshy hole].

Karny Kirk Sanday: chapel site on the farm of 'Skaill' [perhaps, as Marwick suggests, a dedication to St. Catherine].

Katespells (see 'Cattispells').

Katta Geo Birsay: [Norse *keyta* foul water, perhaps from rotten seaweed trapped here (see 'Rotten Gutter')].

Kearfa Sandwick: (see below).

Kearfea Rousay: in the northeast corner of the island, the highest hill on the island, 235 metres high [Norse *kýr* cattle, *fjall* hill].

Keases Point Sandwick, Appieteen: [Norse *kös* a heap of stones (with English plural): (see also 'Rerness', an alternative name)].

Kebro Orphir: on the brow of a hill in the 'Tuskerbister' district, north of the 'Loch of Groundwater' [Norse *kví* enclosure, 'brock' a form of Norse *brekka* slope, found principally in the 'West Mainland'].

Keefa Hill Swona: near the top of 'Wasbister Hill' (see 'Kearfea' above).

Keek Evie: on 'Vishall Hill' near the standing stone here (see 'Whistle-Keek': compare 'Glower').

Keelylang Hill Firth/Orphir: this hill forms the boundary [Norse *kjöl* a keel-shaped range of hills or mountains, *langr* long].

Keengabeen Rousay: a jagged promontory of rocks on the coast between 'Scockness' and' Faraclett' [Norse *bein* bone, *kinn* 'cheek'? *kinn* is strictly 'cheek' but also had the possible meaning 'chin', hence 'chin bone' as a protruding part of the face (see 'Mull')].

Keeval Harray, Grimeston: a hill slope east of 'Horraquoy' [Norse *kví* enclosure, *fjall* hill].

Keigar Deerness: earlier 'Calgarth' as in 'Calgarth', Rousay: 'South Keigar' in Deerness is known as 'Sookey', a contraction of 'South Keigar'].

Keld, The Sanday: the stretch of water between 'Spurness' and the 'Holms o Spurness' [Norse *keila* a narrow sound].

Kelda Ber Westray: coastal placename 'Noup Head' [(see *kelda* above), Norse *berg* rock: the name seems to relate to a well in the rock surface here].

Kelda Brae Harray: [Norse *kelda* well, Scots *brae*].

Kelda Reedy Birsay, Hundland: a well, [see above: origin of 'reedy' uncertain, unless it is a corruption of 'reekie' below].

Keldaback Birsay, Geerny; Rousay: [Norse *kelda* a well, *bakki* a slope].

Keldalays Sanday, Elsness: early 18th century [Norse *kelda* well, Scots *leys* unploughed land].

Keldamurri Wyre: a well [Norse *kelda* well: the 'murri' element suggests a well dedicated to the Virgin Mary].

Keldapringle Stronsay: vanished quoy [Norse *kelda* well, Scots surname 'Pringle' was recorded in Orkney in Stromness in the 1840s: Pringle was a preacher but there is no record of his staying in Stronsay].

Keldareekie, Burn o: Birsay: near the 'Burn o Lushan': [Norse *kelda* a well, 'reeky' = Scots smoky which refers to a low mist lying here in certain damp conditions].

Kelday Holm: [Norse *kelda* well].

Kelderknowe Sanday: a mound, Park district, Northwall [Norse *keldur* Wells, Scots *knowe* knoll].

Kelderngate Sanday: a path north of 'Skelbrae': another stretch of this path is called the 'Tun Road' [Norse *keldurnar* the wells, *gata* path].

Keldernwell Sanday: a well near 'Skelbrae' [Norse *keldurnar* the wells].

Keldillie North Ronaldsay: [Norse *kelda* well, *hlíð* slope].

Keldro Rousay, Tratland: [Norse *keldur* wells].

Keldroseed Sandwick, Lyking: a field name [Norse *keldur* wells, *sjóða* to cook but really 'to boil' in this instance: a 'vigorous spring'].

Kell, The (see 'Keld, The').

Kellaquoy Deuas Stenness, Germiston: [Norse *kelda* well, *kví* enclosure: 'Germiston' is adjacent to 'Dowascarth' which was owned by *Tófi* and it is possible that he also owned this nearby enclosure].

Kellyan Birsay: near the Palace, Birsay Bay [Norse *kel(di)n* the well].

Kellyan Brae Sandwick: to the east of 'Queenalonga' (see above).

Kelp Factory Sanday: also called 'The Pit o Riv', only a depression in the ground and some bricks are visible [an attempt by the laird to industrialise kelp production, burning wet kelp with coal: it stood near 'The Riv': the chimney was struck by lightning and destroyed in the early 20th century].

Kelp Too Sanday: an alternative name for 'The Temple': it probably looked like a heap of kelp [Norse *þúfa* heap].

Kelsbir Stronsay: old house site [location and meaning unknown].

Kennisquoy South Ronaldsay, Hoxa: [from the surname 'Kennedy', Norse *kví* enclosure].

Keppers Westray: [possibly from the Scots surname 'Kepper' where the suffix 's' represents a curtailed form of 'house' which is very common in Orkney: (alternatively see 'Caperhouse')].

Kergurn Harray, Netherbrough: a large area on the edge of the 'Harray Loch' [Norwegian *kjarr* boggy land, Norse *gormr* mud or ooze].

Kerlin Skerry Orphir: (see 'Barrel of Butter').

Kerragloup Birsay: a narrow geo with steep sides on the north Birsay coast [origin of 'kerra' uncertain, perhaps Norwegian *kjarr* boggy land, Norse *gloppa* a big hole in the ground often caused by rock collapsing some distance from the cliff face].

Kerse, Burn o Birsay: one of many streams which combine in their marshy upper reaches to form the 'Burn o Beaquoy' [Norwegian *kjarr* boggy land: the suffix 'se' is not understood: perhaps 'Kerse' = Scots 'carse' (see 'Carse o Henzie Hunt')].

Kestro Westray: a mound [Norse *köster* heap or pile, the suffix 'o' represents Norse *haugr* a mound].

Kethisgeo Stenness: [Old Scots *caddas* lint, but also used to describe cotton grass (for 'geo' see Geo in the Appendix)].

Kettin Harray: [Norse *keyta-n* the foul, stinking stretch of water].

Kettle, The Pentland Skerries: [Norse *ketill* a cauldron but used here metaphorically of a hollow: on the coast these hollows were sometimes used for evaporating sea water to make salt].

Kettles' Point Stronsay: ['kettles' were used for boiling bark for nets].

Kettletoft Sanday: a village on the island: the location of the original placename is unknown [Norse personal name *Ketill*, *topt* site of an old house].

Kevaday Rousay: part of a hill above 'Furse' with a small sheet of water (see 'Chuivity', North Ronaldsay).

Kewing Rendall: [Norse *kví* enclosure with definite article suffix, hence *kví-n* the enclosure].

Kews Evie: stretches of moorland hillside – on the eastern flank of the 'Hill of Huntis' [Norse *kví* enclosure, the plural of which is *kvíar* enclosures, giving such Orkney placenames as 'Quire' in Stenness and Sanday and 'Quear' in Firth: in this case the English plural 's' is used as in the case of the many 'Quoys'].

Keys, The South Ronaldsay: a coastal feature [Norse *kös* a heap of stones].

Keys Geo Rousay: (see 'Cheese Geo').

Kibbens Geo Eday: a small indentation on the west side of Eday north of 'Greentoft' [origin of this name unknown].

Kierfold Sandwick: [Norse *kýr* cow, *fjall* hill].

Kierlie Sanday: a shoal off 'Bea Ness' [Norse *keyra* to whip, also used of the tossing movement of the sea, Norse *lega* a place where something is laid, e.g., creels].

Kilbarn Sanday, Newark: Lady parish [the barn with the grain-drying kiln].

Kildingie, Well o Stronsay: an ancient well said to have healing properties, with pilgrims coming from Denmark and Norway in former times: there was a local saying that 'the dulse of Guiddin (Geo Odin) and the water from this well would cure any illness with the exception of the Black Death': the saying is quoted by Sir Walter Scott in his novel *The Pirate*: there is the site of a chapel nearby, probably dedicated to the Virgin Mary, hence it will rank with the several 'Mary Wells' found elsewhere on the islands, e.g. 'Keldamurri' above [Norse *kelda* well, the other element of the placename refers to the Scandinavian god *Ingi*].

Kilheugh Harray, Grimeston: a field with a well in it, close to the farmhouse of 'Biggings' [Norse *kelda* a well, Scots *heugh* a pit].

Kili Holm Egilsay: a small, long island at the north end of Egilsay separated by a narrow channel [Norse *kjöl* a keel, hence shaped like keel (see 'Keelylang')].

Killopeter Harray, Overbrough: a folk tale says that a man called 'Peter' drowned in a well in this field [Norse *kelda* well, Norse *pyttar* pools: (see 'Peterditch' for another example)].

Kiln, The North Faray; Sanday; South Ronaldsay; Switha: (see 'Kilns o Brim-Noven' below for an explanation).

Kiln Geo North Ronaldsay: (c.f. above).

Kiln o Dusty Rousay: (see 'Kilns o Brim-Noven' above for an explanation).

Kilnbarn Skerry Sanday: coastal feature near 'Tafts' [named from 'Kilnbarn', Norse *sker* reef].

Kilns o Brim-Noven Rousay: (perhaps Brimn-Oven?) in storm conditions sea spray blows over the cliffs and gives the impression of smoke coming from a grain-drying kiln [Norse *brim-gang* dashing surf, *ofn* furnace: (see 'Kilns o Rowamo', Harray)].

Kilns o Rowamo Harray: maps show only the head of a stream in this location, but the name suggests that in the distant past there were small lochs here which, in certain atmospheric conditions, would get covered in mist, giving the impression of smoking, grain-drying kilns (see placenames with the prefix 'sinn', especially 'Sinnisinkar').

Kilns o Skae Birsay: (see 'Skae').

Kiltyan Harray: location unknown [Norse *kelda-n* the well].

Kinabeen/ Kanabeen Sanday, Lopness: field name, (see 'Keengabeen').

King William's Hall Birsay: a large sea cave: there is no local tale to explain the name: [William III died in 1702: the naming of this cave must relate to a period immediately before when war broke out between Catholics and Protestants in Scotland and the suggestion is that some significant Orkney dignitary hid here to avoid capture].

King's Craig Papa Westray: a rocky point on the shore just south of Backaskaill: there is no cliff here [the 'king' element must relate to the surname 'King', long established in Westray and Papa Westray].

King's Hard Flotta: a rocky point on 'Stanger Head' where King George V landed on 9th July 1915 to inspect the troops stationed there.

Kingarly Rousay: a vanished croft in Sourin district named after the hill on which it stood [origin unknown].

Kingielang Hoy: a long stony hill ridge to the west of 'Chalmer's Hope' and travelling in a northwest-southwest direction [perhaps a scribal error for 'Keelylang'].

Kings Dale Firth: (see above).

Kingsdale Birsay, Southside: a fanciful name first recorded in the late 16th century, now vanished ['dale' = Norse *dý* marshland].

Kingshall Sanday: a cottar house near Garbo [a fanciful name, Scots *ha* cottage].

Kingshouse 1. Harray: fanciful name apparently changed from an original 'Mydgarth' to 'Kingshouse' sometime after the year 1500.

Kingshouse 2. Stromness, Ootertoon; Orphir; Hoy; Sandwick; South Ronaldsay, Burwick: [a fanciful name applied originally to a poor dwelling to give it status].

Kinloch Sanday: same house as 'Lettan No. 1' [a name suggested by a Highland lighthouse keeper based at 'Start Point' in the 1950s].

Kirbest Egilsay: a large farm [Norse *kirk* church, *ból-staðr* farm].

Kirbist 1. North Ronaldsay: (see Busta).

Kirbist 2. Westray, Kirbisttown: also in records referred to as 'Kirbuster' (see 'Kirbest' above).

Kirbister Orphir (see 'Kirbest'); Kirbister (Stromness bordering the parish of Sandwick); Kirbister (Walls, in the 'Longhope' area) 'Kirbuster, (a portion of 'Everbist' tunship, Stronsay) Kirbuster (Shapinsay, on the south side of the island in which the parish church is sited) Kirbuster, (Deerness, a former district in the northwest of the parish) Kirbuster (Birsay, well known because of the farmhouse which retained the old practice of having the fireplace in the middle of the floor: it is now a museum).

Kirfea Hill Rousay: [Norse, *kýr* cattle, *fjall* hill].

Kirk 1. Birsay: a vanished house beside the 'Burn o Lushan', it is said that there was formerly a chapel there.

Kirk 2. Orphir: marked on the 1813 Map of the Division of the Commonty of Orphir but it is not clear whether the reference is to the area near the 'Round Kirk' or the kirk which was built out of the stones of the original Round Kirk. The 'new kirk', (even the site) has vanished.

Kirk 3. South Ronaldsay: this name which predates 1600 lay in the Eastside district of South Ronaldsay but there is no record of any church there which represents a real puzzle.

Kirk and Kill Sanday: twin mounds, Westside, Northwall [a juxtaposition of Norse and Celtic names, Norse *kirkja* church, Gaelic *cill* church].

Kirk Geo 1. Birsay: tributary of the 'Hillside Burn' where an old chapel reputedly stood (for 'geo' see 'Geo' in Appendix).

Kirk Geo 2. Evie: near ruins of Peter's Kirk [Norse *gjá* ravine].

Kirk Noust Rousay: [Norse *naustr* a sheltered part of a beach where a boat might be secured in wintertime].

Kirk o Buggery Evie: a very unpleasant nickname (probably given by Protestants to Catholics) to this isolated chapel in the hills.

Kirk o How Sanday: alternative name for 'Kirk and Kill' [Norse *haugr* mound].

Kirk o Howe/Hoo Papa Westray: the ruins of a chapel which survived until the 1840s [Norse *haugr* mound].

Kirk o Norrisdale Evie: near 'Savedale' [origin of 'Norrisdale' unknown].

Kirk Sheed 1. Firth: [Old Scots *schedd* a piece of land distinctive in some way or other].

Kirk Sheed 2. Sanday, Elsness: field name, early 18th century (see above).

Kirk Swarfs Sanday: shoals east of the 'Inner Holm o Ire' [Norse *svarf* tumult, a reference to the roughness of the sea].

Kirk Taing 1. North Ronaldsay: just north of 'Dennis Ness' [a chapel is said to have existed here (see 'Kirk Taing' below)].

Kirk Taing 2. Sanday, Tresness: there is an old chapel site here [Norse *tangi* point of land].

Kirk Taing 3. Sanday: coastal feature, the famous 'Chapel o Cleat' stood close by [Norse *tangi* point of land].

Kirk Taing Ire, Sanday: there is an old chapel site here [Norse *tangi*, point of land].

Kirkabreck Rendall: (see 'Kirkbreck').

Kirkabuster Sanday: a farm mentioned in the Commissariot Record, of 1615; vanished, position unknown [Norse *kirkju ból-staðr* church farm].

Kirkasteethe Birsay: field name, 'Fea', Abune-the-Hill [Norse *kirkju-staðr* site of a chapel].

Kirkbanks Sanday: beach feature, Tresness, it lies near a former chapel.

Kirkbreck Holm: [Norse *kirkja* church, *brekka* slope].

Kirkgair St. Andrews: an old farm which lay near the 'Mill o Tankerness' and took its name from the path which led to the kirk [Norse *gata* path, *götur* paths (see 'Messigate')].

Kirkgate Rousay; Harray: [Norse *kirkju* church, *gata* path].

Kirkgeo Sanday: coastal feature [Norse *kirkja* church; there is an old chapel nearby].

Kirkha, Kirkhall Sanday: near Sanday Kirk Manse [Scots *ha* cottage].

Kirkhall Stronsay: east of 'Muckle Water' (no known association with a kirk).

Kirkholm/Curcum Birsay: in the Abune-the-Hill district [Norse *kirkja* church, *hólmr* island but not an island in this case. It seems to refer to an elevated piece of land in what was formerly a marshy area].

Kirkhoose Sanday: [former 'Poor House' beside Cross Kirk; now a store].

Kirkhouse 1. Deerness; Westray, (Skelwick district): there is no church in Skelwick today and there is no record of such: the name was used for farms established near churches but also for dwellings for the poor supported by the church.

Kirkhouse 2. Westray: near 'Newark' in the district of Skelwick [there is no 'kirk' near here: the reference must be to a vanished chapel].

Kirkie Hill South Ronaldsay: southeast of 'Widewall Bay' [origin of 'kirk' here perhaps same as above].

Kirkisetter Sanday: stood to the east of 'Skeeticauld', vanished [Norse *kirkju-setr* settlement near a church].

Kirkland o Tougar/Towagar North Ronaldsay: (see 'Towagar').

Kirkland of Orkeness North Ronaldsay: (see 'Orkeness').

Kirkley Sanday: field name near 'Viggar', Burness parish [Norse *kirkja* chapel, *hlíð* slope: there is no kirk or chapel here today (see 'Viggar')].

Kirkness Sandwick: a large peninsula which juts out into the north of the 'Harray Loch' [it was the site of an old chapel and it was from this 'ness' that the farm of 'Kirkness' was named].

Kirkquoy Harray: [Norse *kví* an enclosure, some of the produce of which was given to the church].

Kirkshed Orphir: (see 'Kirk').

Kirkton Shapinsay: nearby lay a late Norse medieval chapel the remains of which are now a scheduled monument: it lies between 'Kirkton' and 'Linton' farms.

Kirkuster/Curcasetter Sanday: a field name north of 'Parlgo': this placename suggests that the field was the site of a vanished chapel.

Kirkwall St. Ola: [Norse *kirkja* chapel, *vágr* bay: the chapel referred to is 'St. Olaf's Chapel', the remains of which, in the form of an arched gateway, can be seen in a narrow lane known as 'St. Olaf's Wynd'].

Kirn South Ronaldsay: [applies to the churning of the sea at coastal points in Grimness and Hoxa].

Kirn, The Birsay: on the coast (see above).

Kirn o the Rue North Ronaldsay: on the coast of 'Dennis Head', south of the house of 'Rue' [the name describes the churning of the sea here].

Kirn Stane Shapinsay: [on the east coast is a small rocky island around which the sea 'churns'].

Kirnie Geo Sanday: part of 'Whal Geo' [Norse *kirna* a churn, used frequently in Orkney placenames and refers to the churning of the sea].

Kirrie Millies Orphir: vanished, location unknown ['Kirrie' is a Scots girl's name and 'Millie' a surname found in Scotland: the placename suggests a poor dwelling occupied by a spinster].

Kirves Harray, Grimeston: a long field south of 'Langskaill' [origin unknown].

Kist, The South Ronaldsay: a box-like rock on the coast, marking the southern edge of 'Hoston Bay' [Norse *kista* a chest].

Kistaklett Sanday: a ridge of rocks, Lettan district [Norse *klettr* rock, *kista* a box or chest: compare 'Kist o Brure', a box shaped rock in Shetland].

Kistins Sanday: a former enclosure, Garbo, also known as 'The Toomal' [Norse *kista-n* the box (with English plural)].

Kitawee Birsay, Swannay: [Norse *keyta* foul water, Norse *kví* enclosure, 'wee' = quoy].

Kitbola Birsay, Southside: vanished farm, last recorded in 1727 [Norse *boeli* a night time secure area for cattle: (see below for 'kit' element)].

Kitchen Holm: (see above).

Kitchen o Brecks Deerness: [(see above for 'kitchen'), Norse *brekkur* slopes].

Kitchen Park Evie: [Norse *keyta* foul water, *tjörn* small stretch of water].

Kithuntlins Birsay: located on 'Kithuntlins Burn' [the house (no record of which exists) is said to be named after a strong woman who lived here: attempts have been made to interpret her name, for example by calling her 'Kit Huntly': she was in fact an ogress, her name shared at one time by Shetlanders on the island of Fetlar where she was called 'Keddhontla'. The name in translation means 'half cat, half dog', in other words a 'monster'!].

Kitilnekkid Evie: a house which stood above 'Broar' [the name literally means 'tickle naked' and most certainly refers to an occupant who used this phrase in some context or other and it became his/her nickname. When it came to naming the house, it was given his/her nickname! (compare 'Heathercowespunk' in Burray)].

Kitloch Walls: a small pool in the hill west of 'Wee Fea' [Norse *keyta* foul water, Scots 'loch' pool of water: (note that this a variation of 'kitchen' forms above)].

Kitta Taing South Walls: [local dialect *kitto* a kittiwake, Norse *tangi* a point of land].

Klaimer (see 'Claymer Road' and 'Clamer').

Klett Birsay: [Norse *klettr* rock but here specifying a particular rock e.g., for fishing].

Klett, The Rousay: an outlying rock on the most easterly point of 'Scockness' [Norse *klettr* rock].

Klett o Saythe Geo North Ronaldsay: a rock on the south side of 'Saythe Geo'.

Klettar /Cletter Papa Westray: rocks on the beach to the west side of the island [Norse *klettar* rocks].

Klettber Rousay: a noted fishing rock in 'The Leean' area [Norse *klettr* rock *berg* rock, a good example of a tautological placename, a few of which exist in Orkney (see Meery-Mawry)].

Klevowern Rousay: a small field on the farm of Corse near the shore [Norse *klif* a path down a steep incline, Norse *aurinn* the gravel].

Klimmer Sand (see 'Climmer Sand').

Kliv Geo Birsay: [Norse *klif* a path down to the shore].

Klogang o the Boons Sanday: an old name for the hill common of 'Stove' [Norse *klauf* cattle, Norse *ganga* to go about, Scots *boons* boundaries: the word 'klogang' is extended in meaning to 'familiar territory'].

Klondyke 1. Burray: named by some local person who sought his fortune in the gold rush to Klondike and returned to build a cottage!

Klondyke 2. Sanday: possibly a renaming of 'Little Cleat' after the famous goldrush.

Kloonaber Birsay: rocks below the Lighthouse on 'The Brough' [Norse *klungr* used metaphorically to describe rocks as for example in *klettar ok klungr*, crags and rocks, Norse *berg* rock].

Klucks Papa Stronsay: field name, south of 'Doocot' [origin uncertain unless it was a field given over to hens!].

Knap Knowes Rousay: a vanished house in Sourin area: a good example of a tautological placename [Norse *knappr* mound, Scots *knowe* mound (a house in the vicinity today is called 'Knapper')].

Knap o Bars/Knap o Girse Sanday: field name, Upperhouse, 'Orties' [Norse *knappr* knob/mound, Scots 'girse' = grass].

Knap o Girndish Sanday: Tresness ['knap' = mound as above, Norse *groen* green, *dýs* mound].

Knap o Howar Papa Westray: Neolithic farmstead dating from 4th millennium B.C. [Norse *haugr* mound, 'knap' as above].

Knap o Trowie Glen Hoy: [Norse *knappr* knob/mound (see 'Trowie Glen')].

Knapper (see above).

Knarston 1. Rousay: on the southeast coast of the island [Norse *Knarrar-staðr* an estate owned by *Knörr*].

Knarston 2. Harray: a district to the east of 'Dounby' (origin as above).

Knarston 3. St. Ola: part of 'Lingro' farm (origin as above).

Knee, The Rousay, Faraclett: [a prominent rock face which can be seen as the 'knee' of a seated person: a similar feature is found on the Westside, known as the 'Knee o Skaebrae'].

Knees, The Calf of Eday: two precipitous projecting points of land on the 'Gray Head' (see above).

Knitchen Rousay: at 227 metres high, 'Knitchen' is the highest hill in Rousay: the hill takes its name from the small loch near the summit [Norse *knutr* knob (referring to the hill), *tjörn* small loch].

Knitchen, Loch o Rousay: (see above).

Knockan North Ronaldsay: [Norwegian *knugg* a knob (or mound), the suffix suggests the definite article 'the mound'].

Knockday/Knockdry South Ronaldsay, St. Margarets Hope: a vanished house [Gaelic *cnoc* lump, *dý* marsh or *drit* filth, in other words a very poor piece of land].

Knockhall 1. Sanday [Gaelic *cnoc* lump ('Knockhall' in Stromness is a good illustration of this), Scots *ha* cottage].

Knockhall 2. South Ronaldsay: ['hall' = 'ha', a very simple cottage (see above)].

Knockhall 3. Stromness: (see above).

Knocking Stone Geo Evie: a recess in the cliff where rock suitable for making 'knocking stones' was mined. Masons would carve the rock into a concave shape and it was on this stone that the grain 'bere' (a type of barley) was pounded to make 'bere meal'.

Knogdale Birsay, Southside: vanished, position unknown [Norwegian dialect *knugg* a knob, hence a 'mound' as in Gaelic *cnoc*].

Knowe Stenness: a croft which stood to the southeast of 'Settersquoy' [Scots *knowe* knoll].

Knowe, The Sanday: Burness parish [Scots *knowe* knoll].

General information relating to 'Knowe' forms.

In their detailed study of features of archaeological interest in Orkney published in 1946, the Royal Commission on Ancient Monuments noted that there were 60 'knowes' in the islands; the writer has added 22 from other named sources, to bring the number up to 82.

The word 'knowe', meaning 'knoll', was introduced by the Scots and replaced the Norse word *haugr*, mound, a word not familiar to the Scots. The Norse word persisted in many cases and where there were distinctive mounds, the nearby settlement would be called How, Howan (meaning 'the mound') or Howar if there were two mounds in the vicinity. In some cases, it can be seen that a mound is described in both Norse and Scots, a good example being the Knowe o Aiverso in Papa Westray where 'knowe' is Scots, 'aiver' is Norse *álfar* 'elves' and the final 'o' represents Norse *haugr*! The reader will notice that many of the mounds listed below end in 'o' which letter represents Norse *haugr*.

It is not practical to list these mounds in detail and therefore the approach of the Royal Commission on Ancient Monuments is adopted and explanations of the name of the mounds are found in the general glossary.

Aiverso; Angerow; Backiskaill; Bain; Bakitaing; Bakkan Swarto; Bea; Bosquoy; Buckquoy; Burland; Merrigar; Burristae; Burrian; Coynear; Crue; Crustan; Cuean; Dale Birsay and Rousay; Cott; Cottorochan; Desso; Dishero; Enyan (The); Esco; Euro; Eversty; Flaws; Forsakelda; Gairso; Garroquoy; Gemashowe; Geoso; Goltsquoy; Gorn; Hamar; Hammar; Holland; Hooan/Howan; Hucklin; Hunclett; Ingacoup; Lairo; Lingro; Lingro; Links Park; Lyron; Makerhouse; Mayback; Midgarth; Moan; Nisthouse; Netherskaill; Newark; Onston; Queeancrusty; Queen o Howe; Ramsay; Redland; Ryo; Samilands; Saverough; Scartan/Hillhead; Scogar; Scorn; Scottie; Skulzie; Smirrus; Steeringlo; Stenso; Sunloft; Smersso; Trinnawin; Trotty; Wheatlaws; Yarrow; Yesco; Yonbell.

Knowes, The Sanday: vanished [Scots *knowe* knoll].

Knows Evie: [Scots *knowe* knoll].

Knucker Hill Westray: [related to Norse *knykill*, Shetland *knugel* a lump].

Knugdale/Knokdale Westray, Dykeside: on 'Knucker Hill' (above).

Koipitten, Kirn o Birsay: [Norse *kirna* a churn referring to the swirling of the sea here, *pytt-inn* the pool, 'koi' element = Norse *kví* enclosure].

Koldeross Rousay: [Norse *kaldr* cold, Norse *rass* arse, i.e., it is too uncomfortable for an angler to sit down (see 'Sockersie')].

Kongie Geo Rousay: an inlet on 'Saviskaill Head' [the word 'kongie' is used in the North Isles to describe a rounded boulder, a version of Norwegian *kongle* the cone of a fir tree (see other examples of the use of this word in 'Conglibist' North Ronaldsay and 'Congie' Sanday)].

Koogro Rousay: [Norse *kví* enclosure, *gröf* stream which in Orkney is usually a slow running stream in a marsh: (compare 'Spurdagro', Birsay)].

Korkquoy Westray: (see 'Curquoy').

Kornslap Sanday: ridge of land, Park district [English 'corn', Scots *slap* gate].

Kothero Stronsay, Holland: field name [origin of first element doubtful (see 'Caither Lea') final element 'o' = Norse *haugr* mound].

Kowaquoy Rousay: [Norse *kua-kví* cattle enclosure].

Koyes, Brae o Birsay, Howe: [Norse *kví* enclosure (with English plural)].

Kraa-tooies Papa Westray: 40 burial mounds on slopes of 'North Hill' and 'Errival' [Norse *kró* enclosure, *púfa* heap or mound (with English plural)].

Kraffen Stromness: [Norse *kró* enclosure, *fen* marsh].

Krapin/Crapin Sanday: now a field name north of 'Thrave' [Norse *kró* enclosure, English 'pen': there was a house 'Cra Pen' in Rendall].

Krassy Waal Rousay: [possibly 'krassy' = 'grassy' but unlikely, dialect 'waal' = well].

Kribbany Rousay: coastal feature: a fishing rock on the 'Leean', on the coast of 'Saviskaill Bay' [see 'Kripady-Kroo' (below) for an attempted explanation].

Kringlamaya/Cringamaya North Ronaldsay: a stretch of sandy beach [Norse *kringla* a circular feature, *melr* sand: it is not clear what the circular feature refers to].

Kringlaquoy, Waal o Birsay, Marwick: [Norse *kringla* a circle used frequently to describe damp places in the landscape, 'waal' = 'well'].

Kringlo 1. Birsay: Abune-the-Hill district [a deep hole (see above)].

Kringlo 2. Birsay: between the 'Burn o Swartageo' and 'Gyron' (see above).

Kringlo 3. Stenness: a damp area in a field referred to as 'The Meadow o Kringlo' [Norse *kringla* a circle].

Kringlo, The Wyre: a circular feature near the coast: no other information (see above).

Kringlo, Willie Work's Rousay: a feature in the burn near 'Breval': [Willie Work lived nearby in the middle of the 19th century'].

Kripady-Kroo Birsay: a spring near the high cliffs on the Birsay/Evie border [Norwegian *krubbutt* narrow, Norse *dý* marsh, *kró* enclosure: it is impossible to untangle the relationship between these three elements].

Kroddy Rousay: in lower 'Leean' (see 'Cruaday' for derivation).

Kromerandeem Sanday: (see 'Crue Maaron Deme').

Kru Sanday: coastal feature, 'The Riv' [this feature is in fact a small reef and the dialect word *kru*, Norse *kró* pen, must refer to an old beach enclosure].

Kruik/Crook Sanday: beach near 'Hucklinsower' [Norse *krókr* bend or curve, a reference to the shape of the beach].

Kruikalis Sanday: field name near 'Marygarth' [probably 'crooked leys', Scots *leys* unploughed land].

Krus Sanday: corner of a field near 'Hellihow' [Norse *kró* pen (with English plural)].

Kuikobba South Ronaldsay: a farm, position unknown: mentioned in a document in the Norse language in 1329 [Norse *kví* enclosure, 'kobba' suggests a personal name, perhaps a diminutive of *Jakoba*].

Kuim Birsay: a large rock lying off the south coast of the 'Brough' [origin unknown].

Kuithe Oil Rock Birsay: a fishing rock off the coast [Ork. dialect 'cuithe' a young saithe: the significance of 'oil' here cannot be explained].

Kuive Rousay: (see 'Kyevidi' below).

Kunquoy Rousay: a field on 'Saviskaill' [Norse *kúna-kví* cattle enclosure].

Kuppa Stronsay: a field at the beach on 'Rothiesholm' [Norse *koppr* hollow].

Kuppa Taing Rousay, Scockness: ['kuppa' as above, Norse *tangi* point of land].

Kuppielow Birsay, Marwick: [Norse *koppr* hollow, *lón* marsh].

Kurkister/Kirkuster/Curcasetter Sanday: a field name: north of 'Parlgo' [Norse *kirkju-setr* the placename indicates the site of a vanished chapel].

Kusigar Gairsay: [Norse *kussi* bullock, *garðr* enclosure].

Kuters Mire North Ronaldsay: [Norse *keytar(s)* stinking water = mire, Norse *mýrr* marsh: 'keytar' is the genitive of 'keyta' and an English genitive has been added].

Kuthies Birsay, Fea: Abune-the-Hill district [origin unknown].

Kuthina Geo Birsay: [Norse *kóð* the fry of trout but used in Orkney as the young of saithe, *gjá* sea inlet].

Kuthiny Klett Rousay: [Norse *kóðna* (of the saithe), *klettr* rock, i.e., a good location to fish for 'cuithes'].

Kuttivatigar North Ronaldsay: a grassy hollow near 'Westness' [Norse *kot* dwelling, *vatn* loch, *garðr* enclosure: it seems that at one time the hollow contained a small loch].

Kweevnie Geos Papa Westray: [Norse *kvínar* enclosures, *gjá* sea inlet].

Kyevidi Rousay: [a complete corruption of Norse *djúp* deep, *dý* marsh (see 'Jubaday' forms)].

L

Lace Skerry South Ronaldsay: [Norwegian *fles* a skerry: in Orkney the initial 'f' is normally dropped].

Lade o Swingerday Birsay: a valley on 'Marwick Head' [Norse *leid* a track, *svína-dý* pig marsh].

Lady Sanday: one of the three original parish divisions of Sanday: the parish takes its name from the 'Lady Kirk' (see below).

Lady Kirk 1. Sanday: built on a prehistoric site: the valuable pre-Reformation communion cup of this church still exists and is in regular use.

Lady Kirk 2. Stronsay: parish kirk near 'The Bay' (a farm).

Laetties Sanday, Breckan: field name [Norse *hluti* share/division (with English plural)].

Laftlie Point South Ronaldsay, Herston: [Norse *lopta* to lift used in Shetland in the sense 'rising up'].

Laga Evie: [it is difficult to find any Norse word which directly explains this placename other than to say it is associated with water as in the Shetland placename 'Laga Brune' a well north of 'Ladie' in Yell: the word is related to English 'lake' (see 'Laketh' Birsay)].

Lair Geo Rousay: [Norse *leirr* clay].

Laird's Geo Sanday: coastal feature, Laminess [Scots *laird* landholder, Norse *gjá* ravine: the significance of 'laird' here is unknown].

Laird's Square Sanday, Brabuster: field name.

Lairo Shapinsay; Rousay: the latter is called after the nearby chambered cairn (Norse *haugr*) [this cairn is built of stone so the explanation cannot be Norse *leirr-haugr* clay mound, but rather *hlíðar-haugr* the mound on the edge of a slope].

Laith Sandwick: [Norse *hlíð* slope].

Laits o Hillya Stronsay: on the southwest corner of 'Rothiesholm' [origin unknown].

Laits o Lambness Stronsay: high ground at the point of 'Lamb Head' [origin unknown].

Lakequoy Westray, Cleatown; St. Andrews: (see 'Laga').

Lakequoy, Skerries o St. Andrews [Norse *sker* reef].

Laketh Birsay, Northside: (see 'Laga': the suffix 'th' indicates a neuter gender).

Lally South Ronaldsay: [Norse *hlað* cairn, *hlíð* slope].

Lamaness Sanday: Burness parish [Norse *lamb* lamb, *nes* a point of land].

Lamaness Firth stretch of sea between Sanday and Calf of Eday (now 'Lashy Sound').

Lamaquoy 1. Harray: [Norse *lamb* lamb, *kví* enclosure].

Lamaquoy 2. Orphir: north of 'The Bu' (see above).

Lamb Bay Stronsay.

Lamb Cot Sanday: part of the bay immediately below 'Measer'.

Lamb Head Stronsay.

Lamb Holm Holm: an island off the parish of Holm.

Lamba Ness Stronsay: the southeast point.

Lamesquoy Firth, Binscarth: (see above: with English plural).

Lamiger Rousay: [Norse *garðr* farm or merely enclosure].

Laminess Sanday: a group of six houses in the Laminess, Cross parish.

Laminess/Lamba Ness Sanday: coastal feature, there is a mound here and tradition speaks of a chapel [Norse *lamb* lamb, *nes* point of land].

Lamira Firth, Binscarth: [Norse *lamb* lamb, *mýrr* moorland].

Lammer Geo, The North Ronaldsay: [Norse *hlað-hamarr* a natural rock jetty, usually written *hlað-berg*].

Lampal Sound Sanday, Foulan: [Norse *hlamma* to thud (used here of the waves), 'pal' may be a corruption of *baa* or *ball* = Norse *boði* a common word for a shoal].

Landers Sanday, Elsness: field names, early 18th century [Norse *lendur*, lands or estates (with additional English plural)].

Landward Ley North Ronaldsay: [landward = inland, Scots *ley* meadow].

Landward Taing Sanday: coastal feature, Ire (see 'Langware') [Norse *tangi* point of land].

Lang Geo Hoy; Sanday, Ire: [Norse *langr* long, Norse *gjá* ravine].

Lang Ridden Shapinsay: a point of rock west of Balfour village [possibly a corruption of 'riggan' from Norse *hryggr* a ridge: (see 'Point of Ridden' Egilsay and 'Long Rigging' Auskerry)].

Lang Sand Sanday, Newark: field name [long (stretch of) sand].

Lang Stein St. Ola, Kirkwall: the bridge over the 'Burn o Pabdale', hence 'Bridge Street': a long stone resting on pillars, medieval style, is now obscured, or perhaps removed.

Lang Taing Sanday: coastal feature, 'Rusness' and 'Sty Wick' [Norse *tangi* point of land].

Langabar Holm; Flotta: [Norse *langr* long, *berg* rock].

Langadee Sandwick: a long narrow hollow, south of 'Roundadee' [Norse *dý* marsh)].

Langadie Birsay, Southside: near 'Breck' [Norse *langr* long, *dý* marsh].

Langadrum/Longatrim Birsay, Southside: vanished [Norse *langr* long, *þruma* outskirts].

Langaland Sandwick: a field below 'Appieteen' [Norse *langr* long, *land* field etc.].

Langalour Firth: [Norse *langr* long, *ló(n)* marsh: in plural form possibly *lóar* marshes].

Langamay Stronsay: beach near Housebay [Norse *langr* long, *melr* sand].

Langamay/Langomay, Sanday, Northwall: vanished but the site of this house remains [Norse *langr* long, *melr* sand].

Langamow Harray: [Norse *langr* long, *mór* moorland].

Langanagrana Birsay: coastal name [the 'gran' element suggests 'a green place', Norse *graena*].

Langbanks Sanday: coastal feature ['long banks'].

Langespells Sanday, Hellihow: field name [Norse *langr* long, Orkney 'spell' or 'speld' is frequently used to describe fields (see 'Sava Speldo')].

Langie Orphir: [Norse *langr* long: it seems that this adjective has lost its noun (see 'Gamla' for another instance)].

Langie Fea Hoy: [Norse *langr* long, *fjall* hill].

Langie Geo Sanday: coastal feature (see 'Lang' Geo').

Langigar Firth: [Norse *langr* long, *garðr* enclosed area].

Langmire North Ronaldsay; Sanday: [Norse *langr* long, *mýrr* moorland].

Langskaill Birsay, Marwick, Boardhouse area, vanished; Stromness, Quholm; Westray, Skelwick; St. Andrews, Sanday, Burness, vanished, on the land of 'Northskaill', buried under sand!; The Ness, Burness, derelict; Gairsay, the home of Svein Asleifsson; Rousay, Wasbister; Harray, Grimeston: [Norse *skáli* a fine building, a long house].

Langtas 1. Sanday: formerly a tunship in the Newark area, also known as 'The Linties' [Norse *langr* long, Norse *teigr* small field (with English plural)].

Langtas 2. Sanday: formerly a tunship, 'Everbist' (see above).

Langware Ley North Ronaldsay: the most northerly point of 'Seal Skerry' [Norse *langr* long, Scots *ware* seaweed: (see 'The Leys o Coorse')].

Langware Taing Sanday: coastal feature, 'Start' [Scots *lang* long, Scots *ware* seaweed].

Langwell Orphir: [Norse *langr* long, fjall hill].

Lanquoy Westray, Broughton: [Norse *land* ground/estate, *kví* enclosure].

Lanta Sanday, Stove: field name [Norse *langr* long, *teigr* small field].

Lantie Gate, The Sanday: an old track west of 'Scar' [Norse *gata* path: (for 'lantie' see above)].

Lanties Sanday, Rue: field name (see 'Langtas').

Lapland Birsay: a ruin above 'Netherbigging' in 'Greeny' [origin unknown].

Lash, The 1. Graemsay: (see below).

Lash, The 2. Orphir: (see 'Lashy Sound').

Lashy Sound stretch of water between Sanday and the Calf of Eday [Norse *fles* skerry: the initial 'f' is lost in many Orkney placenames].

Lashy Taing Calf of Eday: (see above).

Latan Stronsay: a point on the east side of 'Rothiesholm' [Norse *láttr-inn* the place where seals lie].

Latha Skerry Birsay, Marwick Head: [seems to have been named from 'Lath-abreck' above].

Lathabreck Birsay: hilly ground near top of 'Marwick Head' [Norse *leðja* mud or ooze, *brekka* slope].

Lavacroon Orphir: a mound [Norse *kró-in* the enclosure: the first element 'lava' is unknown].

Lavey Sound North Fara: a narrow, shallow stretch of water between 'Holm of North Fara' and Fara [origin unknown].

Laxhow Harray: [Norse *haugr* mound: the origin of the first element 'lax' is unknown].

Laxigar Hunda: on the east side of Hunda, Burray [Norse *lax* salmon, *garðr* fence, in other words a salmon trap].

Lay Taing South Ronaldsay: [Norse *tangi* a point of land, *leggja* to lie i.e., where seals lie].

Layburn Rendall: [seemingly named after a vessel 'Leyburn' from a place of that name in Yorkshire: the former name of this croft was 'Goltsquoy'].

Layes, The Sanday, Elsness: field names, early 18th century [Scots *lays* unploughed land under grass].

Layhammer Sanday: a sea inlet and ridge of rocks at 'Otterswick Bay' near 'Seater' [Norse *hlað* load, *hamarr* rock].

Lea/Lie Birsay: alternative name 'West Plank' [Norse *hlíð* slope].

Lea Shun Stronsay: a loch close to beach near Holland [Norse *hlið* passageway (between the loch and 'Sand of Crook')].

Leabreck Birsay, Southside: [Scots *breck* poor quality land which became part of 'Lea/Lee' above after the Division of the Commonty].

Leadberry Eynhallow: a rock in east of the island [Norse *hlað-berg* literally load rock, a natural pier for loading and unloading goods, animals etc.].

Leadmine Sanday: lies to the northeast of 'Leavisgarth', this lead mine was worked in the 1880s.

Leafea Stromness: [Norse *hlíð* slope, *fjall* hill].

Leager Stromness, Ootertoon: vanished [Norse *hlíð* slope, *garðr* farm].

Lealand Sanday: origin uncertain (see 'Leyland').

Lean Westray, Dykeside: [Norse *hlíð-in* the slope].

Leaquoy 1. Birsay, Marwick; North Fara; Shapinsay; Stronsay: [Norse *hlíð* slope, *kví* enclosure].

Leaquoy 2. Sanday: Cross parish, formerly 'Fieldquoy' and 'Botany Bay': the present name is not old.

Leary/Learaquoy Birsay, Marwick: [Norse *leara* a field with clay soil, *kví* enclosure].

Leata/Leatan Sanday: [almost certainly an older form of 'The Lettan'].

Leavisgarth Sanday: [Norse personal name *Leif*, Norse *garðr* farm].

Leavo Loch Sanday: a small loch on the narrow neck of land which joins the 'Ness of Brough' to the rest of Cross parish [origin unknown].

Lecky Skerry Sanday: a reef to the south of 'Kettletoft' [Norse *sker* reef: origin of 'lecky' element unknown].

Ledya Brae Harray: [Norse *leið-(völlr)* place where a 'leet' was held].

Lee Sandwick; Rousay; Stromness: [Norse *hlíð* slope].

Lee/West Plank Birsay, Southside: (see 'Lea').

Lee Hammer Rousay: rocks at beach below 'Tratland' [Norse *hlíð* slope, *hamarr* rock].

Lee Hellia Evie: flat sloping rocks off the coast of the 'Knowe o Ryo' [Norse *hlíð* slope, *hella* flat rocks].

Lee o Copinsay Copinsay: sheer rock faces on the east of the island [Norse *hlíð* slope (excessive in this case)].

Leean 1. North Ronaldsay: a small knoll southeast of 'Westness' [Norse *hlíð-in* the slope].

Leean 2. Westray: east of the 'Bay of Noup' [Norse *hlíð-in* the slope].

Leean, The Rousay: steep sloping land between 'Sourin' and 'Wasbister' [Norse *hlíð-in* the slope].

Leeans, The Rendall: [Norse *hlíð-in* the slope (with English plural): position unknown but probably in the area of 'Ayrean'].

Leeants o Oycelee Birsay, Swannay: [Norse *hlíð-in* the slope (with English plural): note the intrusive 't' common in Birsay placenames, Norse *óss-hlíð* stream mouth slope].

Leeatangie North Ronaldsay: a fishing rock [Norse *hlíð* slope, *tangi* point of land].

Leeber Birsay: a pillared rock formation on the north side of 'Saed Geo' [Norse *hlíð* slope, excessive in this case (compare 'Lee o Copinsay'), *berg* rock].

Leegliv Birsay: a cleft in the rocks on the coast [Norse *hlíð-in* the slope, *klif* a path down a steep slope].

Leeng Burn Rousay: [Norse *hlíð-in* the slope: a gentle slope in this case].

Leeniesdale Hill Eday: [up until 1841 there was a Lennie family in 'Stenoquoy': to the west of Stenoquoy was 'Lenniesdale Hill'].

Leeon Firth: a pronounced slope to the west of the village of 'Finstown' and formerly used by children sledging [Norse *hlíð-in* the slope].

Leesburn Westray, Broughton: on the southeast coast of the 'Bay o Pierowall' [Norse *(f)les* a flat, rocky point of land, *borg-inn* the rock].

Leeshany Rousay: sloping land on 'Faraclett' [Norse *hlíð* slope, *tjörn* small loch].

Leeskro Birsay: a rock face on 'The Brough' sloping down to the sea [Norse *hlíð* slope, *skriða* a land slip].

Leian Sanday, Elsness: field name, early 18th century [Norse *hlíð-in* the slope].

Leigh Firth: [unknown position].

Leisburn Firth, Burness: (see 'Leesburn' above).

Leith 1. Burray: first recorded in 1627 (see below).

Leith 2. Evie/Rendall: near 'Cot-on-Hill' [Norse *hlíð* slope].

Lenady St. Andrews: a moor in Tankerness [Celtic *linne* a pool, *dý* a marsh].

Lenahowe/Linnahowe Sandwick: south of 'Stockan' [Celtic *linne* a pool, Norse *haugr* mound, a reference to an elevated area near the farm called 'The Castle'].

Lenay, Point o Stronsay: on the south side of 'Mill Bay' [Norse *hlíð-in* the slope].

Lenders Dale Hoy: [Norse *lenda* land or fields, *dalr* valley].

Lengmire Westray, Kirbistown: [Norse *langr* long, *mýrr* moor].

Lensmire North Ronaldsay: [Celtic *linne* a pool, *mýrr* moor].

Lensty Flotta: [Celtic *linne* a pool, Norse *stía* a sty].

Lenswick North Ronaldsay: (see 'Lindswick').

Leon Harray: [Norse *hlíð-in* the slope].

Leoquoy South Ronaldsay: (see 'Leaquoy' forms).

Lerchan Westray: formerly an ale house, now a field name, 'Cleat' (see 'Lergin').

Lerely Sandwick: [Norse *leir* clay, *hlíð* slope].

Lergin Sanday: on 'Northskaill' land [Norse *leir* clay, *tjörn* pool].

Lermond's Geo Sanday: coastal feature, Ire [surname 'Learmonth', Norse *gjá* ravine].

Lerquoy Stromness; Orphir; Rousay; Rendall, (on the land of 'Upper Ellibister'): [Norse *leir* clay soil, *kví* enclosure].

Leslie's Ditch Evie: on glebe land [dug during the ministry of Reverend Leslie].

Lesshammer northwest of Eday [Norse *(f)less* a reef, *hamarr* rock].

Lettaly Firth: originally 'Clettaly' [Norse *klaet* some kind of built structure, *hlíð* slope].

Lettan Sanday: district in Northwall, originally a row of unnamed cottar houses [Norse *hlutr-inn* the allotment, share].

Lettan, The Sanday: now a field name, 'Links o Warsetter'; earlier 'Leata' and 'Leatan' [Norse *hlutr-inn* the allotment, share].

Letties Sanday, Northskaill: field name (see 'Laetties').

Leuan Rendall: coastal feature near 'Skaill' [Norse *hlíð-in* the slope].

Leval Flotta: [apparently named after a town in northern France or the surname: related perhaps to Napoleonic prisoners of war? Somewhere around Scapa Flow was a likely place for internment].

Leverahall Stronsay: vanished house recorded in 1735 [perhaps the Scots surname 'Leverick', Scots *ha'* cottage].

Ley North Ronaldsay: (see below).

Leyan Harray: (see 'Lean').

Leygarth Sanday: a farm mentioned in the 1841 Census [origin of 'ley' here uncertain: Norse *garðr* farm (compare 'Leager')].

Leyland Sanday: originally 'Lerland' [Norse *leir* clay, Norse *land* land].

Leyni Geo South Ronaldsay: [Norse *hleinn* a rock projecting like a pier into the sea].

Leys Sanday, Beafield: field name [Scots *lays* arable land under grass].

Leys, The Wyre, Rusness: a field [English 'ley' an arable field under grass].

Leys o Coorse North Ronaldsay: [Norwegian *laegja* a lair: deep channels where lobster creels can be set (see 'Coorse')].

Leys o the Green Skerry North Ronaldsay: (see 'Ley o Coorse' above).

Lian Birsay, Northside: (see 'Leon').

Liberness Birsay: coastal feature, position unknown [origin uncertain].

Libuster Rousay: vanished: location unknown but probably on what is now the land of 'Langskaill' [Norse *hlíð* slope, *ból-staðr* farm].

Lickers Gate Stronsay, Airy: field name [Norse *gata* path (to a well in this case?): origin of 'lickers' uncertain: Norse *laekr* is a stream].

Lidda St. Andrews [Celtic *lod* pool, Norse *dý* a marsh].

Liddell/Luddale South Ronaldsay: [doubtful origin: perhaps related to Norse *loðinn* shaggy but with the sense 'coarse grass', dale= *dý* marsh or moorland].

Liddie, Point o the St. Andrews: (see 'Lidda' above).

Lidyoes Rousay: submerged rocks off Garsnigo, 'Faraclett' ['yoes' element probably represents 'geos': origin of 'lid' here uncertain].

Liensquoy Birsay, Northside: an enclosure attached to 'Lian' (see above).

Lighthouse Birsay, Southside: near 'Glower' (see below).

Lighthouse Geo Sanday: near 'The Riv' ['lighthouse' was applied in Orkney to parts of the coast used as a fishing mark: Norse *gjá* ravine].

Lily Skerry Sanday: coastal feature [Norse *leir-hlíð* clay slope, Norse *sker* reef].

Limbo South Ronaldsay: [the borderland of Hell! Pejorative name for this simple (turf?) cottage, (compare 'Hell' and 'Purgatory' elsewhere)].

Lime Banks South Ronaldsay, Grimness: [so called because of calcareous secretions on the rocks here].

Lime Geo Evie: southeast of 'Aikerness' (see 'Lime Banks' above).

Lime Kiln South Ronaldsay: south of 'Hoxa', where peat was used as the fuel.

Limmers Burn Rousay: a small stream near 'Sacquoy', the extreme north point of Rousay (see below).

Limra Firth: Bridgend, between 'Bridgend' and 'Nabban' [Norse *ljómi* a light, in this case a reference to the flickering light sometimes seen in marshland, i.e., Will o the Wisp: recorded in Birsay as 'limro'].

Linahow Sandwick: [Celtic *linne* pool, Norse *haugr* mound].

Lincro, Geo of Westray: [Celtic *linne* pool, Norse *kró* enclosure].

Linda 1. Flotta: (both this and the above are close together) [Celtic *linne* pool, Norse *dý* marsh].

Linda 2. Harray: southeast of 'Nisthouse' [see 'Pow o Linda' which confirms origin of 'lin' element as Celtic, 'pow' = Scots 'pool' as in 'Linda' (above)].

Linda 3. Sandwick: (as above).

Lindagoe South Ronaldsay: [Celtic *linne* pool, Norse *dý* marsh, *gall* marsh].

Lindamire Sanday: field name; now the site of 'Quivals Garage' (see 'Linda' above) [Norse *mýrr* moorland].

Linday Geo Sanday: coastal feature [(see 'Lindamire'), Norse *gjá* geo].

Lindisbreck Evie: location unknown [Celtic *linne* pool, Norse *brekka* slope].

Lindrake Evie: [Celtic *linne* pool: origin of 'drake' element unknown].

Lindswick/Lenswick North Ronaldsay: [Celtic *linne* pool, Norse *vík* bay].

Linegar South Ronaldsay, Hoxa: now a ruin [Norse *hlíð-in* the slope, *garðr* enclosure].

Ling Holm Hoy: [Norse *lyng* heather, *hólmr* island].

Ling Ness Rousay: (see above).

Linga Fiold Sandwick: [Norse *lyng* heather, *fjall* hill].

Linga Stronsay: an island [Norse *lyng* heather, *ey* island].

Lingall Flotta: [metaphorical use of Norse *gall*, English 'gall' in the sense of 'bitter', 'sour' land: (see 'Geo' in Appendix)].

Lingavi Geo Shapinsay: a small bay on the east coast of the island [Norse *hlíð-in* the slope, origin of 'gavi' element unknown, *gjá* ravine].

Lingawheen Harray: [Norse *lyng* heather, *kví-n* the enclosure].

Lingklett Brae Westray: on 'Testaquoy' (see 'Linklett' under 'Cleat' in Appendix).

Lingmira Stromness: [Norse *lyng* heather, *mýrr* moor].

Lingo 1. Flotta: on 'Kirk Bay' (see 'Lingall').

Lingo 2. Orphir: east of 'Buxa' (see 'Lingall').

Lingro 1. Birsay, Abune-the-Hill: built by family evicted from 'Lingro' in Swannay (see below).

Lingro 2. St. Ola; Rousay; Shapinsay; Birsay, Swannay: [Celtic *linne* pool, Norse *gröf* a stream which has embedded itself].

Lings, The Stronsay, Airy: field name [no doubt a form of Scots *links*, a sandy shoreline].

Linkataing Eday: a prominent point of land on the west coast with a well in it: [Norse *lyng* heather, Norse *tangi* point].

Linklater 1. Sandwick: [*klettar*, the plural form of *klett*, is shown here (see Appendix under 'Cleat' for origin)].

Linklater 2. South Ronaldsay: (see above).

Linklet 1. Deerness: field on 'Hall of Brecks' ('Mirwick' is part of the same field) [Celtic *linne* pool, (for 'klet' element see 'Cleat' in Appendix)].

Linklet 2. Deerness: field on 'Kitchen of Brecks', the 'Well of Hammar' is on same field [Celtic *linne* pool, (for 'klet' element see 'Cleat' in Appendix)].

Linklet North Ronaldsay: (see above).

Linkletten Brae Birsay: between 'Burn of Kerse' and 'Glims Moss' [in this case the definite article provides a suffix, hence *klett-inn* (see 'Cleat' in Appendix)].

Links of Aikerness Evie: (see above).

Links Park Stronsay: west of 'Housebay' (see above).

Links Westray, Pierowall, Dykeside, Rackwick; Sanday: (see above).

Links, The Birsay; North Ronaldsay: (see above).

Linkses Sanday: field name near 'Ortie' [Scots *links* the additional 's' is puzzling, perhaps a contraction of 'Linkshoose'?].

Linkshoose/Linksie Sanday, Tresness: field name [Scots *links* a stretch of undulating coastal sand].

Linksness Stronsay; St. Andrews: [Scots *links* coastal sand flats or dunes].

Linkwell Stenness: to east of the Stenness Hotel [Celtic *linne* pool, the 'kvell' element is probably a corruption of Norse *kelda* well (the field on which the present Stenness Hotel is located was called 'Lundagoe')].

Linna Harray: [Celtic *linne* pool, the final 'a' is probably Norse *á* stream].

Linnabreck Birsay, Ravie Hill, Marwick, Beaquoy; Stronsay: [Celtic *linne* pool, Norse *brekka* slope].

Linnadale Orphir: [Celtic *linne* pool, Norse *dý* marsh].

Linney North Ronaldsay: [Celtic *linne* pool, Norse *á* water].

Linnieth Harray: [Celtic *linne* pool: the final 'th' represents the orthography of the Orkney form of the Norse neuter definite article. This shows that in the Norn language local people accepted *linne* as a Norse word (see 'Ayrean', Evie, for another example)].

Lint Brae Orphir: [cotton grass was seen as 'lint' (see 'Kethisgeo')].

Lint Pows South Ronaldsay: [lint = linen, pow = pool: these were pools for soaking flax when it was grown in the islands].

Linta Sanday: a farm in the 17th century Commissariot Record [identity uncertain: perhaps the same as 'The Linties'].

Lintie Stronsay: east of the 'Loch of Matpow' (see below).

Linties, The Sanday: an alternative form of 'Langtas', near Newark.

Lint-lus North Ronaldsay: [flax, Norse *(f)lói* marsh].

Linton Shapinsay: [Celtic *linne* pool, Norse *tún* home (field)].

Linylaga Firth: in the Burness/Quatquoy area [Norse Norse *hlið-inn* the slope (see 'Laga' for second element)].

Lippa Burray: a sand bar between Burray and South Ronaldsay in the entrance to 'Water Sound' [Norse *hlið* passageway, *boði* reef].

Liscups Firth: above Redland [Norse *koppr* hollow (with English plural): origin of 'lis' unknown].

Lithan Skerry Birsay: a reef between 'Sae Geo' and 'Fay Geo' [Norse *hlið-inn* the slope, which must refer to the cliff to the east].

Lithy Birsay: a narrow channel through which boats can pass between the south side of the 'Brough o Birsay' and a shoal [Norse *hlið* a passageway].

Little Ber Sanday: coastal feature, Lady parish [Norse *berg* rock].

Little Geo (see 'Peedie Geo').

Little Less Papa Westray: one of two shallow adjacent rock features between Papa Westray and the Holm of Papa Westray, the other rock feature being 'Big Less' [Norse *fles* a reef: note that in the case of *fles* the initial 'f' is always missing in dialect].

Little Linga Stronsay: an island off the northwest tip of the island [Norse *lyng* heather, *ey* island, *lítill* small].

Little Seatter Sanday: Cross parish, vanished: it stood near 'Boloquoy' (see 'Seater').

Little Water Stronsay: a loch near Kirbister, there is a similar placename in Rousay [Norse *lítill* small, *vatn* loch].

Lity Well North Ronaldsay: [Norse *lita* to dye: a well where yarn can be dyed].

Livaness Shapinsay: southeast of 'Elwick Bank' spelt in many different ways [suggests Norse *hlíf* shelter, i.e., providing a shelter from the west wind].

Livera Tongue Evie: east of the 'Knowe o Ryo' [the OS surveyor in the late 19th century says that the name derives from a kind of seaweed found on the flattish rocks here: presumably a red seaweed].

Loadberry Shapinsay: [Norse *hlað-berg* a rock where goods can be loaded/unloaded].

Loan, The 1. Birsay: northeast of 'Greeny Hill' [Celtic *lòn* marshland].

Loan, The 2. Stromness: a marshy area northwest of the parish [Celtic *lòn* marshland].

Loany, Lonnie Sanday: Cross parish, vanished [Celtic *lòn* marshland].

Loba Birsay, Muce, Sabiston: [Norwegian (Nynorsk) *lodda* damp depression].

Loba, The Harray: [Norwegian (Nynorsk) *lodda* damp depression].

Lobady Birsay, Dirkadale: [Norwegian (Nynorsk) *lodda* damp depression, *dý* marsh or moor].

Lobath Evie: high ground west of 'Burn o Millhouse' (same as above?).

Lobban Harray: [marshy area before it was drained: site of Dounby School (see 'Lobba' above)].

Lober Rock South Ronaldsay, Hoxa: natural rock jetty [Norse *hlað-berg* a rock where goods can be loaded/unloaded].

Lobust, The Rousay: rock pillar [origin unknown].

Loch Aber Sanday: [Gaelic *eabar* mud, puddle; Irish *abar* marshy land: Orkney dialect *iper*, midden ooze: the loch is now completely drained].

Loch o Baseley Sanday: Lady parish (see 'Bazlie' east of 'Silverhall').

Loch o Bludgeon Sanday: now drained; it stood on 'Hermisgarth' land near Howland Road [Norse *bleyta* marsh, Norse *tjörn* lake].

Loch o Brockan Rendall: (see 'Brockan').

Loch o Gin Harray: [Norse *tjörn* small pool].

Loch o Grutchen North Ronaldsay: [Norse *grjót* stony, *tjörn* small loch].

Loch o Hyan North Ronaldsay: a small loch near the old site of 'Hayan'.

Loch o Matpow Stronsay: near 'Errigar' (see 'Matpow').

Loch o Roo Sanday: (see 'Roos Loch').

Loch o Skjaiver/Skivar North Ronaldsay: on 'Dennis Head' [origin unknown].

Loch o the Riv Sanday: (see 'Riv, The').

Loch o Vastray Evie: east of the 'Hill o Swarmo' (see 'Vastray').

Loch Park Sanday, Scar: field name [there was at one time a loch in this field].

Lochmailing South Ronaldsay: [Scots *mailing* a tenanted farm].

Lochs o Sketchan Evie: two small lochs on the northwest coast of Woodwick Bay which are sometimes flooded by sea incursion: [Norse *tjörn* small loch, the 'sket' element has a number of meanings: here it is a metaphorical use of Norse *skíta* excreta and means 'marsh' (see 'Skiddy')].

Lochsheen South Ronaldsay: [Norse *tjörn* small loch].

Locklith Birsay, Leary: field name [Scots loch? Norse *hlíð* slope].

Loeta Sanday: a farm mentioned in the Commissariot Record in 1671: perhaps the same as 'The Lettan'].

London Eday; Rousay; Sanday; South Ronaldsay: [Norwegian (Nynorsk) *lón* watery meadow flat (see Appendix), Scots *donk* a marshy place (related to English 'dank')].

Longa Tong Rousay: [Norse *langr* long, *tangi* tongue of land].

Longa Tonga Evie: (see above).

Longaback Birsay, Greeny Hill: [Norse *langr* long, *bakki* a slope].

Longabar Birsay: coastal placename [Norse *langr* long, *berg* rock].

Longagleeb Geo Birsay: a very deep, rocky geo, formed perhaps from a collapsed gloup [Norse *langr* long, *gloppa* a big hole, *gjá* ravine].

Longapol Rousay: a rocky pier-like shelf in the 'Lean' district [Norse *pallr* a step].

Longar North Ronaldsay: north of Ancum Loch (see 'Longiger' Rendall).

Longatrim/Langadrum Birsay, Southside: vanished: it lay to the west of 'Newbigging' [Norse *langr* long, *tromr* edge of a district etc. (see 'Trumland')].

Longbigging Sanday, Eastin district; Westray, 'Swanson's Park': [Scots *bigging* building].

Longhope Walls: [Norse *langr* long, *hóp* bay].

Longiger Rendall: [Norse *langr* long, *garðr* enclosure].

Longland o Ness Sanday, 'Stove': field name.

Longlands Birsay, Bea: (as above).

Longrigging Auskerry: [for 'rigging' read 'ridging', i.e., ridge and furrow].

Longsheed Rendall, 'Overhouse/Iver house'; Birsay, Eastabist: [Old Scots *schedd* a piece of land distinctive in some way or other].

Longstane Rousay: Frotoft, a Neolithic standing stone 2 metres high and still in its original position.

Longtaing Sanday: coastal feature [Norse *tangi* point of land (see 'Longa Tonga')].

Longtownmail St. Andrews: [Norse *langr* long, *tún-völlr* home field].

Lonnie (see 'Loany').

Looath Sandwick: [Celtic *loth* marsh].

Lookout Rendall: field near 'Brookfield'; site of an old croft in the 1800s (see 'Nisnaquoy').

Looma Shun Evie: (see above).

Loomachun Rousay; Holm: [Norse *tjörn* pool, *lóm* the red throated diver which favours lonely hilltop pools to nest].

Loomi Shuns/Loomachuns Walls: (see above).

Loonan Birsay: south end of 'Swannay Loch' [Norwegian (Nynorsk) *lón* watery meadow flat (see Appendix)].

Loons, The Birsay; Stromness; Harray: (see above).

Loop o Geoholdis Stronsay: (see above).

Loop o Kroo/Crooie Birsay: coastal feature (see above) [Norse *kví* enclosure].

Loop o Saverday Sanday: coastal feature, Northwall (see above and 'Sowerdie').

Loop o the Ayre Sanday: coastal feature, 'Roos Wick' [English 'loop' a sweeping curve, used to describe bays].

Loopie, The Birsay: [a 'loop like' feature on the 'Dirkadale Burn'].

Loos, Burn o Orphir: (see 'Lows').

Lopness Sanday: coastal feature [Norse *hlaup* a leaping out, Norse *nes* headland].

Loppack Pentland Skerries: (see below).

Lotche Sanday: farm mentioned in the Commissariot Record, 1624: position unknown but may be the same as 'Loeta'.

Loth Sanday: west of 'Spurness' [Norse *hljóð* sound (of the sea)].

Lothan Evie: (see 'Luthan').

Lother Rock South Ronaldsay, Burwick: [Norse *flaeðr* flood tide, i.e., a reef which becomes intermittently flooded].

Lotheran/Lowtheran Sanday: coastal feature, point of 'Ire' [Norse *flaeðr-in* the flood tide].

Lotherin Sanday: area of large stones on the shore, Park district (see above).

Lounders Fea Hoy: [Norse *lundar* puffin with English genitive (compare 'Lyradale')].

Loup o Braesgar Sanday: beach name north of 'Taftsness' [English 'loop' curve of a beach (see 'Braesgar')].

Loup o Skeegeo Sanday: coastal feature near Muir [English 'loop' curve of a beach, Norse *gjá* rock fissure (see 'Skeebanks' for 'skee' element)].

Loup o the Quoynagreenie Sanday: coastal feature, 'Taftsness' [English 'loop' curve of a beach].

Louther Skerry Pentland Skerries: [Norse *flaeðr* flood tide, i.e., a reef which becomes intermittently flooded, *sker* a reef].

Low Fiold Harray: [an elevated tract of rough pasture on the west side of the 'Kame o Corrigall': 'low' in relation to the higher 'Kame'].

Low's House Rousay: vanished house in 'Wasbister' [named after a Low family].

Lower Breck Sanday, Newark: field name, also known as 'Binkly' [Norse *brekka* slope].

Lower Dinnies Rendall, Hogarth: field name (see 'Dinnies').

Lowrie's Water Evie: [personal name 'Lowrie' (Laurence), Norse *vatn* pool].

Lowther (see 'Lotheran').

Lowther Rock Sanday: on the Warsetter shore, Cross parish [Norse *flaeðr* flood tide, i.e., a reef which becomes intermittently flooded: here, as in many other instances the initial 'f' is missing].

Luafield Rousay: [Norwegian (Nynorsk) *ló* muck/marsh].

Luan Evie/Rendall: [Norwegian (Nynorsk) *ló-in* the marsh].

Lucknow Shapinsay: [a number of cottages were named after battles fought by the British forces. In this case it was the Battle of Lucknow in India in 1857].

Lucky Nose Evie: a cliff marking the coastal boundary between Birsay and Evie parishes [doubtful origin: probably the cliff profile is similar to the profile of the head of the Orkney witch 'Lucky'].

Ludd Birsay: part of the beach northeast of 'Choin' [a variant of Norse *lón* water meadow/marsh (according to the Norwegian etymologist Torp) and may have been the original name of 'Choin', giving it a similar interpretation to 'Marwick'].

Ludenhill Birsay: [the final 'en' of 'ludd' here is the definite article and demonstrates that 'ludd' was originally a Norse/Nynorsk word].

Lug Swona: [Scots *lug* ear, referring to a projecting part of the coast in this instance].

Luim House Birsay, Northside: it lay between 'Westerhouse' and 'Fidgarth' [Scots *lum* chimney: the reference must be to a cottage which had a chimney when most others still had a central fireplace with a hole in the roof].

Luisber Rousay: crags west of the 'Knee o Faraclett' [Norse *berg* rock, *ljós* brightness caused by seabird guano].

Lum Head, The Westray: a chambered cairn to the northwest of 'Iphs' [origin unknown].

Lunan 1. Firth/Stenness: lies on the boundary of Firth and Stenness near the Kirkwall to Stromness road: (see below).

Lunan 2. Harray: a hollow area covered with heathy pasture, southwest of Huntscarth [Norwegian (Nynorsk) *lón* 'marsh' or more specifically 'water meadow'. The suffix is the definite article 'the', hence *lón-in*].

Lundagoe Stenness (site of the present hotel) [Norwegian (Nynorsk) *lón* marsh, *dý* marsh, Norse *gall* used metaphorically to describe a marsh (see Appendix)].

Lundigo Orphir: position unknown (see above).

Lunga Skerries Auskerry: two long shaped skerries to the west of 'North Taing'.

Lunnadale Orphir: [Norwegian (Nynorsk) *lón* marsh, Norse *dalr* valley].

Lurand/Lurn North Ronaldsay: a point of low water rocks on the west coast, south of 'Tuin Ness' [Norse *flaeðar-in* with loss of initial 'f' which is common in coastal features].

Lurdy Flotta: (see above).

Lurdy/Lerdie Burray: [Norse *ler* clay, *dý* marsh].

Lurn North Ronaldsay: (see 'Lurand' above).

Lurns o the Soond North Ronaldsay: (see 'Lurand' above).

Lushan, Burn o Birsay: a tributary of the 'Hillside Burn' [a contraction of 'Loomachun' where the burn rises].

Lussamae Sanday: coastal feature [*luss* represents Norwegian *fles* Skerry, with loss of initial 'f' (compare 'Lashy Sound'), Norse *melr* sand/gravel].

Luthan/Lothan Evie: position unknown, most likely a coastal name (see 'Loth').

Lyachoin Birsay, Flaws: a pool (*tjörn*) which appeared after heavy rain [this name and the one below suggests that the 'lya' element means merely 'marsh' since there is a well here].

Lyapitten Birsay: 'Makerhouse', Dounby [Norse *pytt-inn* the pool: (see' Lyachoin' above)].

Lyawheena Birsay, Kirbister: [(see 'Lya' forms above), Norse *kví-n* the enclosure].

Lyber Rousay: a ridge of rock visible at low tide in southeast 'Saviskaill Bay' [Norse *berg* rock: origin of 'ly' element unknown].

Lyde Firth: the road from Harray to Rendall passes through a saddle in the hills [Norse *leið* road].

Lyde, The Birsay: the road from 'Marwick' to 'Sandwick' (see above).

Lydes o Tingwall Rendall: (see above).

Lye Holm Sanday, The Riv: [dialect *ley* part of the coast where lobster creels may be set, Norse *lega* a resting place, Norse *hólmr* island].

Lyers/Lyres Breck North Ronaldsay: [Norse *líri* manx shearwater, *brekka* slope].

Lyking Holm; Sandwick; Rendall: [Norse *leik* play, *eng* meadow: sport was very popular for the Norse and special fields were usually set aside for this purpose: the tradition was kept up in Orkney (see 'Gamon Park')].

Lylie Birsay, Northside: does not appear in records before 1881 [origin uncertain].

Lynaber Birsay: good fishing rock [Norse *hlein* a rock projecting like a pier into the sea, *berg* rock].

Lynedardy Hill Stromness: north of 'Garth' and west of 'Brunt Hill' [a very difficult name to interpret: Celtic *linne* pool and *dý* marsh/moorland are straightforward but no suggestions can be offered for the 'dar' element].

Lyness Walls: [possibly Norse *hlíð* slope, *nes* point of land].

Lyradale, Hill o Orphir: [Norse *líri* manx shearwater, *dalr* valley].

Lyrawa Bay Walls: [Norse *líri* manx shearwater, *vágr* bay].

Lyrawall South Ronaldsay, Herston: [a transferred name from the above].

Lyre Back Falls South Ronaldsay: near 'Stews' [Norse *líri* manx shearwater, *bakki* slope: the word 'falls' relates to a stream, which, after heavy rain, develops here and falls over the cliff].

Lyre Cliff Sanday: coastal feature ['lyre' appears elsewhere in Orkney placenames: possibly Norse *líri*, manx shearwater].

Lyre Geo Hoy; Sandwick: [Norse *líri* manx shearwater, *gjá* ravine].

Lyren Stronsay: a shoal on west side of Rothiesholm [perhaps Norse *flaeðr-in* periodically flooded].

Lyron Rendall: [Norse *hlíðar-in* the slopes].

Lythe 1. Hoy: [Norse *hlíð* slope].

Lythe 2. South Ronaldsay, Barswick: one of the earliest recorded Norse farm names, recorded in 1329 as '*Lið*' and later as 'Quoyleith' [Norse *hlíð* slope].

Lythes South Ronaldsay, Walls: [Norse *hlíðar* slopes (with English plural)].

Lythes Ness Birsay: near 'Skippie Geo' [a noted place for catching lythes or pollacks: Norse *lirr* lythe].

M

Maat Flas Stronsay, Airy: field name ['mat' = malt, Norse *flá* strips of meadow land: where malt was steeped for brewing ale?].

Mackum Rocks Sanday: on the shore at 'Lamba Ness', [dialect 'Mekum' = Malcolm (see below)].

Mad Geo Papa Westray: a small narrow geo on the west coast of the island [origin unknown].

Mae Ness Egilsay: northeast of the island [Norse *melr* sand, *nes* point of land].

Mae Sand Westray: [Norse *melr* a sand/gravel bank].

Maeback Papa Westray: [Norse *melr* sand, *bakki* bank (i.e., sand bank)].

Maes Taing Gairsay: (see 'Mae Sand' above: the suffix 's' is the genitive case).

Maeshowe Stenness: (see Appendix).

Maesquoy Harray: near 'Currcabreck', i.e., church slope [Norse *messa* mass, *kví* enclosure].

Maesry/Maesrie Sanday: (see 'Mount Misery') mound on 'Start Point' (see Appendix).

Maesygate Orphir: [Norse *gata* path: 'maesy' must relate to 'mass', hence 'path to church': (see 'Messigate' forms)].

Maggie Broon's South Ronaldsay: a cottar house, now a field name near 'Grindley'.

Maggie Burnie's South Faray: vanished [it lay near the old school: according to the 1891 Census: she was a teacher living at 'South Cot'].

Maids Geo (see 'Meadis Geo').

Main Slap Wyre: between 'The Bu' and 'Hawn' [Scots *slap* gateway].

Mainland, The the principal island of the Orkney group, often confused with 'The Mainland of Scotland' [Norse *megin-land* principal island (of Orkney)].

Mainlands Sanday: one of the 'Laminess' houses [named after a former occupant].

Maizer Sanday: in the Everbist area, originally 'Measetter' [Norse *melr* sand, *setr* home stead].

Makabist/Meckabist Sanday: a large mound, 'Langamay' [Norse *maki* partner, Norse *ból-staðr* farm (compare 'Tiffmaka', Stronsay)].

Makerhouse Dounby: [Norse *maki* partner (see above examples)].

Malesburgh/Malisburgh Deerness: it was located about the centre of the parish and described by the Ordnance Surveyors in 1880 as a 'crofter's dwelling house'; vanished? [Norse *melr* gravel here, rather than sand: significance of 'burgh' not understood].

Mallies 1. Birsay: above 'Evrabist' (see below).

Mallies 2. Birsay: above 'Stara', Marwick [a pet name of 'Mary'; simple cottar houses occupied by spinsters were often named after the occupant: (see 'Hannahs')].

Mallow Banks Sanday: grassy banks off 'Saville' [Scots *mallow* eel grass].

Mame, The Stronsay: rock islet below the coast of 'Finyo', Odin Bay [Celtic *màm* rounded hill].

Mammersdale Birsay, Lochside: a low depression locally called the 'Sinkie o Mammersdale' [Middle English *synke* a water-filled hole in the ground, dale = Norse *dý* marsh: origin of 'mammer' uncertain, perhaps Norse *málm* goldish colour, referring to the vegetation].

Mamru Geo Birsay: a narrow geo [the same explanation as above, i.e., a shining gold colour].

Man o Finyie Rousay: (see Appendix).

Mananeban, Forses o Harray; Overbrough/Netherbrough boundary [Norse *fors* torrent or rapid on the 'Burn o Netherbrough' (see Appendix for 'man' element)].

Manclett Walls: (see Appendix).

Manitoba South Ronaldsay: fields to the east of 'Gaira': originally a house, now vanished [possibly built by a returned emigrant who had worked for the Hudson Bay Company].

Mannobreck Birsay, Swannay: field name (see Appendix).

Manse Well Birsay: near 'Boardhouse' [a traditional tale says that water from this well was used to wash the body of St. Magnus: a more reasonable explanation is that this well was frequented by someone by the name 'Mans' i.e., Magnus].

Manseboat Eday: [the name suggests that this small cottage was originally an upturned boat lived in by Mansie: there were several instances of this in the islands].

Mansie Bichen's Hill Rousay: the hill above 'Corse' [Magnus Bichan lived in Rousay in the late 1600s].

Mansie's Knowes Rousay: mounds southwest of 'Kierfea Hill'.

Mansmas Hill Rousay: [no explanation can be given for the origin of this name, but it can be assumed that an annual festival celebrating the life of St. Magnus was held here: compare Georgemas in Caithness].

Manso Pow Evie: location unknown [= Magnus' Pool].

Mantelpiece o Risday Evie: Everbie, a ledge on a cliff [two stones rested here, placed by seamen as a feat of daring; destroyed in a storm in late 1990s (see 'Risday')].

Maraber Rousay: part of the rocky coastline south of 'Queenalonga Ness' [Norse *berg* rock, *merr* mare, usually applied to a coastal rock feature: (compare 'The Mares' in South Walls, below)].

Maraquoy 1. Sandwick: a field below 'Ness' (see below).

Maraquoy 2. Stromness: southeast of 'Brunafea' [Norse *mara* water-logged but 'marsh' in this case].

Mare Evie: launching site of inshore fishermen's boats (see 'Maraber' above).

Mares, The Walls: three rocky pillars on the west side of 'Brims' (see 'Maraber' above).

Margaret's Kirk Stronsay: an old chapel which lay south-southeast of 'Clestran': vanished.

Marisgoe/Morisgoe Sanday: [no further details].

Mark, The 1. Rendall, Orquil: almost certainly a markstone [Norse *mark* boundary (see 'Markstone Moss' below)].

Mark, The 2. Rendall: Cott (see above).

Marka Ber Deerness: a small rock stack east of 'Creya' [Norse *mark* boundary, *berg* rock].

Markstone Moss Holm: east of 'Hemp Stack' (see 'The Mark' above).

Marlaryar Rousay: hill ground in 'Frotoft' above 'Mount Pleasant' [(see 'Maraquoy' above for 'mar' element) origin of 'laryar' unknown].

Marlow Holm: Kili Holm: a rocky stretch of coast on the west side of the Holm [the placename seems to relate to a pool here which is flooded by the sea: Norse *lo* a marshy area, *mar* a marsh (see Marwick below)].

Marwick Birsay: a tunship [(see 'Marlow' for 'mar' element), Norse *vík* bay].

Marwick Head Birsay: a precipitous cliff in the north of Marwick, 87 metres high.

Mary Kirk 1. Rendall, Grind: ruins are still visible.

Mary Kirk 2. Sanday: alternative name for the Sanday kirk, a dedication to the Virgin Mary.

Mary Park Sanday, Newark: field running down to the shore [an old building lay in this field which might have been a dedication to the Virgin Mary].

Mary Stairs Sanday: rocks below 'Meur' ['Mary' is a corruption of 'Meur', 'stairs' relates to the rock formation here].

Mary Well 1. Evie: a well dedicated to the Virgin Mary.

Mary Well 2. Rousay: 200 yards west of 'Mary Kirk', the former parish church of Rousay

Marygarth/Marrigar Sanday: [nearby stood an old chapel which was perhaps dedicated to the Virgin Mary].

Masser Rock South Ronaldsay: 'Harborough Head' coastal feature [origin unknown].

Masseter/Morsetter South Ronaldsay, Windwick: [Norse *mór* moor, *setr* settlement].

Mat Pow Stronsay: southeast of St. Catherine's Bay ['mat' = 'malt', Scots *pow* pool, where malt was steeped for brewing ale?].

Matches Crag North Ronaldsay: a fishing rock at the end of 'Matches Dyke' (see below).

Matches Dyke North Ronaldsay: one of two prehistoric turf/stone walls which divide the island into three [can be only partially explained: probably related to Norse *meta* to measure in different senses e.g. for tax purposes etc.].

Mathi's Glen South Ronaldsay: a small valley near 'Upper Serrigar': said to be haunted by an old man and woman [Scots *glen* valley].

Mathieson's Tumal Stronsay, Aith: 1639 [Norse *tún-völlr* home field i.e., near the dwelling].

Matman Firth: a pool in the stream, 'Nabban', near Bridgend (see Appendix).

Matthew's Hoose Sanday: a seamark northwest of Holms of Ire [refers to the 'West Manse' and a former occupant, Rev. Matthew Armour].

Maud Geo Sanday: coastal feature [origin of 'Maud' uncertain (compare 'Mad Geo')].

Maulto Birsay: marshy area near 'Hinchaquoy', Hundland Loch [origin uncertain, perhaps malt hole? keeping the original 'l': (compare 'Matman' above)].

May/Mae Sand Rousay: Scockness [Norse *melr* sand].

May Scottie's South Ronaldsay, Grimness: vanished; at one time the surname Scottie was found all over Orkney but it has now died out.

Mayback 1. North Ronaldsay: (see below: location uncertain).

Mayback 2. Papa Westray: on the east of Papa Westray [Norse *melr* sand, *bakki* bank].

Maygie Birsay: an outlying rock [origin unknown].

Mayvie Rousay, Trumland: [Norse *melr* sand, *vágr* bay].

Mea Banks Deerness: (see 'Mayback', Papa Westray, above).

Meadisgeo/Maidsgeo Sanday: coastal feature near Rue [origin uncertain; perhaps Norse *miðs*, genitive of *mið* a sea mark, Norse *gjá* ravine].

Meadow Betts Birsay: between 'Swartageo' and 'Lushan' [Norse *beit* pasture (with English plural)].

Meadow o Kringlo Stenness: (see 'Kringlo').

Meal 1. Deerness, Newark: [Norse *melr* sand].

Meal 2. Holm: the name was changed to 'Graemeshall' by the Graeme family in the latter part of the 17th century [Norse *melr* sand].

Meal Meadow Birsay, 'Howally' [origin of 'meal' here uncertain].

Meaness Shapinsay: west of 'Burrowstone' [Norse *mjó-nes* the smaller point of land].

Mearo Stronsay: south of 'Lower Leaquoy' [Norse *mýrr* marsh, the suffix is a diminutive].

Measer Sanday: earlier spellings 'Maizer' and 'Maisouer': earlier (1601) 'Measetter' [Norse *melr* sand, Norse *setr* homestead].

Measetter (see 'Measer' above).

Meckabist (see 'Makabist').

Meean Burn Rousay: (see 'Essaquoy').

Meean Well Rousay: [Norse *migandi* to wee, i.e., to pass water].

Meera Muggla Harray: [(for 'Meera' see 'Mearo' above) Norse *mykill* large].

Meeran Rousay: [Norse *mýrr* marsh (with definite article suffix, i.e., 'the marsh')].

Meero Stronsay, Holland: field name (see 'Mearo' above).

Meery-Mawry Birsay: a wet hole between 'Leabreck' and 'Herpsa' [Norse *mýrr* marsh with a rhyming duplicate].

Mefra Geo Birsay: [origin unknown].

Meikle Sheed Stronsay: west of 'Coppa' [Scots *schedd* a piece of land distinctive from its surroundings].

Meikle Water Stronsay: [Norse *vatn* small loch].

Meikleplank Birsay: [Scots *muckle* large, Old French *planchet* introduced through Scots, a unit of arable land: this word was used very much in the Division of the Commonty].

Meiklequoy Birsay, Southside: [Norse *kví* enclosure].

Meil Geo North Ronaldsay: [Norse *melr* sand].

Mekum's Waal Sanday: a well near 'Cuvan', Burness parish [Malcom Scott lived at 'West Thrave' nearby].

Mel Fea Hoy: [Gaelic *meall* hill, Norse *fjall* hill].

Melberry Walls: [Gaelic *meall* hill, Norse *berg* hill].

Mell Evie: low tide skerry [origin unknown].

Mells Kirk Stronsay: a sandy stretch of coast to the west of Holland; near the beach lay a vanished kirk [Norse *melr* sand].

Melsetter Walls: [Norse *melr* sand, *setr* residence].

Merchant's Pier Evie: a natural pier from which salt pork was shipped to Kirkwall.

Meriday Sanday: a flat mound in 'Tirlees', cultivated land, Northwall [Norse *mýrr* moor, *dý* marsh].

Mermaid's Chair Stronsay: a rock shaped 'chair' off the coast: position uncertain.

Mero Swanney's Sanday: former name of 'Warbreckan' [Mary Swanney was a former occupant].

Merons Birsay, Northside: vanished: it stood near 'Wattle' [a personal name based on a 'Mary' form e.g., 'Marian'].

Merry Pow Sanday, Bellevue: field name [probably Scots *miry* marshy, Scots *pow* pool].

Merryhoose Sanday: [Norse *mýrr* moor, Norse *hús* house].

Mervar Stronsay: rocky beach, east side of Rothiesholm [origin unknown].

Mesmes Geo Rousay: Quandal district, near 'Kiln o Dusty' [origin unknown].

Messager Deerness: [Norse *messa* chapel, *götur* paths (to the chapel)].

Messigate 1. Birsay: path to St. Magnus Kirk [Norse *gata* path].

Messigate 2. St. Andrews: [lower road to the chapel of St. John].

Messigate, The Papa Westray: [vanished pathway to St. Tredwell's Chapel].

Messigate Road North Ronaldsay: (see above).

Messquoy Harray: (see 'Maeshowe' in the Appendix).

Mester Grip (see 'Grip o Loonan') [mester = principal (stream)].

Mestergate Sanday: (see below).

Mestragate Road St. Andrews: the road from 'North End' to St. Andrews Kirk [mestra = master = principal, *gata* path].

Meur Sanday: Northwall [Norse *mór* heathland].

Mewie Hill Stromness: (see 'Miffia').

Mickle Cloack Sanday, Elsness: field name, early 18th century (see 'Cloak').

Micklequoy Stenness: [Norse *mykill* large, *kví* enclosure].

Mid Hill 1. Birsay/Evie: a hill marking the boundary between Birsay and Evie.

Mid Hill 2. Orphir: forms part of the boundary between Stenness and Orphir.

Mid Holland Sanday: mentioned in 1601 Udal Book (see' Holland', 'Scar').

Mid Mire Sanday: district [Norse *mýrr* moor].

Mid Tooin Rendall: at 224 metres, the highest point of the range of hills which sweep down the West Mainland [Norse *þúf-in* the mound].

Midbea Westray: a district, on the southern slopes of 'Fitty Hill' [Norse *mið-boer* the middle farm].

Midbigging Firth: [Scots *bigging* building].

Midgarth 1. Rousay, Sourin: [Norse *mið* middle, *garðr* farm].

Midgarth 2. Stromness: (see above).

Midgarth 3. Stronsay: (see above).

Midgarth, Knowe o Rendall: (see 'knowe' in Appendix).

Midhoose Sanday: now a field name on the land of 'Stumpo', near 'Ruthie Taing'.

Midhouse Westray; Stenness; Shapinsay; Harray; Firth, The Lyde; Deerness; Evie: [the name can mean the middle house of a single dwelling but more usually the middle house of three separate units].

Midland 1. Orphir: a district to the west of what is now 'Houton Bay'.

Midland 2. Rendall: adjacent to the border with Evie [the 'mid' reference relates to the border as it does in 'Mid Hill' (see above)].

Midland, Hill o Orphir: directly north of 'Houton Bay'.

Midland Haven Orphir: now called 'Houton Bay'.

Miffia Stromness: [Norse *mið* middle, *fjall* hill].

Milagar Orphir: marked on 1813 map southwest of 'Kirbister Loch' [Norse *milli* between, garðar farms].

Milahamer Firth: [Norse *milli* between, *hamarr* rock/s: this probably refers to the rocky outcrop to the east of 'Binscarth House' which became a quarry as did the quarries to the west of 'Binscarth House', above 'Wasdale'].

Milahawen Firth, Binscarth: [Norse *milli* between, *haugar* mounds i.e., between the mounds].

Milgarth Westray: it was probably sited near the 'Mill o Rapness'.

Milgeos Firth, Binscarth: [a deep entrenchment through which the burn flows to the 'Mill', Norse *gjá* a ravine].

Mill Brae Sanday: a flag was hoisted here when a ship arrived with cargo at 'Kettletoft': a windmill formerly stood in this location].

Mill Grip Sanday: site of an old mill near 'Newark' [Scots *grip* a ditch].

Mill Hallow Harray, Grimeston: [Norse *helga* made holy i.e., the land, not the mill: 'St. Mary's Kirk' lay close by].

Mill Loch Sanday: existed at one time in the middle of the parish of Burness; now drained (see 'Stinkpow').

Mill o Bea Sanday, How: now demolished.

Mill o Clappag South Ronaldsay: [a click mill in the 'Cleat' area, the stream of which has been diverted: 'clappag' is diminutive of 'clap' the sound made by the turning of this small type of mill wheel (see 'Click Mill')].

Mill o Dilto Sanday: Cleat district, this mill, unusually, was tidally powered [Norse *deild* division, boundary, *á* stream].

Mill o Rusness Sanday, Rusness: a water mill fed from 'Langamay Loch' and a windmill stood near 'Rusness Kirk'.

Mill o Stousater Sanday: alternative name for 'Mill o Cruiko'.

Mill o Woo Sanday: near Scar (see 'Woo').

Mill Sheet Sanday, West Brough: field name [possibly the site of a Windmill: *sheet* a variation of *sheed*, a common Orkney field name].

Mill Toomal Rendall: Upper Ellibister [Norse *tún-völlr* the field near the mill].

Milldam Sanday: Burness parish, a house, now derelict and North Ronaldsay, where it is also known as 'Powstink'.

Millgoes Rendall: [Norse *milli* between (marshes, see Appendix) it forms the boundary between the parishes of Harray and Rendall].

Millivenier Westray: [Norse *ver* a fishing place, *milli* between].

Mills Sanday: formerly 'Eggletoor' [called 'Mills' today, from the name of a former inhabitant].

Millstone Geo South Ronaldsay: [millstones were cut from the sides of the geo just as they had been at 'Yesnaby'].

Milyasundee Birsay, Marwick: exact location unknown [Norse *milli* between, *sund* a channel/stream/ditch, *dý* marshland].

Minehill Stromness: [the name relates to an attempt to mine lead probably in the 18th century: in 1880 'Minehill' was a small farm east of 'Yelda'].

Mingero/Mingro Stronsay, Rothiesholm: a house at the south end of the ayre in what was a swampy area [Norse *gröf* literally a pit but used in Orkney as a stream (which has embedded itself) flowing out of the 'Loch o Rothiesholm', the 'min' element is perhaps a form of *minni* (see above)].

Minister's Flag Papa Westray: [a flat rock where the parish minister alighted before a pier was constructed].

Minister's Geo Sanday: coastal feature [Norse *gjá* ravine; this 'geo' is near the manse].

Minna Geo Birsay: [Norse *minni* the smaller].

Minyin Deerness: cultivated bog on 'Holland' (see 'Mingro').

Miravalhvi Firth, Binscarth: [Norse *mýrr* moorland, 'vi' = *fjall* hill: 'val' element and location unknown].

Mirber, Skerries o Birsay: [Norse *berg* rock: origin of 'mir' element unknown].

Mirbister Harray: a district east of 'Hourston' in Sandwick: recorded earlier as 'Myrkumbister' [Norse *myrk* darkness with definite article suffix, hence *myrkann*, Norse *ból-staðr* farm].

Mire South Ronaldsay: a vanished house which lay near St. Margaret's Hope [Norse *mýrr* moorland, usually found in English plural form 'Mires' as below].

Mires o Linties Sanday: near 'Measer' (see 'Langtas').

Mires o Stangasetter Sanday: near 'Smithscott' (see 'Mires' and 'Stangasetter').

Mires o Whip Sanday: a flat area of land to the west of 'Whip'.

Mires Sanday, Everbist: formerly known as 'Nether Gorn' (see 'Mires' above).

Mires/Myres Sanday: field name near 'Beafield' [Norse *mýrr* swamp or bog (with English plural)].

Mirk Evie/Rendall: [Norse *myrk* darkness of soil or, more likely, vegetation cover].

Mirkady Deerness: [Norse *myrk* darkness of vegetation, *dý* marsh].

Mirkholes Deerness: a farm in the 1880s just north of 'Upper Stove': birthplace of the celebrated poet and writer David Vedder [Norse *myrk* darkness, *hol* a depression].

Mirkitchen Westray: a loch on 'Noup' farm [Norse *mýrr* swamp or bog, *keyta* foul water, *tjörn* small loch].

Mirky Geo Sanday: coastal feature [Norse *myrkr* dark, *gjá* ravine].

Mirkyhole Westray: (see 'Mirkholes' above).

Mirran Harray: [Norse *mýrr* moorland with added suffix 'n', hence 'the moorland'].

Mirth Hilly Holm: a rocky cliff 'Roseness' [origin of name unknown].

Mirwick Deerness: [Norse *mýrr* moor, *vík* bay].

Miry Spelds Sanday, Stove: field name [Scots *miry* marshy (see 'Sava Speldo')].

Misbister Geo South Walls: a geo close to the above.

Misbister South Walls: a small farm to the west of 'Kirk Hope' [*ból-staðr* farm: the element 'mis' cannot be explained].

Mistra Evie: [possibly Norse *mið* middle, *setr* dwelling].

Mithist Harray: [Norse *mið* middle, *hús* house, with neutral suffix 'it' hence *húsit*].

Mithouse Evie: [Norse *mið* middle].

Mithquoy Harray: [Norse *mið* middle, *kví* enclosure].

Mithvie Rousay: (see 'Eastafea').

Mittens/Newhouse Birsay: [Norse *mið* middle, *tún-völlr* home field (with English plural): the name was changed to 'Newhouse'].

Mittun Stronsay: a field on Grobister [Norse *mið* middle, *tún-völlr* home field].

Mo Westray: [Norse *mór* poor sandy or gravelly soil].

Moa Stenness; Rendall; Westray: [Norse *mór* heathland].

Moan Firth; Graemsay; Harray; Rousay; Sandwick; Birsay: [Norse *mórin* the moorland].

Moaness 1. Hoy: [Norse *mór* moor, *nes* a ness].

Moaness 2. Walls: a small stony point at the extreme east end of 'Longhope' [Norse *mjó* narrow, *nes* point].

Mobisyord Sandwick: 'Stove' region, one of three contiguous parcels of land recorded in the early Rentals of Orkney with personal names attached ['yord' = land since we find the name also written as 'Mobis land', Norse personal name *Móbil*].

Moclett PapaWestray: [(see 'Mo' above) Norse *klettr* rock, the whole name suggesting that at one time there was a standing stone or stone structure here].

Moda Harray: Corrigall district, an area of peat moss on the southwest slope of the 'Kame o Corrigall' [Norse *mór* moor, *dý* poorly drained land].

Mogar Birsay, Kirbister area; Harray, near 'Nistaben' in Russland [it is doubtful if the later name is original since the earliest and only reference the writer can find to 'Mogar' is a school photograph dated 1895].

Moi Fea Walls: [Norse *mór* heathland, *fjall* hill].

Moi Geo 1. Cava: on the east of the island (see above).

Moi Geo 2. South Ronaldsay: Herston district (see above).

Mon South Ronaldsay, St. Margarets Hope: vanished [an unusual spelling of 'Moan' (see above)].

Moncliff/Monscliff/Moo Cliff Orphir: a bold rocky headland near 'Roo Point' [Norse *mórin* the moor, *klif* a cliff].

Monivey Westray: on the southern flank of 'North Hill' [Norse *mór* moor, *fjall* hill].

Monquhanny Shapinsay: [a placename introduced by the Balfours from one of their lands in Fife].

Montreal Birsay, Greeny: one of several Canadian placenames to be found in Orkney [These were given by Orkney emigrants who prospered in Canada and who returned to build a house (see 'Canada)'].

Moo Geo Sanday: coastal feature [Norse *mjó* narrow].

Moo Taing Orphir: forms the western boundary of Stenness and Orphir [Norse *mjó* narrow, *tangi* point of land].

Moo/Mue Geo North Ronaldsay: a small inlet to the west of 'Twinyes' [Norse *mjó* narrow].

Moodies Sanday, How: field name ['Moodie' was a local surname and this is probably an old house site].

Moolie Rousay: west end of a hill ridge above 'Muckle Water' [Norse *múli* snout of an animal and used figuratively for a projecting land feature (c.f. 'Mull Head', Deerness)].

Mooness Holm: a small farm north of 'Little Dawn' [there is no 'ness' in the locality so perhaps a transferred name from 'Moness' on Hoy].

Moonlight Evie/Rendall; Harray: [fanciful names, some perhaps relating to moving house in moonlight after a day's work!].

Moor Fea Hoy: [Norse *fjall* hill].

Moor o Toosness Sanday: formerly uncultivated land to the west of 'Toosness'.

Moorican-Mansie's Hole Rousay: [most probably a hollow where a tramp by the name 'Moorican-Mansie' often lay: (compare 'Faldaral's Hole', Harray)].

Moosie Ha' Sanday: near Howland [Scots *ha* cottage: a pejorative nickname 'mouse cottage': (compare 'Conninghole')].

Moostrings Stronsay: a track across the 'Moss o Mossfield' [a rare use of Norse *strengr* literally 'string' to apply to a narrow straight path, it is applied more commonly to a narrow sea channel (see 'The String')].

Mopier Birsay: a watery hole northwest on Kirbuster Hill [Norse *mór* moor, the 'pier' element presents a problem, perhaps originally *pyttar* pools].

Mor Stein Shapinsay: a large standing stone in the east of the island. There is no tradition attached to it but no doubt it was an ancient place of assembly.

Morris Geo Sanday; South Ronaldsay: [the origin of 'morris' cannot be explained].

Morsetter Shapinsay: [Norse *mór* moor, *setr* dwelling].

Mosbister Stronsay: north of 'Midgarth' [Norse *mosi* moorland, *ból-staðr*, farm].

Moss 1. Birsay, Ingsay: field name.

Moss 2. Holm; Orphir; Hoy: [Norse *mosi* dampish moorland].

Moss, The Birsay: part of Greeny Hill.

Moss o Broonalanga Firth.

Moss o Catagreen Rousay.

Moss o Cruan Firth.

Moss o Hattamoa Evie.

Moss o Hyon Firth.

Moss o the Whitestanes Hoy.

Moss on Crook Orphir.

Mossbank Westray.

Mossetter 1. Birsay, Beaquoy: (see above).

Mossetter 2. Rendall: a cottage now mainly in ruins (see 'Setter').

Mosside Westray: Garthstown.

Mossland Westray.

Mossquoy Rendall, field in Hackland district; Orphir; Deerness.

Mou Ness Firth: a point of land south of the Bay of Isbister': a farm called 'The Lighthouse' stands on it [Norse *mjó* narrow, *nes* point].

Mount 1. Evie: a small cottage west of 'Creya' in Woodwick ['Mounts' are probably curtailed forms of 'Mount Hoolie' etc. placenames].

Mount 2. Westray: Midbea, south of 'Bresco' (see above).

Mount, The Hoy: a small cottage in Rackwick (see above).

Mount Misery 1. Like Mounthoolie, Mount Misery is recorded outside Orkney. In England there is even a 'Mount Misery Farm'! The origin of this placename is unknown: it seems to be associated with hard work.

Mount Misery 2. Birsay: a mound on 'Birsay Bay'.

Mount Misery 3. Sanday: a mound on Start Point.

Mount Misery 4. Westray; Stromness; Evie; Eday.

Mount Pleasant 1. There are a number of 'Mount Pleasant' names in Orkney and a good scattering throughout England. There are many hundreds in the USA. Originally, they seem to have had religious associations. An alternative name for a Mount Pleasant house in Birsay for example was (Mount) Pisgah in the Bible, which lay to the east of the Jordan River. Below are other Orkney examples:

Mount Pleasant 2. Rendall, Green Hill; Rousay; Sandwick; Harray, Birsay, west of Kirbister, Greeny, Beaquoy; Westray, Rackwick, Fribo; Stronsay.

Mounthoolie these placenames appeared in Orkney in the early 1600s: they are names chosen to give a cottage an air of respectability sincemany of them were ale houses such as Mounthoolie in Kirkwall where the name is still retained in 'Mounthoolie Lane'. The name 'Mounthoolie' is also found outside Orkney.

Here are other examples below:

Mount Hoolie 1. Birsay, Southside: Garson, not far from 'Mount Misery'.

Mount Hoolie 2. Birsay, Swannay.

Mount Hoolie 3. Stronsay: old house site near 'Tiffmaka'.

Mount Hooly 1. Orphir.

Mount Hooly 2. Shapinsay.

Mount Hooly 3. South Ronaldsay.

Mountholy Sanday: Stove).

Mounthoolie Sanday: now a field name, Bellevue.

Mounthooly Evie.

Mountvedo Evie: [seems to be a form of 'Montevideo' in Uruguay: a name probably brought to Orkney by a sailor who returned to the islands].

Moursi North Ronaldsay: a hollow near 'Dennis Loch' [Norse *mýrr* moor, the second element 'si' is difficult to interpret, perhaps *sae* sea, which is very close].

Mousebrae Westray: [English 'mouse'].

Mousetter Copinsay: [Norse *mór* heath, *saetr* a temporary hut used seasonally].

Mousland Westray, Cleatown; Stromness; Sandwick.

Mousound Walls: near Crockness, Rinnigill, at the extreme east end of Longhope [Norse *mjó* narrow, *sund* narrow passage].

Mouster Head South Ronaldsay: a headland on the east coast of the island near 'Stews'.

Mu Geos Eday: a farm name: there are certainly no geos here with that name ['geo' must refer to a marsh (see Appendix for explanation), the 'mu' element is probably Norse *mór* heath].

Muce 1. Birsay, Dounby (see below).

Muce 2. Birsay, Marwick: [a corrupted form of 'Midhouse'].

In all the following entries 'muckle' means 'big'. The word can have its origin in Norse *mykill* or in Scots *muckle*.**Muckle Bar** Sanday: coastal feature, it stands beside the 'Little Ber' [Scots *muckle* large, Norse *berg* rock].

Muckle Billia Fiold Evie.

Muckle Cloack Sanday.

Muckle Dyke 1. Rendall, Scottshall: ['dyke' usually referred to an old earthen boundary wall].

Muckle Dyke 2. Rendall: a field on 'Scottsha'.

Muckle Furs Birsay, Skelday: ['furs' = Norse *fors* waterfall, but is used in Orkney to describe 'rapids' in burns].

Muckle Geo Evie.

Muckle Gersty North Ronaldsay: (see 'Gersty').

Muckle Gurness Evie.

Muckle Kiln Sanday: [Scots *muckle* big: a cave in Burness parish: the English word 'kiln' is often found in coastal placenames in Orkney where storms produce a spray akin to the smoke given out by the old, large, grain-drying kilns on Orkney farms].

Muckle Linga Stronsay: old name of 'Holm o Midgarth'.

Muckle Moss Harray.

Muckle Pow Evie: [Scots *pow* pool].

Muckle Sand Sanday: seabed feature, Rooswick.

Muckle Sheed o Marykirk Sanday, Elsness: field name, early 18th century (see 'Sheed').

Muckle Tuna Evie: grassy projecting ledge near cliff top [Norse *þúf-in* the mound].

Muckle Water 1. Rousay.

Muckle Water 2. Stronsay: a loch in the middle of the island ['water' = Norse *vatn*].

Muckle Well North Ronaldsay.

Mucklehoose Birsay, Hundland.

Mucklehouse/Greathouse South Fara.

Muckleplank Birsay, Northside: [Scots *plank* a field].

Muckquoy 1. Firth: (see below).

Muckquoy 2. South Ronaldsay: [Norse *mór* moor, *kví* enclosure].

Muddisdale St. Ola: [Norse personal name *Móði*, Norse *deild* division/allotment].

Muestack Stronsay, Kirbister: [significance of 'mu' here is unknown].

Mugar South Ronaldsay: [Norse *mór* moorland, *garðr* farm].

Muglafurse Harray: [Norse *mykill* large, *fors* rapid in a stream].

Mugly Rousay: Swandal, originally 'Queenamuckle' [Norse *mykill* large: there are several instances in the North Isles of the placename being abbreviated by loss of the noun to which the adjective applies].

Mugly Meadow Birsay, Eastabist: [Norse *mykill* large].

Muir Sanday: [Norse *mór* moorland].

Mull Head Deerness: [Norse *muli* snout of an animal but also used metaphorically of a jutting crag].

Mull o Papa Papa Westray: (see above).

Mullar/Melr Geo North Ronaldsay: [Norse *melar* gravel, normally referring to the head of the geo].

Muller Geo Shapinsay: (see above).

Muller Taing Stronsay: south point of 'Holm o Huip'.

Mullery Geo Sanday: coastal feature, Ire, and Northwall [Norse *melar* sand or gravel banks, Norse *gjá* ravine].

Mullery Point Sanday: north of West Ayre Loch, 'Sellibister' [Norse *melar* sand or gravel banks].

Mungistiff/Mungister Stronsay: a field on Aith with a hillock of burnt stones [the name suggests that the 'g' should be a 'k', hence Munkistiff/Munkister: origin unknown].

Munkerhoose Papa Westray: old stone structures in vicinity of 'St. Boniface's Church' [believed to be associated at one time with monks].

Munkermae Sanday: a large mound near 'Queensbrig', which used to be the site of the annual ba' game [Norse *múnkar* monks, Norse *melr* sand].

Munsie Rousay: a deserted house on a lower slope of St. Magnus Hill [probably a corruption of Magnus: 'Mansie' is the nickname of anyone with the personal name 'Magnus'].

Murder South Ronaldsay: a field name near Brough Ness [probably in the sense 'difficult to work': compare English field names called 'Hell'].

Murka Hole South Ronaldsay: small hole in the cliff top, 'Harrabrough Head', Herston [Norse *myrkr* dark].

Murous/Murons Orphir: extreme north of 'Veness Hill' [Nors *mýrr* moor, *hús* house].

Murra Hoy: Braebister district, in the 1880 survey it was a small farm [Norse *mýrr* moor: the 'a' suffix is common in Orkney placenames, e.g., 'Queena'].

Murren Rousay: between the 'Braes o Moan' and the sea [Norse *mýrr* moorland plus the definite article 'in' suffix].

Murton St. Andrews: a small indentation in the coast near the 'Gloup' and 'Churn' but must have originally applied to a vanished house [Norse *mýrr* moor, *tún-völlr* a field attached to the house].

Musapul North Ronaldsay: pasture land along Senness Loch [Norse *mosi* moss, *pollr* pool].

Musbister Stronsay: old tunship between Huip and Whitehall, [Norse *mosi* moss, *ból-staðr* farm].

Musland Westray: [Norse *mosi-land* moorland].

Muslandquoy South Ronaldsay: (see above).

Mussaquoy Orphir; Deerness: [Norse *mosi* moss, *kví* enclosure].

Mussater Stronsay, Airy: field name.

Mussel Ebb Sanday: Skitho Bay [Scots 'ebb', foreshore (see below)].**Mussel Ebb o Lussamae** Sanday: near 'Ortie' [bait was dug for long line fishing here (see 'Lussamae')].

Mussetter Eday: [Norse *mosi* moss, *setr* dwelling].

Mussies, The Birsay, Beaquoyside: a wet area, perhaps with pools [Norse *mór* marsh: the English plural is not common (compare 'The Loons')].

Mustardish Sanday: only the farm buildings remain now [Norse *mór* moorland, Norse *setr* dwelling, Norse *dys* a mound].

Mustardquoy Orphir: (see above).

Muzie Orphir: exact location unknown (perhaps same name as 'Mussaquoy' below).

Mydhouse Evie: a house in Garth tunship, vanished.

Myers North Ronaldsay: [Norse *mýrr* a bog (with English plural)].

Myre Orphir; Rousay: [Norse *mýrr* a bog].

Myres Birsay, near Slinghorn; Rousay: [Norse *mýrr* a bog (with English plural)].

Myrtlelane Sanday: formerly known as 'Dog Too', a fanciful name.

Mystray Evie: [Norse *mið* middle, *setr* temporary shelter: (see 'Mistra')].

N

Nabban Firth, Bridgend: [Norse *nabbi* a protuberance (i.e., a mound), Norse *nabbi-nn* the mound].

Nabissa Stromness, Quholm: 1642 [('nab' as above); 'issa' element unknown].

Naggles o Piapittem Sanday: coastal feature, northeast Sanday [Norse *Knykill* small knob, 'Piapittem' = 'Pow o Pitten', Scots *pow* pool and Norse *pyttr-inn* the pool].

Nap Burray: a house (see 'Nabban' above).

Nap Park Evie: (see 'Nabban' above).

Napogirs = Knap o Girse Sanday: field name, Upperhouse, Orties [Norse *knappr* knob/mound, Scots *girse* grass].

Narr Ness Westray: [definition uncertain].

Narrow Geo Sanday: coastal feature, Park district [Norse *gjá* ravine].

Nava Stronsay: the field on which 'Benni Cumul' stands, west of Housebay [the 'nav' form here and below suggest that the word is a form of 'nab/nap' mound].

Navere Geo Sanday: Lady parish, coastal feature [Norse *nafarr* a gimlet: may have referred originally to a rock with a hole in it, *gjá* ravine].

Naversdale Orphir: [Norse personal name *Nafarr* and *deild* a portion (of land), *dalr* valley].

Navershaw Stromness: west of 'The Bu' [Norse personal name *Nafarr* and *haugr* mound].

Navo Sanday: Cross parish, a small headland [Norse 'nab/nap' mound].

Navsy, The Stronsay: mound at beach 'Grobister' [Norse 'nab/nap' mound, *haugr* mound].

Neagar Rousay: (as above).

Neagarth Westray: (as above).

Neager Shapinsay: [Norse *nýr* new, *garðr* farm].

Neares Shapinsay: [a contraction of 'Netherhouse' (see below)].

Nearhoose 1. Sanday village: a grocery shop at the end of the 19th century ['near' is usually a contraction of 'nether' from Norse *neðri* lower].

Nearhoose 2. Sanday, Howland; Rendall; Evie; Orphir; St. Andrews; Birsay, Marwick; Rousay: [Norse *neðri* lower].

Neb Longa Stromness: [Norse *nabbi* a protuberance, *lunga* long].

Neban Point Stromness: (see 'Nabban').

Nebban Sanday: coastal feature, 'Seater', Sellibister [Norse *nabb-inn* the projecting point, used also of mounds].

Nebbie Geo Sandwick: [both this placename and the name below relate to Norse *nabbi* mound or point but the significance is not understood, *gjá* ravine].

Nebby Geo Stronsay, Kirbister: (see above).

Nedyar Stronsay: a field on 'Hunton' [a contraction of 'Newgarth'].

Neebasa Birsay: a cliff used as a sea maithe [notice the similar placename below which is not on the coast: origin of both unknown].

Neebister 1. Sanday: on 'Warsetter' land; in the 1890s it was used as byres for the farm of Warsetter [Norse *nýr* new, Norse *ból-staðir* farm buildings].

Neebister 2. Sanday: [old house site at a mound near 'Airy'].

Needlo's Sanday: an old name for 'Westbank' ['Needlo' was the nickname of a tailor who lived there].

Neeoquoy North Ronaldsay: [Norse *nýr* new, *kví* enclosure].

Neigarth 1. Evie: (as below).

Neigarth 2. Sanday: [Norse *nýr* new, *garðr* farm].

Neigley/Niggly Evie: there was a public house here in the 1900s [Norse *knykill* a mound].

Neil's Helly Papa Westray: [probably Norse *hella* a flat rock: the attachment of a personal name suggests that it was favoured by a 'Neil' perhaps as a landing stage].

Nellan Wyre, The Bu: it later became a school [origin unknown but the suffix 'n' suggests that it is some lost Norse word related for example to English 'knoll'].

Nello Firth: [origin uncertain but see below: the suffix suggests 'o' Norse *haugr* mound].

Neo/Quoynania Rousay: [Norse *kvín* the enclosure, *nýr* new].

Nesgar/Nestyar Sanday: beach name between 'The Riv' and 'Foulan' [Norse *nes* point of land, *garðr* farm].

Nesodden Papa Westray: [Norse *nes* point of land: a dedication to *Odin*].

In the following entries 'ness' usually refers to a coastal point but rarely also refers to the shape of a field.

Ness 1. Birsay, Netherbigging, Greeny: field name.

Ness 2. Birsay, Southside: near Sallies.

Ness 3. Harray.

Ness 4. Papa Westray.

Ness 5. Rendall: near Puldrite.

Ness 6. Sandwick.

Ness 7. Shapinsay.

Ness, The 1. Sanday: area name and collective name of a row of houses, Burness parish.

Ness, The 2. St. Andrews.

Ness Geo Sanday: coastal feature.

Ness Muir North Ronaldsay: (see 'Muir').

Ness o Brough Sanday: [Norse *borg* stronghold or 'broch'].

Ness of Boray Gairsay.

Ness of Gairsay Rendall.

Ness of Hangaback Orphir [Norse *hengi* steep, *bakki* slope].

Ness of Ork Shapinsay.

Ness Sand Sanday, Otterswick: coastal feature.

Ness Shift Sanday, Gresmay: field name [Norse *skipti* a division of land].

Ness Toon North Ronaldsay.

Nessan Geo Stronsay: in the southwest of Rothiesholm [origin unknown].

Nessbreck Harray: [*brekka* slope].

Nessgarth Sanday: beach name [Norse *garðr* farm].

Nest Stromness: [short for 'Crow's Nest': location unknown].

Nethabooth Evie: north of 'Fibla Field' ['booth' is Norse *búð* a temporary summer residence: nearby is *Ayrean* (Gaelic *airigh*) which carries the same meaning].

Nether Sether Sandwick, Lyking: field name [Norse *neðri* lower in position, *seyðir* is a fire pit and is also known in Iceland as a placename, e.g., *Seyðisfjörðr* an important seaport on the east coast of the island. The meaning of the placename is not known].

In the 'nether' samples below, only short details of the original farm or field, where appropriate, are given. The main entries are to be found in the text.

Nether Breck North Ronaldsay.

Nether Breckan Sanday: [Norse *neðri* lower, Norse *brekka-n* the slope].

Nether Button Holm: [Norse *botn* end (of a field) for example].

Nether Cott North Ronaldsay.

Nether Dealy (see 'Dealy').

Nether Gorn Sanday: former name of 'Mires'.

Nether How Sanday: [Norse *haugr* mound].

Nether Howar Sanday: possibly one of the 'Howars' of Sanday but uncertain (see 'East Howar').

Nether Howland Sanday.

Nether Inkster Rendall: an old house on the farm of Inkster.

Nether Keldalays (see 'Keldalays').

Nether Linay North Ronaldsay.

Nether Treb North Ronaldsay.

Netherbigging Birsay, Greeny; Stenness; Firth: ['bigging' = Scots 'building'].

Netherbow Sandwick: a hill ridge southwest of 'Uppadie' [origin of 'bow' here unknown].

Netherby Deerness: vanished [Norse *bae* farm of importance].

Netherdale Birsay: 'Loons'.

Netherfaulds Burray: [Scots *fauld* a small enclosure].

Nethergarth Westray: Garthstown.

Netherhouse 1. Birsay: near Skelday.

Netherhouse 2. North Ronaldsay; Westray; Harray.

Netherhouse/Nears Birsay: near Stara, Marwick.

Netherskaill Birsay, Marwick.

Netherton Holm; Birsay, Nether Toon, Farafield, Skelday: [Norse *tún* field].

Netlater/Noltclet Harray: (see 'Klett' in Appendix).

Netletar Sanday: (see above).

Neuks 1. Sanday, Northwall: formerly called 'Park' [Scots *neuk*, English 'nook', used to describe an enclosure].

Neuks 2. Westray, Fribo: (see above).

Nev, The North Faray; North Ronaldsay: [Norse *nef* nose, a narrow point of rocks on the coast west of the farm of 'Skaill'].

Neva/Navi, The Stronsay: fishing ground off Holland [clearly related to *nefi* forms above but its application here is not understood].

Neven Craig Westray: [the gender of *nef* is neuter, hence 'Nevith' (above) which is correct: the 'neven' forms below show a gender shift to feminine which in Norse produces *nef-in* forms].

Neven o Grinni Westray: a green promontory on a high cliff southwest of 'Knucker Hill' (see above).

Neven Point Eday: (see above).

Nevi Skerry Flotta: a rock east of 'Roan Head', sometimes submerged, which carries a tall navigation beacon.

Nevi, The Graemsay: a small headland on the extreme south of the island (see above).

Nevin North Ronaldsay: (see above).

Nevith Stromness, Garth: another name for 'Appieteen Point', Sandwick [Norse *nef-it* the point].

New Zealand South Ronaldsay: vanished [one of the many instances of cottages built by returned emigrants and named after the area in which they had prospered].

Newan Birsay, Northside: [origin unknown].

Newark Rousay; Westray; Sanday; Rendall; Deerness; South Ronaldsay, (vanished): [Scots 'new work'].

Newbigging 1. Birsay, Southside; Stronsay; Sanday; Evie; Orphir: [Scots *bigging* building].

Newbigging 2. St. Ola, vanished (see 'Tofts'); Sandwick; Westray.

Newbreck Rendall: remains may still be seen (see 'Breck', Rendall).

Newdyke Naust Sanday: coastal feature north of 'Tafts' [Norse *naustr* boat shelter, 'new dyke' may refer to a wall of 'Tafts' farm].

Newgarth Sandwick: [Norse *ný-garðr* new farm].

Newhouse/Bum Birsay: Kirbister area (see 'Bum').

Newpark Loch Sanday: on the peninsula which goes out to 'Start Point'.

Nibister Sanday: vanished, location unknown [Norse *ný-ból-staðr* new farm].

Nichol's Croo, Point o Wyre: (see above) [Norse *kró* small enclosure].

Nickle Head South Ronaldsay: [Norse *knykill* a hillock].

Nicol Point Birsay: (see 'Nickle Head' above).

Nicol's Toorie Sandwick, Lyking: field name [origin unknown].

Nidgarth (see 'Neigarth') Evie; Rousay; Sanday: [Norse *ný-garðr* new farm].

Niggle Point South Ronaldsay: (see 'Nickle Head' above).

Niggly 1. Evie; Holm: [Norse *knykill* a knuckle used as a description of a raised surface, i.e., a mound in this case].

Niggly 2. St. Andrews; Evie: [Norse *knykill* a hillock].

Nine Rigs Rousay, Langskaill: field name [the name must precede the old system of agriculture before the Division of the Commonty in the 19th century].

Nirlies, The Rousay: two hillocks on the 'Head of Wasbister' [Orkney dialect 'nirl' a swelling, a form of English 'knurl'].

Nisnaquoy Evie: a coastal feature [Norse *njósn* 'a looking out' but the significance is unknown: *kví* enclosure].

Nistaben Stenness; Harray: [Norse *neðsta* lowermost, Scots *bigging* building].

Nistabreck Harray: [Norse *neðsta* lowermost, *brekka* slope].

Nisthouse Evie; Birsay; Stenness; Harray: [Norse *neðsta* lowermost, *hús* house].

Nistigar Evie; Westray: [Norse *neðsta* lowermost, *garðr* farm].

Nistoo Rendall: [Norse *neðsta-tún* lowermost farm in relation to 'Appietoon'].

Nistow Rendall: (see 'Stoo').

Nobagrand Stenness: 1760, location unknown but may be guessed [Norse *grandi* a shingle bank which locates the placename on the 'Bay of Ireland': it may be an old name for a prominent mound now called 'Cummany Howe', near the farm of Cummaness, Norse *nabbi* a mound].

Noland North Ronaldsay: [Norse *ný* new? no other information].

Noltland 1. Sanday: field name, east of 'Aboondariggs' [Norse *naut* cattle].

Noltland 2. Westray; Deerness: (see above).

Nor Hellia Rousay: [Norse *norðr* north, *hella* flat rock].

Norhouse Birsay: Hayon [*norðr* north].

Norquoy Stronsay, Holland; Firth, Savil; Orphir: field names [Norse *norðr* north, *kví* enclosure].

Norsmerchant St. Andrews: [Norse north, *smjör* (old) butter used figuratively to describe a stinking mess, *tjörn* pond: (see 'Smerchants' Birsay)].

Nort Kup Sanday: small elevation, Park district, Northwall [*norðr* north, origin of *kup* uncertain; related to Old English *copp*, hill?].

Norton Birsay, Greeny: [*norðr* north, *tún* field].

Nose of the Yard Hoy: [origin unknown].

Only some samples of 'north' are included below.

North Burry Brae Orphir: [Orkney dialect 'burry' a type of coarse grass].

North End, The Sanday: formerly 'Northwall' or 'Nortwa'.

North Ettit Rendall.

North Faray island: uninhabited (see 'Fara, North').

North Flat Sanday: a long flat ridge off North Harbour, Start Point.

North Gravity North Ronaldsay: (see 'Gravity').

North Gue Rendall: (see Geo in the Appendix).

North Harbour Sanday: at Start Point, it was here where lighthouse provisions were landed.

North Holm 1. North Ronaldsay: (see North Holm below).

North Holm 2. Sanday, Sellibister: field name [Norse *hólmr* island (perhaps formerly in a marsh)].

North Howar Sanday: [Norse *haugar* mounds].

North Kews Evie: [kews = quoys].

North Leavisgarth (see 'North Hoose').

North Lettan Sanday, Northwall: (see 'Lettan').

North Letty Sanday: field name [Norse *hluti* part or share].

North Leys Sanday, Boloquoy: it is possible that this was an alternative name for 'Boloquoy'.

North Lodge Sanday: formerly the lodge of 'Geramount'.

North Loup Sanday: coastal feature, Northwall [English 'loop' in common use throughout Sanday for a curving, sandy bay].

North Mire Sanday: the birthplace of Walter Traill Dennison.

North Moa Rendall.

North Right South Faray: west of the island, the name of the shore to the west of 'Back Burn' [Norse *réttr* a seasonal enclosure where sheep are counted and the fleece is removed].

North Ronaldsay An island [earlier 'Rinansey', St. Ninian's Isle, a name changed during the Norse occupation to avoid confusion with 'Rognvaldsey', i.e., 'South Ronaldsay': an unusual island in that it is surrounded by a wall to keep the sheep off farmland since they live on seaweed: population 72 in 2011].

North Shalds Sanday: shoal off Newark [Scots *shald* a shoal, from Old English *sceald* shallow].

North Skomie Sanday, Newark: field name [Norse *skamr* short].

North Thrave Sanday: (see 'Treb').

North Wads Evie.

North Yard North Ronaldsay: [Norse *jörð* a stretch of land. This word is rarely used in Orkney placenames].

Northdyke Sandwick: the name of the northern part of the parish ['dyke' must relate to an ancient turf boundary wall: (compare 'Matches Dyke' in North Ronaldsay)].

Northgarth Sanday.

Northquoy 1. Deerness: (see 'Norquoy').

Northquoy 2. Sanday; Deerness: [Norse *kví*, enclosure].

Northskaill Sanday: [Norse *skáli* hall].

Northwall Sanday: district name in the northeast; formerly 'Waas' or 'Nortwa'.

Nortie Evie: a land [no further information].

Nose o the Bring Hoy: ['nose' is a translation of Norse *nef* used elsewhere in the text to describe a cliff].

Nose o the Harper Evie.

Nose o the Head Evie.

Nose o the Ridge North Ronaldsay.

Notster 1. Deerness: a small inlet near south of the 'Querns o the Mull (Head)' origin unknown but it is possible that the name stems from an inland Norse *naut* cattle and *stíar* enclosures.

Notster 2. Holm: (see 'Notster' above).

Noup 1. Birsay, Linnabreck, Beaquoy: [Norse *gnúpr* cliff makes no sense here: it must be a transferred name].

Noup 2. Eday: [Norse *gnúpr* a headland].

Noup, The Westray, Dykeside: (see above).

A noust [Norse *naustr*] provides safe storage for a boat during the winter: sometimes it is roofed but, for the most part, unroofed. In a number of areas, nousts occur in groups, in which instances, they are found in the Norse plural form *naustar* but since naust is neuter and does not change in the plural this shows a change of gender in the form of the Norse language spoken in Orkney. Some nousts have a prefix (e.g., 'Gray's Noust' in Stromness). These are not included below.

Noust 1. Sanday, Elsness: field name.

Noust 2. Westray; Orphir; South Ronaldsay.

Noust, Eric Orlon's Orphir: [origin unknown: no record of this French inhabitant!].

Noust o Ayre Sanday: coastal feature.

Noust o Bewan Papa Westray: vanished.

Noust o Blossom Papa Westray.

Noust o Boloquoy Sanday: coastal feature (see 'Boloquoy').

Noust o Bothikan Papa Westray.

Noust o Howar North Ronaldsay.

Noust o Hundland Papa Westray: vanished.

Noust o Links Papa Westray: vanished.

Noust o Midgarth Rousay.

Noust o Moclett Papa Westray.

Noust o Pow Rousay.

Noust o Sandback North Ronaldsay.

Noust o Tafts Sanday, Tafts: coastal feature.

Noust o Taphland Westray.

Noust o Via Papa Westray: boat shelter.

Noust o Whitehowe Papa Westray.

Nouster 1. North Ronaldsay: (see above).

Nouster 2. Papa Westray: (see above).

Nouster 3. Sanday: [Norse *naustar* winter shelters for a boat].

Noustfield Sanday, Hermisgarth: field name.

Noustigar Rousay: [Norse *garðr* enclosure].

Nousts o Backiskaill Papa Westray.

Nousts o Castle Geo Westray.

Nousts o Cott Papa Westray.

Nousts o Mayback Papa Westray.

Nousts o Nistaben Papa Westray.

Nousts o Nouster Papa Westray: [the area around has taken its name from the nousts].

Nousts o Quoyolie Papa Westray.

Nousts o Rapness Westray.

Nousts o Shorehoose Papa Westray.

Nousts o Skennist Papa Westray.

Nousts o Sponess Westray.

Nousts o Tuquoy Westray.

Noutland Westray: (see 'Noltland').

Novan Rousay: the hillside northeast of 'Muckle Water' [a difficult name to interpret: if we consider that 'b' and 'v' are often interchangeable, the original may have been *nob-an* the mound, the hillside being named after the mound now vanished (see 'Nabban')].

Nowt Bield Hoy: [Scots *nowt* cattle, Scots *bield* protection for animals in the form of a turf wall or temporary building].

Nuggle Rousay: a mound on the hill ridge west of 'Wasbister' [Norse *knykill* a mound].

Nurdie Sanday: Lopness Farm, now a field name [Norse *nyrðri* the more northerly].

O

O (see 'Woo' and 'Westove').

Oacles, The Sanday, Elsness: field name, early 18th century [Norse *öxl*, the shoulder joint].

Oba Orphir: [same as 'Oback'?].

Oback Deerness; Harray; Evie; South Ronaldsay; Orphir, formerly a house where two dangerous! old women lived [Norse *á* stream, *bakki* bank].

Oback Quarries North Ronaldsay: (see below).

Occlester St. Andrews: [Norse *öxl* shoulder joint, i.e., shoulder of a hill, *setr* settlement].

Od Point o St. Andrews: [Norse *oddi* a point of land].

Odderaber, Geo of Papa Westray: [origin unknown].

Oddi Orphir: (see 'Od' above).

Oddie Field Stronsay: northwest of 'Odie'.

Oddie Stronsay: farm at base of point known as 'Linksness'.

Odin Ness Gairsay; Stronsay: (see Appendix).

Odin's Wick Sanday: former name of 'Otterswick' [Norse personal name *Auðin* and *vík* bay].

Odinsgarth Sanday: [(see *Auðin* above), Norse *garðr* farm].

Odinstone Shapinsay: a distinctive stone on the beach in 'Veantrow Bay'.

Odness Stronsay: a contraction of 'Odiness' southeast of 'Hescombe' (see above).

Odny Toomal Sanday: part of a field on 'Stove' land [Norse *odd-inn* the triangular point of land, *tún-völlr* home field].

Oessen Skerry Auskerry: [origin unknown].

Ogru Burn Graemsay: [Norse *á* stream, *gröf* pit, hole or stream which has dug itself a trench].

Oinysetter/Onziesetter Sanday: now only a name applied to the area east of 'Bea Loch' [Norse personal name *Örn*, Norse *setr* dwelling].

Oirne Firth: below the farm of 'Redland' [gravelly soil? (see below): (c.f. 'Arnesk' Evie)].

Okkambae/Okamby Sanday, Lopness Farm: field name [Norse personal name *Hákon*, Norse *boer* farm].

Olad 1. South Ronaldsay, Widewall: [Norse *á* stream, Norwegian *lad* a flat stone, probably originally stepping stones over the 'Oback Burn'].

Olad 2. South Ronaldsay: Sandwick district (see above).

Olath Harray: (see 'Olad', South Ronaldsay).

Old Boat Geo Birsay, Marwick: this noust had to be abandoned because of a wrecked ship in the vicinity and a new noust was formed to the south.

Old Butt Target Sanday: 'Plain o Fidge' [the rifle range for the Old Volunteers at the beginning of last century].

Old Man of Hoy Hoy: a 137 metre rock stack off the west coast of Hoy

Oldman Rousay: an old cottage [origin unknown].

Oliecorsquoy Westray: [an enclosure owned/tenanted by 'Oliver Corse'].

Oliver's Quoy/Quoyolie Evie: (see above).

Ollyer Tong Rousay: Leean [Ollyer = Oliver, Norse *tungi* point of land].

Oman, Pow o Harray, Netherbrough: deep pool in burn on shore of Harray Loch (see Appendix).

Omand, Well o Birsay: (see Appendix).

Onbrid Firth, Redland: [origin not known].

Ontoft South Ronaldsay: Hoxa district, vanished [Norse personal name Örn and *topt* old house site].

Onyo Firth, South Heddle: [Norse *örn* is sea eagle but the significance here is unknown since it is far from the sea].

Onziebust Egilsay; Wyre: [Norse personal name Örn and *ból-staðr* farm].

Oo/Ooin/Oot Cletts North Ronaldsay: ['cletts' is Norse 'rocks': the other element cannot be translated].

Ool, The Switha: a bold rocky point on the south end of the island [origin unknown].

Ootbarry Birsay, Marwick: [Norse *barð* a projecting cliff].

Ooter toon Stromness; Stronsay, a field on Holland [Norse *tún* cultivated enclosure in this instance].

Ooter Trula/Troola Birsay: fishing rocks on the coast [some unknown association with trolls].

Ootfreedom Birsay, Leaquoy: ['freedom' is a piece of land not allotted to a superior].

Ootlie Sanday: a small slope in the corner of 'Loch Park', 'Scar' [outlying?].

Ootslap Birsay, Northside: [Scots *slap* gate].

Ootspay Stronsay: a projecting rock [a form of Scots *spit* a point, English 'spit' a piece of land jutting out. e.g., 'Spurn Head' in Yorkshire].

Ootsuir Birsay: beach on the north side of 'Ramna Geo' [Norse *út-suðr* 'out south'].

Ootwall 1. Sanday: (see 'Newbigging', Sanday).

Ootwall 2. Sanday: east of 'Stangasetter' ['outside the wall', in this instance the tunship wall of Skelbrae].

Orakirk Orphir: small chapel dedicated to St. Peter lay at the 'Burn o Coubister' [Norse *ár* genitive of *á* stream].

Oralie/Orally South Ronaldsay: vanished [Norse *ár-hlíð* stream slope].

Orchin Egilsay: name of part of the beach in the east of the island [Norse *tjörn* small pond or loch: origin of the 'or' element unknown].

Ore Walls: [somehow or other related to Norse *á* stream: there is a stream flowing into the bay here].

Ore Lee South Ronaldsay: [Norse *eyar* islands, skerries in this case].

Orem's Fancy Stronsay: a (special?) house on the ridge of the island: William Orem lived in Orkney at the end of the 17th century.

Orgill Hoy: on the banks of a stream [Norse *ár-gil* bank of stream].

Ork Shapinsay: (see Introduction).

Ork (Big and Little) Flotta: short reefs of solid rock jutting out from shore (see Introduction).

Orklandquoy Holm: [origin unknown].

Oro, Well of Rousay: a strong spring below 'Knarston' [origin uncertain].

Oroquoy Orphir: to the west of the 'Swanbister' area [no suggestions for the 'oro' element].

Orphir a parish [originally *Örfirisey*, ey referring to the small island, the 'Holm o Houton': Norse *ör-fjara* ebbing dry, applying to offshore skerries].

Orr Shun Sandwick: [Norse 'ár' genitive of *á* stream].

Orrledge Sanday: flat rock on the beach, Lopness, and used as a pier by small local fishing boats [Norse *oyrr* gravel ridge, English 'ledge'].

Ortie Sanday: three houses all with the same name [Norse *aurr* gravel soil].

Orwick St. Andrews: [Norse *vík* bay: 'or' = ár, genitive of *á* stream, in other words, 'bay of the stream'].

Osk Shapinsay: [location and meaning unknown].

Osmundwall /Augmundr-vágr Walls: [Norse *Asmund's* Bay].

Ossamae Sanday: a dune capped spit extending east from 'Styabanks' [Norse *óss* stream mouth, *melr* sand].

Ossen Stronsay: at beach on west side of Rothiesholm [Norse *áss* a rocky ridge].

Ossen Skerry Auskerry: a small rock lying off the west coast of 'Auskerry' [possibly the same as above].

Ossi Taing South Ronaldsay: [Norse *áss* a rocky ridge, *tangi* point of land].

Ossin Egilsay: [Norse *áss-in* the rocky ridge].

Ossquoy South Ronaldsay: [Norse female personal name *Ásleif* and *kví* enclosure].

Ostie/Oslie Geo Rousay: [a small indentation in the coast near 'Corse': origin unknown].

Ostoft Shapinsay: small farm referred to as 'Osted' by the Ordnance Survey in the 1890s [Norse personal name *Asmund*, Norse *topt* an old house site].

Otter's Had Westray: [Scots *had* a shelter/safe place].

Ottergill Stenness; Orphir: [Norse *otr* otter, *gil* an incised stream or valley].

Otterswick 1. Sanday: [the farm name seems to be a back formation from 'Otterswick'].

Otterswick 2. Sanday: a bay, formerly 'Odin's Wick' [Norse personal name 'Otar': a Sanday legend says that 'Otar' lived at 'Skartan'].

Oudengar/Ounsgar Sanday, Rue: field name [Norse personal name *Auðinn*, Norse *garðr* farm].

Oumist Breckan Sanday: another name for 'Upper Breckan' [obsolete dialect *oumist* uppermost].

Our Ness Westray: eastern entrance to the 'Bay o Noup': the placename should be read as 'Howar Ness' [Norse *haugar* mounds].

Ouraquoy Firth: [Norse *aurr* clay, *kví* enclosure].

Ourequoy Burray: (see above).

Ourie Head South Ronaldsay: [Norse *eyar* islands, referring to offshore reefs].

Ourns, Loch o Wyre, Onziebust: an area with gravelly soil [Norse *aurr*].

Ours o Stews South Ronaldsay: (see 'Ourie Head' above).

Ouse, The 1. Firth; the mouth of 'Binscarth Burn' (see below).

Ouse, The 2. Sanday: landlocked bay [Norse *óss* (see 'Ossamae')].

Ouse Ber Rousay: flat rocks near the northern part of 'Scaquoy Head'.

Ouse Birsay: coast, mouth of 'Swannay Burn' (see above).

Ouse Point Sanday: coastal feature (see 'Ossamae').

Ouse Pow Sanday: narrow sea channel extending inland from 'Otterswick' to a short distance southeast of the farm of Knowe (see 'Ossamae').

Ouse/Ousiehoose Sanday: near 'The Ouse' (see 'Ossamae').

Ouseness Westray, Rackwick: east of Gill Pier [significance of 'ouse' element unknown].

Out Reef Stronsay: southeast of 'Cliva'.

Outer Clump Sanday: rock on 'Ire', a sea mark [English 'clump'].

Outer Colligan Sandwick, Lyking: field name (see 'Colliness').

Outer Creeso Sanday: outer rocks of 'Point o Creeso', 'Taftsness'.

Outer Curcatae Sanday: chapel site on Elsness [Norse *kirkja* church, *teigr* strip of land].

Outer Hangie Sanday: coastal feature, Stove.

Outer Holm Sanday, Ire: [Norse *hólmr* island].

Outer Hushan Sandwick, Lyking: field name [origin unknown].

Outer Set Sanday, Foulan: outer position for setting creels.

Outer Sound Sanday, The Riv: [Norse *sund* channel].

Outer Tolmus Stronsay: northeast of Clestran [origin unknown].

Outerbogs Stronsay: to the north of 'Housebay' [English].

Outerdykes Rousay: [outside the wall of the tunship].

Outerscaws South Ronaldsay: [Norse *skjá* a temporary building normally used seasonally].

Outertown Stronsay: a field northwest of 'Leashun'.

Outshore Point Birsay: [Norse *út-suðr* literally 'out south': it is the most southerly point of the 'Marwick' shore].

Outspay Stronsay: north of 'Burgh Head', a projecting point of rock.

Over Oacles (see 'Oacles').

Overbigging/Iverbigging Stenness: ['higher than the other bigging', i.e., Tormiston farm].

Overbist/Everbist Sanday: [now a district name Norse *efri* upper, *ból-staðr* farm].

Overbrough Harray: [the upper 'broch'].

Overdale Evie: attached to 'Dale' and 'Newfield'.

Overfaulds Burray: ['over' = 'upper', Scots *fauld* fold].

Overhouse Sandwick; Rendall, ruinous: [over = upper].

Overhow Sandwick: (see 'Housegarth').

Over-the-Water Sanday: Lady parish [similar to other forms found in Orkney placenames such as 'Abune-the-Hill,' in Birsay and 'Beneath-the-Hill' in Hoy].

Overton Orphir: [over = upper, Norse *tún* enclosure].

Ow Evie: (see 'Woo').

Owar/Ower Rendall: between 'Moa' and 'Hinderayre' [Norse *ár* streams (see 'Orquil')].

Owendsatir Shapinsay: in 'Sands' tunship, recorded in 1492, then vanished [Norse *Øyvends setr* the settlement of *Øyvend*].

Owerlan/Ourlan North Ronaldsay: [Norse *aurr* poor pebbly soil, lan = land].

Owerliddens Birsay, Millbrig: [Norse *á* stream (in genitive form), Marwick suggests that the element 'liddens' relates to meadow flats].

Owern Rousay, Langskaill: field name [Norse *aurr* gravelly soil].

Owld Lighthoose North Ronaldsay: on Dennis Head.

Ownes North Ronaldsay, Greenwall: field name [origin unknown].

Owrens Sanday, Rue: field name [Norse *aurr-inn* the clay soil (with English plural); there is a fieldname 'Owren' in Rousay].

Oxan, Point o Graemsay: [Celtic *iska* water: (see 'Axnaday')].

Oxen, Geo o Shapinsay: (see above).

Oxna Geo 1. Stronsay: 'Holms o Midgarth' (see above).

Oxna Geo 2. Stronsay: west side of 'Muckle Linga' (see above).

Oxtro Birsay: broch site [Norse *haugr* mound, *saetr* dwelling].

Oyce Sanday: (see 'Ossamae').

Oyce, The Birsay, Swannay: the mouth of the Swannay Burn.

Oyce o Herston South Ronaldsay.

Oyce o Huip Stronsay: south of 'Huip' farm.

Oyce o Isbister Rendall.

Oyce o Quindry South Ronaldsay.

Oyce-end Birsay, Hundland: the northwest end of the 'Hundland Loch' where streamlets from the meadows enter the loch [Norse *áss* mouth/end of a stream, *endi* end].

Oycelee Birsay, Swannay: [Norse *lón* a piece of marshy land].

Ozen Stromness, Stank: field name [origin unknown].

P

Packhoose North Ronaldsay: in the extreme north of the island south of 'Green Skerry' [origin of 'Packhouse' uncertain: perhaps related to barrelling pickled herring].

Padachun, Harray, Mirbister: [Norse *padda-tjörn* toad pool].

Paddie Navo/Paddy Norran Sanday: field name near 'Greenquoy' [Norse *padda* a toad: both adjectives have 'lump' as a meaning referring to their warty skin].

Padoo Moss Harray, Grimeston: [Norse *padda* a toad].

Pallion Sanday: coastal feature, Northwall, an area of flat rocks where roofing flags could be easily quarried at low tide [Norse *pallr-inn* the step (in the rock)].

Pan Flotta: the reference is to 'salt pan'.

Pantland Craigs Evie: [origin unknown].

Papa Stronsay An island off the northeast of Stronsay, originally inhabited by early missionaries and within recent years inhabited by a religious order [Norse *papi* (Celtic clergy), *ey* island].

Papa Westray: a large productive island off the northeast of Westray. originally inhabited by *papi* (see above): population 90 in 2021: famous for its 'Knap o Howar' an almost perfectly preserved Neolithic dwelling dating from a period 3,500 B.C. and said to be the oldest standing domestic dwelling in Northern Europe.

Papdale St. Ola: pronounced 'Pabdale', a piece of land originally allotted to the clergy [Norse *papi* clergy].

Papey Grunyie Papa Stronsay: a shoal northeast of the island [Norse *grunn* shoal].

Paplay 1. Holm: part of Holm parish, a large district in the east of the parish much of which was clearly given over to the Celtic clergy.

Paplay 2. South Ronaldsay: an area given over to the early Celtic missionaries: the main church of St. Peters was established here.

Paplay-hoose Eday: a small croft in the 'Cusvie' area [origin of 'Paplay' here is uncertain: perhaps the surname 'Paplay'].

Paradise Sanday: a fanciful name [many houses in England and Wales carry such a name].

Park 1. Sanday: district between Lopness and Start.

Park 2. Sanday: former name of 'Neuks'.

Park 3. Westray, Rackwick: ['Park' in Orkney placenames often refers to a very large, enclosed field, apparently of administrative rather than agricultural use].

Park o Basso Rendall: near 'Appietoon'.

Park o Cara South Ronaldsay.

Park o How Sanday, Stove: field name.

Park o Ire Sanday, Bellview: field name (see 'Ire').

Park o Sootan Swona: [Norse *suðr* south, *tún* enlosure].

Parkaway Sanday, Newark: field name [origin unknown].

Parkhouse Sanday: old name for the house of 'Quivals'.

Parkiehoose Sanday: recorded in the 1841 Census (same as above?).

Parks o Moan Stenness: use of the plural form here not understood.

Parlgo Sanday: Broughstoon [a derogatory name for a cottage, dialect 'pirl' or 'parl' sheep dung; (for 'go' element see 'Geo' in Appendix)].

Parliament Square Pentland Skerries: a gathering place for cormorants!

Pass, Geo o Evie: [origin unknown].

Patie's Hoose Sanday: field name [the name refers to the burial chamber at 'Ruthie Taing': 'Patie' is a dialect form of 'Peter' but may be a local name for a sprite].

Patience Westray, Midbea: a fanciful name like 'Paradise' above.

Peat Geo Evie: [peats were brought here from Eynhallow and landed in this geo, Norse *gjá* ravine].

Peatbanks Sanday, Newark: field name [a shallow basin of peat alluvium lies/lay here].

Peatgate Birsay, Northside: [Norse *gata* path (to the peats)].

Peatwall Westray, Aikerness: [origin of 'wall' here uncertain].

Peckhole/Peekhole North Ronaldsay: an old farm south of the 'Knowe o Samilands' [Scots *peck* a small unit of land].

Peeblesquoy South Ronaldsay: [the Scots surname 'Peebles', Norse *kví* enclosure].

Peedie Geo Sanday: coastal feature, also known as 'Little Geo' [dialect 'peedie', little].

Peedie Kiln Sanday: coastal feature, a sea inlet ['kiln' is a reference to the spume here resembling a smoking kiln].

Peedie Pert Sanday: coastal feature, Burness parish [Orkney dialect *peedie* small, *pert* part].

Peedie Sea 1. Sanday: a lagoon cut off by 'Elsness' and 'Ouse Point'.

Peedie Sea 2. St. Ola, Kirkwall: [formerly 'Peerie Sea': a shallow lagoon created by a shingle bank known as 'The Ayre' which blocked off the exit of the streams draining into it].

Peeky Firth, Lyde: [suggests a high elevation where it is possible to 'peep down' at the surroundings (see 'Keek' Evie)].

Peeno Rousay: a vanished house in Sourin ['pin' with diminutive 'o': (see 'Corsey's Pin')].

Peerie Breast Westray: a small, projecting cliff ['peerie' is an earlier form of 'peedie'].

Peerie Hill Stromness: ['little hill'].

Peerie Tuna Evie: grassy projecting ledge near cliff top [Norse *púfa* mound with definite article suffix 'in'].

Peerie Water Evie: [Norse *vatn* loch, dialect 'peerie' small].

Pegal Burn Walls: a stream which flows eastward reaching the sea at a point facing 'Rysa Little' [origin of 'Pegal' uncertain].

Peiblis Cott Birsay, Northside: [Scots family names 'Peebles'].

Pelkie's Hole Firth: ['Pelkie' was a nickname for the Devil].

Pelt South Ronaldsay: a field name in the Windwick area [Scots *pelt* worthless].

Pentland Firth a stretch of water separating Orkney and Caithness [originally it was called '*Péttland*' from '*Petti*' Norse for 'Pict'].

Pentland Skerries South Ronaldsay: large reefs off the southeast of the island: at one time it accommodated eight families: uninhabited since 1994.

Perk Sanday: field name [common dialect variation of English 'park'].

Perk Door Sanday: on 'Outer Holm', Ire [the 'door' to the 'park' on 'Outer Holm'].

Perks, The Rendall: field on 'Lower Biggings'.

Perks, White Rendall: fields on 'Biggings' ['white' probably relates to 'cotton grass'].

Pernealy, Head of Eday: a point of land projecting into the sea on the northeast coast of the 'Calf of Eday' [origin unknown: possibly the Scots surname 'Parnally'].

Perteens Sanday: coastal feature, Ire [English 'partings', i.e. division, in this instance the division relates to seaweed allotment].

Perth Westray: Rapness district, originally 'Prettie' in 1492 [Norse *pretta* to cheat (over a land transaction?)].

Peter/Coubuster Skerry Orphir: [Norse *sker* reef].

Peter Kirk Sanday, Garbo: field name, formerly a large ecclesiastical building containing a well stood here.

Peter Kirk, Waal o Sanday: [a well near 'Peter Kirk': dialect *waal* well].

Peter Wylie's Hunda: the only house on 'Hunda', a small island off Burray, it never had a name!

Peterditch Road Sanday Burness: [Norse *pyttar* pools].

Peterheillye/Peterhellyo Sanday: rocky shore of 'Inner Sound', Ire [Norse *pyttar* pools; there are many pools in this area, Norse *hella* flat rock].

Peterkirk Evie: remains of, northeast of 'Muckle Pow'.

Peterkirk Westray: chapel site.

Petertown Orphir: [after the old kirk of that name].

Phislegar North Ronaldsay: (see 'Fisligar').

Piapittem Ebb Sanday: coastal feature [Scots *ebb*, foreshore: 'piapittem' is a corruption of 'pow o pitten' Scots *pow*, pool, Norse *pyttr-inn*, the pool].

Pickadyke North Ronaldsay: ['dyke' = earthen wall, 'pick' is the Orkney dialect form of Norse *pettr* Pict, the name given to the Celtic inhabitants of Orkney before the arrival of the Norse].

Pickaquoy St. Ola: (see above).

Pickasquoy Harray: evidence of something ancient locally suggested that this enclosure might have been established by the Picts.

Pickletellum Deerness: a ruin called locally Picktill [a village in Fife just across the River Tay from Dundee].

Pickling Skerries Swona: [where herrings were gutted and packed tightly in barrels].

Picto Evie: an old hill dyke (c.f. 'Picky Dyke': see below).

Pictou Westray: a mound said to be of Pictish origin [Norse *þúfa* mound].

Picts' Hoose Sanday: near Start Point [dialect *Picts' Hoose* applied to any ancient building of obscure origin].

Picts' Hoose Field Sanday, Elsness: field name [the field takes its name from 'Quoyness' chambered cairn nearby].

Picts' Waal Hoy: [believed to be a well, used by the Picts].

Pierowall Westray: principal settlement on the island [properly 'The pier o Wall' where 'wall' is a corruption of Norse *vágr* bay].

Piggar Orphir: [an unusual placename, several of which exist: a very early use of the word 'pig' instead of 'swine': Norse *garðr* enclosure].

Pigger Westray: Cleatown (see above).

Piggiger North Ronaldsay: recorded in 1653 (see above).

Pikanestie Sanday, Stove: field name [Norse *Pettanna* genitive plural of *Pettr* Pict, Norse *staðr* farm].

Pinap Birsay, Swannay: location and site unknown [a house that had been 'pinned up'?].

Pincod Sanday: former name of 'The Rock' [dialect *pincod* pincushion: the significance of this name is unknown but compare 'Needlo's'].

Pirlo Birsay, Swannay: vanished, position unknown [dialect pirl sheep dung, in other words a 'filthy place'].

Pisgah Westray: location unknown ['Pisgah' is a Biblical name: it lay to the east of the Jordan River: use of the name here is not understood].

Pisgah/Mount Pleasant Birsay, Abune-the-Hill: nearby lies the 'Well of Jericho'!

Pit o the Riv Sanday: a pit specially constructed for the treatment of kelp when Sanday was an important producer of this material (see 'Kelp Factory').

Pitagrana Harray, Netherbrough: field name [Norse *pytt* pool: origin of 'grana' not known].

Pitcho Rousay: Frotoft district, a small loch [Norse *pyttr* pool, *tjörn* loch].

Pitgreys Sanday: land on Westove [Norse *pyttr* pool: nearby is 'Greasgate'].

Pitnabornaquoy Birsay, Hayon: field name [a difficult name to interpret, perhaps Norse *pytt-in* the pool on *Bjarni's* enclosure].

Pitten Birsay, Marwick: (see 'Sellibister' below).

Pitten 1. Birsay: coast [Norse *pyttr-inn* the pool: there are many rock pools on the coast in this area].

Pitten 2. Evie: (see Sellibister below for origin).

Pitten 3. Sanday, Sellibister: [Norse *pyttr-inn* the pool].

Pitten Swarto, Pow o Rousay: [literally 'The pool of the black', Norse *pyttr-inn* the pool, *svartr* black, Scots *pow* pool].

Pitten, Point o Rousay, Kili Holm: (see 'Pitten' forms above).

Pittos o Dale Evie: [Norse *pytt* pool (with English plural)].

Place, The 1. Birsay: village [corrupted form of 'The Palace' and invariably used locally].

Place, The 2. Burray: = the Bu, Burray.

Plank, The Rendall Fields on Upper/Lower Biggings, Gitterpitten, Hogarth (see below).

Plank, The Sanday, Elsness: field name, early 18th century [French *planche* strip of land, through Old Scots].

Plantie Crues North Ronaldsay: small enclosures for growing kale [Norse *kró* enclosure].

Plittro Birsay: Sabiston [dialect 'plittro' a muddy mess].

Ploverbrake South Ronaldsay: [the name of this moorland bird was frequently used to give names to poorly built 'cottages' on the fringe of settlements].

Ploverha Evie; Eday: (see above).

Ploverhall Rousay; Wyre: (see above).

Pockie Spelds Sandwick: [Norwegian dialect *spjell* a strip of land, 'pockie' seems to be Scots in the sense 'small'].

Point o Queehammeron Evie: [Norse *kví* enclosure, *hamarr* rock with definite article suffix].

Point o Runas Sandwick: field below Ness [Norse *raun* stony ground].

Point o Spindle Orphir: (see 'Spindil').

Pole/Pool Westray: [Norse *pollr* pool].

Pole/Poolsherp Burray: now 'Pole' [Norse *pollr* pool, *skarpr* dry and barren: the meaning seems to be 'poor land with pool in it'].

Pomels Birsay, Northside: [the only record of the surname 'Pomel' in Orkney].

Pomona Inn (see 'Finstown').

Pontooth Sanday: Tresness [also called 'Point o Touthey': Norse *þýfðr* hillocky].

Pool Sanday, Laminess; Deerness; South Ronaldsay: [Norse *pollr* pool].

Pool Geo Sanday: coastal feature, Ire [Norse *pollr* pool, *gjá* ravine].

Poolow Evie: [Norse *pollr* pool, for 'low', Norwegian (Nynorsk) *lón* watery meadow flat].

Poor Hoose Sanday: the former 'Poor House' of Sanday (see 'Riverside').

Pootch, The Rendall: on the land of Biggings; a watery hole [Scots *pootch* badly drained land'].

Port o Aikerness Evie: a rocky jetty providing a link to Rousay.

Port Selr Sanday: a small stony creek west of 'Rivesbank' and guarded by two small rocks [Norse *port* gate, Norse *selar* seals].

Portingale Sanday: Cleat district [a fanciful name 'port in gale'].

Pow Sandwick; Rousay; North Ronaldsay; Sanday; Evie; Harray; Westray: [Scots *pow* pool].

Pow o Puldee(k) Sanday: [Scots *pow* pool, Norse *dokk* depression].

Powshed/Powsheet Sanday, Warsetter: field name [Scots *pow* pool, there is a well in the middle of this field, Scots *schedd* a piece of land distinctive in some way].

Powstink 1. North Ronaldsay: alternative name for 'Milldam' (see below).

Powstink 2. Westray: [English 'stink' suggesting stagnant water].

Prattsfauld/Sprattsfauld Sanday: ['Pratt', earlier 'Parrat' an old Sanday Surname, Scots *fauld* an enclosure].

Pressquoy Stromness: ['priest's quoy'? (see 'Priest's Loch' below)].

Pretty Westray: (see 'Perth').

Pretty/Standpretty Rousay: [fanciful name popular in the 19th century].

Prettykirk Evie: (see 'Peter Kirk').

Priest's Loch South Ronaldsay: [no information].

Priory, The Sanday: name applied to the corner of an old building which stood in Lady Kirkyard [origin unknown].

Puckquoy Eday: [(for 'Puttquoy'?) Norse *pyttr* a pit or hole in the ground].

Puddeney Knowe Sanday: coastal feature to the north of Kistaklett, Lettan [a mound which looks like a pudding].

Puil Birsay: coastal point north of 'Snushan' [Norse *pollr* pool: such pools can be very wide bays].

Pulaber Geo Birsay: ravine with a narrow entrance but widening further in, making a kind of pool [Norse *pollr* pool, *berg* rock].

Pulaland Rendall, Hall o Rendall: field name [an area covered with pools: originally a croft: also known as 'Clankvengeance'].

Pulbuskus Birsay: on the coast [Norse *pollr* pool: the name 'biskus' is also found in the Marwick area: origin unknown].

Puldrite Sanday: coastal feature, Foulan [Norse *pollr* pool, Norse *drit* filth: there is also a 'Puldrite' in the parish of Rendall].

Pulgreasy Birsay: Marwick Head, a ledge in the cliff face [Norse *pallr* bench: second element cannot be interpreted].

Pulkitto Evie: [Norse *pollr* pool, Norse *keyta* foul water].

Pullaice Evie: 17th century [probably a form of 'pools'].

Pullan Stenness: location uncertain [Norse *pollr* pool with definite article suffix].

Pulpit Evie: [Norse *pollr* pool, *pyttr* hole or pit in the ground].

Pulram Birsay: coastal feature, Snushan [Norse *pollr* pool, Norse *ramr* bitter in the sense 'rotten'].

Pulse Skerry Stromness: a rocky area south of the Sand of Warbeth ['pulse' = 'pools'?].

Pulswarto Rendall: a swampy area near Blubbersdale [Norse *pollr* pool, *svart* dark].

Pultisquoy Stromness: [Norse *kví* enclosure, 'pult' is a nickname of the owner based on Norse *piltr* boy].

Pulwilla Birsay: a deep hole in the Curcum area [Norse *pollr* pool, *hvíla* resting, which suggests a quiet pool].

Pund North Ronaldsay: [English 'pound' an enclosure].

Purgator 1. Sanday: former name of 'Hillhead', Sellibister [a name usually applied to ale houses].

Purgator 2. South Ronaldsay: sometimes used metaphorically of land that was difficult to work but more often applied to ale houses.

Purgatory 1. Birsay, Beaquoy: [an ale house?].

Purgatory 2. Firth, Lettaly: it was situated near the site of the parish gallows!

Purgatory 3. Sanday: it stood near 'Mary Kirk' and was an ale house; there were frequently ale houses near parish churches.

Purgatory/Pug/Sailor's Home Birsay, Northside: (see below).

Purmha Eday: (see 'Needlo's', 'Pincod', etc.) the house of a tailor [Scots *purm* a cotton reel].

Purtabreck North Ronaldsay; St. Andrews: [Norse *brekka* slope: (for 'purta' see below)].

Purtaquoy Shapinsay: [Norse *kví* enclosure (see below for 'purta')].

Purtna Lurtna Birsay: coastal name [rhyming Norse words, both of which carry the meaning 'filth': 'purt' is an Orkney and Shetland Norn word meaning filth or dirt and Norse *lort* is filth: the suffix represents the definite article as in the case of 'Queena' for example].

Purvis South Ronaldsay: field name, originally a cottage by this name [English 'purvis' the holy area in front of a cathedral, hence this name falls into a group of old house names such as 'Mounthoolie', etc.].

Putt Steeven North Ronaldsay: a hole or channel between the shore and an outlying rock called the 'Steven o Papy' [there must be some confusion in the naming of this rock. The name 'steven' is found in several parts of Orkney: Norse *pyttr* a hole, *stúfr* a bit cut off, *fen* marsh].

Q

Quacko Evie/Rendall: [a piece of soft 'quaking' moor: location uncertain].

Quackquoy Birsay, Marwick: a difficult name to interpret, similar to Quatquoy in Firth ['white'? enclosure, referring to cotton grass or to sparse leached turf].

Quadraa Rousay: Sourin district [Norse *kví* enclosure: the element 'draa' cannot be explained].

Quam Orphir: [Norse *hvammr* a rounded valley].

Quan Westray: [a variation of the name above].

Quandal Rousay: [Norse *hvammr* rounded valley, *dalr* valley].

Quanoo Orphir: [Norse *hvammr* (as above), 'oo' element may relate to 'stream' as in 'Woo', Evie].

Quanterness St. Ola: [Norse *nes* point of land: origin of 'quanter' unknown].

Quarrel Geo South Ronaldsay: there was a quarry here at one time which provided good, thin roofing flags.

Quarrel, Point o Wyre, Helziegitha: probably relates to an old quarry.

Quarrelbraes Evie: there was an inn here in the early 1900s [English 'quarry'].

Quarrelhouse Orphir: built near quarries.

Quarry o Linn Sanday: near Hettle (see 'Lindamire').

Quarrybraes/Braes Rousay: Sourin area, the site of former quarries: now usually referred to as 'Braes' only.

Quarryhall Sanday: entered in the 1841 Census, position unknown; [perhaps the same as 'Quarryhoose'].

Quarryhole Rendall: home of Annie Harper, hawker, famous itinerant collector of eggs, etc.

Quarryhoose Evie; South Ronaldsay; Sanday, it lay southwest of 'Scarrigar' on Warsetter land: material for roadmaking was obtained from a nearby quarry.

Quatquoy Firth: [Norse *hvítr* white, *kví* enclosure: the white element probably refers to thin, leached turf].

Quavie/Quivie Sanday, Northwall: also written 'Wheevie' [Norse *kví* enclosure, *vegr* road].

Quean Sandwick; Harray: [Norse *kví* enclosure with definite article suffix].

Quear Firth; Birsay; Rousay; Westray: [Norse *kví-ar* enclosures].

Queear Birsay, Greeny: [Norse *kví* in plural form = *kvíar*].

Queekirsay Harray: [Norse *kví* enclosure plus personal name 'Christie'].

Queen's Howe, Knowe o Westray: [Norse *haugr* mound].

Queena Birsay, Abune-the-Hill, Twatt; Stenness; Firth; Sandwick: 'Queen' means 'the enclosure' [Norse *kví* with the definite article suffix, to give the form *kví-n*. The final 'a' is a local and meaningless addition, akin to Italian 'o' at the end of many words].

Queena Howe Westray: enclosure near a probable broch mound [Norse *haugr* mound].

Queenabreckan Birsay, Gelderhouse, Barony; Harray; Westray: [Norse *brekka-n* the slope].

Queenaday Birsay: Skelday [Norse *kví-n* the enclosure, *dý* moorland or marsh].

Queenafinieth Harray: [Norse *fen* marsh with definite article 'it' suffix, usually written 'ith' in Orkney].

Queenafiold Birsay, Southside; Harray: [Norse *fjall* hill].

Queenalanga Sandwick: [Norse *langr* long].

Queenalia Evie: [*hlíðar* slopes].

Queenalonga Birsay: (see above).

Queenamarion Stenness: [personal name 'Marion'].

Queenamidda Rendall: [last element suggests Norse *miðr* middle].

Queenamilyoar Firth: a field on Binscarth [Norse *milli* between, *ár* streams: west of Binscarth Farm, now drained].

Queenamoan Stenness: [Norse *mór-in* the moor].

Queenamuckle Rendall: [Norse *mikla* big].

Queensbrig Sanday: [Norse *kvín* the enclosure, 'brig' is a Sanday variant of 'breck' from Norse *brekka* slope; (compare 'Inyan Brig')].

Quegar Sanday: Cleat district, location unknown [Norse *kví* enclosure, Norse *garðr* farm].

Quern Geos Calf of Eday: (see above).

Quern o Grithin Rousay: (see 'Grithin').

Quern o Whisber Rousay: a rock on the beach south of 'Skaebrae Head' [it probably behaves like a quern at high tide].

Quern Swarf Sanday: rocks, northeast Burness parish [Norse *quern* a hand mill, *svarf* tumult, a reference to the churning of the sea].

Quholm Stromness: (see above).

Quholm/Holm Shapinsay: [Norse *hvammr* a rounded valley].

Quholmslie Stromness: [Norse *hvammr* a rounded valley, *hlíð* slope].

Qui Ayre Sandwick: [Norse *kví* enclosure, *eyrr* gravel spit].

Quilaverans Firth, Grimbister: [personal name *Laverans* = Laurence].

Quildings Quoy Stromness: old name of 'Quildon' (see below).

Quildon Stromness: [Norse *hvíld* resting place for a funeral party].

Quina Ho Sanday: coastal feature, 'Backaskaill Bay' [Norse *kvín* the Enclosure, Norse *haugr* mound].

Quina Westray; Stenness; Stromness: (same as 'Queena').

Quinagreena Westray: [the 'green enclosure', Norse *groena* green].

Quinamuckinshay Westray: [Norse *kvín* the enclosure, *myki-n* the dung, 'hay' = how = Norse *haugr* mound].

Quinania/Neo Rousay; Stenness: [Norse *nýr* new].

Quindry South Ronaldsay: [Norse *kví-n* the enclosure, *drit* marsh in this instance].

Quinni Rendall; Birsay: [Norse *kví-n* the enclosure, *nýr* new].

Quinnimoan Evie: [Norse *mór-in* the moor: (see 'Quinni' above)].

Quire/Quoire Sanday: in 1877, this was a ruin situated at the northeast corner of Kettletoft Bay [Norse *kvíar* enclosures].

Quitamoa Orphir: [Norse *hvítr* white, *mór* moorland: white with bog cotton or leaching].

Quithagoathe Evie/Rendall: [Norse *hvítr* white: (for 'goathe' see Geo in Appendix) (compare 'Guithe') the placename means 'bog cotton marsh'].

Quivals Farm Sanday: formerly 'Parkhouse' [Norse *kví* enclosure, *völlr* field (with English plural)].

Quiven Sanday: [Norse *kví* enclosure, Norse *fen* marsh].

Quoire (see 'Quire').

Quoy North Faray; South Ronaldsay; Sanday: [Norse *kví* enclosure].

Quoy/Queefiglamo Birsay: 'Burn of Lushan' [Norse *mór* moorland: origin of 'figl' unknown].

Quoy Bano Evie: [origin of 'bano' element not understood].

Quoy Biscas Birsay, Southside: [bishop's land?].

Quoy Hokka Birsay, Southside: [Norse *haugr* mound = 'Howquoy'].

Quoy Liddie Sanday, Colligarth: field name [Norse *hlið* gate].

Quoy o Horonsay Harray: [possibly a transferred name from 'Horraldsay' (pronounced 'Horonsay') in Firth].

Quoy o Mounthoolie Evie: (see 'Mounthoolie').

Quoy o Slap Evie: [Scots *slap* gate].

Quoyangry/Angerquoy Westray; Orphir; South Ronaldsay: [Norse *engjar* meadows].

Quoyayre Sanday: Elsness [Norse *kví*, enclosure, *eyrr* gravel spit].

Quoyball South Ronaldsay: [Norse *ból* resting place for animals].

Quoybanks St. Ola; North Ronaldsay; Sanday, coastal feature: [Norse *kví* enclosure, English 'banks'].

Quoybarrow Harray: [Norse *borg* a reference to one of the many Iron Age towers in this area].

Quoybeezie Firth, Redland: [Norse *báss* stall in a byre, hence 'animal pen'].

Quoybelloch Deerness: [Norse *ból* resting place for animals with local diminutive].

Quoybernardis Holm: [the personal name 'Bernard'].

Quoyberstane St. Ola: (see 'Berstane').

Quoybewmont St. Andrews: [from the surname 'Beamond' recorded locally].

Quoybirse Westray, Broughton: [personal name *Bersi*].

Quoyblackie Rendall: (c.f. 'Blackbraes', Stenness).

Quoybleers Stronsay: field north of Holland [origin unknown].

Quoyboon South Ronaldsay: Sandwick area [Scots *bund* border].

Quoybora Stronsay: [origin of 'bora' unknown].

Quoybreckan Westray: (see 'Breckan').

Quoybrown South Ronaldsay: earlier 'Quoybrownaris' [personal name 'Bernard'].

Quoybuise Westray: Broughton ['buise' represents the Orkney surname 'Bews'].

Quoybunds Birsay, Bea: [Scots *bund* border].

Quoyburing Deerness: [Norse *borg-in* the broch].

Quoyburray St. Andrews: [from the Orkney surname 'Burray' or transferred name from the island of Burray].

Quoyburrigar Westray: [Norse *borg* broch, *garðr* farm].

Quoybutton South Ronaldsay, Hoxa: [Norse *botn* end, of a field, for example].

Quoycanker 1. Birsay: a house mentioned in the witch trial of Annie Taylor in 1624; probably one of the 'Canker' placenames (see 'Canker').

Quoycanker 2. Deerness: now 'Daystar' (see 'Canker').

Quoycanker, Pows o Birsay, Ravie Hill: [Scots *pow* pool: (see 'Canker')].

Quoycare Rousay: near 'Brough' on Westside, vanished [Norse *kjerr* boggy land].

Quoyclerks Orphir: [English 'clerk'].

Quoycous South Ronaldsay: vanished, it lay in the Eastside district (see 'Keys').

Quoycrude Sanday: farm mentioned in the Commissariot Record of 1619; location unknown; [perhaps the same as 'Crudy'].

Quoycrusda Deerness: [Norse *kró* enclosure, *dý* marsh].

Quoycuip South Ronaldsay: [Norse *koppr* hollow].

Quoycuise South Ronaldsay: [Norse *kös* a heap of stones].

Quoycurris Westray: [origin of 'curris' element unknown].

Quoydandy St. Ola [Scots surname 'Dandy'].

Quoydoun South Ronaldsay: ['doun' may mean 'lower' here (see 'Dounby')].

Quoydyke Swona: like most other islands Swona was divided into three by dykes.

Quoyeden South Ronaldsay: [girls' name 'Eden'].

Quoyenis South Ronaldsay: [personal name Inga?].

Quoyer/Queer Westray; Stenness: [Norse *kvíar* plural of *kví* enclosures].

Quoyerriga Harray: [Norse *eyrr* gravel spit, *garðr* farm].

Quoyestre Rousay: [easter quoy].

Quoyfaras Rousay: (see 'Faro').

Quoyfaulds Eday: [Scots *fauld* enclosure].

Quoyfea Deerness: Norse *fjall* hill].

Quoyfeggie Evie/Rendall: [Icelandic *feygja* to let decay, i.e., to abandon?].

Quoyfree Rendall: (see 'Freedom').

Quoygelding Birsay, Northside: [Norse *geldingr* wether, a castrated ram].

Quoygeo/Wheygeo Sanday: coastal feature [Norse *kví* enclosure, Norse *gjá* ravine].

Quoygrava Evie: [Norse *gróf* hollow].

Quoygray Rousay: no record of a 'Gray' surname in Rousay [origin of 'gray' element unknown].

Quoygrinnie Rousay: [Norse *groena* green].

Quoyhenry Rendall: [personal name].

Quoyhorrie Birsay: [Norse *horr* really nasal discharge, but here probably has the Old English meaning 'filthy' referring to wet, marshy land].

Quoyhorsetter South Ronaldsay: earlier 'Quoyschorsetter' [Norwegian (Nynorsk) *skur* hut, *saetr* a seasonally used hut, i.e., a shieling].

Quoyinga South Ronaldsay: [girl's name 'Inga'].

Quoyingabister Holm: [personal name 'Inga', *ból-staðr* farm].

Quoyinnimoan? Evie: [Quinnimoan?].

Quoyita Harray: [origin of 'ita' element unknown].

Quoyjenny Rousay: [Norse *tjörn* pool].

Quoykea 1. Harray: [Norse *kýr* cattle].

Quoykea 2. St. Andrews; Harray: [Norse *kýr* cattle].

Quoykilling Westray: [Norse *kel(d)a* well, *eng* meadow (compare 'Kilheugh')].

Quoykua Deerness: (see 'Quoykea' above).

Quoylanks Deerness: ['lanks' element unknown: perhaps a corruption of 'links'].

Quoylealand Sanday: formerly 'Hobbister' (see 'Lealand').

Quoyleith South Ronaldsay: [Norse *hlíð* slope].

Quoylet Westray: [Norse *hluti* share (see 'Lettan' forms)].

Quoylinga Orphir: [Norse *lyng* heather].

Quoylonga Birsay, Marwick: ['longa' = Norse *langr* long].

Quoyloo South Ronaldsay; Sandwick: [Norwegian (Nynorsk) *lón* a marshy area].

Quoymorhouse Shapinsay: [Norse *mór* moor].

Quoymos Deerness: [Norse *mosi* moss].

Quoymyrland Deerness: Mirland [Norse *mýrr* a bog].

Quoynagreenie Sanday: beach name, Taftsness [Norse *kvín* the enclosure, *groenn* green].

Quoynaknap Graemsay: [Norse *nap* mound].

Quoynalonga Rousay, Ness: [Norse *kvín* the enclosure, *langr* long].

Quoyneip Setter Walls: [Norse *gnípa* protruding point, *setr* dwelling].

Quoyness/Quoyaness Sanday: a beach name [Norse *nes* point of land].

Quoyock Sanday: [perhaps 'ock' is a local diminutive, hence 'small enclosure'].

Quoyolie Papa Westray: [personal name 'Olaf'].

Quoyorally South Ronaldsay: [Norse *ár-hlíð* slope of the streams].

Quoyostray Rousay: [Norse *austri* to the east].

Quoypecko Birsay: above Skelday [Scots *peck* a small unit of land].

Quoypetty Deerness: [origin of 'petty' unknown].

Quoyribs Sanday: beach name, Newark [Norse *kví* enclosure, 'ribs' = Shetland dialect 'rips', used to describe strips of fields].

Quoyruina/Runa Birsay: Kirbister area [Norse *raun* stony ground].

Quoyrush Deerness: [Norse *hrossa* horse/mare].

Quoys Birsay, Beaquoy; Westray, Dykeside; Hoy; Walls; Evie; Burray; Graemsay; Orphir; Stromness; Rousay; South Ronaldsay; Sandwick: [English plural of *kvíar* enclosures].

Quoys o Quinea Birsay, Kirbister: ['nea' = Norse *nýr* new].

Quoys o the Hill Birsay, Northside: this hill area produced good roofing flagstones.

Quoyschoirt Evie: [from the Orkney surname 'Shoart'].

Quoyscottie Birsay, Beaquoy: [from lost surname 'Scottie'].

Quoyscows Rousay: [Icelandic *skjár* a hut: (see 'Scews')].

Quoysharps South Ronaldsay: it probably lay near Cara [Norse *skarpr* dry and barren soil].

Quoysheed Sanday, Hermisgarth: field name [Norse *kví* enclosure, Scots *shed*, a piece of land different in some respects from its surrounding].

Quoyshoir Evie: [17th century Orkney surname Shoart?].

Quoysin Sandwick: [possibly 'sean' Norse *tjörn* pool (see 'Dyke o Sean')].

Quoyskega Westray: [Norse *skeggi* rough (land) probably covered with scrub].

Quoysmiddie South Ronaldsay: ['smiddie' = 'smithy'].

Quoythom Holm: [from the surname 'Thom'].

Quoytoans Harray: [Norse *púfa* mound (with English plural)].

Quoytob St. Andrews: (see 'Toab').

Quoyturben Deerness: [possibly Norse (see 'Treb')].

R

Rabbitha Westray; Rendall: an old house near 'Riff' [a name given in jest].

Rackwick Westray; Hoy; Stromness: [Norse *rek* flotsam, *vík* bay].

Raff's Quoy Sanday, West Brough: field name [personal name 'Ralph', Norse *kví* enclosure].

Ragan Firth, Redland: a small cottage [Norse *raki* damp (of the land)].

Ragan, Well o Firth: (see above).

Ramberry St. Ola: a point of land on the shore near Quanterness [Norse *berg* rock: origin of 'ram' uncertain].

Rami Geo Eday; South Ronaldsay; Pentland Skerries: [probably carries the same meaning as 'ramli' below].

Ramli Geo Birsay: coastal feature [Scots *ramle* broken stones, Norse *gjá* ravine].

Ramna Geo/Risdae Evie: a rowing boat can enter this geo until it becomes too dark to proceed [Norse *hramn* raven].

Ramray Graemsay: [unknown origin].

Rams Geo Shapinsay: a small indentation on 'The Galt' [origin unknown].

Ramsay Rousay; Westray, earlier 'Ramyshow': [Norse personal name *Hramn*, *haugr* mound. Where a personal name is attached to a *haugr* the *haugr* is usually written 'ay' (see 'Horraldsay')].

Ramsdale Orphir: [perhaps Norse personal name *Hramn* and *dalr* valley].

Ramsquoy Stenness; South Ronaldsay: [Norse personal name *Hramn* and *kví* enclosure].

Randa Birsay, Brockan, Marwick: field name [Norse *rönd* boundary (see 'Stane Randa')].

Randi-Keely Rousay: a well in a field of 'Ervadale', Sourin [Norse *rönd* boundary, *kelda* well].

Ranga Sanday, Elseness: field name [Norse *rangr* crooked, a reference to the shape of the field].

Rangeger Harray, Netlater: [Norse *rangr* crooked, *garðr* wall or farm].

Rangie Sanday, West Brough: field name (see above).

Rango Sandwick: [Norse *rangr* crooked, Norse *á* stream].

Ranisgarth Westray, Skelwick: vanished [Norse personal name *Hramn*, Norse *garðr* farm].

Ranscow, Burn of South Ronaldsay: [Norwegian (Nynorsk) *skjaa* a hut made of loose boards in which meat etc. was placed to dry: origin of 'ran' element not known].

Ransgarth Harray: (see 'Ranisgarth' above).

Rantan Birsay, Swannay: [a house named after the occupant who had the nickname 'Rantan' i.e., carousing].

Rapness Westray: a district name [most probably Norse *hreppr* district].

Rattany Brae Sanday: mound on the east side of Taftsness [obsolete dialect 'raton' rat].

Rattle Up Birsay; Sanday: the former name of 'Strangquoy' [dialect *rattle up* to build quickly; a house which was 'rattled up'].

Rattlypots Sanday, Tresness: field name, named after a vanished house [origin unknown].

Ravie Hill Birsay: [the 'vie' element represents Norse *fjall* hill: the 'ra' element is uncertain].

Readypenny Stromness: coast near the old lead mine, a good place to catch sillocks [origin unknown].

Reanna Skerry Birsay: a long skerry off the Birsay coast [origin unknown].

Red Craig Birsay; Sanday: [sandstone cliffs, iron-stained].

Red Face Flotta: [low iron-stained cliff].

Red Glen Hoy: a deep hollow with a stream passing through it ['red' probably relates to a ground cover of red moss].

Red Quarry Birsay, Quoyhorrie: ['red' = iron-stained].

Red Rigs Evie: [probably related to iron-stained earth].

Redd, The Swona: [Norse *hroði* rubbish (heap), probably of flotsam].

Redgarth Rendall: an old house which stood near 'Queenamuckle' [origin of 'red' not known].

Redland 1. Evie: also written Rothland, an old urisland embracing 'Flaws', 'Nistigar', 'Quoys' etc. [Norse *rauðr* red probably relating to soil colour].

Redland 2. Firth: originally 'Rennaland'/'Raynland' [Norse *renna* a flowing stream].

Redland 3. Stromness: (see above for possible explanation).

Redriver Evie/Rendall: [named by a returning employee of Hudson Bay Company].

Ree, Point o Graemsay: [Scots *ree* a sheepfold].

Reefs o Turrigeo South Ronaldsay: (see 'Turrie Geo').

Reekie Brae Copinsay: [a smoking fire was raised here to notify the boatman in Deerness that an islander wished to cross].

Reekiebraes Birsay: old name of Canada West: [probably relates to low-lying mist that appears in certain atmospheric conditions (c.f. 'Kilns o Rowamo')].

Reeky Knowe Rousay; Evie: [a mound below Westness farm where a smoking fire was lit to communicate with the inhabitants of Eynallow].

Refuge 1. Harray: [a croft established on common land by a family who had been evicted from Eday].

Refuge 2. Rendall: on Layburn's land; a few remains may still be seen: (see above).

Relief Birsay: Kirbister area [probably carries the same meaning as 'Refuge' (above)].

Rendal Rigs Birsay, Gelderhouse [Gaelic *rinndeal* the old allotment of land before the enclosures].

Rendall a parish: historically very important in early saga times: site of Tingwall: domicile of Svein Asleifsson on Gairsay [Norse *renna* a flowing stream, *dalr* valley].

Rendall Papa Westray: [named after family with the surname 'Rendall'? (compare 'Swanson's')].

Renni's South Ronaldsay: [a house occupied by a family with the Scots surname 'Rainy'].

Rennibister Firth: [Norse *renna* a flowing stream, such a stream flows Nearby, *ból-staðr* farm].

Rental, The Swona: [Gael *rinndeal* (see 'Rendal Rigs')].

Rerness, Point o Sandwick: also called 'Keases Point' [Norse *hreyrr* cairn, *kös* cairn].

Rerwick St. Andrews: [Norse *hreyrr* cairn, *vík* bay].

Resting Hill Eday: [a resting place for pall bearers: normally takes the Norse form *hvíl(d)*].

Rethie/Ruthie Taing Sanday: Burness parish [Norse *rauðr* red, presumably relating to seaweed: compare the Scots word 'redware' = seaweed].

Rice Meadow Sandwick: below the 'How o Burrian' [Norse *hrís* brushwood].

Rickerha Rendall: on 'Brookfield' farm [Scots *ruckle* a loosely constructed heap (of a house in this case)].

Rickie's Brae Sanday: site of a house, Westside, Northwall [probably a personal name].

Rickla Harray: (see 'Rickerha' above).

Rico Evie: [origin unknown].

Ridden, Point o Egilsay: the northern part of 'Kili Holm' (see 'Ridgarth' below).

Ridgarth Evie/Rendall: [Norse *hryggr* ridge, *garðr* farm].

Rievi Hill Walls: (see 'Ravie Hill').

All Riff forms below = Norse *rif* reef.

Riff Rendall: near 'Puldrite' [the name relates to a rocky shoreline].

Riff/Reef Dyke North Ronaldsay: [a dangerous skerry to the southeast of the island, where the Swedish East Indiaman 'Svecia' was wrecked in November 1740].

Riff, The 1. Holm: a rocky beach on 'Rose Ness'.

Riff, The 2. Rousay: the northeast extremity of 'Faraclett Head'.

Riff Geo North Ronaldsay: [a geo spanned by a natural arch: the meaning here is 'roof' rather than 'reef'].

Riff o Lythe Rousay: part of the shore in 'The Leean' [Norse *hlíð* slope].

Riff o Rive Sanday: at the extremity of 'The Riv' [Norse *rif* reef].

Riff o Skaebrae Rousay: rocks off 'Skaebrae Head' on the west coast of the island.

Riff o the Foulan Sanday: coastal feature, 'Foulan' [Norse *rif* reef (see 'Foulan')].

Rig Betwixt Towns, The Sanday, Elsness: field name, early 18th century [Scots *rig* a strip of arable land, Norse *tún* enclosure].

Rigbister Pentland Skerries: [English 'rig' strip of land, Norse *ból-staðr* farm but can hardly mean 'farm' on the skerries despite the fact that quite a number of families lived here: 'enclosure' would be more suitable].

Rigersland Rousay, Wasbister: [Norse *hryggir* ridges (of land)].

Rigg 1. South Ronaldsay: vanished, it lay near 'Masseter' [Norse *hryggr* a strip of land].

Rigg 2. Stromness: west of 'Brig o Waithe' (see above).

Rigga Rendall: coastal feature, northwest of 'Queenamuckle'.

Rigs o Lint South Ronaldsay, Halcro Head: [flax was grown in Orkney for a short period].

Rima Sanday: farm mentioned in the Commissariot Record, 1664 [the same as 'Rummie'?].

Rimmer Hole, The Birsay: an old quarry on Kirbister Hill [origin unknown].

Rimmers, The North Ronaldsay: [Norse *rimi* a raised strip of ground (with English plural)].

Rimmon Birsay, Swannay: a small farm in the 1890s [origin unknown].

Rims, The Birsay: east of the 'Wilderness' [Norse *rimi* a raised strip of ground].

Rin, Stanes o Birsay: a semi-circlar ring of boulders in Marwick Bay which forms 'The Choin' [Norse *hraun* a heap of stones].

Rinan/Runnan Rendall: near 'Appieteen' [an abbreviated form of 'Runabout' which suggests the dwelling of a beggar (see 'Runabout')].

Rinansey the old name of North Ronaldsay [Norse *Rínansey* believed to be a form of St. Ninian, hence 'St. Ninian's Isle', which has a Shetland equivalent].

Ring Westray, Dykeside: [the name suggests a 'ringed' enclosure instead of the normal quadrilateral].

Ringie Geo North Faray: [a geo which has semi-circular shape].

Ringsquoy Westray: [*kvi* an enclosure, attached to the farm of 'Ring'].

Riniber South Ronaldsay, Hoxa: [Norse *hraun* stony ground, *berg* rock].

Rinna/Runnan Rendall: stood near 'Appietoon' [an abbreviated form of 'Run-about/Rinnabout'].

Rinnabout 1. Shapinsay: [the dwelling of a beggar who rarely stayed at home: compare English 'gadabout'].

Rinnabout 2. Evie/Rendall: (see above).

Rinnabreck, Baa Green o Sanday: a shallow reef lying off the coast of 'Ire', Burness ['Baa Green' normally refers to a field given over to games but in this instance 'baa'= Norse *boði* a reef, and 'green' = Norse *grunn* shallow water].

Rinners o Breckan Harray, Bimbister: the name refers to watering places in a very marshy area [Norse *renna* a stream, here in plural form *rennar*].

Rinniegill Walls: [Norse *renna* stream, *gil* a valley, sometimes deeply incised].

Rinyo Rousay: a field name above 'Bigland' [Norse *hraun* a stony heap and refers to a Neolithic mound here where a 'beaker' shard was discovered].

Risday Birsay: a valley on Costa Hill [Norse *hrís* brushwood, *dý* marsh].

Ritquoy Birsay, Marwick: [Norse *rettr* a sheepfold used particularly for 'rooing' the sheep (i.e., removing their fleeces) on 'Sheepright Day'].

Rittack Hill South Walls: [a hill favoured by 'ritticks', Norse *rytr* the black headed gull].

Ritten/Rittin Evie: low, wide cave in 'Sole Geo' [origin unknown].

Riv South Ronaldsay: (see below).

Riv, The Sanday: coastal feature [Norse *rif* Faroese *riv* a reef].

Rivacliff, Geo o Evie: (see 'Rives Geo' below).

Rivers Birsay, Marwick: in the Old Boat Geo [Norse *rífar* marks made by boats being hauled up: (see 'Old Boat Geo')].

Rives Geo Sanday: coastal feature [Norse *rifa* fissure, *gjá* ravine].

Roan Head Flotta: a headland on the east end of Golta [Norse *hraun* a heap of stones].

Roan, The Papa Stronsay: (see 'Roan Head' below).

Roana Bay Deerness: (see 'Roan Head' below).

Robbie's Hole Sanday: on 'Scar Links' [origin unknown].

Robbie's Loch Evie: (see above).

Robie Geo Walls: [origin of personal name applied here is unknown].

Robie's Knowe Evie: (see above).

Rock o Hangie North Ronaldsay: (see 'Hangie').

Rock Sanday: near 'Pincod' [a fanciful name].

Rock, The 1. Birsay: near Cooperhouse, Marwick, vanished [reason for the application of this name unknown].

Rock, The 2. Sanday: former name of 'West Garth'.

Rockerskaill South Ronaldsay: [Norse personal name *Hrókr* and *skáli* hall or cottage: with the personal name attached, more likely to be 'hall'].

Rocko Birsay, Lochside: [perhaps for 'Rockquoy'].

Rocks o Smeargeo (see 'Smeargeo').

Roe Ness Egilsay: a point of flat rocks [*rauðr* red?].

Roe, Hole o St. Andrews: (see above).

Roeberry South Ronaldsay: [Norse *rauðr* red, *berg* rock].

Roland's Geo Papa Stronsay: [reason for the application of this unusual personal name unknown].

Roma dale Evie: 1681, Romerdaill in 1653: also recorded as 'Rummerdale' (Burn of) a small stream east of 'Shortie' [origin unknown].

Romps, Geo o Rousay: the Ordnance Survey in the 1880s entered this name applied to a small bay at 'Hullion' [origin unknown].

Ronaldsay, North earlier 'Rinansey', the most northerly of the Orkney archipelago: it is famous for its Sheep Dyke which surrounds the island and was constructed to keep the seaweed-eating sheep off the arable land: the population in 2011 was 72.

Ronaldsay, South An island made up of two parishes, St. Peter's in the north and St. Mary's in the south [Norse personal name *Rögnvald* and *ey* island].

Ronney Sanday: coastal feature, Holm o Elsness [Norse *hraun* bare rocks: 'Roni' is a common placename in Shetland].

Ronsvoe South Ronaldsay: applies to a district west of the 'Bay of St. Margaret's Hope': pronounced Ronsa, a name rarely used now [it is called *Rögnvalds vágr* in the *Orkneyinga Saga*, *vágr* = bay].

Roo (see 'Rue').

Roo Howan Birsay, Dounby: [Norse *hrugr* a heap, *haugr* mound with the definite article suffix].

Rookals o Digger Rousay: peculiarly shaped stones on the beach below 'Digger' [Norse *hrukka* wrinkle].

Rooman Hill Evie/Birsay: [origin unknown].

Roondback Evie: launching site for boats of inshore fishermen ['roond' = 'round', *bakki* bank].

Roos Loch Sanday: (see 'Rue').

Roos Wick Sanday: [(see 'Rue'), Norse *vík* bay].

Roost, The Papa Westray: at the north end of the island [Norse *röst* rough tideway].

Root, Gloup o South Ronaldsay: the old name of the 'Gloup o Halcro' [Norse *rjóta* to roar: this gloup makes a persistent roaring sound even in calm weather (see 'Gloup')].

Roothe Birsay: a field on Netherskaill, Marwick [dialect 'ruithy girs' (grass), corn spurrey, a troublesome weed which invades corn fields].

Rora Head Hoy: [Norse *hreyrr* a cairn of stones].

Rosemire Sandwick: [Norse *hross* horse, *mýrr* moor].

Rosen Brayo Sanday, Brabister: field name in Burness (see above).

Rosen Breya Sanday, Elsness: field name, early 18th century [Norse *hröysi* a cairn, *breiðr* broad: (compare 'Brisni Brayo')].

Roseness Holm: in the extreme south of the parish [Norse *hröysi* a cairn, *nes* point of land].

Rossmire Firth: [Norse *hrossa-mýrr* horse moor].

Rossmyre South Ronaldsay: (see above).

Rothiesholm Stronsay: ['holm' used in ancient sense of big lump of an 'island': the usage is very old (compare Bornholm in Sweden)].

Rotten Gutter Flotta: [a hollow on the beach where seaweed rots].

Rotten Loch Walls: [a loch where there is little movement of water but a strong smell from algae].

Rouansmouch Birsay, Hayon: field name [origin unknown].

Rough o Kame South Ronaldsay, Grimness: a good fishing spot [Norse *rif* a reef, *kambr* a ridge of land to the west].

Rounda Harray: a round damp area in a field usually caused by bad drainage [Norse *dý* marsh].

Roundadee Sandwick (see above).

Rousay An island, famous for its extraordinary collection of Neolithic and Iron Age remains: [Norse personal name *Hrólf* and *ey* island: population in 2011 was 212].

Rousay's Pier Sanday: also known as 'Garsons Pier', near Nouster [not a pier but the remains of an old wall (which is revealed by the name 'Garson' = Norse *garðs-endi*, wall end) apparently no connection with the island of Rousay but rather the surname 'Rousay'].

Rousay's Sanday: (see 'Laminess').

Routhum Sanday, Seater: field name, Sellibister [Norse *rauðr* red, Norse *hólmr* island, originally an 'island' in a marsh].

Rovacova Harray [Norse *rófa* animal tail (see below): origin of 'cova' element unknown: perhaps a mere rhyming word (see 'Meery-Mawry')].

Roveland Westray: Noltland area [Norse *rófa* animal tail, used to describe elongated features, such as a field in this instance].

Rovi Westray: the name of a field on the 'Glebe' (see above).

Row Head Sandwick: [Norse *rauðr* red, referring to the colour of the rocks].

Row Taing Flotta: [Norse *rauðr* red (of seaweed), *tangi* point of land].

Row, Hole o 1. Flotta: on 'Stanger Head', a dangerous 'gloup' or hole in the cliff face which inspired terror in the soldiers who were encamped near here in World War l (see above).

Row, Hole o 2. Sandwick: a prominent hole in the cliffs here [Norse *rauðr* red: an abbreviated form of 'Koppie Row', the red headed spirit who haunted the Orkney coastline (see 'Cubbie Roo's Rock')].

Rowamo Firth/Harray: a stretch of moorland [Norse *rauðr* red, *mór* moor].

Rowan's Sanday: formerly 'Brough Hill' [named after a Rowans family, circa 1861].

Rowbar Sanday: coastal feature, 'Warsetter' [Norse *rauðr* red, Norse *berg* rock].

Rowbeam Holm: [origin unknown].

Rowen Eday: a small headland northwest of 'Greentoft' [Norse *rauðr* red: the origin of the suffix is unknown].

Rowgar Rousay: near 'Skaill' [Norse *rauðr* red, *garðr* farm or enclosure: probably relates to soil colour].

Rowland Holm: slightly to the northeast of St. Mary's Village [Norse *rauðr* red of the earth?].

Roy Holm: on 'Roseness Headland' [Norse *hröysi* a marked cairn nearby].

Roy's Well North Ronaldsay: Scots surname 'Roy', rare in Orkney: no further details known (compare 'Winster's Well' in Flotta).

Ruberry Walls: a point of land north of 'Rysa Bay' [Norse *hrúga* heap, *berg* rock].

Rue North Ronaldsay: in the east of the island: a name adopted from a local feature [Norse *hrúga* heap].

Rue/Roo Sanday: [Norse *hrúga* heap; the 'Hill o Rue' is a large hillock in Papa Stronsay].

Ruebreck Birsay, Marwick: [(see above for 'Rue'), *brekka* slope].

Ruff Burray: a derelict house, formerly known as 'Sheepquoy'.

Ruff, The South Ronaldsay: a skerry in the entrance to St. Margaret's Hope Bay [Norse *rif* reef].

Ruin Sanday: also known as 'Storehoose o Foulan' [Norse *hrun* ruin: this name is recorded elsewhere in Orkney].

Rumin Hoy: [Norse *rimi* a strip of land with definite article suffix, i.e., *rimin*].

Rumly Point South Ronaldsay: [dialect 'rumle' to rumble, describing the noise made by small boulders as they are rolled by wave action: there are several 'Rumly Points' in Orkney].

Rummie Sanday, Lettan: probably same place as above [Norse *rimi* a strip of land].

Runa 1. Birsay, Twatt: (see below).

Runa 2. Harray: [Norse *raun* stony ground].

Runa/Quoyruina Birsay: west of Kirbister (see above).

Runabout Shapinsay: [Scots 'rin' English 'run about': used in Orkney in the sense 'dwelling of a beggar'].

Runalith Birsay: field name Abune-the-Hill, vanished: originally a house name [Norse *hraun* stony ground: there are several interpretations of the 'lith' element, probably *hlíð* slope].

Runas Hoy: [Norse *raun* stony ground].

Runcigill Hoy: a stream flowing into Rackwick Bay [Norse *gil* stream, first element unknown].

Runnabreck Sanday: [Norse *hraun* stony heap, *brekka* slope].

Runnaclett/Rimmaclett Sanday: there was formerly a mound here which, presumably, was used as a bleaching green (see 'The Bleaching Green') [Norse *hraun* stony heap, *klettr* rock].

Runnan/Rinnan Evie: [possibly a form of 'Runabout' (above)].

Runnarto Hoy: a small bay south of the 'Old Man o Hoy' [Norse *hraunar* heaps, *þúfa* heap].

Runtha Eday: [Scots *runt* a contemptible term applied to a disagreeable old Woman, Scots *ha'* a cottage].

Runthall Stronsay: (see above).

Rur South Ronaldsay, Grimness: vanished [Norse *reyrr* a cairn].

Rus(s)land Stronsay; Harray; Westray: [Norse *hross* horse, *lenda* fields].

Rushabreck Evie: [Norse *hross* horse, *brekka* slope].

Rushacloust Eday: [Norse *hross* horse, English 'cloist(er)' with it original meaning, 'an enclosed place' (see 'Clouster')].

Rusht, Burn o Birsay: the name of one of the earlier stages of the 'Burn o Dirkadale' [Norse *rust* hill ridge (from where the burn flows)].

Rusk Holm Westray: (see above).

Rusky Hill Orphir/Stenness boundary: [Norse *hross* horse, Norwegian (Nynorsk) *skjaa* a hut made of loose boards in which meat etc. was placed to dry but in Orkney the word was used in the sense 'shieling'].

Rusness 1. Sanday: district name, many houses in this area had no name: today (2024) only four houses fall into this category.

Rusness 2. Wyre; Gairsay: (see above).

Russa, Burn of Orphir: also known as the 'Burn of Drummy' [Norse *hross* horse, Norse *á* stream].

Russadale Stenness: [Norse *dalr* dale].

Russamoa Holm: [Norse *mór* moor].

Russamyre Orphir: [Norse *mýrr* marsh].

Russapond Sanday: a stretch of drystone wall beside the road between 'Otterswick' and 'Myrtle Lane' [Norse *hross* horse, *pund* pound for animals].

Russness Sanday: area of land which projects into 'Cata Sand' near 'Measer' [Norse *hross* horse, *nes* point of land].

Russoo Harray: (see above).

Russoo Myres Harray, Corston: [(for Russoo see above), Norse *mýrr* marsh].

Russquoy Sanday: field on Elsness estate, early 18th century [Norse *hross* horse, Norse *kví* enclosure].

Ruthie South Ronaldsay: a field bordering the shore at 'Kirkhouse', Widewall [dialect 'ruithie' corn spurrey].

Ruthie Taing Sanday: coastal feature [Norse *rauðr* red, *tangi* point of land; 'red' refers presumably to the 'redware' or seaweed].

Rutto Castle Birsay: rock pillar(s), near 'Skipi Geo': name noted by Ordnance Surveyors in the 1880s but unknown today ['castle' is commonly used in Orkney to describe tall rock pillars].

Ryas Geo North Ronaldsay: position unsure ['Ryas' is a Scots surname but there is no record of this surname in North Ronaldsay].

Rymman/Rymmon Evie: the old name of 'Whitemire', Evie [origin unknown (see 'Rimmon', Birsay)].

Ryo, Knowe o Evie: a round broch-like feature west of Burgar [the final 'o' represents Norse *haugr* mound: no explanation can be offered for the initial 'ry' element].

Rysa Walls: an island east of Hoy: sometimes called 'Little Rysa' in relation to its much larger neighbour: probably inhabited up until the 19th century [Norse *hrís* brushwood, *ey* island].

S

Sabay 1. St. Andrews: [Norse *saer* sea, *boer* farm].

Sabay 2. South Ronaldsay: a vanished house which lay in 'Herston' [probably a transferred name from above].

Sabiness North Ronaldsay: [origin unknown].

Sabiston Birsay: [Norse personal name *Sabjorn* and *staðr* estate].

Sabraes Evie: near 'Mistra': mentioned in a Land Tax Roll in 17th century [origin unknown].

Sacquoy Head Rousay: northernmost point of Rousay [Norse *saer* sea, *kví* enclosure].

Saddle, The Stronsay: coastal feature 'Lamb Bay' [origin unknown].

Saed Geo Birsay: 'Sae Geo', coastal indentation [Norse *saer* sea, *gjá* ravine].

Saeva Ness Shapinsay and Helliar Holm: [Norse *saevar* genitive of *saer* sea, *nes* point of land].

Saever Howe Birsay: a prominent mound on 'Birsay Bay' [Norse *saevar* (as above), *haugr* mound: (compare 'Saverock')].

St. Andrews parish in the East Mainland [the parish church is dedicated to St. Andrew]

St. Augustine's Chapel Sanday: [on Ortelius' map of Orkney, a chapel dedicated to this saint is marked near Burrian, Park district].

St. Boniface's Church Papa Westray: old parish church in use until 1920.

St. Colm's Chapel Sanday: Burness, Ire district.

St. Colm's Kirk Sanday; the church has vanished but the churchyard still exists and continues to be used.

St. Columba's Sanday: an alternative name (now disused) for what is Sanday parish, named from the dedication of the parish church which no longer exists.

St. Gile's Chapel North Ronaldsay: vanished, location uncertain.

St. John's Geo South Ronaldsay.

St. John's Head Hoy: at 335 metres, it is the highest vertical cliff in Britain [it was here where Johnsmas bonfires were lit].

St. John's Hill Stronsay: in the north of the island (see above for explanation).

St. Magdalene's Sanday: site of chapel, Everbist district.

St. Magnus Cathedral St. Ola, Kirkwall: founded in 1137 by Earl Rognvald in memory of his martyred uncle Magnus. The cathedral is unique in that it does not belong to a Church but to the community.

St. Magnus Kirk Birsay, Northside: the present church was built towards the end of the 17th century on the site of an earlier, 11th century foundation. No longer in use by the Church but kept in good repair and used for community activities.

St. Margaret's Chapel South Ronaldsay: vanished, it gives its name to the village.

St. Margaret's Hope South Ronaldsay: [named after the chapel there dedicated to St. Margaret, little trace of which remains, Norse *hóp* bay].

St. Mary's Kirk 1. Rendall: located near 'Grind', ruinous.

St. Mary's Kirk 2. Sanday: derelict, the 'Lady Kirk' which gives its name to the 'Lady' district of Sanday.

St. Mary's Village Holm: named after the parish church dedicated to St. Mary.

St. Marys 1. Holm: a village in the parish of Holm.

St. Marys 2. South Ronaldsay, Burwick: the original name of what is now 'South Parish'.

St. Peter's Pool Deerness/St.Andrews: the innermost part of 'Deer Sound', named after St. Peter's chapel which lay nearby.

St. Peters South Ronaldsay: the original name of what is now 'North Parish'.

St. Thomas' Kirk Rendall: also known as 'Tammas Kirk', vanished: it lay at the 'Hall of Rendall'.

St. Tredwell, Loch of Papa Westray: named after the medieval chapel dedicated to St. Tredwell.

St. Tredwell's Chapel Papa Westray: ruins of a late medieval chapel and formerly a celebrated pilgrimage centre.

Saintear Westray: vanished but the name 'Loch Saintear' remains near 'Quoybirse' [apparently there was a chapel dedicated to St. Tear near Wick in Caithness. Nothing more is known of this particular saint].

Saither Birsay, Dounby: [Norse *soetur* plural of *soeta* a midden but here it is used in the sense 'stinking marsh': there are many instances in Orkney of words used in Norn to describe miry ground].

Salt Hellyie Rousay, Leean: [Norse *salt-hellur* salt rocks: salt would not have been produced here but perhaps temporarily stored].

Salt Ness Shapinsay, Walls: (see below).

Salt Pan Orphir: [where salt was produced from sea water by evaporation].

Salta Taing Rendall; South Ronaldsay: (see above) [Norse *tangi* point of land].

Salthouse Westray, Dykeside: (see above).

Salties/Salthoose Sanday, Lettan: perhaps where salt was stored? (compare 'Flesh-hoose' and 'Fishoose').

Saltings Sanday: beach name in three different parts of Sanday [a legacy of the days when Orkney folk produced salt from the sea by evaporation].

Samaria South Ronaldsay, Widewall: 1871, vanished: Biblical placename; ancient capital of Israel; there were several such old house names in Orkney: (compare Jericho in Dounby and Babylon in Stenness, both vanished).

Samilands, Knowe o North Ronaldsay: [Scots *knowe* mound, Norse *saman-landir* property held in common].

Samson's Lane Stronsay: a house, former Post Office and inn in the centre of the island [the surname 'Samson' is recorded in Orkney though not in Stronsay: the house is situated at the end of a lane].

Sand North Ronaldsay; Sanday.

Sand Ayre Sanday: coastal feature [Norse *sandr* sand, *eyrr* sand bank].

Sand Geo Evie; Birsay; Egilsay; Rousay; Wyre.

Sand Holm Sandwick: a small island in the 'Harray Loch' just north of the 'Ring o Brogar' [Norse *hólmr* island].

Sand o Gill Westray: ['Gill' is a farm in 'Pierowall': a huge sandy beach appears here at low tide].

Sand o London Sanday: an area to the northeast of Skaill (see 'London').

Sand o Saville Sanday: (see 'Saville').

Sand o the Owran Sanday, Roos Wick: [Norse *aurr-inn* the clay (soil)].

Sand Spels Sanday: [Norwegian dialect *spjell* a strip of land].

Sandaiken Deerness: recorded by the Ordnance Survey as a 'small farm' in the 1880s: situated in the extreme west of the parish [the last element is the common Deerness surname 'Aitken' but the name is an unusual format].

Sanday 1. Third largest island in the Orkney archipelago: named after its extensive sandy beaches: famous for its extensive Neolithic and Iron Age remains. Population in 2011 was 494.

Sanday 2. Deerness: [Norse *sandr* sand, *eið* isthmus, a reference to the narrow stretch of sand which separates the parishes of St. Andrews and Deerness. The parish of St. Andrews at the other side of the isthmus also has its 'Sanday'].

Sanday/Sandyha Rendall: on the southwestern flank of 'Gorseness Hill' [origin of name not understood].

Sanday Sound the stretch of water between Sanday and Stronsay [Norse *sund* a channel].

Sandaygates Sanday: [origin doubtful: possibly a transferred placename, there is a 'Sandaygates' in Fife (compare 'Fintray')].

Sandback North Ronaldsay: east of 'Garso Loch': it has a fine 'noust' [Norse *sandr* sand, *bakki* bank].

Sandber 1. Holm: south of St. Mary's Village: only the 'Bay of Sandber' is remembered today [Norse *berg* rock].

Sandber 2. Rousay: [a fishing rock at the mouth of 'Lair Geo' where the bottom is sandy, Norse *berg* rock].

Sandbister, Bight of North Faray: [Norse *sandr* sand, *ból-staðr* farm].

Sander 1. North Ronaldsay: (see above).

Sander 2. Sanday: beach name, 'Scar' (see above).

Sander 3. Sanday: district name [Norse *sandar* sands].

Sandfiold Sandwick: [Norse *fjall* hill].

Sandgarth Shapinsay: [Norse *sandr* sand, *garðr* farm].

Sandgeo Sanday: coastal feature, Hermisgarth [Norse *sandr* sand, *gjá* ravine].

Sandgin Flotta: [Norse *tjörn* a small loch].

Sandi Sand St. Andrews: 'St. Peter's Pool' forms part of this extensive stretch of sand.

Sandkrumma Birsay: a small sandy geo [the 'krumma' element seems to carry the meaning 'squeezed together' hence narrow: compare dialect 'krom' a constriction in the throat].

Sand-Lelyie Rousay: coastline on the east side of 'Sacquoy Head' [origin uncertain].

Sandlogate North Ronaldsay: [the origin of this name is not understood].

Sandoyne Holm: [origin doubtful: Norse *ey-in* the island?].

Sandquoy Eday: (see above).

Sandquoy Sanday: 'Warsetter' and 'Tresness' [Norse *kví* enclosure].

Sands o Erraby Sanday: a tombolo connecting 'Tresness' to the main island of Sanday (see 'Erraby').

Sands o Evie Evie.

Sands of Piggar Orphir: (see 'Piggar').

Sands/Flenstath Deerness: the only 'estate' name in Deerness [Norse personal name *Fleinn* and *staðr* estate].

Sandsend coastal name, 'Foulan', Sanday and 'Garthstown', Westray.

Sandsheen North Ronaldsay: a small loch [Norse *tjörn* small loch].

Sandside 1. Deerness: a corrupted name: originally 'Sandsend'.

Sandside 2. Graemsay: a corrupted name (see above for an identical shift in language).

Sandwick 1. a large fertile parish in the West Mainland, famous for the Neolithic village of 'Skara Brae' [Norse *sandr* sand, *vík* bay].

Sandwick 2. Deerness; South Ronaldsay: (see above).

Sandy Geo North Ronaldsay.

Sandy Myres Evie: [Norse *mýrr* moor].

Sandyhole Westray, Rackwick.

Sandytae/Sandytee Sanday: 'Warsetter Links' [Norse *teigr* strip of land].

Sane Sanday: on the land of 'Saville' [Norse *tjörn* pool, a placename which appears in many guises in Orkney].

Sane Sheet Sanday: on Saville land: the field on which the house of 'Sane' stood (see below) ['sheet' = Scots *schedd* a piece of land distinctive in some way].

Sang North Ronaldsay: [a corruption of 'sand'].

Sangar North Ronaldsay; Westray; Burray: [Norse *sand-garðr* a farm built on sandy soil].

Sangwish, Point o Shapinsay: [last element 'wish' not understood].

Sanlya Birsay: Marwick coast, a small sandy geo [element 'lya' is not understood].

Sanquoy Westray, Cleatown: [Norse *sand-kví* sand enclosure].

Santhy Sanday: Cleat district [origin uncertain: its position near Cleat could suggest a Celtic origin; compare Welsh *sanctaidd* sacred].

Santoo/Sandtoo Head Hoy: a rock face west of 'Whitefowl Hill' [Norse *sandr* sand, *púfa* a mound: the significance of these two is not known].

Saoul Less Papa Westray: location unknown ['less' = Norse *fles* skerry].

Sarraquoy/Serraquoy Flotta: in 'Pan Hope': recorded as a small farm by the Ordnance Survey in the 1880s [there is a farm of 'Serrigar' (a corruption of *suðr-garðr* south farm) in South Ronaldsay but this name cannot apply here].

Sat Skerry Birsay: [a small skerry lying off the 'Old Boat Geo' where shallow pools evaporated leaving salt which could be harvested].

Saughiquoy Harray, Knarston: vanished [Scots *saugh* willow, Norse *kví* enclosure].

Sava Speldo Sanday, Stove: field name [Norse *sef* rush or sedge, dialect *speld* a field; compare Icelandic *spilda* a strip of land].

Savaquoy Shapinsay: [Norse *saevar-kví* an enclosure by the sea].

Savaskaill Papa Westray: 'Wasbister' [Norse *saevir-skáli* a hall by the sea].

Savday Evie: on 'Vinquin Hill' [Norse *sef* rush or sedge, *dý* marsh].

Save Geo North Ronaldsay: a long, narrow geo on Torness in the north of the island [Norse *seiðr* saithe].

Savedale Stenness: (see above for derivation).

Savenick Holm: [Norse *sae(var)* sea: the 'nick' element suggests a mound, a word related to Norse *knykill*].

Saverday (see 'Sowerdie').

Saverock St. Ola: [Norse *saevar-haugr* sea mound].

Savers Geo Sanday: coastal feature, Taftsness [Norse *gjá* ravine].

Saversdale/Saversdeel Sanday: ['saver' is normally translated 'of the sea' as in 'Savers Geo'; inappropriate here: perhaps Norse personal name *Sjólfr* and Norse *deild*, division of property].

Saverton Westray, Dykeside: [Norse *saevar-tún* sea farm].

Savi Geo South Ronaldsay: [Norse *sae* sea, *gjá* ravine].

Savigair Rendall: stood between 'Skiddy' and 'Hacco'; no remains [Norse *sef* rush or sedge, *garðr* farm].

Savil Sanday: [Norse *sae* sea, *völlr* field].

Savil Less Papa Westray: [(see above), Norse *fles* skerry].

Saville Firth: [Norse *völlr* grassy field, Norse *sef* sedge].

Savillegreen Sanday: [Norse *sef* sedge, *völlr* field].

Savisgarth Evie: [Norse *saevar-garðr* sea farm with English genitive'].

Saviskaill Rousay: [Norse *saevar-skáli* hall by the sea, again with English genitive].

Sawa-steethe Rousay: a portion of beach on the Quandal shore [Norse *staðr* position or site (see above for 'sawa')].

Sawa Skerry Rousay: [origin of 'sawa' unknown].

Sawaskeel Rousay: a geo on the south side of 'Scabra Head' [relation to Saviskaill unknown].

Saythe Geo North Ronaldsay: [*Norse seiðr* saithe].

Scabra Head Rousay: [Norse *skeifr* askew but used in Orkney to describe a steep slope, Norse *breiðr* broad].

Scad Head Walls: [Scots *scald* to burn (of heath cover in this instance)].

Scaesgar South Ronaldsay: in the Sandwick area, vanished [Orkney Norn *skeifr* a steep slope, *garðr* farm].

Scair Tacks/Scairdacks (see 'Skate Dykes').

Scaland Orphir: [probably Norwegian (Nynorsk) *skjaa* a hut made of loose boards in which meat etc. was placed to dry but in Orkney the word was used in the sense 'shielin' (see 'Rusky Hill', Orphir)].

Scamilie Stronsay: field southeast of Airy [(for 'sca' element see above) Norse *milli* between, but between what? It seems that part of this placename is missing].

Scapa St. Ola: [the Norse name in the *Orkneyinga Saga* was *Skalpeið*: Norse *eið* is isthmus referring to the narrow neck of land between the West Mainland and the East Mainland, Norse *skálpr* a type of boat: both sides of this isthmus made suitable harbours and this seems the best explanation among a number of alternatives].

Scapa Flow [Norse *floi* a stretch of water, marsh etc. compare the 'Flow Country' in Caithness].

Scar 1. Hoy: a dwelling house south of 'Quernstones', west of Rackwick [reason for appellation unknown].

Scar 2. Sanday: [Norse *skör* rim or edge, in this instance the seashore (in the parish of Stenness there was a farm 'Scar o the Rims', now a fieldname)].

Scaraber Rousay: (see 'Scaraber, Point of' above).

Scaraber, Point o North Faray: extreme south point of the island [Norse *skarfr* cormorant, *berg* rock].

Scarabreck Rousay: 'Faraclett' area, a vanished house [Norse *skör* rim or edge, *brekka* slope].

Scarataing Evie; Rousa; Sandwick; Wyre: [Norse *skarfr* cormorant, *tangi* point of land].

Scaratin Orphir: (see 'Scaratain' forms above).

Scare Gun St. Andrews: a low water reef [Norse *skarfr* cormorant: origin of 'gun' here not understood].

Scarf Skerry South Ronaldsay: there are several instances of this placename in Orkney (see above).

Scarf Taing: South Ronaldsay: (see 'Scarataing' above).

Scarfha Sanday, cottar house, Newark; Westray, Broughton: [dialect skarf (Norse *skarfr* cormorant), Scots *ha* cottage, a derogatory reference to the cottage or perhaps to the food eaten by the occupants: cormorants were formerly eaten in the 'North Isles'].

Scarma, Bight of Stronsay: to the west of 'Lea Shun' in Torness [origin unknown].

Scarpan Harray: Grimeston district, poor, usually thin soil [Norse *skarpr* barren: although an adjective it seems to have developed as a noun too in Orkney, hence *skarp-in*].

Scarpigar St. Andrews: [Norse *skarpr* barren, *garðr* farm].

Scarpsquoy Firth, Binscarth: [Norse *skarpr* barren: the English genitive form shows again that *skarpr* developed a nominative form, *kví* enclosure].

Scarra Sandwick: (see below for possible interpretation).

Scarradale/Scoradale Orphir: a saddle in the Orphir hills west of 'Crya' [Norse *skor* a rift in a rock face].

Scarrigar Sanday: 'Warsetter' [Norse *skarð* notch or rift, in this instance refers to a saddle in the hill, *garðr* farm (see 'Skarray')].

Scarrigeo Sanday: coastal feature, west of Backaskaill Bay (see above) [Norse *gjá*, ravine].

Scarry Geos Evie: [indentations in the rock faces (see above)].

Scarsa Hoy: a cleft in the rocks allowing passage down to the 'Old Man o Hoy' [Norse *skarð* rift, the 'sa' element could be *sae* sea].

Scartan Point Pentland Skerries; Flotta: [Norse *skarfr* cormorant, *tangi* point].

Scarton Walls: [perhaps a contraction of 'Scarataing' (see above)].

Scarvie Clett Shapinsay: a low water rock on the south coast of the island [Norse *klettr* rock, *skarfr* cormorant].

Scarwell/Skorwell Sandwick: the earlier name of what is now 'Stove' [a difficult name to interpret: the last element is *völlr* field: the first element 'scar' suggests Norse *skör* rim or edge and this agrees with an alternative name for this area 'Fermandikis' which translates as Norse *farman* merchant, and Scots *dykes*. Stove was occupied by the Kirkness family who were well-known merchants].

Scat Wick Flotta: a bay in the south of the island: [Norse *vík* bay, Norse *skattr* toll charge: visiting vessels had to pay a toll: (compare 'Tollhop', now 'Toab')].

Scathquoy Orphir: [Norse *kví* enclosure: meaning of 'scath' element uncertain: related to words 'to split', e.g., Gothic *skaidan* hence the meaning 'to split boards' to make a certain structure e.g., a hut].

Scatlands of Sandstown Sanday: [those lands which paid the Norse tax 'skatt'].

Scatt Riggs Sanday, Elsness: field name, early 18th century [Norse *skattr* tax, Scots *rigg* a strip of land].

Scaun Westray: [a projecting rock with a natural arch: (see 'Scuan')].

Scaval Stronsay: [Norwegian (Nynorsk) *skjaa* a hut made of loose boards, *völlr* field].

Scews Walls; South Ronaldsay: [Icelandic *skjár* a hut made of slats: (with English plural)].

Schoolha Evie: (see below).

Schoolhoose Sanday: may well have been one of the simple 18th century schools (compare 'Damaschool', Evie).

Schusan South Ronaldsay: pronounced 'Skoosan' [same origin as 'Scews' (above) but with definite article in plural form].

Sco Taing South Ronaldsay: [Norse *scagi* point of land, *tangi* point of land!].

Scoban Harray, Netherbrough: a large squared-off field, named after a hut which must have stood here [Icelandic *skjár* a hut: origin of 'ban' element uncertain].

Scockness Rousay: earlier 'Scowness' [Norwegian (Nynorsk) *skjaa* a hut made of loose boards: (see 'Scow' forms)].

Scofferland Sanday: Park district [origin uncertain; perhaps Norse *skeifr*, askew, a reference to the field shape (compare 'Ranga')].

Scomer Holm: location and meaning unknown but suggests [Norwegian (Nynorsk) *skjaa* hut made of loose boards, Norse *mýrr* moorland].

Scommie (see 'Skommie').

Scone Brae Sanday, Nouster: where cow dung pats were built to dry in those days when animal dung was used for fuel [Norse *myki-skán* dung].

Sconie Brae Sanday, Newark: (see above).

Scorn Birsay: a low breach in the Marwick Hills [Norse *skör-in* the breach].

Scorpaw Sandwick: = Scorpol = Skorwell?

Scorradale Orphir: marked valley in the west of the parish through which the main road passes [Norse *skör* a defile].

Scotsha Rendall; North Ronaldsay: the Rendall cottage was formerly called 'Blink'.

Scotties Grip Sanday, Northwall: the outlet from 'Langamay Loch' [Scots *grip* a ditch, 'Scottie' relates to the surname 'Scott'].

Scottigar North Ronaldsay: (see above).

Scottigar Taing North Ronaldsay: [surname 'Scott' (above), Norse *garðr* farm, *tangi* point of land].

Scottish Brae Sanday, Kettletoft: [the name was transferred from a house in Dunrossness, Shetland].

Scotto Westray: Rackwick area, a narrow rocky promontory north of 'Swartaback' [origin unknown].

Scotts Rendall, 'Quoyblackie': field name [the surname 'Scott' is well established in this parish].

Scoulters Stronsay: [Norse, metaphorical use of *skoltar* skull to apply to a mound].

Scows Orphir; Walls; South Ronaldsay, Cara: [Norwegian (Nynorsk) *skjaa* hut made of loose boards (with English plural)].

Scrapsquoy Firth, Binscarth: a corrupt form of 'Scarpsquoy' [Norse *skarpr* barren, *kví* enclosure].

Scrimpo Rousay: a rocky point at 'Berry Head', Scockness [origin unknown].

Scruit Birsay: former name of 'Lochside', Swannay [related to Norse *skrúfr* a haystack but with the sense 'mound', Norse skrúf-*it* is 'the stack': (see 'breck' and 'Scrutoo'): compare Norse *dys* a cairn and local dialect 'diss' a small haystack].

Scrutoo Harray, Overbrough: to the west of what was the Free Church [(see 'Scruit' above), Norse *tó* mound, literally 'tuft'].

Scuan Stenness: [Icelandic *skjár* a shed with definite article suffix, *skjá-n*].

Scupper Hole Horse o Copinsay: Deerness [English 'scupper' a hole on the deck of a boat level with the deck].

Scurroes, Point o the Westray: [origin unknown].

Scuthi Head Sanday: coastal feature [Norse *skúta* to project].

Scuthvie Bay Sanday, Northwall: [Norse *skúta* to project, Norse *vágr* bay].

Scuttas o Curcaday Sanday, Elsness: field name, early 18th century [Norse *skúta* to project (see above): (see also 'Curcaday')].

Sea Pows Sanday: 'Oyce' [Scots *pow* pool].

Seal Skerry Eday; Rendall; North Ronaldsay; Sanday, Holm o Elsness: [Norse *sker* reef].

Seamill Sanday: to west of the 'Mill o Dilto': at the end of last century, it was used as a kelp store [the 'Mill o Dilto' was a tidal mill or 'seamill'].

Seasbanks Sanday: part of the beach at the Burrian end of 'Whaevy', Park district.

Seater Walls, in a former tunship; Hoy; Sanday, Sellibister; Firth; Harray; St. Ola; Stromness; Birsay, Abune-the-Hill (a name transferred from 'Setter' in Swannay): [Norse *setr* temporary summer hut].

Seaterquoy Rousay, Wasbister: it lay near 'Fealquoy' [Norse *setr* temporary summer hut, Norse *kví* enclosure].

Seatter's Ebb Sanday: on the 'Boloquoy' shore [Scots *ebb* foreshore].

Sebastapol South Ronaldsay: 'Myrtle Villa' was built on the old site [one of many houses built during the Crimean War and named after battles fought there].

Sebay St. Andrews; South Ronaldsay, Herston district, vanished: a transferred name from St. Andrews [Norse *saer-baer* sea farm].

Seekabout Evie/Rendall: [the dwelling of a beggar: compare 'Runabout'].

Segal Hoy: a glen south of the 'Cuilags' [origin unknown].

Seggie Spot Birsay, Whitemire: [dialect 'seg' a type of flag iris].

Seider/Seither, The North Ronaldsay: the highest part of 'Seal Skerry' and a gathering place for cormorants [Norse *soeta* a midden, referring to the mess made by these birds].

Selchie Geo Sanday, Ire: [dialect *selkie* seal, Norse *gjá* ravine].

Selkeragoe Birsay: coast, a corruption of 'Selkie Geo' (see above).

Selki Skerry Swona: (see below).

Selkie Skerry Sanday: coastal feature near the 'Point o Creeso' [dialect *selkie* seal, Norse *sker* reef].

Sellibister Sanday: district name, containing 'Garbo', 'Hillhead' and cottar houses [Norse *selja* willow (see below), *ból-staðir* farm buildings].

Sellyland Burray: [Norse *selja* willow'].

Selta, Burn o Hoy: it flows into the 'Bight o Mousland' on the west coast of the island [origin of 'selt' unknown: Norse *á* stream].

Selwick Hoy: [Norse *sela-vík* bay of seals].

Semolie Holm: a coastal indentation east of 'Cornquoy' [origin unknown].

Senness North Ronaldsay: in the north of the island [offshore lies 'Seal Skerry' hence probably originally 'seal ness', Norse *sela-nes*].

Sennikelda Firth: a well in the Redland area [Norse *kelda* well, Norwegian *sine* to dry up].

Seraquoy/Soraquoy Flotta: [origin unknown].

Sergeants Deerness: an old name for 'Little Millhouse' [clearly a military man lived here at one time].

Serrigar South Ronaldsay: [originally *suðr-garðr* south farm].

Settersquoy Stenness: [named after a Seatter family, Norse *kví* enclosure].

Settin Meadow Birsay, Dirkadale: [origin unknown].

Settiscarth Firth: [Norse *setr-i-skarði* settlement in a hill saddle].

Settling South Ronaldsay, South Parish: vanished, a contemptuous name for a house or inhabitants ['settling' = dregs].

Sgoilamar Swona: [despite its Gaelic appearance it is a corruption of Norse *skjól* shelter and *hamarr* exposed rock face: there are several stone shelters in this area].

Shacy, Kirns o Birsay: coast near Sir William's Hall [seems to be same as 'Kilns o Skae'; 'sk' being pronounced 'sh'; (compare 'sheer' old Orkney pronunciation of Icelandic *skýr* a type of yoghurt)].

Shald Sheed Sanday, Elsness: field name, early 18th century [Scots *shald* shallow (soil)].

Shaltaquoy Shapinsay: [Norse *hjalt* (dialect 'sholt') a young horse or pony, *kví* enclosure].

Shalter Rousay: [origin unknown].

Shanna Harray: [Norse *tjörn* pond, *á* stream].

Shapinsay a large island, the first recording in 1375 being 'Scalpandisay' [Norse personal nickname *Hjálpandi*, i.e., a helpful person: population in 2021 was 307.].

Sharnymire South Ronaldsay: [Norse *skarn* dung (used metaphorically here to describe a wet marsh), *mýrr* marshland. Note: Norse *skjárn* shelters/huts].

Sheansbreck/Sheensbreck/Shinbreck Sanday: on Newark land [Norse *tjörn* pool (with English plural)].

Shearer's Hole Stronsay: coastal feature north of Burgh Head ['Shearer' is a common Stronsay surname but the reason for the name is unknown].

Sheep Dyke North Ronaldsay: a Grade A listed structure to keep sheep off the grassland and encourage them to feed on seaweed. It was built two hundred years ago and completely surrounds the island.

Sheep Geo Sanday: coastal feature [perhaps from where sheep were shipped (compare 'Horse Geo'), Norse *gjá* ravine].

Sheep Punds Sanday: old enclosure near the shore, Taftsness [dialect *pund* pound (for animals)].

Sheep Skerry Egilsay; Rousay; Walls: [reefs used for grazing by sheep at low tide].

Sheepal Rousay: a stretch of hill ground in Sourin [sheep hill?].

Sheepheight Papa Westray: a ruinous farmhouse on the 'Head o Moclett' [reason for the name unknown].

Sheepquoy Burray: [Norse *kví* enclosure].

Sheepright Geo Westray: ['right' = Norse *rettr* a sheepfold, used especially at a time when the old fleeces were removed].

Sheepy Kirk Westray: nickname of old United Presbyterian Church [reason for the name unknown].

Shelha Sanday: [a cottage built on land with a high proportion of shells: (see 'Cockleha')].

Shelly Knowe Sanday, Northwall: [from the large numbers of shells it contains (compare 'Cockleha'): Shelly Knowe is also known as 'Girso Wasses'].

Shelto Sanday: location unknown [perhaps an alternative name for 'Shelly Knowe' where 'to' is Norse *þúfa* mound, literally 'tuft'].

Sherry Geo Sanday: coastal feature, Spurness [origin of 'sherry' unknown, perhaps from smuggling days (compare 'Tobacco Rock'), Norse *gjá* ravine].

Ship Dock Sanday: coastal feature [ships came formerly to 'Saville' to load seaweed].

Ship Geo North Ronaldsay: [(compare 'Skippie Geo' Birsay), Norse *gjá* ravine].

Ship's Waal Sanday, Saville: [Scots *waal* well: it was here where the kelp ships watered].

Shippy Rock Birsay: [a long narrow oblong rock off the coast resembling the hull of a vessel, hence its association with a shipwreck].

Shirhue Birsay Coastal feature near 'Snushan' [origin unknown].

Shodybanks Sanday: coastal feature, Burness parish [English 'shoddy': this is a good description of the coast here].

Shoeha Eday: [a cobbler's cottage (compare 'Purmha')].

Sholtisquoy North Ronaldsay: [Norse personal name *Hjalti,* Norse *kví* enclosure].

Sholtoquoy Shapinsay: [Norse *hjalti* pony/horse].

Shoramere Birsay: Hundland, near 'Skesquoy' [Norse *saurr* swampy tract, *mýrr* moor].

Shorewindows South Ronaldsay, Garth: [Norse *vindr* wind, *hús* house, English 'shore' i.e., an exposed house at the shore].

Shortie Evie: a corruption of Norse *svartr* black (see below), [probably a reference to vegetation cover (compare 'Blackbraes')].

Shortie Geo South Ronaldsay: [Norse *svartr* black, *gjá* ravine].

Shua Geo Birsay: a small inlet in a rugged part of the shore [perhaps Norse *skúfr* skua ('sk' was formerly pronounced 'sh'), *gjá* ravine].

Shuber Evie: coastal feature [origin of 'shu' element unknown, Norse *berg* rock].

Shun, The Harray: [Norse *tjörn* small loch].

Shunnan, The Hoy: [Norse *tjörn-in* the pool].

Shurameea Evie: = Shuramira (the equivalent of 'Shoramere' above).

Shutbehind Flotta: [a peculiar name for a cottage: the cottage must have stood near a gate to the commons (usually called by the Norse name *grind)*. It was very important to keep this gate shut, especially in summer to prevent cattle straying onto the crops: it is surprising that 'behind' is used here rather than dialect 'ahint'].

Shuttleha Eday: [a weaver's cottage (compare 'Purmha')].

Sibbies Geo North Faray: [personal name 'Sibella': the reason for her association with the ravine, is unknown].

Siebergeo Sanday: coastal feature, Tresness [Norse *saevar* genitive of *sae* sea, Norse *gjá* ravine].

Sillar o Fay Geo Birsay: an indentation in the side of 'Fay Geo' [seems to be a corruption of Norse *hellir* a cave].

Sillerdyke South Ronaldsay; Burray: [named after the practice of splitting herrings and laying them on a wall to dry which gave the impression that the wall was silver].

Sillerha Stronsay; Eday; Sanday: (see 'Sillerdyke' above).

Sillery Geo Birsay: [a ravine frequented by shoals of herring].

Sillock Geo Sanday, Brough: [dialect *sillock* a coalfish in its first year; sillock fishing is a popular summer sport in Orkney, Norse *gjá*, ravine].

Simblestersquoy Westray: [seems a corruption of the Sanday placename 'Simbuster', *kví* enclosure].

Simbuster/Symbustar Sanday: earlier recorded as 'Synbustaith' [Norse *sunn* southern, *ból-staðir* farm buildings].

Simegreenie Sanday, Newark: field name [origin of 'sime' unknown, Norse *groenn* green (compare 'Hinegreenie', 'Queenagreenie' etc.)].

Simlesker Rousay: a small loch near 'Moan' [Norse *tjörn* pool: origin of 'lesker' unknown].

Simon's Holm Sanday: northeast [Norse *hólmr* small island, an indication that Simon's boat ran foul of the rocks there].

Sin(n)isinkar Harray: [apparently a 'sinkie' (Orkney dialect 'depression') which, in special weather conditions, retains a fine mist cover giving the area the impression of being a smoking, grain-drying kiln].

Sinchman Birsay: a fishing site near 'Katta Geo' [origin obscure].

Sinclair's Geo/Blow Geo Birsay: a small ravine with a cave [reason for the name unknown].

Sindiber/Sulliber North Ronaldsay: a fishing crag: [origin of first elements Unknown, Norse *berg* rock].

Sinians o Cutclaws Rousay: (see above) [Orkney surname 'Cott' and personal name 'Nikolas'].

Sinians o the North Hoose Rousay: also known as the 'Kiln o Dusty' ['sin' is an obsolete local name for a kiln (in Swedish dialect the verb 'sina' is to dry out): this entry and the entry below refer to blow holes in the cliff face which, in stormy weather, act like smoking, farm grain-drying kilns].

Sinilie South Ronaldsay: [Norse *hlíð* slope: (for 'sin' element see above): the name seems to suggest an area with parched, thin soil].

Sinkie o Mammersdale Birsay, Lochside: [Orkney dialect 'sinkie' = depression in the land: origin of 'Mammersdale' unknown].

Sinmire South Ronaldsay: [dialect 'sina' to dry up, *mýrr* moor].

Sinnaclett Deerness: [local dialect 'sina' to dry, Norse *klettr* rock does not make much sense: perhaps it refers to stretches of rocky beach which dry out at low tide].

Sinnakilda Firth, Redland: [local dialect 'sina' to dry, Norse *kelda* a well, hence a dried up well].

Sinnayclift Westray: [location and origin unknown].

Sinnenspells Sanday: [dialect 'sina' to dry up, dialect *speld* a field].

Sinngifu Orphir: [location and origin unknown].

Sinnisting Flotta: ['ting' = 'taing', Norse *tangi* point of land, nes *point* of land, dialect 'sina' to dry up hence parched or unproductive].

Sinsoss/Sins Röst North Ronaldsay: [Norse *röst* rough tideway].

Sinyan Hammers, The Rousay: [dried grass (dialect 'sina' to dry) in an area of projecting rocks, Norse *hamarr*].

Sivers Geo Sanday: coastal feature, Elsness [Norse *saevar* genitive of *sae* (sea with additional English genitive), Norse *gjá* ravine].

Skae Deerness; Rousay; South Ronaldsay: [Norse *skeifr* oblique but used in Orkney in the sense 'steep' of a slope].

Skae, Kilns o Birsay: [holes in the cliff top through which spume breaks, giving the appearance of a grain-drying kiln in action (see 'Skae' above)].

Skae Hill Westray: (see above).

Skaebrae/Skeabrae Rousay; Sandwick; Sanday: [Norse *skjald-breiðr* literally 'shield-broad' and describes an extensive piece of land that resembles a shield: this term is also used in Norway].

Skagar Westray: location unknown [Icelandic *skjár* a shed, *garðr* enclosure].

Skaifles South Ronaldsay: a reef off the 'Taing o Knockhall' [origin of 'skai' here uncertain, unless it is point of land, Norse *fles* a skerry].

Skaigram, Skerries o South Ronaldsay: [Norse *scagi* projecting point, 'ram' element is probably a corruption of Norse *raun* stony ground].

Skailbister Orphir: [Norse *skáli* hall, *ból-staðir* farm buildings].

Skaildaquoy Point Holm: extreme south of the parish [(the same origin as 'Skelday' in Birsay), Norse *skáli* hall, *dý* marsh/moorland].

Skaill Rendall; Eday; Orphir; Egilsay; Sandwick; Holm; Rousay; Westray; Sanday; Deerness: [Norse *skáli* hall: the Orkney surname 'Scollay' retains the original pronunciation of the Norse name for a 'hall'].

Skailtoft Holm: [Norse *skáli* hall, *þúfa* mound often representing an old house site].

Skaith Orphir: [a gate made of strips of wood: Norse *skíð* a strip of wood].

Skaitherlie South Ronaldsay: [a gate made of strips of wood (the exact equivalent of 'Grindally'), Norse *hlíð* slope].

Skanaquoy/Skinnaquoy Birsay, Marwick: [Icelandic *skjá-n* the shed, *kví* enclosure].

Skar Rousay; Sanday, Burness: [Norse *skör* rim or edge, in this case the seashore. In Stenness there was a farm 'Scar o the Rims', now a field name].

Skara Brae Sandwick [a puzzling name: perhaps Norse *skör* edge, marking the boundary of old between North Sandwick and South Sandwick, *breiðr* broad].

Skarpoquoy Stronsay: on Burgh Hill [Norse *skarpr* barren, referring to the Soil, *kví* enclosure].

Skarray Sanday: position unknown but recorded in 17th century sasines; (may be same as 'Scarrigar').

Skartan Sanday: mound near the beach, Hillhead, Sellibister (probably the site of 'Skartane', below).

Skartane Sanday: a local legend says that a great Viking hall stood here.

Skarvatanga Birsay [Norse *skarfr* cormorant, *tangi* point of land].

Skateland Skerry Stromness: a rock near the 'Bu' which appears at low tide [it is impossible to explain this placename which was recorded by the Ordnance Survey in the 1880s].

Skatequoy Rousay: [Norse *skíð* gate, *kví* enclosure].

Skathquoy Orphir: (same origin as above).

Skaysan/Skeo Sand Birsay: extreme north of Marwick Bay [Norwegian (Nynorsk) *skaa* wooden shed used for drying meat/fish etc., *sandr* sand].

Skea Deerness: (see above).

Skea Hill Westray: (see above for origin).

Skea/Skae Birsay: [Norse *skeifr* oblique but used in Orkney in the sense 'slope'].

Skeaness Westray; Gairsay: [Norse *skeifr* oblique i.e., sloping, *nes* point of land].

Skebigo South Ronaldsay: [the South Ronaldsay equivalent of Birsay 'Skippie Geo', i.e., a ravine where it is possible to haul boats up and beach].

Skecking Hill Hoy: [origin of 'skecking' unknown: may be a local unrecorded word].

Skedgibist Sanday, Braeswick: the earlier name 'Sketyibuster' may provide a clue to the origin of the name [Norse *skíð* gate or fence of boards, *ból-staðr* farm].

Skedgibist(er) Orphir: (see 'Skedgibist' above).

Skee Banks Sanday; Birsay, Greeny: [Norse *skeifr* slope, seen as 'askew', English 'banks'].

Skeegeo Sanday: coastal feature, 'Meur' [('skee' as above), Norse *gjá*, ravine: i.e., land sloping down to a ravine].

Skeeticauld 1. North Ronaldsay: (same as above).

Skeeticauld 2. Sanday, field name, [Norse *skytja* a little nook (possibly a small hut/cottage), *kaldr* cold].

Skeetie Bowan Birsay: [probably refers to a reef at the mouth of this geo, Norse *skit* (bird*)* excrement, *boði-inn the* reef].

Skeggabiarnarstath Deerness: [Norse personal name *Skeggbjarn*, Norse *staðr* estate: an estate mentioned in the *Orkneyinga Saga* and believed to be in Deerness: not positively identified].

Skeithva Sandwick: [origin uncertain].

Skelbist Gairsay; Graemsay; Rendall: (same origin as below).

Skelbister Orphir; Sanday, earlier 'Scale Butter': [Norse *skáli* hall, Norse *ból-staðir* farm: the 'butter' form may be a corruption, otherwise it could be Norse *bygðir* settlements].

Skelbrae Sanday: [Norse *skáli* hall, *breiðr* broad].

Skeld o Gue North Ronaldsay: a stretch of high, grassy ground between 'Doo Geo' and 'Gue', the largest ravine in North Ronaldsay [probably a metaphorical use of *skjöldr* a shield but the significance of its use is not understood].

Skelday Birsay; earlier 'Skalder' [origin unknown].

Skeldela St. Andrews/Holm: 1653, position unknown (see 'Skeld o Gue' below).

Skeldigar Westray, Fribo (see 'Skeld o Gue', above).

Skelho Sanday: (same name as 'Shelly Knowe'?).

Skelperha North Ronaldsay: [Scots 'skelper' a gadabout, usually a beggar: (compare 'Seekabout'), Scots 'ha' a simple cottage/hovel].

Skelwick Westray: a large district south of 'Pierowall' [Norse *skáli* hall, *vík* bay].

Skennist Papa Westray: [Norse *skeið-n* a type of boat (with definite article suffix), *naust* an indentation in the coast where boats can be drawn up and wintered].

Skenstoft Shapinsay: [Norse *skeið-n* the boat, *topt* old house site: N.B. the placename here should read 'Skennistoft'].

Skently Sanday, Elsness: field name, early 18th century [Norse *skammr* short, Norse *hlíð* slope?].

Sker Nosey/Sker Aiven Birsay: a rock just off the Garson shore [neither of these names can be interpreted].

Sker Tam Birsay: skerries are frequently associated with names of those who were particularly associated with them e.g., running aground [Norse *sker* reef, personal name 'Tam'].

Skerandas Birsay: [Norse *sker* a reef, 'andras' may be a form of the personal name 'Anders' (see 'Anderswick')].

Skerhua Birsay: [Norse *sker* reef (in this case a rock), the origin of the 'hua' element is uncertain].

Skerloom South Ronaldsay: [Norse *sker* reef, *hjlómr* to resound, of the breaking sea].

Skerp Walls: [Norse *skarpr* poor thin soil].

Skerpie Burray: (see above).

Skerrilee South Ronaldsay: [Norse *sker* reef, the latter element probably represents *hlíð* slope].

Skerrobreck Birsay: vanished, it stood in one of the fields of 'Lingro' [Norse *skör* a depression, *brekka* slope].

Skerry o the Soond Evie: [rocks (*sker*) allegedly dropped by the spirit 'Cubbie Roo'; his footprints are said to be on the Evie shore, Norse *sundr* a channel].

Skerry Sound [Norse *sker* a reef between 'Lambholm' and 'Glimps Holm', *sundr* a channel].

Skersi Wyre, Rusness: a point of land (see below).

Skersi, Ayre of Wyre, Russness: [Norse *sker* reef, the element 'si' may represent 'sea'].

Skerter, The Sanday: coastal feature, 'The Riv' [Norse *sker-garðr* a belt of rocks in the sea].

Skesquoy Birsay, Hundland: unlikely to be surname 'Skea': perhaps from a nickname [Norse *skessa* apart from meaning a spirit it also meant in Iceland a coarse looking woman].

Skethaquoy Stenness; Westray, Dykeside, southeast of the 'Bay o Noup': [Norse *skíð* gate or fence of boards, *kví* enclosure].

Skethebuster Shapinsay or Stronsay: 1653 [Norse *skíð* gate, *ból-staðir*, farm].

Skethouse Harray: 1841 [Norse *skíð* gate].

Skethquoy Sandwick: (see above).

Skethway Firth, Coubister: [Norse *skíð* gate, 'way' is almost certainly a corruption of *kví* enclosure which would have been pronounced 'why'].

Sketquoy Rousay: (see 'Skethquoy' above).

Skett o Fincus/Sketifinsos North Ronaldsay: rigs of land in 'Sennes', the most northerly district in North Ronaldsay [Norse *skíð* gate, *fen* marsh, the 'sos' element may be related to dialect 'ses', the slurry which runs in the channel of the old cowsheds, used figuratively to describe a morass].

Sketterings Stronsay: southeast of 'Scoulters' [origin unknown].

Skettholter North Ronaldsay: [Norse *skíð* gate, Icelandic *holter* a rough stony ridge].

Skibby Geo Evie: (compare 'Skippie Geo').

Skibowick St. Andrews: [Norse *skip* ship, *vík* bay].

Skiddy Rendall: [Norse *skit* excrement, used figuratively, *dý* marsh].

Skiderhoose North Ronaldsay: [Norse *skit* (as above): a most uncomplimentary name for a cottage/hovel].

Skidge Birsay, Southside: [Norse *skíð* gate (compare 'fit' and fidge names)].

Skidgibist Orphir: [Norse *skíð* gate, *ból-staðir*, farm].

Skidsabister Sanday: (origin as above).

Skifflatooan Harray: the area around 'Huntscarth' [origin unknown].

Skiftabacon Stenness: 1760 [Norse *skipti* a division of land, *bakka-n* the slope].

Skingum South Ronaldsay: a small knoll near 'Kirk Ness' in the Eastside [Norse *skygni* shelter, *hólmr* a word also used on land for an elevated piece of ground in marshland (see 'Ancum')].

Skipi Geo South Ronaldsay: (see above).

Skippers Sanday: field name Elsness, early 18th. century [Norse *skipting-ar* divisions of land (with English plural)].

Skippie Geo Birsay: the largest geo in Birsay Northside where boats may be drawn up [Norse *skip* boat or ship].

Skird Hill Walls: near 'Heldale's Water' [origin unknown].

Skirlo Birsay, Swannay: [origin unknown unless it refers to a simple, early windmill: children use this name for a windmill toy].

Skirpo Birsay: near 'Hell' [Norse *skarpr* barren, i.e., poor, shallow soil].

Skirps Harray: (see above).

Skirvie Harray: [origin unknown].

Skirvil Taing Shapinsay: on the east side of 'Veantrow Bay' [Norse *sker* Reef, origin of 'vil' element unknown, *tangi* point of land].

Skitho Sanday: [Norse *skíð* gate/fence: the 'o' is probably meaningless].

Skitho's Laytey Sanday: field name [Norse *hluti* part or share].

Skithva Sandwick: [Norse *skíð* a hut made of strips of wood, *kví* enclosure].

Skitter Skerry position cannot be ascertained (see below).

Skitterha Sanday: it lay between 'Stumpo' and 'West Thrave' [vulgar dialect *skitter* diarrhoea, Scots *ha* cottage, a most uncomplimentary nickname].

Skittibuen Birsay: [Norse *skít* excrement, *boð-inn* the reef: a skerry covered with bird dung].

Skogar Birsay, Twatt: [Icelandic *skjár* a hut made of loose boards for drying fish, lamb etc., *garðr* farm/enlosure].

Skokness Rousay: in the northeast of the island [Norse *scagi* projecting point of land, *nes* point].

Skolimar Swona: a rock face [Norse *skjóli* shelter, *hamarr* exposed rock face].

Skooan Rousay: [Icelandic *skjár* a shed with definite article suffix, i.e., *skjá-n* (see 'Scuan')].

Skooany Rousay: (see 'Skooan').

Skorags, The Swona: jagged rocks on the west coast [Norse *skor* a rift in a rock wall plus local diminutive 'ag' or 'ack'].

Skorwell Sandwick: (see 'Scarwell').

Skowsetter South Ronaldsay: [Icelandic *skjár* a shed, Norse *saetr* seasonally used hut].

Skrimpo Rousay: a rocky point [origin unknown].

Skroo/Skrue North Ronaldsay; Rousay, Faraclett: [Norse *skrui* a landslide].

Skrowa Skerry Stromness: a rocky promontory off the 'Black Craig' [origin unknown].

Skrutabreck Birsay, Northside: [Norse *brekka* a slope: origin of 'skruta' element unknown: (compare 'Scruit' above)].

Skuan Harray; Birsay, Dirkadale: [Icelandic *skjár* a shed with definite article suffix, i.e., *skjá-n*].

Skuant Birsay: marshy area west of Loch o Isbister (same as 'Skuan' above, see 'Huant' for explanation of final 't').

Skulehoose Ebb Sanday: coastal feature, Foulan [relates to the schoolmaster's right to extract sand, collect seaweed, etc.].

Skulto Birsay: a skerry lying off 'Sma Geo' [Norse *skolt* a skull i.e., a flattish reef].

Skurro Sanday: coastal feature west of 'Grunavi Head' [Norse *skor* a rift in a rock].

Skuthie Geo Rousay; Sanday: overhanging cliffs [Norse *skúta* to jut out].

Skuttos o Benyiecot Rousay: a small division of land [Norse *skúta* to jut out].

Sky Fea Walls: [Norwegin *skaa* a hut, *fjall* hill].

Sk-yeos Swona: [same as above in plural form].

Slack Hoy; Orphir: [Scots 'slack' a saddle in the hills].

Slap Burray: [Scots 'slap' a gateway, usually a gateway between arable and common land].

Slap o Grindela Birsay, Northside: [combines both the Scots and Norse names for a gateway in a hill dyke (see 'Grindally')].

Slap o Mark Rendall: on 'Queenamuckle's' land [Scots 'slap' gateway, Norse *mark* a boundary].

Slapahagar Stromness Garth: [Scots 'slap' gateway].

Slates o Hest South Ronaldsay [Norse *slettr* smooth (rock), *hestr* stallion, used metaphorically as a rock face].

Slates o the Altar Swona: [Norse *slettr* smooth rock: nearby is an 'altar' shaped rock and 'The Bishop Rock'].

Sleds Taing Sanday: coastal feature, Ire [see *sleds* (above), Norse *tangi* point].

Sleds, The Sanday: area of flat rocks near the 'Sleds Taing' [dialect *sled* a flat stone, Norse *slettr* flat].

Slett o the Heel Hoy: extreme north of the island of Hoy (see 'slett' above).

Slett South Ronaldsay: (a form of 'sledd', above).

Sley, The Firth: old farm building near 'Turrieday', Heddle [origin unknown].

Slids Sanday: beach name 'Lopness Farm' [dialect *sled* a flat stone, related to Norse *slettr* flat].

Slinghorn Evie/Rendall; Birsay: [it seems to originate in an obscure dialect word meaning 'tramp', in other words Slinghorn is a hovel where a tramp stayed: another name for this dwelling was 'Holodyke' which should be consulted above: 'Skethorn' was a famous Orkney tramp but the name may not be connected].

Slite Face Birsay: [dialect 'slite' = smooth, referring here to a smooth rock face caused by a rock fall].

Slite Moss Birsay: Itherigeo [a smooth covering of moss (see above)].

Slounks, The Rendall: swampy area near Orquil [Scots *slunk* a depression in the ground].

Slumps, The Sanday, Ire: pockets of deep water close inshore [Scots *slump* a swamp].

Sly Hill Stronsay: on the east side of 'Rothisholm Head' [Norse *slý* bog cotton].

Sly Well South Ronaldsay: [Norse *slý* slime, like algae].

Smaa Geo Birsay: [dialect 'sma' small].

Smear Geo Sanday, Newark; Westray: coastal feature [Norse *smjör* butter, perhaps figuratively from the froth churned by the sea, *gjá*, ravine].

Smeesber Rousay: cliffs on the east of 'Sacquoy' ['ber' = *berg* rock, the origin of 'smee' is unknown].

Smeravill Firth, Redland: [Norse *smári* clover, *völlr* field].

Smerchan Harray: [Norse *smjör* grease, *tjörn* pond: ponds in marshy areas often have oily surfaces].

Smerchants Birsay, Northside: [as above (with English plural)].

Smerdale Orphir: [Norse *smár* clover, *dalr* valley].

Smergeo Sanday: coastal feature (see 'Smear Geo' above).

Smerhoose Rendall: a field on the 'Hall of Rendall' [probably originally 'Smeravillhoose', a house standing in a clover patch].

Smero Spot Evie: [Norse *smári* clover].

Smerquoy Birsay, Cauldhame; St. Ola; Sandwick: [Norse *smári* clover, *kví* enclosure].

Smerricky Piece Deerness, Horries: [the same origin as 'Smero Spot' (above)].

Smerskeal Westray: [Norse *smári* clover, *skáli* cottage: suggests a cottage set in a clover field].

Smersso, Knowes o Evie: [in olden days butter used to be buried in the ground to keep it in good condition: there is a record in the Sagas of butter being buried in a mound: the final 'o' represents Norse *haugr* mound].

Smewan, Knowes o Harray: [Norse *smuga* a hole in a wall allowing sheep to pass through, *smuga-n* = the hole].

Smirrus, Knowe o Birsay: [Norse *smári* clover, *hús* house].

Smithfield Dounby: the latter building was long associated with a public house.

Smithquoy St. Andrews: [probably surname 'Smith', Norse *kví* enclosure].

Smithscott Sanday: a blacksmith lived here at the end of the 19th century (see 'Bengie's Corner').

Smittaldy Westray, Garthstown [Norse *dý* marsh, *smita* to infect (originally to strike), the suggestion being that those who enter this marsh may be 'struck' by some kind of illness].

Smoan Harray: (see 'Smewan' above).

Smogar Firth: [Norse *smá* small, *garðr* farm].

Smoo, The Swona: [Norse *smuga* a hole, probably part of the 'Gloup'].

Smoo Field Evie: [probably a field named after a gap in the wall to allow sheep to pass].

Smoo, Geo o Evie: a hole in a rock face in this ravine [Norse *smuga* a hole].

Smoogro Orphir: [Norse *gröf* an embedded stream, 'smoo' suggests that this stream passes down a hole and reappears again].

Smook Rousay: a vanished house in 'Quandal' [dialect 'smook' sea spray: there would have been plenty of 'smook' on this wild coast from time to time].

Smornie Sanday: [origin unknown].

Smossaber Birsay: a rocky fishing site near 'Ramla Geo' [first element unknown].

Smugglers' Hole South Ronaldsay.

Snaba Hill Firth: [Norse *snaer* snow, *ból* a resting place for cattle].

Snash Ness North Ronaldsay: [Norse *snös* a projecting rock or point].

Sneb South Ronaldsay: [Scots *snab* a steep, short slope].

Sneck, The Papa Westray: [Scots *snug* the shoulder or slope of a hill].

Sneckie's Hole Sandwick, Lyking: field name [Scots '*Sneckie*' the devil].

Snelsetter Walls: [Norse personal name *Snjallr*, Norse *setr* a dwelling].

Sneuk Westray: low water rocks which divide the 'Bay of Cleat' from the 'Bay of Swartmill' [here, the placename 'Sneuk' suggests 'projecting' (piece of land)].

Sneuk Head Hoy: (see 'The Sneck' above).

Snippigar Deerness: [Norwegian *snipp* a corner (of a field in this case), *garðr* farm].

Snoddies Sanday: former name of 'Daisy Cottage' [called after a former inhabitant Maggie Snoddie, born 1818] a Sanday children's (skipping?) rhyme runs:

Maggie Snoddie, puir buddy,

Caa'd her tae on a curly doddie.

Ap she got, doon she fell

Caa'd her tae in a cockleshell!

Snuffy Hole North Ronaldsay: [probably related to English 'snuff' to suck air through the nose, hence a small blow hole].

Snushan, Point o Birsay: [Norse *snös* a projecting rock or point].

Sockersie South Ronaldsay: a rocky shelf on the coast ['sockersie' is a rock that soaks the arse of the angler if he sits down (c.f. 'Koldeross' in Rousay)].

Sole Geo Evie: [Norse *sollr* (really swill or blood): used figuratively to describe the contents of the water trapped in the geo].

Somiar Sandwich, Dounby area: [Norse *suðr* south, *mýrr* swamp].

Soo Taing South Ronaldsay: [Norse *sauðr* sheep, *tangi* point of land].

Sooknavel Firth: close to 'Cursetter Quarry' and also in Evie where it lay between the 'Cott of Dale' and 'Woodwick Burn' [the dwelling of a fool who got off to a bad start in life!].

Sorquoy South Ronaldsay: Paplay district [Norse *saur* used in the sense 'swampy land', *kví* enclosure].

Sorton Firth: position unknown [Norse *saur* swamp, *tún* home field].

Sotland Holm: vanished [possibly Norse *sót* soot, a reference to the colour of the soil].

Souamira Dounby: old spelling of 'Somiar'.

Soulisquoy St. Ola: [Norse personal name *Solli*, *kví* enclosure].

Souly/Sowlie Orphir: [Norse *sauðr* sheep, *hlíð* slope].

Sound 1. Egilsay: the most northerly farm on the island [named after the channel which separates Egilsay and Kili Holm].

Sound 2. Shapinsay: a large area now part of 'Balfour Mains' [named after the stretch of water between Shapinsay and 'Carness'].

Sound, The North Ronaldsay: (see 'Lurns').

Sourin Rousay: district in the east of the island [Norse *saurr* boggy land, plus nominative suffix, i.e., *saur-inn*].

Sourpool/Sorpool Orphir: [Norse *saur* swampy, *pollr* pool].

Sourpow Stromness: (see below).

Soutan South Ronaldsay: (same word as above).

South Kews Evie: (see 'North Kews').

South Laytey Sanday: field name, Summerdale [Norse *hluti* part or share].

South Ronaldsay one of the largest of the Orkney Islands and closest to the Scottish Mainland: it is linked to the Orkney Mainland by the 'Churchill Barriers': it is well known for its Neolithic Chambered Cairn containing many sea eagle bones, hence its common name 'Tomb of the Eagles': population in 2021 was 909.

Southan Sanday: a shoal to the west of 'Prattsfauld', formerly known as the 'Bow o Hermaness' [dialect 'South One'?].

Southerbie (see 'Sutherbie').

Southwall Sanday: the land around Braeswick, Cross parish: the name is no longer used [wall = Norse *vágr* bay].

Sow, The Hoy: (see below).

Sow, Geo o The Hoy: a small indentation in the coast north of the 'Old Man o Hoy' [Norse *sauðr* sheep, *gjá* ravine, i.e., an indentation favoured by sheep].

Sow Skerry Copinsay; Graemsay; Deerness: [Norse *sauðr* sheep, *sker*reef].

Sowa Dee Sandwick: [Norse *sauðr* sheep, *dý* moorland].

Sowasker Geo Birsay: (see 'Sow Skerry' above).

Sowerdie Rousay: exists only in the form 'Bay of Sowerdie' [Norse *saurr* Mire, Norse *dý* marsh].

Sowlisyord Sandwick: Stove area [Norse personal name '*Solli*' and *jörd* earth, really 'land' (see 'Soulisquoy')].

Sowluran North Ronaldsay: an outlying rock on the west side of 'Twinyes' [its association with Norse *sauðr* sheep suggests that it is periodically submerged: Norse *(f)laeðr* flood tide with nominative suffix 'n', hence *(f)laeðr-in*].

Spaney Geo Sanday, Spurness: coastal feature [dialect *spenye* bamboo cane for catching small coalfish, Norse *gjá*, ravine].

Spannis Myre Deerness: [(as below): perhaps the allotted area given over temporarily to the survivors was a piece of moorland, Scots *mire* moorland].

Spannysquoy Westray: [Scots *Spannis* 'Spanish', related in some way to a stranded Spanish vessel: perhaps a special temporary area given over to the survivors].

Sparrow Inn Evie/Rendall: very few ale houses are mentioned in old documents though many existed [the name suggests that this was a poorly built cottage, the inhabitant making a living through selling ale].

Sparrowhall Sanday: [a nickname given to a poorly built cottage (compare 'Moosie Ha', 'Conninghole' etc.)].

Speldie Grasses Birsay, Hayon: (see below).

Spelds, The Sanday, Elsness: field names, early 18th century [Orkney dialect 'speld' a field].

Spindil/Spindle Orphir: [the house of a 'spinner'? (compare 'Needlo's)].

Spithersquoy/Spethisquoy Evie: [the earliest recording is 'Spittalsquoy' which suggests that this was a house which cared for the sick, especially lepers: there was a similar arrangement in Caithness where the name 'Spittal' still exists].

Sponess Westray, Lochend: [Norse *spói* a curlew, surprisingly one of only two recordings of this bird's name in the placenames of Orkney].

Spoot Hoops South Ronaldsay: [local dialect 'spoot' razor fish, Norse *hóp* bay in the sense here of small indentation].

Spord, The Sandwick: to the west of 'Vestrafiold': a small indentation in the coast [the name suggests a stream in this locality (see 'Spurdagro')].

Spots Sanday: lobster set.

Spout o Hammar Rowe Birsay: a coastal name [English 'spout' suggesting a small blow hole].

Sprattsfauld (see 'Prattsfauld').

Sprillen Sanday: [location and origin unknown].

Spuifield Westray, Broughton: [Norse *spói* a curlew].

Spur o the Isle Eynhallow: a point on the west of the island.

Spurdagro Birsay: [Norwegian *sprut* to stream or gush, *gröf* a hole].

Spurn Evie: [nearby is 'Hull' which suggests that these crofts were built by retired seafaring men].

Spurness Sanday: [Norse *spori* spur, *nes* headland, point].

Spurquoy Stronsay: location unknown [Norse *spori* spur, *kví* enclosure].

Staas o Gridgar Birsay: indentations in the cliffs, Marwick [English 'stalls'].

Stable, The Birsay: a rock on the coast [probably a corruption of Norse *stöpull* a (rock) stack].

Stacalbrae Sanday: beach name and mound, 'Lopness Farm' [Norse *stagl* rack, implying that something was stacked here, most probably dung fuel].

Stack, The Westray: [Norse *stakkr* (rock) stack].

Stack o Chung Sanday: near 'Gorn' [Norse *tjörn* small loch].

Stack o Kame South Ronaldsay: [Norse *stakkr* rock stack (see 'Kame')].

Stack o Roo Sandwick: a 50-foot-high rock pillar just south of the Birsay/Sandwick boundary (see 'Roo').

Stackaback Papa Stronsay: [the rock stack at the back (see above)].

Stackaday Burn [no information].

Stackasteeth Harray: Nettletar district: a small area of peat [thought to have been a resting place for peat carriers].

Stackber Rousay: columnar rocks near the 'Knee o Faraclett' [Norse *stakk-berg* pillar rocks].

Stackie Geos Eday: [ravines with small rock stacks in them].

Stacks o the Isle Eynhallow: peats were boated from here.

Staff, The North Ronaldsay: a small rocky island off Tor Ness [origin uncertain].

Stainzie Stronsay: north northeast of Housebay (see 'Stensy').

Stancro Westray, Rapness: a farm, slightly north of Peterkirk [Norse *steinn* stone, *kró* enclosure].

Standard Evie: coastal feature (see below).

Standard/Castle o Gullslate Birsay: coastal feature: an outlying rock pillar [Norse *standa* to stand (upright): (see 'Gulslate')].

Stane South Ronaldsay: in the Linklater/Windwick area [probably related to a lost standing stone].

Stane o Quoybune Birsay: [Norse *kví* enclosure, *bón* petition, in the sense of prayer].

Stane Randa/Randy Birsay, Newan: [Norse *rönd* a border or in this case a boundary].

Staneisbul South Ronaldsay: coastal feature [Norse *steinn* stone, *ból* resting place for cattle].

Stanekelda Birsay: [Norse *steinn* stone, *kelda* a well i.e., a stone-built well].

Staneloof St. Andrews [Norse *steinn* stone, *hlífa* to shelter: suggests a stone-built shelter for animals].

Stanemora Swona: relates to a stretch of rocks on the coast: [Norse *steinn* stone, possibly *mór* heathland].

Stanesber Birsay: coast, a fishing rock [Norse personal name *Steinn,* Norse *berg* rock].

Staney Hill Hoy; Harray.

Stangabreck Birsay: a field on Boardhouse land: [Norse *stöng* a pole, used perhaps as a boundary mark, *brekka* slope].

Stangasetter Sanday: [(see above: see also 'Stensgist'), Norse *setr* dwelling].

Stanger Birsay, Southside: [Norse *steinns-garðr* 'stone farm', where the reference is to the nearby 'Stone o Quoybune'].

Stanger Head 1. Flotta: (see above).

Stanger Head 2. Westray: (see above).

Stanigoe Westray, Aikerness: in the extreme north of the island [Norse *steinn* stone(y): (for the 'goe' element see 'Goe' in Appendix)].

Stank Stromness: [Scots *stank* a wet hole or stretch of marshy land: modern French *étang* pond].

Stansger South Ronaldsay: Windwick district, vanished (see 'Stensigar').

Stany Ayre Sanday: beach feature, Spurness [Scots *stany* stoney, Norse *eyrr* gravel spit].

Stanyiron, Stye of Rousay: [Norse *steinn* stone, *stía* sty, Norse/Gaelic *erg* a shieling with nominative 'n' suffix].

Star of Lopness Sanday: [Jo Ben writing in the 16th century referred to 'The Start' by this name: it is very likely that the form 'Star' is incorrect].

Stara Birsay, Marwick, Beaquoy; Harray: [Norse *stíar* animal pens: in the 17th century, a dwelling in Marwick was called 'Stierhouse', now 'Stara': 'The Steer' is recorded in Harray, 'Starilie' in South Ronaldsay, 'Sterlie Ness' in Gairsay, Rendall].

Stara Fiold Evie/Birsay: [Norse *stíar* animal pens].

Starabir Orphir: [Norse *stíar* animal pens, *berg* rocky cliff: slightly to the west is a sheepfold].

Starilie South Ronaldsay, Grimness: [(see 'Stara' above), Norse *hlíð* slope].

Starling Hill Evie/Birsay: [starlings favour nesting in old rabbit burrows in peat].

Starrie Geo Sanday: coastal feature, Hacksness [Norse *starri* starling, *gjá*, ravine].

Start Farm Sanday: (see below).

Start Point Lighthouse Sanday, Start Point: erected 1802-1806; the tower was rebuilt in 1870.

Start Point Sanday: coastal feature, the most easterly point of Orkney [figurative use of Norse *stertr* tail: in Old English the same figure of speech was used as shown by the placename 'The Start' (Old English *steort*) in Devon].

Staura-meirie/Stouramira Rousay: location unknown [Norse *stóra-mýrr* big stretch of moorland].

Staveley Firth, Binscarth: [Norse *stafr* stave or post: used metaphorically in Norway for points of land but in Orkney, more likely keeping its original meaning, a boundary post, *hlíð* slope].

Staves Stronsay: [a substantial building built of logs: compare the 'stave' churches of Norway or, at a simpler level a *stave-naust* a strong boat shelter].

Steaquoy Shapinsay: [Norse *stía* an animal shelter, *kví* enclosure].

Steaver/Stevand Stromness: originally a farm south of 'Streather': the Ordnance Survey named it 'Stevand' and this name remains today [Norse *stúfr* a bit cut off, *fen* marshy ground].

Stebb Hill Stronsay: an elevation near 'Dishes' [Norse *steypðr* rising high].

Stedyaquoy Birsay, Marwick: [originally 'Stagaquoy', Norse *stigi* a step, probably in the sense 'embankment': 'Stedyaquoy' might derive from Norse *stedda* a 'mare', *kví* enclosure].

Steedie, Point o Egilsay: north of 'Netherskaill' [origin uncertain].

Steenathy Rousay: Leean district [Norse *steinn* stone, origin of 'athy' uncertain].

Steenie-Vestifal Rousay, Sourin: [Norse *steinn* stone, *Vestifal* = west hill: it is believed that there was a standing stone here in the 1770s].

Steer, The Harray: near Winksetter [Norse *stíar* animal enclosures].

Stees/Stees o Steegolt Harray: [Norse *stía* animal enclosure is repeated here, *göltr* boar but used in Orkney in the sense 'pig', hence 'pig enclosure'].

Steethe o the Erse Rousay: a maithe [one bearing was the 'Knee o Faraclett' on the 'Head of Saviskaill'].

Steeths, The Westray: a small, sandy indentation on 'Weatherness' [probably named after ruinous buildings on the point].

Steincavan Birsay, Farafield: (see 'Cavan').

Steinsa, Geo of Shapinsay: [Norse *steinn* stone, *á* stream (see 'Goe' in Appendix)].

Steirhouse Birsay, Marwick: (see 'Stara').

Stembister St. Andrews: [Norse *steinn* standing stone (the following 'b' of 'bister' changes the 'n' to 'm')].

Stenaquoy Eday; Harray: [Norse *steinn* stone, *kví* enclosure].

Stenchmae Sanday: beach name and mound, 'Lopness' [English 'stench'? (compare 'Stumpo'), Norse *melr* sand].

Stendals Sanday: field name [Norse *steinn* stone, Norse *deild* division, a reversal of Norse *deilis-steinn* boundary stone].

Stenigar Stromness: [Norse *steinn* stone, *garðr* farm].

Stennabreck North Ronaldsay: a farm on 'Bride's Ness' [Norse *steinn* stone, *brekka* slope].

Stenness a parish famous for its Neolithic monuments and 'Maeshowe'. [literally 'stone ness'].

Stennie Hill Eday: ['steenie' = stoney].

Stennigor Stromness: (see 'Stinniger').

Stennisgorn Rousay: a vanished farm which lay in the Wasbister area [Norse *steinn* stone, *garðr* farm, or in this case *garð-inn*, the 'n' suffix representing the definite article: the change of vowel from *garðr* to *gorðr* is most unusual but there is a great number of 'Gorn' farms in Orkney].

Stensgist Sanday: a house recorded in the 1841 Census (perhaps 'Stangasetter').

Stensigar South Ronaldsay: Sandwick district [Norse *steinn* standing stone, *garðr* farm].

Stenso Evie: [Norse *steinn* standing stone, Norse *á* stream].

Stensy/Stainzie Stronsay, Houseby: [Norse *steinn* stone, *saer* sea (compare 'Sebay')].

Stephen o Papy North Ronaldsay: an outlying rock off the coast of 'Howmae Brae': the name must relate to the coastal area itself which, at the time of surveying would have been marshy [Norse *stía* small animal enclosure, *fen* marsh: (see 'Putt Steeven'), origin of 'Papy' not understood].

Stephen's Gate Eday: an indentation in the coast [origin unknown].

Sterlie Ness Gairsay: stands in a narrow channel facing 'Sweyn Holm' [Norse *stíar* animal pens, *hlið* a passageway, *nes* a point of land].

Stevedun Evie: it lies on the border of Birsay and Evie parishes at 'Crismo' [Norse *stúfr* a bit cut off (see 'Stews' below), *dýna* a marsh].

Steven Stromness: [Norse *stúfr* a bit cut off, *fen* marsh].

Stewart's Sanday: alternative name for 'Gallow Hill' [named after a former occupier, Stewart Drever].

Stews South Ronaldsay: [Norse *stúfar* stumps (of standing stones): that regrettably, was the fate of many standing stones in Orkney].

Stiff Braes Sandwick, Easter Voy: field name [English 'stiff' describing perhaps the nature of the soil].

Stiglister Sanday: [Norse *stikill* a form of *stilkr* stalk, perhaps in this case a boundary marker, *setr* dwelling].

Stine Croonie/Stino Rousay: [Norse *steinn* stone, *kró(k)-inn* the enclosure].

Stines Moss Stenness: [Norse *steinn* stone, *mosi* moss or moorland].

Stinkanie Geo Birsay; Rousay: [Faroese *stinka* to smell (in this case rotting seaweed), Norse *gjá* ravine].

Stinkpow Sanday: it lay to the north of 'Stumpo', on the northern edge of the now vanished 'Mill Loch' [English 'stink', Scots *pow* pool].

Stinniger/Stenigar Stromness: a stone wall which began at a small ravine here separated Ootertoon from 'Innertoon' [Norse *steinn* stone, *garðr* wall (see 'Geo o Stinniger')].

Stjurmiclett Onziebust Wyre: rocks at the shore: [Norse *straumr* tidal stream, *klett* rock].

Stockan Evie; Sandwick: [as in the case of English placenames, the word 'stock' has not been successfully explained: it seems to mean nothing more than 'place' or 'building' in which case Stockan would mean 'the place/building' from Norse *stokk-inn*].

Stoddisyord Sandwick: Quoyloo area, only one recording in 1492 [personal name *Stóði*, Norse *jörd* piece of land].

Stoen North Ronaldsay: [Norse *stöðin* the boat shelter].

Stoif/Stove Birsay, Southside: (see 'Stove' below).

Stoka Stromness: on 'Streather' (see 'Stockan' above).

Stokaquoy Stronsay: (see 'Stockan' above).

Stone of Scar Sanday: [large erratic block left after the retreat of the Ice Age near the house of 'Savil': between the years 1879 - 1880, it was attempted to move all 14 tons of it at great expense to 'Scar' but the carriage transporting it collapsed. N.B., there is also such an erratic under a steep cliff on the Birsay/Sandwick boundary but it can only be seen at very low water. Yet another erratic lies/lay on the west coast of Westray].

Stone Star Westray, Dykeside: exact location unknown.

Stoneflit 1. locally a tale is told that to build 'Stoneflit', stones were 'flitted' from an old house on 'Esphany'. The fact that there was another house, equally old, named 'Stoneflit' in St. Andrews would seem to disprove this story.

Stoneflit 2. St. Andrews: northwest of Horrie: a transferred name? (see above).

Stonequoy South Ronaldsay.

Stony Milders Birsay, Lochside, Swannay: field name [English 'small broken muldered' stones: (see 'Stymilders')].

Stony Ranner Birsay, Skesquoy: [origin of 'ranner' unknown].

Stonybreck Westray: [Norse *brekka* slope].

Stony-Gro Birsay: [Norse *gröf* a stream].

Stonyhall Westray: ['hall' = Scots 'ha' a small cottage].

Stoo 1. Evie: northwest of 'Pow' (see 'Stoo' below).

Stoo 2. Rendall: an old house near 'Appietoon' [many Orkney placenames were contracted, the best example being 'Snea' in Sandwick, a contraction of *'hús nya'* (see 'Nistoo')].

Stoo Flats Evie: south of Peter's Kirk [relates to flattish rocks on the shore].

Stoo Slass Evie: at the edge of the 'Burn o Pow' near 'Stoo' [perhaps obsolete English 'slash' wet and miry ground].

Stooun Evie: coastal feature [Norse *stoðin* the boat house].

Storehoose Deerness (now 'Shorehouse'); Sanday, How, Foulan, Geo o Tresness, Nouster: a fish drying and storage building Sanday, 'Saville', Sanday, was a kelp/fish store. There is some doubt about why these substantial storehouses were built: no doubt their function changed over the years.

Stour Meadow Rousay: [Norse *stóra* big].

Stouramira Rousay: [Norse *stóra-mýrr* big stretch of moorland].

Stourdale Hoy: [Norse *stóra* big, *dalr* valley].

Stours Kinora Hoy: coastal feature just north of the 'Old Man o Hoy' [Celtic *stùrr* a pinnacle, *ceann* a headland: 'or' element not understood, perhaps *orag* young cormorant].

Stoursdale Stenness: [Norse personal name *Storr*, Norse *dalr* valley].

Stouster Sanday: near Boloquoy [probably the 'Stursetter' of the 1601 Udal Book].

Stout Farding Holm: [English 'farding' a quarter of a stretch of land in this case: surname 'Stout'].

Stout's Waal North Ronaldsay: [Orkney surname 'Stout', dialect 'waal' a well].

Stove Deerness; Sandwick; Stromness; Stronsay; Orphir; Sanday, (Stoveby above): [these were apparently houses with a heated room and belonged to a wealthier set of people].

Stove/Stoveby Sanday: after Crofters' Commission report in 1888, this farm was subdivided and separate parts given to ex-servicemen after World War I.

Stow, Tails o Birsay: [Norse *stöð* the old boat shelter in Marwick: 'tails' is used here in the English sense 'ends' and it is not clear to what the word refers in this case but see 'Rivers'].

Straenia Water Stronsay: at the edge of the sea in the south of Rothisholm [Norse *strönd* beach].

Straither Stromness: [from a lost Norse word related to Old English *stroð* marsh. In Middle English *strother* also carries the meaning 'marsh'].

Straits Westray, Broughton: [a small cottage perhaps named by a returned whaler who had been to the Davis Straits, Greenland].

Straits o Dover Evie: flagstones in a burn near 'Trophers' [a corruption of Norse *sléttr* smooth of stone etc.].

Strandygate Rousay: a road on the east side of Saviskaill Loch [Norse *strönd* beach, *gata* path].

Strangquoy Sanday: Braeswick, formerly known as 'Rattle Up' [named after 'Strangquoy Taing' (above)].

Strangquoy Taing Sanday: coastal feature, Braeswick [Norse *strönd* beach, *kví* enclosure].

Stratisgarth/Strettagarth Sanday: [Norse *straeti* street (see 'Streethouse' below), Norse *garðr* farm].

Streethouse Sanday, Stove: [farm labourers' cottages were built like a 'street' of houses (c.f. 'Queen Street' in Stromness)].

Streets, The Wyre, Russness: [origin of 'streets' in this instance not known].

Stremulo/Strelums Sanday: beach name, Newark [Norse *strönd* beach, Norse *melr* sand].

Strenzie/Strenyie Stronsay: originally a large area in the north of the island now known as 'Whitehall': 'Papa Sound' provides an excellent sheltered harbour where, in the past, fishing went on commercially for hundreds of years and where, before the days of piers, beaches served as loading areas [Norse *strandir* beaches].

String, The Shapinsay: the channel of water between 'Helliar Holm' and 'Carness' (see below for interpretation).

String, The o Vinko Sanday: a tidal race off 'Strangquoy Taing' [Norse *strengr* swift current, 'Vinko' is a fishing mark or maithe, relating to the 'Hill o Vinko' in Eday].

Stripe o Sandgar North Ronaldsay: [English 'stripe' referring to the shape of the field].

Strom Ness North Ronaldsay: [Norse *straumr* tidal stream, *nes* point].

Stromberry Shapinsay: coastal point to the southwest of the island [Norse *straumr* tidal stream, *berg* rock].

Stromlie Point South Ronaldsay, Herston: [Norse *straumr* tidal stream, *hlið* gap, relating probably to the entrance to 'Widewall Bay'].

Stromness an important ferry port serving the Scottish Mainland and the South Isles: population approximately 2,500 in 2021.

Stromness Taing Wyre: (see above) [Norse *tangi* point of land].

Stron, Braes o Rendall: on land of 'Mill Farm' near the Loch o Brocken [Norse *strönd* beach].

Strone, The South Ronaldsay: an alternative name for 'Ayre o Burwick' [Norse *strönd* beach].

Stronsay (*Strjónsey* in the *Orkneyinga Saga*) a large island: at one time famous for its trade in herring fishing [the 'strons' element seem to be the genitive case of a rare first name] population in 2021 was 349.

Strynd St. Ola, Kirkwall: a narrow lane to the north of St. Magnus cathedral: it was formerly a small stream [Scots *strynde* stream].

Stuan, The Sanday: beach feature [Norse *stöðin* the boat shelter or landing place (compare 'Stuin')].

Stucka Deldays Sanday, Elsness: field name [Norse *stúka* sleeve, used here in the sense extended part of a field, Orkney surname 'Delday'].

Studja Fiold Evie: [Norse *steði* anvil or *stedda*? Mare, *fjall* hill].

Stumpatanga Birsay: a small rocky ridge on the coast of 'Birsay Bay' [Norse *stumpr* stump, *tangi* point of land].

Stumpo Sanday: [originally 'Stinkpow'; the 'p' changes the preceding 'n' to 'm' (compare 'Okkambae') Scots *pow* pool].

Stumpo Geos Sanday: coastal feature, lies below land belonging to 'Stumpo'.

Stursetter Sanday: mentioned in the 1601 Udal Book; possibly 'Stouster' [Norse *stórr* big, Norse *setr* dwelling].

Stursie Stronsay, Linksness: 400 metres west of 'Odie' [origin unknown].

Sty Shapinsay; Rendall, now 'Sweenalay' [Norse *stía* small animal enclosure].

Sty Taing Stronsay: [Norse *tangi* point of land].

Sty, Grip o the Birsay: a small stream flowing into the 'Burn o Lushan' [Scots *grip* a ditch].

Styabanks Sanday: an alternative name for 'Stywick'.

Stye Deerness: (see 'Sty' above).

Styes o Aikerness Evie: (see below).

Styes o Brough Sanday: coastal mounds, west Sanday [Norse *stía* sty].

Styes o Steenie-iron Rousay: [English 'sty', Norse *steinn* stone, *erg-in* a shieling: note change of gender: it ought to be *erg-it* since *erg* is neuter. There are several changes of gender shift in Orkney Norn].

Styes, Point o The Sanday: (see 'Brough' above).

Stymbro Evie: [Norse *steinn* stone, *brú* bridge: the 'bridge' is likely to have been made of stepping stones].

Stymilders Stenness: [Norse *steinn* stone, English 'moulder' to crumble away, i.e., a field with a preponderance of broken stone].

Stywick Sanday: bay in south [Norse *stía* sty, Norse *vík* bay].

Sucko Birsay, Howally: a deep hole in the Hillside Burn [Norwegian *søkk* a depression or hollow].

Suckquoy South Ronaldsay: (see above): the name also appeared as 'Surquoy' in old records [Norse *saurr* marshy, boggy ground].

Suez Orphir: a small croft east of the Free Church, vanished [no doubt so-called by a retired seafaring man].

Sugarhoose North Ronaldsay: [a corruption of 'south garth house'].

Sui Fea Hoy: [Norse *sauðr* sheep, *fjall* hill].

Sule Skerry An island over 30 miles west of Orkney [Norse *súla* pillar].

Sule Stack 8 kilometres west of the above: famous for its colony of gannets [Norse *súla* gannet].

Sulland Westray: [according to earlier records, a corruption of Norse *suðr-land* southern land].

Sulliber North Ronaldsay: [no information].

Sultigo Stenness: one of three areas in Stenness in close proximity: the other two are 'Kethisgeo' and 'Lundagoe' [here the 'geo/goe' forms mean 'marsh' (see Appendix), Norse *sultr* famine, in the sense of unproductive land: (compare 'Hungerquoy')].

Summer Ayre North Ronaldsay: on the eastern side of 'Garso Wick' [Norse *eyrr* shingle spit, significance of 'summer' here not known].

Summer Geo Sanday: coastal feature, Ire [Norse *sumar* summer, *gjá* ravine: 'summer' might allude to its use in summer for fishing].

Summer o Hoy Walls/Hoy: it marks the boundary between Walls and Hoy [Norse *suðr* south, *mark* boundary].

Summer Skerry Birsay: a small skerry on the west coast [Norse *suðr* south, *mark* boundary, probably denoting the southern boundary of the parish of Birsay].

Summerdale 1. Stenness: site of the only recorded battle in Orkney in 1529 (see 'Summerdale' below).

Summerdale 2. Stronsay; Sanday: land area [Norse *sumar* summer, *deild* division (of land used for summer pasture)].

Summery Walls: to the west of North Bay [(see 'Summer of Hoy' above): the significance of this boundary is not known].

Sundiehoose Rendall: mentioned in the trial of the alleged witch, Jonet Rendall, in 1629 [Norse *sunn* south, *dý* marsh/moor].

Sunless Geo Hunda, Burray.

Sunnybank (see 'Grindyha').

Surhouse Taing Papa Westray: a prominent stretch of rock on the coast, east of 'Cott' [Norse *tangi* point of land: 'Surhouse' is vanished, possibly Norse *saurr* marsh].

Suro North Ronaldsay, Sanger: lay in 'Hunton' area, vanished.

Surrie Geo North Faray: [Norse *saurr* mud or marsh, *gjá* ravine].

Surrigarth Westray: [Norse *saurr* marsh, *garðr* farm].

Surtaday Birsay, Swannay: [Norse *saurr* mud or marsh, *dý* marsh, referring to the vegetation cover].

Surtagen Birsay, Hyval: field name [Norse *saurr* mud or marsh, *tjörn* pool].

Surtan Evie: on the east bank of the 'Woodwick Burn' in a marshy area [Norse *saurr* marsh, *tún* home field].

Surtan, Bog o Birsay, Kithuntlins: [Norse *saurr* marsh: (see 'Kithuntlins')].

Surto Sanday: lobster set, Park district [Norse *svartr* black: the reference may be to dialect *swart* a large tangle].

Surton Evie: a vanished farm near 'Nidgarth' (see 'Surtan', Evie).

Suso Burn Rousay: an old name for the 'Sourin Burn' [origin unknown].

Suthergill South Ronaldsay: now called 'Breck' [Norse *suðr* south, *gil* stream running in a narrow channel].

Sutherland Burray; Flotta: [Norse *suðr* south + land].

Sutherquoy Sandwick: an extensive area to the south of Sandwick [Norse *suðr* south, *kví* enclosure: one of the largest *kví* areas recorded in Orkney: the name is no longer used].

Suthirbie/Southerbie Sanday: vanished tunship which included the farms of 'Backaskaill' and 'Knowes' [Norse *suðr-boer* southern farm].

Suthirgarth Graemsay: [Norse *suðr* south, *garðr* farm].

Suthirquoy Holm: (see 'Orklandquoy').

Swalkie, The Orphir: on the 'Burn o Drumy' [Norse *svelgr* a swallow hole: the only swallow hole recorded in Orkney].

Swaltipot Westray: recorded by the Ordnance Survey in the 1880s as 'a small farmhouse' [origin unknown but suggests a variation of 'Swalkie' (above) and Norse *pyttr* pit or pool].

Swanaland Rousay: [Norse *svín* pig + land].

Swanbister Orphir: [Norse *svín* pig, *ból-staðr* farm].

Swandale Rousay, Sourin: [Norse *svín* pig, *dalr* valley].

Swandro Rousay: [Norse *svín* pig, *þró* a water trough?].

Swannay Birsay: [Norse *svín* pig, the origin of the 'ay' element is uncertain].

Swannay's South Ronaldsay: [from the surname 'Swanney'].

Swannayland Birsay, Marwick: to the west of 'South Waird' [Norse *svín* a pig].

Swannies Burray: (see above).

Swannies Geo North Faray: [from the surname 'Swannie', Norse *gjá* ravine].

Swannies Point Burray: [from the surname 'Swannie'].

Swanson Westray: a puzzling, long established farm and house name. There were two buildings here in the late 19th century — 'East' and 'West' 'Swanson', one being a house for the poor, the other a small farm [called after the surname 'Swanson' but oddly enough, with no first name].

Swaquoy South Ronaldsay: ['swa' is probably a corruption of Norse *svartr* black].

Swarback Falls South Ronaldsay: near 'Stews': after very heavy rain, water pours over the cliffs here to make a distinctive waterfall [Norse *svartr* black (a reference to the rock?), *bakki* slope].

Swarf Sanday: rocks off Elsness [Norse *svarf* tumult].

Swarsquoy St. Andrews: (related perhaps to 'Swartaback' below).

Swart Hellia Geo Shapinsay: [Norse *svartr* black, *hellur* rocks, *gjá* ravine].

Swartaback Orphir; Westray; St. Andrews: [Norse *svartr* black, perhaps a reference to the heather cover, *bakki* slope].

Swartageo Birsay: [Norse *svartr* black/dark of the *gjá* ravine].

Swartaquoy Shapinsay; Holm; South Ronaldsay: [Norse *svartr* black/dark of the vegetation perhaps, Norse *kví* enclosure].

Swarthammar Sanday: on the coast near 'Boloquoy' [Norse *svartr* black, *hamarr* crag].

Swarthowe Holm: [Norse *svartr* black, *haugr* mound: 'black' here probably means 'sinister/superstitious'].

Swartie Sanday: a rabbit warren, Hogsha, Rusness [Norse *svartr* black; the land is slightly blacker here than the predominantly sandy soils around].

Swartifield/fiold Rousay: there are two such placenames in Rousay, in Frotoft and on Kierfea [Norse *svartr* black/dark of the vegetation, *fjall* hill].

Swartland Birsay, Ingsay; Sandwick, Dounby; Walls: [Norse *svartr* black + land].

Swartmeil Westray, Lochend: [Norse *svartr* black, *melr* sand].

Sweenalay Rendall; [Norse *svín* pig, *hlíð* slope (see 'Sty')].

Sweero Evie; Rousay: a well [origin unknown].

Swein Geo Walls: [Norse *svín* pig, *gjá* ravine: animal names were often used for coastal features].

Swenabo Orphir: [Norse *svín* pig, *ból* animal resting place].

Sweyn's Castle Gairsay: [named (erroneously) after Sveinn Asleifsson].

Sweyn's Watch Tower Gairsay: (see above).

Swinetaing Orphir: [Norse *svín* pig, *tangi* point of land].

Swinge Geo Rousay: (probably the same as 'Swein Geo', above).

Swinste Spelds Sanday: (see below) [Scots *speld* field].

Swinstie Eday: [Norse *svín* pig, *stía* small animal enclosure].

Swinta Sanday, Elsness: field name, early 18th century [Norse *svin-teigr* a strip of land given over to pigs].

Switha Walls: an island: inhabited until the 20th century [Norse *sviða* a burning, used in the Norse language as 'clearing by burning', but there could have been little to clear here: the placename is related to Orkney dialect 'swee' a burning pain].

Swona An island: uninhabited since 1974 [Norse *svín* pig: animal names were frequently applied to landscape features by the Norse].

Syblisterquoy Westray, Fribo: the equivalent of the Sanday placename 'Simbister' [Norse *sunn* south, *ból-staðr* farm].

Sygle Holm (now called 'Holm o Huip').

Syraday/Syradale Firth: a valley to the north of 'Seatter' [Norse *saurr*marsh, *dý* marsh].

Syraday, The Hammers o Firth: rocks protruding from a valley in the hillside [Norse *hamarr* rock].

T

Taaber Well Evie: [Celtic (Gaelic) *tobar* a well].

Tack South Ronaldsay: South Parish, vanished [Scots *tac* land or house held on lease].

Tafnichill South Ronaldsay: Widewall district, vanished [Norse *topt* old house site, Faroese *knikil* a knoll].

Taft Birsay: North Hammar, Greeny [Norse *topt* old house site].

Taftend Westray: a farm in Rapness [Norst *toptir* old house site].

Taftinga South Ronaldsay: St. Margaret's Hope [believed locally to have been the site of a 'Thing' because of the 'ting' element in the placename but it is more likely that the 'Inga' element represents the Norse personal name 'Inga' (see 'Taft' above)].

Taftland Westray: [Norse *topt* old house site + land].

Taftnica Burray: (see 'Tafnichill' above).

Tafts Sanday; Westray; Rousay: [Norse *topt* old house site: sometimes the Norse plural is retained (see 'Tufter')].

Tafts/Taftshoose Sanday: now a farm steading, formerly 'North Tafts'.

Tafts Ness Sanday: coastal feature, Northwall [(see 'Tafts' above), *nes* point of land].

Taftshurrie South Ronaldsay, Grimness: [Norse *topt* old house site, Orkney surname 'Shurie' a form of 'Sigurd'].

Taftsshucky South Ronaldsay: [Norse *topt* old house site: Norse personal name 'Siggie', a form of 'Sigurd' though not recorded in Orkney].

Taid Ha Birsay, Swannay: [Scots *taid* toad, used of an objectionable person and then applied to the house, Scots *'ha'* simple cottage].

Tail o the Skerry Birsay: [English 'tail' = end: rocks which appear at the north end of 'Leeskro' on 'The Brough'].

Tails o Sgoilamar Swona: (see above for 'Tail' and 'Sgoilamar').

Tails o Stow Birsay: a rocky part of the beach where the old noust, 'Rivers', existed [Norse *stöð* a place where a boat can be wintered: unsure of the meaning of 'tails' here].

Taing o Corkatae Sanday: coastal feature, Elsness [Norse *tangi* point of Land, *kirkju-teigr* strip of church land].

Taing, The Wyre: [Norse *tangi* point of land].

'Taing', in a variety of spelt forms is a very common coastal name. Here are a few instances: Crudy South Ronaldsay; Tor Ness Orphir; Roo Sanday; Crow Sanday; Leaskana Geo Birsay; The Pund Sanday; The Clett St. Andrews; Torsker Sanday; Westove Sanday; Burgar Evie; Gairsay; Midgarth Rendall; Corkatae Sanday.

Tainga South Ronaldsay: a variation of 'taing'.

Taingapoos Orphir: in the west of Orphir Bay [Norse *pollr* pool (with English plural)].

Taings o the Holm Sanday: coastal feature, 'The Riv' [Norse *tangi* point (with English plural), Norse *hólmr* island].

Tam's Pund Stronsay: coastal feature southeast of the 'Vat of Kirbister' [Scots *pund* animal pound].

Tamas Kirk Rendall: a field on 'Hall of Rendall' [the site of the old kirk dedicated to St. Thomas].

Tammy Cowie Birsay: a rock visible at low water [said locally to be named after a boy who survived a shipwreck: this surname has been recorded only once in Orkney].

Tammy Reid's Swarf Sanday: coastal feature [Norse *svarf* tumult (of the sea in this case): Tammy Reid's boat fell foul of this reef].

Tammy's Leiti Sanday: field name, exact location unknown [Norse *hluti* share].

Tanga Birsay: coast, [a variant of 'taing'].

Tangana Graena Geo Birsay: [Norse *tangi* point of land (with definite article appended), *groena* green (covered with green seaweed), *gjá* ravine].

Tangbrae Sanday: on Backaskaill land [dialect *tang*, seaweed which grows above the low water mark, Scots *brae* small elevation].

Tanger Sanday, Ness: field name [Norse *tangi* point of land, *eyrr* gravel spit].

Tankerness St. Andrews: the northern part of the parish [Norse nickname *Tannskári*, *nes* point of land].

Tankley Sanday, Newark: field name [Norse *þang* seaweed, *klettr* rock].

Taphland Westray: Skelwick [Norse *þaefa* to stamp, of the hooves of cattle etc., i.e., to make a muddy mess: (see 'Klogang')].

Tarf Tail Swona: (see 'Tails o Sgoilamar').

Tarland South Ronaldsay: [Norse *þari* seaweed, i.e., a field regularly manured with seaweed].

Tarracleat/Tarracliff Deerness: [Norse *þari* seaweed, *klettr* rock].

Tarri Clett Glims Holm: (see 'Tarracleat' above).

Tarristae Westray: (see above).

Tarristy Sanday: beach feature [Norse *þari* seaweed, *teigr* strip of land].

Task South Ronaldsay: Sandwick district, vanished [probably in the sense 'land difficult to work': (compare 'Murder' in South Ronaldsay and the 'Hardhill' places in Orkney)].

Taverso Tuick Rousay: a Neolithic burial chamber [Norse *taufr* witchcraft, the terminal 'o' represents *haugr* 'mound', 'tuick' is Norse *þúfa* a mound with local diminutive 'ick'].

Teengie Sker Rousay: [a form of Norse *tangi* point of land, Norse *sker* reef].

Teengsie Sanday: in Lady parish, a ruin lying between 'Hillside' and 'Castlegreen' near 'Sparrowha' [origin uncertain perhaps the nickname of an inhabitant: dialect *teengs* is 'tongs', formerly a favourite tool for chasing away unwanted suitors!].

Teeoma, Burn o Birsay: a small stream flowing into the 'Burn o Kirkgeo' [Norse *mór* moor, for 'teeo' element, see 'Teeve Well' (below)].

Teevath Harray; Birsay, Dounby: [a complete corruption of Norse *djup-it* literally 'the deep marsh': the neuter article 'it' is always pronounced 'th' in Orkney: (compare 'The Teeve' below where the English definite article is used)].

Teeve, The Birsay, Twatt: (see 'Teevath' above). **Teeve Well** Holm: [a powerful spring in a marshy area (see above)].

Teevicks Deerness: a marshy area west of 'Mire' on 'Horries' [(see above) the suffix 'icks' represents the local diminutive].

Teevieha Deerness: [(see 'Teevath' above), Scots *'ha'* simple cottage].

Teing Westray, Cleatown: a house [a variant of Norse *tangi* point of land].

Teist Stane Hoy: on west coast of the island [Norse *þeist* the black guillemot].

Teistequoy Westray; Wyre: [Norse personal name *Teitr*, *kví* enclosure].

Teisti Taing Papa Westray: (see above for derivation).

Telegraph Cottage Sanday: (see 'Flagstaff').

Temple, The/Kelptoo Sanday: built on 'The Foulan'; lobstermen lived here for six days at a stretch when the ring method of catching lobsters was popular [the 'too' element of 'Kelptoo' is Norse *þúfa* a heap].

Templehall Sanday: ['temple' is probably a nickname given for some unknown reason (compare 'The Temple' above), Scots *ha'* cottage].

Tengagena Harray, Grimeston: a marshy point on the edge of the Harray Loch [Norse *tangi* point of land: the 'gena' element suggests that there was a small pool on this point at one time, Norse *tjörn* pool].

Tennis Court Pentland Skerries: [where cormorants gather: Norse *tangi* point, English 'court' (compare Chaucer's 'Parliament of Fowls')].

Tenston Sandwick: in the south of the parish [one of several *staðr* (estate) names in the West Mainland: the first element is an unknown Norse personal name].

Tenye Sanday: coastal feature, west of the 'Riff o The Riv' [Norse *tönn* a tooth; perhaps a reference to the nature of the rocks].

Terra Cliv South Ronaldsay: [Norse *þari* seaweed, *klufðr* cleft].

Tersabreck Rousay: Wasbister, vanished ['Tersa' is perhaps related to dialect 'tirse' to pull with difficulty, Norse *tríza,* hence 'land difficult to work', *brekka* a slope].

Tew, Quarry o Westray: on 'Tirlot' [Norse *djup* marsh].

Tews, The Wyre, Rusness: field name [Norse *djup* literally 'deep' but used in Orkney in the sense 'marsh' or 'wet area' here (see 'Jewaday')].

Thickbigging Firth: [Norse *þykkva-bygging* suggests a wider building than normal: *þykkvi-baer* thick dwelling, is recorded in Old Norse].

Thieves Holm St. Ola: a small island in 'Kirkwall Bay' [though some native peoples of British Columbia expelled miscreants to desert islands, there is no evidence of this having been done in Orkney: the reason for the name being applied is unknown].

Thorn Westray: on the 'Bay of Swartmill' [English 'thorn': reason for the name unknown].

Thorness Sanday: (see 'Torness').

Thornesshill/Turnesshall Sanday: also known as 'Harpers' (see 'Torness').

Thorodale/Turridale Evie: 'Turido' in 17th century [Norse personal name *Þórðar* and *dý* marsh or moor].

Thrave Sanday: Park district (see 'Treb').

Thurrigar South Ronaldsay: [Norse personal name *Þórðar* and *garðr* farm].

Thurvoe Walls: crofts in the 1880s Ordnance Survey [named after 'Thurvoe' the original name of what is now 'Mill Bay': personal Norse name *Þórir?* and *vágr* bay].

Tick-(h)ip and Fusso a sea mark in the North Ronaldsay Firth [origin unknown].

Tiddley's Reef Sanday: coastal feature, 'Taftsness' [origin unknown].

Tiffyha Deerness: ['tiffy' is a form of 'Teeve' (above), hence 'marshy', Scots *'ha'* simple dwelling].

Tiftaloos North Ronaldsay: [Norse *toptir* old house site, *lo* a marshy area].

Tifter Westray; Papa Westray: [Norse *toptir* old house sites].

Tillydelph Burray: a farm: not an old name, 1871 is the earliest recording: abandoned after the family died of scarlet fever many years ago [perhaps a corruption of Tillyduff in Aberdeenshire: or after a fishing vessel of that name?].

Timmer Dykes South Ronaldsay: [dialect 'timmer' = timber: suggests a fence made of wood].

Timor Hoose Stronsay: just north of 'Linna Brake' [a house made of timber].

Tindisgar, Dam o Rousay: a dammed pond in the hill above 'Hullion', there must have been an enclosure here at one time [Norse personal name *Tindr* and *garðr* enclosure].

Tingley Loup Sanday: coastal feature, Tresness [Norse *þongull* tangle, English 'loop', used commonly in Sanday for a curving bay].

Tingwall Rendall: a prehistoric broch and probably the location of the assembly field in early Norse times [Norse *þing-völlr* parliament field].

Tinkigar North Ronaldsay: an enclosure adjacent to an old chapel [Norse *garðr* enclosure, origin of 'tinki' element unknown].

Tirharrold Rousay, Frotoft: [part of a hillside where, it was said, a woman by the name Harrold died (for discussion of 'tir' element see below)].

Tirlees/Tirlet Sanday: cultivated ground, Westside, Northwall [Scots *tirr* to strip off (turf in this case)].

Tirlot Rousay; Westray, Midbea: [Scots *tirr* to strip, Norse *hluti* allotted part].

Tirrietaing St. Ola: [Norse *þari* seaweed, *tangi* point of land].

Tisly Tumall Sanday, Elsness: field name, early 18th century [dialect *tisly* thistly, Norse *tún-völlr* home field].

Toab St. Andrews: a district of the parish [a compressed form of Tollop which is made up of two Norse words *toll* tax and *hóp* bay i.e., where foreign ships paid a toll and this would include Scottish vessels at that time: foreign ships would also have paid toll at Cantick in South Walls, the earliest recording of which is 'Cantop'].

Tobacco Rock Sanday: southeast point of 'Start' [origin unknown; from smuggling days or a shipwreck? (compare 'Sherry Geo')].

Tober North Fara: a ledge on the shore, the reference must be to a well rather than the ledge itself [Gaelic *tober* a well].

Toburn Sanday, Elsness: field name, early 18th century [may be Gaelic *tober* the well adopted into Norse as the definite article suffix shows].

Todds Zir/Todis Yor Westray: [the final element 'zir' or 'yor' represents Norse *jörð* land or ground, the first element is probably the Norse personal name *Þórðr*, i.e., Thord].

Tofties Sanday: fields on west side of road to 'Stove' [probably Norse *topt* site of a house, *hús* house].

Tofts Rousay; Burray; Egilsay; South Ronaldsay; Sanday: [Norse *topt* old house site].

Toisterburn Rousay: Wasbister, vanished [origin unknown].

Tolland Sanday: vanished, Northwall, remains may still be seen [origin uncertain: perhaps Norse *tollr* toll: foreign vessels visiting Orkney had to pay a toll: compare 'Tollhop' (now 'Toab') and 'Scat Wick'].

Tom Budge's Stone South Ronaldsay: Sandwick area [a fishing rock favoured by some unknown Tom].

Tomison's Academy South Ronaldsay: originally a school donated to the parish by William Tomison who prospered in his employment in the Hudson's Bay Company: the academy is now disused].

Tommy Tiffy Deerness: coastal feature [probably a corruption of Norse *tangi* a rocky point of land and *þófi* felt: it was the practice in some parts of Orkney to thicken or waulk material by securing it on the shore and let the beating of small waves do the task].

Tongabrayie Rousay: [Norse *tangi* tongue of land, *breiðr* broad].

Tongaday/Tongie Rousay; Wyre: [Norse *þang* seaweed, *dý* marsh].

Too Rousay: [Norse *þúfa* a mound].

Too Gill Orphir: location unknown [Norse *þúfa* a mound, *gil* stream running in a narrow channel].

Too o the Head Hoy: [Norse *þúfa* a mound].

Tooacks o the Boy Hoy: not far from the 'Old Man of Hoy' rock pillar [Norse *þúfa* a mound plus local dialect diminutive].

Toofals Westray, Broughton: [a building with a lean-to extension which 'falls to' the main house].

Tooin o Rush(t) Rendall: a small mound on the boundary of Harray and Rendall parishes [Norse *þúfa-n* the mound (with definite article suffix), *rust* hill ridge].

Toomal 1. Evie; Rendall, Biggings; Rousay: [Norse *tún-völlr* home field].

Toomal 2. Sanday: field name, Nouster [Norse *tún-völlr* home field, a common Orkney field name].

Toomal o Eingley Sanday, Stove: field name, also known as 'Tumlins' [Norse *tún-völlr* home field (see 'Eingley')].

Toomal o Quoy Jenny Rousay: (see 'toomal' above and 'Quoyjenny').

Toon Field Rousay; Sanday, near 'Meazer': [Norse *tún* enclosure].

Toon o Milldam Sanday, Bellevue: field name: others include Barnhouse, Howally, Housby, Skesquoy, Yeldabreck, all in Birsay.

Toonis Skerry Sanday: coastal feature near 'Scar' [Norse *tún* enclosure, *sker* reef].

Toonland Rendall: fields on 'Biggings', 'Gitterpitten' and 'Hogarth'.

Toorlie/Toorlo Sanday, 'Whalbrae' Burness: [origin uncertain: 'toor' = tower, *hlíð* slope?].

Toosness alternative name of 'Torness'.

Toots Inn/Tootsinn North Ronaldsay: [no information].

Toppacks o Hess South Ronaldsay: Windwick, three rocks in the sea looking like small haystacks [Scots *top* a conical shape with diminutive 'ick, Norse *hestr* horse, used metaphorically to describe a rock(y) face].

Tor Ness North Ronaldsay; Stronsay; Walls; Orphir: [several coastal regions in Orkney carry the name of Norse gods/goddesses, Norse *Þórr* Thor].

Toressin Firth, Redland: a stretch of land at the other side of the main road from Redland [both elements are related to 'dry' e.g., *þurr* dry and local dialect *sina* to dry].

Tormiston Stenness: [personal name *Þormóð* and *staðr* estate: one of a number of large estates in the West Mainland with personal names attached (see 'Hourston')].

Torness/Toosness Sanday: small promontory, East Sanday [Norse *þurs* (pronounced *þuss*) a giant: (compare 'Hermaness'), *nes* point].

Torrie Firth, Burness: [no information].

Torsker/Tosgarth/Tosger Sanday: Rusness area [Norse personal name *Þórir* and *garðr*, farm].

Tostes Sanday: field name Rusness area [Norse *topt* house site, *staðr* farm: (compare 'Houstais')].

Tougay Westray: recorded in 1653: cannot be identified today.

Touger North Ronaldsay: the 'Kirkland of Touger' is mentioned in the Land Tax Rolls of 1645: location unknown [Norse *þúfa* mound, *garðr* farm].

Toultrie Sanday: stood on a field on 'Galdry' land [dialect *toultrie* ready to fall, which is why it has vanished!].

Toumal o Haan Sanday: southeast of Hillhead, Sellibister [Norse *tún-völlr* home field (see 'Haan')'].

Toumal, The Sanday: on 'Garbo' land: small enclosure (see above).

Toun o Sellibist Sanday: all the cultivated ground between 'Seater' and 'Crudy' [Norse *tún* enclosure (see 'Sellibist')].

Toung South Ronaldsay: a vanished house near a point of land [there was also an old house of 'Toung' in Stenness].

Tounga Birsay: near 'Plittro' Sabiston [a house in a 'tongue' of land: *tangi* point of land].

Toungie Evie [no information].

Tour Rendall: a house, vanished: location unknown.

Touthey Point o Sanday: south Tresness [a corruption of *þúfa* mound?].

Tow/Toou Geo Birsay: [origin unknown].

Toward Birsay: Abune-the-Hill district [because of its hill position the name suggests Norse *varða* a beacon and *þúfa* a mound (compare 'Wart o Crook')].

Towmail is a variant of 'toumal' above [such 'towmails' are found at 'Orkness', 'Prestan', 'Kelldelie', 'Newbigging' and 'Treb', all in North Ronaldsay].

Toyhorns Birsay, Hayon: field name [origin unknown].

Toyness Point Orphir: on 'Swanbister Bay' [origin uncertain: a form of *þúfa* mound?].

Trabaquoy/Trepaquoy St. Andrews: north of 'Langskaill' [Norse *kví* enclosure: (for 'Traba' element see 'Treb')].

Trabbequoys Deerness: on 'South Keigar' (see 'Treb').

Traddletown/Trattletown Shapinsay: to the northeast of 'Strathore' [the basic meaning of 'traddle' here is 'dirt' as in English dialect 'trattle' sheep droppings: (compare 'Turdobreck' on 'Ayrean' in Stromness)].

Trae Geo Pentland Skerries; Swona: [Norse *tré* wood, in the sense of trapped driftwood].

Traisbie Sandwick: 17th century [location unknown: genitive of Norse *tré* tree, *boer* farm which suggests a farmhouse built of timber].

Trance, The South Ronaldsay, St. Margaret's Hope: a lane connecting Front Road and Back Road: [Scots *trance* a lane, from Old French *trance* (see 'The Vennel' for an interesting comparison)].

Trangie, Geo na North Ronaldsay: [Norse *þröngr* narrow, *gjá* ravine].

Tratland Rousay: [Norse *Þræta* to quarrel over, in this case disputed land].

Tratlands Birsay, Eastabist: (see above).

Treb Sanday: Sutherbie (see below).

Treb/Trebb North Ronaldsay: (see 'The Treb' below).

Treb, The Sanday: remains of a massive prehistoric earthen rampart, the origin of which is not known [the placename means essentially 'barrier' as in Norse *þref* loft or þrep ledge: 'Garbo' in 'Sellibister' was formerly called 'Gairbak' where 'bak' = 'balk': Garbo lies on a 'treb dyke'].

Trebb Sanday: it stood near a treb dyke at 'The Knowes' (see above).

Trebisquoy Sanday: in Middle Hill, How: this farm was already a ruin at the end of the 19th century [Norse *kví* enclosure (see 'Treb' above)].

Trebland Westray: (see 'Treb' above).

Trena Loch South Ronaldsay: [origin unknown].

Trenaby Westray, Rackwick: [rare Norse personal name, perhaps *Þrándr*?, Norse *boer* farm].

Trenastie Sanday: [Norse *þróndr* a boar, *stía* a pen].

Tresness Sanday: a peninsula, earlier recorded 'Trosness' [Norse *trés* genitive of *tre* tree or wood, used here presumably of driftwood].

Treta Meadow Birsay, Skelday: [Norse *þraeta* a quarrel: a disputed meadow (see 'Tratland' above)].

Trettigar Harray: [Norse *þraeta* a dispute, *garðr* farm].

Trevan (see 'Bars o Trevan').

Triblo Rousay: 'Sourin' area, vanished [the placename may be a form of 'Treb' but unlikely].

Trifties Birsay: Kirbister area, another name for the dwelling 'Bum' [an instance of a house called after an inhabitant who probably boasted of being 'thrifty'].

Trim Tooers/Tuo North Ronaldsay: a mound near 'Antabreck' [Norse *þúfa* Mound, origin of 'trim' element unknown].

Trin Geo South Ronaldsay: [Norse *þröngr* narrow, *gjá* ravine].

Trinester (see 'Trenastie' above).

Trinielet Sanday: [Norse *þróndr* boar, *hlé-t* the shelter].

Trink Sanday: coastal feature [Scots *trink* ditch or stream].

Trinkie Geo South Ronaldsay: (see above).

Trinnawin, Knowes o Hoy: [Norse *þróndr* boar, *kví-n* the enclosure, Scots *knowe* knoll].

Trinnigar Sandwick: southeast of 'Aith' [Norse *þróndr* boar, *garðr* enclosure].

Trofer Burray: [Norse *traðir* trampled down by cattle (see below)].

Troffers Evie: a lane [Norse *traðir* trampled down by cattle: the same sense is used in Iceland].

Trolla Shun Harray [Norse *troll* demon, *tjörn* small loch or pond].

Trollawatten North Ronaldsay: [Norse *troll* demon, *vatn* loch].

Trolldgeo Burn o Shapinsay: [for 'geo' read 'go' = Norwegian - *gjól*, better shown by Middle High German *gole* meaning 'marsh', Norse *troll* demon: the 'd' reflects dialect pronunciation of 'g' (see 'Geo' in Appendix)].

Trolle Geo Evie: [Norse *troll* demon, *gjá* ravine].

Trongiron Sanday: coastal feature, 'Whitemill Beach' [Norse *þröngr* Narrow, *eyrr-inn* the gravel spit].

Tronston Sandwick: [Norse personal name *Þróndr*, Norse *staðr* estate: one of a number of old estates in the West Mainland, all of which carry personal names].

Troondie Rendall, Queena: field name [Norse *þróndr* boar, *dý* moor/marsh].

Trotty, Knowes o Harray: the largest Bronze Age site in Britain containing sixteen barrows the largest revealing four wafer-thin gold sun discs [may be Norse *Þrúðr* a goddess, daughter of Thor].

Trow's Buil Sanday: a piece of land on 'The Treb' at 'Hillhead' [dialect *trow* troll, evil creatures are invariably associated with boundaries, 'buil' = *ból* animal resting place].

Trow's Close Shapinsay: a small creek northwest of 'Twiness' [Norse *troll*, dialect *kloss* passageway].

Trow's Hole Shapinsay: a cave in 'Luffaness Geo' [Norse *troll*].

Trow's Well Birsay, Westerhouse: [Norse *troll*].

Trowie Geo Rousay: [local dialect 'trowie' a form of Norse *troll*].

Trowie Glen Hoy: (see above).

Trull Geo Eday: a small geo [Norse *troll*, *gjá* ravine].

Trumland Westray; Rousay: [Norse *tröm* edge which suggests a boundary or outskirts].

Trundi Geo South Ronaldsay: [Norse *þróndr* boar, *gjá* ravine].

Trundigarth [Norse *þróndr* boar, *garðr* enclosure].

Trunisty Sanday: [Norse *þróndr* boar, *stía* sty].

Trussans Geo Westray: west of Clestron [Norse *þurs* a giant, one of many mystical creatures recorded on the Orkney coastline: the suffix 'n' represents the definite article].

Tuacks o the Boy Hoy: [Norse *púfa* a mound with local diminutive 'ack': they lie close to the Old Man o Hoy!].

Tuan Westray: [Norse *púfa-n* the mound].

Tuanabackan Evie: coastal feature [Norse *púfa-n* the mound, *bakk-inn* bank].

Tuberry Point Cava: in the southeast of the island [Norse *púfa* a mound, *berg* rock].

Tuffin Firth, Binscarth: [Norse *púfa-n* the mound: perhaps the original name of 'Harper's Howe' the only named mound on Binscarth].

Tufta Harray; Birsay; Sandwick: [Norse *topt* old house site].

Tuftaback Birsay, village: [Norse *topt* old house site, *bakki* bank].

Tufter Birsay; Westray: [Norse *toptir* old house sites].

Tumail Sanday: field name north of Rue [Norse *tún-völlr* home field].

Tumlins Sanday: alternative name for 'Toomal o Eingley', 'Stove' [Norse *tún-völlr-inn* the home field (with English plural)].

Tundar Hole Evie: a place where lovers met! [it lay near the sea which suggests that 'tundar' = 'thunder' relating to the sound of the breaking surf].

Tungan Birsay: coastal feature [Norse *tangi* a point of land].

Tungie North Ronaldsay: (see above).

Tunlins North Ronaldsay: arable land north of the Ness houses [Norse *tún- land* (see 'Toonland)'].

Tuo 1. Sanday: northwest point of 'Ire' (see below).

Tuo 2. Sanday: coastal feature, Foulan [Norse *þúfa* mound].

Tuos Sanday: coastal feature [Norse *þúfa* small mound].

Tuos/Toos Sanday: field name, 'Millhouse', Rusness (see above).

Tuquoy Westray: site of an important Norse medieval settlement [Norse *þúfa* mound, *kví* enclosure].

Tur Geo Holm: [Norse *þurr* dry, i.e., a grass covered ravine].

Turbitail Rousay: [origin unknown].

Turdobreck Stromness, Arion: field name [Norse *tord* dung but such 'foul' words in Orkney placenames usually refer to poor marshy ground].

Turkey Skerry Sanday: coastal feature [Norse *þurka* dryness, hence a skerry which is never submerged, *sker*, reef].

Turnesshall (see 'Thornesshill').

Turridale Evie: (see 'Thorodale').

Turrieday Firth: [origin as above].

Turrieness North Ronaldsay: the northwest point of North Ronaldsay [Norse *þurr* dry, suggesting that it is rarely flooded].

Tuskerbister Orphir: [Norse *torf-skeri* turf cutter, better *torf-stað* where peat is cut, *ból-staðr* farm].

Twargreen Harray: [Norse *þver* across].

Twarspells Harray: [Norse *þver* across, Scots *speld* a field, lying across as opposed to longitudinally].

Twartquoy Orphir: [Norse *þver* athwart, *kví* enclosure].

Twatt Birsay; Stenness: [Norse *þveit* a piece of land].

Twatt Meadow Birsay: Dirkdale (see above).

Tween Burns Rendall: a field on the land of Lettaly ['tween' = between].

Tween the Wicks Flotta: [Norse *vík* bay].

Twiness Westray; Shapinsay; St. Andrews; North Ronaldsay: [Norse *þúfa* mound, *nes* point of land].

Twisting Nevi Deerness: an indentation on the extreme north of 'Mull Head' [English 'twisting', Norse *nef* cliff, literally 'nose'].

Twitheday, Well o Birsay, Twatt: [Norse *þveti-t* piece of land, *dý* marsh].

U

Uimest Hoose Sanday, Elsness: field name, early 18th century [dialect *uimest* uppermost].

Uimis Hass Evie: the house above 'Hass' [obsolete dialect *uimest*, uppermost].

Uiss, The Rousay: [Norse *óss* the outlet of a stream but in Orkney always refers to an obstructed outlet of a stream which forms a pool].

Ulie Bogie Rousay, Frotoft: field name: an 'ulie bogie' was literally a bag for holding fish oil ['ulie' = oily: the reference is not understood].

Ullapow Holm: ['ulla' = oily?, Scots *pow* pool: pools often had oily surfaces caused by decaying vegetation].

Una Burn o Stromness: [Norse *á* stream, origin of the 'un' element not known].

Underhallow Evie: field name north of 'Spithersquoy' [origin unknown].

Unigar Sandwick: earlier 'Owkingarth' [Norse personal name *Hákon* and *garðr* farm].

Unston/Onston Stenness: [Norse personal name *Örn* and *staðr* estate: one of a number of estates in the West Mainland with personal names attached].

Unziebust Wyre: [Norse personal name *Örn* and *ból-staðr* farm].

Uppadie Sandwick: [Norse *uppi* higher, *dý* moor or marsh].

Upper Breckan Sanday also known as 'Oumist Breckan' [Norse *brekkan* the slope (see 'Uimest Hoose')].

Upper Cott Sanday: also known as 'Daisy Cottage' and 'Snoddie's' [there is only one recording of the surname 'Snoddie' on the island].

Upper Lerquoy Rendall, Upper Ellibister: field name, probably site of an old house [Norse *leirr* clay, *kví* enclosure].

Upsale Sandwick: [Norse *uppi* the higher, *salr* hall: an identical name to the Swedish city of 'Upsala'].

Upthra Swona: [obsolete dialect nickname for a house selling ale].

Uraday Rousay: a valley on the southwest slope of 'Ward Hill' [Norse *urð* a rock fall].

Urback Flotta: [Norse *ár-bakki* the bank of a stream].

Urigar Evie: [*ár* genitive of *á* stream, *garðr* farm].

Uttesgarth Holm: [Faroese *uttastur* outermost, *garðr* farm].

V

Va Burn Orphir: the stream is named after the ford: location unknown [Norse *vað* a wading place across a stream].

Vacquoy Rousay: [Norse *vað* a ford, *kví* enclosure].

Vaday Egilsay: [Norse *vað-eið* wading isthmus].

Vager/Vedger Sanday: on Saville land [Norse *vé* sacred, *garðr* farm or wall].

Vahm South Ronaldsay, Hoxa: vanished [Norse *hvammr* a grassy slope].

Vakkles North Ronaldsay: rocks in the sea at the entrance to 'Stuan' [recorded in Shetland as a 'skerry': Norse meaning uncertain].

Valay Holm: [Norse *hváll* a dome, a variant of *hóll* hill].

Valdigar St. Andrews: [at first sight, apparently a variant of 'Veltigar' meaning a 'cultivated enclosure' but perhaps also 'an enclosure belonging to *Vald*'].

Valdiger Holm: (see above).

Valgreen Sanday, Newark: field name [Norse *völlr* field, *groenn* green].

Vam Burn o Orphir: [Norse *hvammr* a grassy slope: (compare 'Vahm')].

Vancouver Birsay, Twatt: vanished [a cottage named by a returning emigrant].

Vanglee Papa Westray: vanished house and associated settlement mound south of Holland [Norse *van* lacking, origin of 'glee' element unknown].

Vany Rousay: a stream name [origin unknown].

Var Hoose North Ronaldsay: [position and derivation unknown].

Varaquoy Rousay: extreme north point of Scockness [Norse *ver* a fishing Place, *kví* enclosure].

Vari Grip Birsay, Hundland: [Scots *grip* a small stream, origin of 'var' element unknown].

Variecott/Verracott North Ronaldsay: west of 'Ancum Loch' [origin of 'varie/verra' elements unknown].

Varmady/dale Rendall, Gorseness Hill; Rousay, Hunclett: [Norse *warmr* warm, *dý* marsh or moor: a strange use of 'warm' for quite exposed areas: compare 'Greenland', an island mainly of ice].

Varrsa, Burn o Rendall, Gorseness Hill: [the terminal 'a' represents Norse *á* stream, origin of 'varrs' element unknown].

Vassaquoy Westray: location unknown [probably a form of 'Vassquoy' (below)].

Vassay 1. Rousay: in the Frotoft area: seems originally to have covered a large area from the 'Geo o Vassay' to a large stretch of hillside to the north [origin unknown].

Vassay 2. Shapinsay: a small loch trapped by a beach formation [the 'vas' element is the genitive of Norse *vatn* loch the 'say' element cannot be explained].

Vassenbrae Rousay: a steep slope on the bank of the 'Sourin Burn'.

Vassquoy Rousay: Scockness area, near a loch [see 'Vassay' (above) to explain the 'vass' element, *kví* enclosure].

Vastray, Point o Evie: [Norse *hvass* pointed or tapering, *tré* wood, in the sense of 'driftwood' (see 'Tresness')].

Vasvia Evie: [Norse *vatns* as in 'Vassay', Shapinsay (above), *vé* sacred or holy place: (see 'Via')].

Vaultness o Ancum North Ronaldsay: [Norse *velta* to turn over (in this case, of soil) i.e., arable land, *nes* point of land (compare 'Veltigar' below)].

Vaval Westray, north of Trenaby; Graemsay: [Norse *fjall* hill, *völlr* field].

Vaxter Geo Sanday: coastal feature [Norse *gjá* ravine (see 'Voxetter')].

Vean Harray, Grimeston; Stenness, east of 'Settersquoy' [possibly a form of Norse *kví-n* the enclosure: (compare 'Wheenabreckan' etc.)].

Veantrow Shapinsay: [Norse *kví-n* the enclosure, 'trow' = dialect 'through' suggesting that this may have been an ale house (see 'Ap-trow')].

Vedder St. Andrews: [Norse *veðr* a ram: it has apparently lost an element such as *kví* enclosure].

Vedesquoy Shapinsay: [Norse personal name *Veðr* and *kví* enclosure].

Vedger Sanday: coastal feature near 'Saville' (see 'Vager').

Vedo Evie: (see 'Mountvedo').

Veesper Sanday: track east of old Sanday Kirk [Norse *vé* sacred, *spor* track].

Vell Westray, Midbea: [Norse *völlr* field].

Vellin Birsay, Marwick: [Norse *völl-inn* the field].

Vellyans Birsay: Southside near 'Wrangleha' [Norse *vellirnir* fields (plus English plural)].

Veltan Birsay, Banks: [Norse *velta* to turn over (of soil in this case) hence ploughed or arable].

Veltie Stronsay: (see above).

Veltigar St. Andrews: (see 'Vaultness o Ancum' above').

Velyie Westray; Sandwick: (see 'Vell' above).

Velzian 1. Birsay: near Makerhouse, Dounby (see 'Vellin' above).

Velzian 2. Harray; Rendall, between Queena and North Ettit.

Veness Hill Orphir: [Norse *vé* sacred, *nes* headland].

Veniba/Vinyba Birsay: Swannay area, high cliffs [Norse *fen* boggy land, *berg* rock (cliffs), pronounced 'ba' locally].

Veniekelday/Vinikelday St. Andrews: [Norse *fen* bog, *kelda* well].

Veniver Shapinsay: east of 'Veantrow Bay', a similar placename exists in Westray in the form 'Millivenier' [Norse *ver* a fishing area].

Vensilly Hill South Ronaldsay: [Norse *fen* bog, *selja* willow].

Ver Geo Stronsay: [Norse *vörr* a landing place for a vessel].

Veran Harray: field name adjacent to 'Midhouse', Huntscarth [Norse *vaera- n* the shelter].

Verbie Stronsay: [(as below), Norse *vörr* a landing place for a vessel: origin of 'bie' in this entry unknown].

Vere Westray, Rackwick: (see 'Ver Geo' above).

Verigens/Virigens Firth: little lochs on 'Wart of Redland' [Norse *vaeri* shelter, *tjörn* pond (with English plural)].

Verpino Rousay: a fishing rock in the Leean district [Norse *varp-in* a net, cast out in fishing].

Verracott North Ronaldsay: Linklet area, west of 'Ancum Loch' [Norse *vaera* a shelter, *kot* a modest house].

Verron 1. Evie: Costa, a broch? mound near the shore [really Norse *varð-in* the beacon but used in the local sense of a 'mound'].

Verron 2. Sandwick, Bay of Skaill: remains of a broch mound (see above).

Verry Geo Evie; Rousay: [Norse *vörr* a landing place for a vessel].

Versa Breck North Ronaldsay: a ridge south of 'Trollawatten' which, like 'The Treb', is thought to be inhabited by an evil spirit: it is now the site of the lighthouse [origin unknown].

Vesker Birsay: a reef which ebbs dry at low tide [Norse *veita* a trench, referring to the channel between the coast and the reef, *sker* a reef].

Vestaber Birsay: a fishing rock [Norse *vest-berg* west rock].

Vestness/Westness North Ronaldsay; Papa Westray: [Norse *vestr* west, *nes* point or headland].

Vestra Fiold Sandwick: [Norse *vestr* west, *fjall* hill].

Vestray Westray, Rackwick: half a mile north of 'Gill Pier' [Norse *vestr* West, origin of 'tray' element here uncertain].

Vetquoy Sandwick: [Norse *vatn* loch, *kví* enclosure].

Veval Graemsay: [Norse *fjall* hill, *völlr* field: (compare 'Feaval')].

Via Papa Westray; Sandwick; Birsay: [Norse *vé* a sacred place].

Vian, The Westray: a large bay in the 'Aikerness' district [Norse *vági-nn* the bay].

Vias Moss Birsay, Makerhouse: a low-lying mossy area [the suggestion is that 'Vias' is the genitive of a 'Via' which at one time must have lain in the locality: (see above)].

Vigga South Ronaldsay; Holm, Paplay; Birsay, Southside, on present site of Barnhouse: (see 'Via' above too).

Viggar North Ronaldsay; Sanday: [Norse *vé-garðr* temple: the field immediately adjacent in Sanday is 'Kirkley': to the north lies an old kirk].

Viggay/Viggie Sanday: now known as 'Clair Lea' (see 'Viggar' for possible Interpretation).

Viggi Stronsay: north of Holland, really the field in which Holland stands (see 'Viggay' above).

Villigar Flotta: a small bay on the north side of 'Pan Hope': the name must relate to a vanished farm on the coast [Norse *völlr* field, *garðr* farm].

Vinbreck Birsay, Northside: [Norse *vindr* wind, *brekka* slope].

Vincoin North Ronaldsay: (see 'Vinquin' below).

Vindon/Vinden Firth: [Norse *fen* a marshy area, *dýna* marsh].

Vinko/Vinquoy Eday: [Norse *vindr* wind, *kví* enclosure].

Vinquin Evie: [Norse *vindr* wind, *kvín* the enclosure].

Vishabreck Evie: [Norse 'Vishallbreck'? (see below), *brekka* slope].

Vishall Evie: [(c.f. 'Upsale' in Sandwick), Norse *vé* sacred or holy, *salr* hall].

Voan Stenness: [refers probably to a mound in the vicinity: origin unknown: (see 'Vean' which may offer an alternative explanation)].

Voderaday Birsay, Gerraquoy: [Norse *dý* marshy ground, origin of 'vodera' element unknown].

Vola Sandwick, Skeabrae; Harray: [Norse *völlr* field].

Voldabrae/Voldibrae Sanday: on Warsetter land [probably a form of 'fiold', Norse *fjall* hill, *breiðr* broad: there is a 'Voldibrae' in Stronsay].

Voldigarth Westray, Lochend: [Norse *fjall* hill (as above), *garðr* farm].

Volespred Rousay, Hurtiso: [origin unknown].

Volgrun Dike Dounby, Hyval: [Norse *völlr* field, *groena* green, Scots/English *dike* wall: suggests a turf-covered wall].

Volla Firth: [Norse *völlr* field].

Volunes referred to in the *Orkneyinga Saga* and occupied by a man 'Bard': position unknown [Norse *völlr* field, *nes* point].

Volyar Sanday, Stove: field name, site of a vanished house [Norse *völlr* Field, Norse *garðr* farm].

Vow Randi Hoy: a long hill west of 'Water o Hoy', near to the Hoy/Walls boundary [Norse *rönd* edge, or boundary in this case: origin of 'Vow' unknown].

Voxsetter Sanday: area around Braeswick (see 'Voy' Sandwick) [Norse *vágs-setr* bay settlement: there is a placename 'Voxter' in Shetland].

Voy Sanday, area around Braeswick; St. Andrews; Sandwick: [Norse *vágr* bay].

W

Wa Westray: the name is now subsumed under 'Pierowa(ll)' [Norse *vágr* bay].

Waa Rendall, Waswick: a vanished house, a name derived from the bay on which it stood [Norse *vágr* bay].

Waal Cottage Westray, Dykeside: ['waal' is the local dialect pronunciation of English 'well'].

Waal o Aan Stenness: location uncertain: marked on the 1760 Division of Commonty map [Norse *á-n* the well].

Waal o Glumsgar Stenness: (see 'Glumsgar').

Waal o Lannigar Stenness: [location and meaning unknown].

Waalhoose Sanday, Warsetter: field name [dialect *waal* well: there is a well in this field].

Waas, Walls/Bu o Walls Sanday, Northwall: house and mound [Norse *vágar* bay (with English plural)].

Waddy o Noustiger Rousay: the channel between rocks at 'Noustiger' and 'Sandbrig' near the mouth of the 'Sourin Burn' which can be easily waded at low water [Norse *vað* a wading place].

Waddy o Skelda Birsay: (see 'Waddy' above and 'Skelda').

Waddy o Skuan/Dirkadale Birsay, Dirkadale: (see 'Waddy' above).

Wadi The Rendall: fields on a number of farms (see 'Waddy' above).

Wads/Wades Evie: [the name suggests Norse *vað* a wading place (with English plural): there were some streams around here in the 1880s: at one time there was a 'Wood' family living here and they were referred to as 'The Wids o Wads', 'wid' being the dialect pronunciation of 'wood'].

Waegoe Sanday: coastal name, Cross parish [Norse *kví* enclosure: (for'goe' element see 'Geo' in Appendix)].

Waird 1. Birsay, Marwick: [Scots *ward/waird* an enclosed piece of ground: one of a few enclosures with walls built of stone].

Waird 2. Birsay, Beaquoy: (see above).

Wairds, Park of Birsay, Wattle: (see above).

Waithe, Brig o Stenness [Norse *vað* a wading place (before the bridge(s)were built)].

Walbroch/Waldibrek/Waldbreck Sanday: possibly on the lands of 'Warsetter' [Norse *hváll* hill, *brekka* slope].

Wald Firth: earlier 'Wathill' [Norse *vaðill* a wading place: there were small streams in this area in the 1880s].

Waldgarth Sanday: Cross parish, mentioned in the early Rental Books: represented by 'Volyar' on the farm of 'Stove' [Norse *vaðill* a wading place, *garðr* farm].

Walerow Birsay, Beaquoy: [no further information].

Walker House Birsay: a house situated near a former fulling mill on the stream which drains the 'Boardhouse Loch' [Scots *'to waulk'* to full cloth].

Walkerhoose Evie: (see below).

Wallies Evie: site of a croft at 'Back Geo' ['geo' here means 'marsh (see Appendix), probably the personal name 'Walter'].

Wallis Farding Holm: [surname 'Walls', 'farding' = farthing, a quarter of a stretch of land in this case].

Walliwall St. Ola: site of a former Kirkwall market and later, a quarry: [Norse *hváll* hill, *völlr* field].

Walls parish comprises more than half of the island of Hoy and includes Flotta: population 1,506: extremely important in two World Wars and earlier in relation to naval activity.

Waltness Shapinsay: [Norse *velta* to turn over (of soil in this case) hence ploughed or arable, *nes* point of land].

Wantonbrae Sanday, Northwall: [origin unknown].

Wappingstreet Sanday: on 'Garbo' land ['street' was applied in Orkney to a long building housing several families e.g., 'Duke Street', Rousay, Queen Street, Stromness].

War Ness Eday: southwest of the island [Norse *varða* normally a beacon site but here applies to an elevated area, in this case a burnt mound: (see 'wart' forms below)].

Warbeth Stromness, Ootertoon: [Norse *hvarf-it* a turning around, i.e., to enter 'Hoy Sound'].

Warbister Hill Swona: the highest point on the island [Norse *varða* beacon, the 'bister' element, normally meaning 'farm', must have the original meaning 'animal shelter' here].

Warbreckan Sanday: [a recent naming of one of the 'Laminess' houses].

Warbuster St. Ola; Hoy: [Norse *varða* beacon, *ból-staðr* farm].

Ward, The o Redland Firth: (see below).

Ward Hill Orphir; South Ronaldsay; Rousay; Eday; Hoy; Sandwick; Shapinsay; Stronsay: [Norse *varða* beacon].

Ward of Houseby Stronsay: a chambered cairn [Scots *ward/waird* an enclosed piece of ground: (see 'Houseby')].

Wards 1. South Ronaldsay, Kirkhouse: (see below).

Wards 2. Walls: [Scots *ward/waird* an enclosed piece of ground].

Wards, The Evie (see above).

Ware Geo Shapinsay: [Scots *ware* seaweed].

Ware Park Sanday: 'The Riv' (see above).

Ware Shore Birsay: [Scots *ware* seaweed].

Warebanks Burray: [Scots *ware* seaweed].

Warren Evie; St. Ola: a piece of ground infested with rabbits [English 'warren' an enclosed area for breeding rabbits].

Warrenhall St. Ola; Eday: [(see above), Scots *ha'* a simple cottage].

Warset Egilsay: a small holding on the highest part of the island (see below).

Warsetter Sanday: originally near a beacon site [Norse *varða* beacon, *setr* dwelling].

Wa(r)squoy Harray, Overbrough: [Norse *kví* enclosure: meaning of 'war' unknown].

Wart 1. Birsay; Burray; Sandwick; Firth, Lettaly: [all 'wart' forms below can be equated with 'ward' forms: most refer to high beacon sites but others on low ground apply to mounds such as the 'North Fara' example below].

Wart 2. North Fara: remains of a chambered cairn known locally as a 'Picts house'.

Wart, Point o the Wyre: 'Onziebust' area ['Wart' must refer to an old vanished mound].

Wart, The 1. Sanday: the highest hill on the island [Norse *varða* beacon: early beacon fires used to warn of the approach of an enemy].

Wart, The 2. South Ronaldsay: [Norse *varða* a beacon (site)].

Wart Holm Westray: it lies off the southwest point of 'Rapness' ['wart' refers to its mound-like shape].

Warth Birsay, Swartland: named after an ancient burial mound, no trace of which remains [Norse *varða* really a high beacon site but used in Orkney for an elevated area such as a mound].

Warth Shore Flotta: (see above).

Warthill Holm: [Norse *varða* a beacon (site)].

Wartie Stronsay: a field around the 'Ward of Housebay', a chambered cairn (see 'Warth').

Warto Rendall: swampy area near 'Blubbersdale' [Norse *svartr* black, often applied to a wet piece of land: (see 'Pulswarto', Rendall)].

Wasbister Rousay; Sandwick; South Ronaldsay: [Norse *vatn* loch, *ból-staðr* farm].

Wasbust Westray: (a form of 'Wasbister' above).

Wasby Stenness: field name, exact location unknown today [Norse *vatn* loch, *boer* farm].

Wasdale Firth: Wansdale, in the 17th century [Norse *vatn* loch, *dalr* valley].

Wasday/Wasdale, Loch of Rousay: [Norse *vatn* loch, *dalr* valley].

Waskera/Wascra; Birsay, Swannay: evacuees built this house near 'Ingsay' using the Swannay name; later called 'Finties/Frowney' [Norse *vatn* loch, *kró* enclosure].

Wasley Sanday, Tafts: field name [Norse *vágs* genitive of *vágr* bay, *hlíð* slope].

Waspitten Birsay, Flecketsquoy: [Norse *vatn* small loch, *pyttr-inn* the pool].

Wassens Sanday, Whistlebrae: field name, [origin unknown].

Wasso Sanday: broch mound, 'Tresness' [Norse *vágr* bay, the final 'o' represents *haugr* mound: (compare 'Yarso')].

Wast Bow Sanday: coastal feature, Ire [Norse *boði* shoal].

Wast Pow Sanday: coastal feature [Scots *pow* pool].

Waster Noust Flotta: ['waster' = 'wester', Norse *naustr* boat shelter].

Wastin, The Sanday: an area of land [dialect *wastin*, the west side (compare 'Eastin')].

Wastlee Moor Walls: [Norse *hlíð* slope, 'wast' = 'west'].

Waswick Rendall: at one time there was a house here called 'Wa' [Norse *vágr* bay, hence 'Waswick' is the bay on which 'Wa' stands but *vágr* has been substituted by *vík* bay].

Waswyns Firth, Wasdale: [origin unknown].

Watch Stone an imposing standing stone, 5.6 metres high, northwest of the Standing Stones of Stenness [the origin of this name is unknown and the interpretation of 'watch' as Norse *vatn* loch is unconvincing: perhaps more reasonable are Norse *vaetti* or Norse *vátta* which would make the monolith a 'stone of witness', an assembly place where oaths were taken].

Water o the Wicks Walls: a small freshwater loch near 'Scad Head':

Waterglen Hoy: in the northeast of 'Ward Hill' [Scots *glen* valley].

Waterhall Sanday: beside 'Bea Loch' [Scots *Hall/ha'* cottage].

Waterloo Rendall: [one of many battle names used in Orkney placenames: now renamed 'Millbrig'].

Watermoss Deerness: also known as 'Grindcheek.'

Waterslap Orphir: [Scots *slap* gate (to a well)].

Watery Speldro Birsay, Netherskaill: [Scots *speld* a field (with 'ro' diminutive)].

Waterygeo Westray: an indentation in the coast visible at low water only.

Watnasker, The Hass o Rousay: the dip in the hill northwest of 'Muckle Water' [Norse *hals* literally 'neck' but used in Orkney in the sense 'constricted' place: 'watnasker' is Norse *vatn* loch, *skarð* a saddle in a hill].

Watten Egilsay: [Norse *vatn* loch].

Wattie's Ship Wyre, Onziebust: a rock in the sea [seen as the vessel of the spirit 'Watty Red/Reid' alias 'Cubbie Roo'].

Wattin Deerness; Egilsay; Sanday, part of Stove land [Norse *vatn* lake].

Wattle Birsay: [Norse *veizle* a farm which provided sustenance for a visiting earl/king].

Watty Reid's Hole Birsay, southwest of 'The Brough'; Stromness: ['Watty Reid' is another name for the spirit, 'Cubbie Roo'].

Waulkmill Orphir: a mill for fulling cloth [Scots *waulk-mill* a mill where cloth is shrunk].

Weardith Stromness: [Norse *verð-it* a beacon site but this is no place for a beacon: the name should be interpreted as a 'mound' but if there was such a mound, it has been cleared].

Wearn Birsay, Ingsay: location unknown (see 'Verron' for derivation).

Weatherness Westray: the southeast point of the island [Norse *veðr* ram, *nes* point].

Weddel Flotta: (see below).

Weddell Burray: [Norse *vaðill* water that can be waded, probably by a horse].

Wee Fea Walls: [Scots *wee* small, Norse *fjall* hill].

Weelan Banks Sanday: banks along the east side of 'Kettletoft Bay', Elsness [Norse *hvíld-in* the place of rest for a funeral cortège: nearby lies 'Curcatae'].

Weelies Taing Papa Westray: on the northern edge of 'North Wick': a broad shingle spit with a loch in the middle [origin of 'weelies' unknown, Norse *tangi* point of land].

Weems South Ronaldsay: east of 'Vensilly Hill' [apparently not connected with 'Weems Castle' which is at the other side of the island: origin unknown].

Whillida Stromness: on 'Fletts' next to 'Briggan' [Norse *kví* enclosure, Celtic *lod* pool)].

Whistlebare Eday; Firth; Sanday; South Ronaldsay: [Scots *whistlebare* poor, hilly exposed land: the original condition of the land].

Whistlebrae Egilsay: (a form of 'Whistlebare' above).

Whistlehigh Evie: [usually applied to a high house where the wind would 'whistle'!].

Whistle-keek Birsay, Northside: an old ale house on 'Eefie Hill' [one of a number of names given in jest to simple cottages near a hilltop, Scots *keek* to peep, in the sense of 'looking down inquisitively'].

Whitagreeth Evie/Rendall: [an error in transcription (see 'Quithagoathe')].

Whitaloo Point Birsay: near 'Longagleeb' [Norse *hvít* white, *lo* a marshy area].

White Brest Hoy: near 'Bring Head' [English 'breast' used to describe a cliff face, significance of 'white' unknown].

White Fowl Nevi Deerness: [Norse *hvíta-fugl* a white seabird, *nef* cliff, literally 'nose'].

White Hamars Hoy: [Norse *hamarr* exposed rocks on a hillside].

White Nev, The Flotta: a headland at 'Pan Bay' [Norse *nef* cliff (literally 'nose')].

White Nose Sanday: (see 'Grunavi').

White Sark Holm: a small bay near 'Backakelday': must refer originally to some land feature [origin unknown].

Whitecleat St. Andrews; Westray; Sanday; Egilsay; Birsay: [Norse *hvít* white, *klettr* rock/stone: painted white for some pagan/early Christian reason].

Whitehall Stronsay: [a house built in the 17th century which gave its name to the village].

Whitehouse Evie: also known as 'Dees' which is probably the original name [Norse *dý* marsh (with English plural)].

Weems Castle South Ronaldsay: Sandwick district [the remains of a broch but it is said locally that this name originally applied to a mansion house which had some connection with the proprietors of Wemyss Castle in Fife].

Weeo Craig Birsay: [local dialect 'weeo' a kittiwake].

Weethick St. Andrews, Tankerness: named after the bay on which it stands [Norse *við* wood (driftwood), *vík* bay].

Weland Shapinsay: [probably Norse *vé-land* sacred (pagan) land: the 'Stone of Odin' lies in the vicinity].

Welcome Evie: recorded only once in 1841 [an unusual name for a house though common on door mats today! No information available on how the house was named].

Well o Aan Stenness: (see 'Aan').

Well o Jericho Birsay: near Pisgah' (see 'Jericho').

Well o Kildingue Stronsay: at one time a famous healing well which drew people from as far away as Denmark [Norse *kelda* a well, personal name *Ingi*].

Well o Nesgar Sanday: an inlet at 'Riv' [Norse *vella* to boil up as in a whirlpool].

Wells o Swona Swona: dangerous whirlpools off the southeast coast of the island [Norse *vella* to boil up].

Werda Birsay, Newhall: [Norse *verða* a mound].

Werne Harray: (see 'Verron').

Wernia Harray, Knarston: (see above).

West Ayre Sanday: coastal feature, Sellibister [Norse *eyrr* gravel spit].

West Lodge Sanday: the lodge for the mansion house of 'Geramount'.

West Shaird South Ronaldsay: [Scots *shaird* a small portion, of land in this case].

West Stove Sanday: [a corruption of 'West O': Norse *á* stream (compare 'Woo')].

Wester Birth Swona: refers to a big sea which strikes the west of the island at flood tide [Faroese *burður* drift of current].

Wester Bows Swona: submerged rocks [Norse *boði a* reef].

Westerbister Holm: [Norse *ból-staðr* farm].

Westermele St. Ola: [Norse *melr* sand].

Westermill/Westermeil Burray: (see above).

Westersands Deerness: formerly 'The Booth'.

Westness Rousay; North Ronaldsay: (see 'Vestness').

Westray A large productive island with imposing relics of Neolithic, Bronze Age and Norse settlements: Population 588 in 2021 [Norse *vestr* west, *ey* island].

Weyland St. Ola; Egilsay: [unlikely to have pagan associations: origin unknown].

Wha Taing Burray: [Swedish *hvaa* foam, probably related to 'Whass' above].

Whaas Geo South Ronaldsay: [Norse *hvass* a wind which whips up the sea].

Whal Brae Sanday: elevated land ['Whal' (as below), Scots *brae* elevation].

Whal Geo Sanday: coastal feature: nearby is the blow hole known as the 'Deed Man's Snore' [dialect *whal* 'whale', Norse *gjá* ravine].

Whal Head Sanday: field on 'Lopness Farm' which at one time had the skull of a whale positioned on it.

Whal Point Sanday: coastal feature (see 'Whal Geo' and 'Whal Brae') [these three 'whal' features are adjacent].

Whal's Back Sanday: coastal feature, shaped like a whale's back: there are at least three rocks of this name in Shetland.

Whale Geo Stronsay; Westray: [possibly trapped or stranded whales].

Whanclet Flotta: [Norse *klett* some kind of cell (see Appendix) 'whan' is probably a form of 'Wheean' (below)].

Wharth Flotta: [Norse *varða* a beacon but in Orkney in many cases such as this, 'mound' or elevation].

Wharvey Sanday, Airon: field name [Norse *hverfi* a cluster of houses].

Whasber Rousay, Skaebrae Head: [Norse *hvass* stormy sea whipped up by the wind, *berg* rock].

Whass Quoy South Ronaldsay: [the exposed part of the point of 'Manse Taing' was apparently a 'quoy' for sheep].

Wheean Evie: [Norse *kví-in* the enclosure].

Wheeawa Birsay, Housebay: [Norse *kví* enclosure: 'awa' element unknown].

Wheecanker, Pow o Birsay: between 'Twatt' and 'Ravie Hill' [Scots *pow* pool: (see 'Canker')].

Wheelbarrow Birsay, Swannay: [reason for this given name unknown].

Wheelco 1. Stenness: on top of Ireland road [a resting place for a cortège; each member of the party had to lay a stone there (see 'Wheelco', below)].

Wheelco 2. Harray/Birsay/Sandwick: that point where the three parishes meet: it was a resting place for a cortège on its way to St. Magnus Kirk in Birsay [Norse *hvíld* rest, *kví* enclosure, in this case a very small enclosure which surrounded a stone boundary mark which was removed during road widening].

Wheelcoupper Harray: [Norse *hvíld* (as above), *koppar* hollows].

Wheelie Creus Sanday: between 'Knowes' and 'Stove' [Norse *hvíld* (as above), *kró* enclosure].

Wheelie-Flaas Birsay, Nether Fea: [Norse *hvíld* (as above), *flag* a meadow].

Wheeling Cross Rendall, Gorseness Hill: [Norse *hvíld* (as above), exact location unknown, 'cross' = creus? (see above)].

Wheelingstone Westray, Aikerness: [stones marking the resting place (*hvíld*) for pall bearers].

Wheems, The Sanday: coastal feature [Norse *hvammr* grassy slope or hollow].

Wheenabreckan Birsay: Gelderhouse, Sabiston [Norse *kví-n* the enclosure, *brekka-n* the slope].

Wheenie-Feels Birsay, Housbay? [Norse *kví-n* the enclosure, 'feels' = fields].

Wheenifiold Birsay, Kirbister: [Norse *kví-n* the enclosure, *fjall* hill].

Wheenobrya Firth, Netherbigging: [Norse *kví-n* the enclosure, *breiðr* wide].

Wheetersinnins Firth, Redland: pasture land [Norse *hvítr* white, *sina* to dry: the derivation seems to mean 'bleached grass'].

Wheethamo Rousay: [literally 'white moor', referring to bog cotton].

Wheetie-Cole Birsay, Hayon: [origin of 'cole' uncertain].

Wheevie Sanday: [Norse *kví* enclosure, *vegr* road].

Whelkie Geo North Faray: (see below).

Whelkmullie Wyre: [English 'whelk', Norse *melr* sand].

Wheppa (see 'Wheppet' below).

Wheppet, Hole o Birsay: coast [Norse *hóp-it* the bay, a pool left on beach at low tide (compare 'Hubbet', Egilsay)].

Whesabreck Stromness: [position unknown: 'whesa' suggests Norse *hvass* a sharp wind, *brekka* slope].

Whey Geo Birsay; Westray: [English 'whey', referring to the churning of the sea in the geo].

Whilliastane Sandwick: near Doehouse: a stone marking the resting place of a funeral party [Norse *hvíld* rest, *stein* stone].

Whitelaw's Holm Birsay, Howally: [after the Whitelaw family who lived at 'Garthsetter'].

Whitelet Westray: [a corruption of 'Whitecleat'? (see above)].

Whitema Hill Eday: [dialect 'whitema' seagull].

Whitemill Bay Sanday: (see below).

Whitemill Skerry Sanday: [Norse *melr* sandbank, *sker* reef].

Whitemire Birsay, Swannay: [Norse *mýrr* moor].

Whitemire, Burn o Birsay: [Norse *hvít* white, *mýrr* moor: 'white' refers to leached soil or bog cotton].

Whitestane Burray: [Norse *steinn* stone: probably a boundary mark].

Whitestanes Shapinsay: a small, rocky promontory near 'Helliar Holm'.

Whitheber Eday: [Norse *veiða* to catch (fish), *berg* rock].

Whiting Point Fara: a point of flat rock [Norse *tangi* point].

Whome Rousay; Flotta; Stromness: [Norse *hvammr* a rounded valley].

Whomslie Stromness; Evie: [Norse *hvammr* a rounded valley, *hlíð* slope].

Whulyo Sand Rousay, Wasbister: [a small sandy beach suitable to draw up a 'whullyo', Orkney dialect for a boat of shallow draft, North English 'keel': in North Ronaldsay a similar boat known as a 'pram' is used].

Whunderless North Ronaldsay: [*hvannir* angelica: plants which were used as a kind of 'hops' in brewing ale (for 'less' see 'Lint-Lus')].

Whupland Sanday: another name for 'Braeswick' [Norse *hóp-it* the bay].

Whurligar Rousay: [Norse *hvirfill* a ring, presumably of flagstones to form a *garðr* enclosure].

Why Geo Rousay: [Norse *kví* enclosure, near a *gjá* ravine].

Wideford Farm St. Ola: [the name refers to the nearby bay, 'Wide Firth' [Norse *viðr* wide, *fjörðr* a bay].

Wideford Hill the second highest hill (after Ward Hill, Orphir) on The Mainland of Orkney, which must have been a beacon site ['wide' is a corruption of Norse *viti* a beacon: the 'ford' element is not easily explained unless it is a corruption of Norse *fjall*, hill: 'Wideford Hill' has no connection with 'Wideford Farm' which is some miles distant].

Widewall South Ronaldsay: [Norse *viðr* wide, *vágr* bay].

Wife's Geo Burray: [the figurehead of a woman from a wrecked vessel was washed up in this geo].

Wilderness Birsay, Beaquoy; Holm: [a Biblical allusion to a barren landscape].

Wilkie's Knowe Westray: mound near Pierowall [Norse *hvíld* rest, referring to pall bearers, *kví* enclosure (compare 'Whilco')].

Willie's Croo (see 'Hoistera', Evie).

Willow Park Sanday: field name (see *selja* another word for 'willow' in 'Sellyland', Burray).

Wind Wick South Ronaldsay: [Norse *vindr* wind, *vík* bay].

Windbreck Birsay, Abune-the-Hill, Marwick; Sandwick; North Ronaldsay; Graemsay; Flotta; Orphir; South Ronaldsay; Rousay: [Norse *vindr* wind in the meteorological sense, *brekka* slope].

Winderness Birsay, Northside, Fidgarth: [Norse *vind* to twist, *nes* a pointed shape of field].

Windi Geo South Ronaldsay: [Norse *vindr* wind, *gjá* ravine].

Windi Mire South Ronaldsay: [Norse *vindr* wind, *mýrr* moorland].

Windmill Papa Westray: south of the farm of Holland, vanished.

Windyha South Ronaldsay: [on an elevated 'windy' site].

Windywalls Westray, Aikerness; Graemsay; Harray; Orphir; Sanday; North Fara; Eday: [a draughty house].

Winehoose Sanday: [a nickname, originally 'Whinehoose', a reference to the 'whining' wind].

Wing, The Walls; South Ronaldsay: [Norse *vaengr* wing in the sense 'extended piece' (of land in this case), compare English 'wing' of a house].

Winksetter Harray: originally 'Wekinsetter' [Norse personal name *Víkingr*, Norse *setr* dwelling].

Winster's Waal a beautiful spring well said to possess healing properties. This may account for the name 'Helliwell' in Flotta, the location of which is unknown.

Winsters Flotta: ruined buildings on the north side of Pan Hope on Roan Head [said to be occupied by a man with the surname 'Winster' but there is no record of this surname anywhere in Britain [Norse *vindr* wind, *setr* a temporary summer shed].

Winter Noust Shapinsay: [Norse *naustr* winter boat shelter].

Wirk, The Rousay: Skaill, Westside: remains of an old fortification [Norse *virki* fort].

Withamo, Loch o Rousay: [Norse *hvít* white, *mýrr* moor: bleached white soil or bog cotton].

Withaquoy Holm: [Norse *hvít* white, *kví* enclosure].

Withigill Walls: a stream flowing into the 'Burn o Bailie Fea' [Norse *hvít* white, *gil* stream running in a narrow channel].

Witter, The Hoy; Walls; highest point on Flotta: [Norse *vitar* beacons].

Woo/Wool, Sanday; Westray; Evie; Rousay: [Norse *á* stream].

Woodhouse Sanday: [named after a 'Wood' family who lived there].

Woodwick Evie: [Norse *við* wood (driftwood), *vík* bay].

Work St. Ola: [Norse *virki* a fortification].

Workwell Orphir: [Norse *virki* a modest building, a word normally used to describe a stronghold, *völlr* field: (see 'Anderswick' in Stenness)].

Wrangleha Rendall; Birsay, Abune-the-Hill, Southside, Marwick: [English 'wrangle' to dispute, usually over land boundaries].

Wyre An island and site of 'Cubbie Roo's Castle': the population in 2011 was 18 [Norse *vigr* a spearhead, a placename which cannot be easily explained but it is not unique: there are islands in Norway and Iceland with this unusual name].

Y

Yairsay St. Ola: in Saverock area, vanished: earliest record is 'Yardshow' [Norse *jörd* enclosure, *haugr* mound].

Yamna(s) Birsay: sea marks off the Marwick coast [Norse *jafn* the same or equal: it is difficult to understand how *jafn* is applied here].

Yarpha Evie; Orphir; Deerness; South Ronaldsay; Sanday; Harray; Eday: [Norse *jörfi* sand or gravel soil which provides a poor peat].

Yarrow Park Sanday: (see 'Knowes o Yarrow').

Yarsdeels o Grew Birsay: a marshy area below the house of 'Grew' [Norse *jörd* enclosure, *deild* a division of land (in English plural)].

Yarso Rousay: (see 'Yairsay' above).

Yeldabreck Birsay, Southside; Burray: [Orkney dialect 'yeld' barren/unproductive (of land in this case) but also of animals, Norse *geldr* barren].

Yeldadee Sandwick: [(see 'yelda' above), *dý* marsh or moor].

Yeldavill Harray: [(see 'yelda' above), Norse *völlr* field].

Yernaseatter Stronsay: [Norse personal name *Jörundr* and *setr* dwelling].

Yesko, Knowe o Harray, Knarston: formerly a large mound containing a cist burial [corruption of Norse *hestr* horse, *kví* enclosure (see below)].

Yesnaby Sandwick: earlier 'Yescannabie' [Icelandic *skjá-n* the shed/protection, *bae* farm: as in the case of 'Hescombe' which was a shed/protection for a horse, Yesnaby must also be a protection for an animal, but no animal name in Norse can explain 'Yes'. It must be concluded that 'Yes' is a corruption of 'Hes', and the name Yesnaby has exactly the same origin as 'Hescombe'].

Yetnasteen Rousay: a large erect stone in a field above the Loch of Skokness [Norse *jötunn* giant, *stein* stone].

Yettna Geo Sandwick: [Norse *jötunn* giant, *gjá* ravine].

Yeulgars Harray, Knarston: field name [Orkney dialect 'Yule-girs' the plant 'meadow sweet': a part of this placename (such as *völlr* field) must be missing].

Yinstay St. Andrews; Firth (1653): [Norse personal name *Jóhan* and *staðr* estate].

Yonbell (Hill) Birsay: a mound on the south side of Marwick [named after the proprietor of the land (Jón Bellie) on which the mound stood: Oliver Bellie is recorded here in 1627].

Yorbrandisquoy/Brance South Ronaldsay: [Norse personal name *Brandr* and *jörd* land].

Yorsaltoun Deerness: [Norse *Jorsal* Jerusalem, *tún* farm: an extremely early use of a Biblical name to describe a dwelling].

Yorstan's Geo Sanday: the Orkney surname 'Yorston' appears in the early records of Sanday [Norse *gjá* ravine].

Youlday South Ronaldsay: (see 'Yeldady' above).

Z

Zion's Loan Firth: a road which takes its name from a cottage which at one time lay at the edge of the old Kirkwall/Stromness road near 'Cursiter Quarry' ['Zion' is another word for 'Jerusalem' but is sometimes used to apply to the whole of Israel].

Appendix

Geo/Goe

A geo is a ravine. Sometimes the initial 'g' of 'geo' is pronounced and transcribed as 'd', which can make interpretation more difficult.

In Orkney, geos are found on the coast, but the word is also used for features inland, where there are certainly no ravines. This has puzzled etymologists, who have found no solution to the problem. These inland geos are often found in the spelt form 'goe', which suggests that we should be looking for another word.

The answer to our difficulty lies on the island of Flotta, where a vanished house, 'Lingo', had the alternative name, 'Lingall'. We must assume that the house was named after the land on which it stood, in which case, 'Go' here is a metaphorical use of Old Norse *gall*, English 'gall'. In other words, the land in this area is 'gall like'. A good illustration of this word is found in Shetland dialect where 'golgrav' describes a urine channel in a byre. In the landscape, 'gol' means 'marsh'. It does not carry this meaning in Old Norse but in Middle High German, 'gole' was a marsh. In modern German, 'galle' is a marshy place in a field. Norse *gall* is neuter so 'the marsh' becomes *gall-it*. Since in Orkney placenames the final 'it' is pronounced as if it were 'ith', a marshy area near the Marwick coast in Birsay becomes 'Gyollath'. Frequently, the double 'l' is missing, which helps us to explain Guithe in Harray and Helziegitha on the island of Wyre.

Klett/Cleat

A *klett* in Norse is a rock found on or near the shore. Inland, however, the word in early days was sometimes spelt *klaet*: in fact, in a document published in Norse in 1329, there was a *Klaete* in South Ronaldsay. Another good example comes from the parish of Sandwick where the farm of Linklater (as shown by the first recording of the surname) was originally referred to as Lingklaet. The fact that this word appears in South Ronaldsay and Sandwick shows that initially its use was widespread. With the arrival of the Scots, the initial 'k' was changed to 'c' and medieval scribes, not being familiar with the dipthong 'ae', changed it to 'ea', with the result that before long, 'Klaet' became 'Cleat', or merely 'Clett'.

So, what was a cleat? One of the most famous chapels in Orkney and a great centre of pilgrimage was the Chapel of Cleat in Sanday. Throughout Orkney, all Cleat farms have associations with ancient chapels and the area in which the chapels were situated paid an extraordinary amount of tax. At first sight, a 'cleat' must be a chapel. This seems confirmed by two Shetland placenames — Prestieclett, 'priest clett' and Mongraclett, 'monks clett'. In the parish of Sandwick is a ruinous house called (Nether) Benzieclett. The first element is Norse *baena* to pray, and so Benzieclett is the exact equivalent of Norse *baena-hús* a chapel. The name 'Benziecot', apparently a variation of Benzieclett, is found in Westray, Sanday and Rousay. It was obviously not necessary to have any stone structure in or at which to pray since there was a mound near Housebay in Stronsay called Benni Cuml, *baena-kuml*, a cairn. There are others such as Benistay, *baena-stöð*, prayer place in Sanday and Benzieroth in Firth. It is pronounced 'Binyaroo', which helps to explain its Norse origin as *baena-hrúga* a prayer cairn.

A broch in Harray is worth mentioning in this case. It is called Netlater but originally named Noltclett. It would have been a place of prayer but in its degraded state a shelter for 'naut' or cattle. The word 'clett' was adopted in Gaelic for stone corbelled houses, similar to those in St. Kilda, where they were used for storing dried meat from seabirds. It was also used for chambered cairns in the Western Isles, e.g., Steinaclete and Breasclete, both near Stornoway. Lastly, we turn our attention to the name Whiteclet. It means what it says — a white place where one can pray. At their lowest level, they would have been lime-washed stones, but they could also have been Whitechapels — a placename known in both Scotland and England. St. Ninian called his own settlement in Wigtownshire, *Candida Casa*, Latin for 'white house'.

Knowe

In their detailed study of features of archaeological interest in Orkney published in 1946, the Royal Commission on Ancient Monuments noted that there were

60 'knowes' in the islands; the writer has added 22 from other named sources, to bring the number up to 82.

The word 'knowe', meaning 'knoll', was introduced by the Scots and replaced the Norse word *haugr*, mound, a word not familiar to the Scots. The Norse word persisted in many cases and where there were distinctive mounds, the nearby settlement would be called How, Howan (meaning 'the mound') or Howar if there were two mounds in the vicinity. In some cases, it can be seen that a mound is described in both Norse and Scots, a good example being the Knowe o Aiverso in Papa Westray, where 'knowe' is Scots, 'aiver' is Norse *álfar* 'elves' and the final 'o' represents Norse *haugr*! The reader will notice that many of the mounds listed below end in 'o' which letter represents Norse *haugr*.

It is not practical to list these mounds in detail and therefore the approach of the Royal Commission on Ancient Monuments is adopted and explanations of the name of the mounds are found in the general glossary.

Aiverso; Angerow; Backiskaill; Bain; Bakitaing; Bakkan Swarto; Bea; Bosquoy; Buckquoy; Burland; Merrigar; Burristae; Burrian; Coynear; Crue; Crustan; Cuean; Dale Birsay and Rousay; Cott; Cottorochan; Desso; Dishero; Enyan (The); Esco; Euro; Eversty; Flaws; Forsakelda; Gairso; Garroquoy; Gemashowe; Geoso; Goltsquoy; Gorn; Hamar; Hammar; Holland; Hooan/Howan; Hucklin; Hunclett; Ingacoup; Lairo; Lingro; Links Park; Lyron. Makerhouse; Mayback; Midgarth; Moan; Nisthouse; Netherskaill; Newark; Onston; Queeancrusty; Queen o Howe; Ramsay; Redland; Ryo; Samilands; Saverough; Scartan/Hillhead; Scogar; Scorn; Scottie; Skulzie; Smirrus; Steeringlo; Stenso; Sunloft; Smersso; Trinnawin; Trotty; Wheatlaws; Yarrow; Yesco; Yonbell.

The Loons

The name 'loon' presents great difficulty in explaining. It has a Celtic explanation, but it also has a Norse explanation. Celtic *lòn* is 'marsh' and Norwegian (Nynorsk) *lôn* is 'marsh' or more specifically 'water meadow'. The best, general translation is 'marsh'. The word is usually written in plural form as in the case above.

Lin

Where placenames begin with 'lin' they relate to water features. The names derive from Celtic *linne* pool. There are many examples in the glossary. A good example is 'Linnieth' in Harray, which shows a neuter definite article as a suffix and hints that 'lin' was adopted into Norse. This name must not be confused with Norse *lyng* heather.

Maeshowe

In most cases, the 'maes' element in Orkney placenames relate to Norse *messa*, i.e., Roman Catholic mass, so they have a connection in one way or another to a religious service. In fact, in obsolete dialect, 'mass' means 'kirk' or earlier, 'chapel'. Let us take as an example, the farm of Curcabreck in Harray. The name means 'chapel slope'. Despite the name, there is no chapel there now but there is a farm by the name Maesquoy, where religious groups would have met. A pathway leading to the old Orphir chapel (the Round Church) is called the Masy Gate, where 'gate' is Norse *gata* path. It seems that formerly in Orkney, 'mass' was pronounced 'maes'/'mess', the best example being the farm of 'Messigate' in Tankerness, where a path would have led to the chapel of St. John. There are also 'Messigate' placenames in Birsay, Papa Westray and North Ronaldsay.

We have to conclude that the meaning of Maeshowe is that it was in the vicinity of this mound that masses were held, until a church was built about 400 yards (365 metres) to the west. This is not the present church, but an ancient church of unusual design, the foundation of which was revealed after an archaeological investigation.

Man

It is extremely difficult to explain the origin of the 'man' element in Orkney placenames. 'Man' cannot be explained in Norse or Celtic, but the meaning of the element is easily explained by deduction. Let us give the simplest example. As part of the brewing process, bere was soaked in a large vat to make malt. Now, in Orkney, any word in which a 't' follows an 'l', the 'l' is frequently missed out, e.g., a sat backie (salt container) used to hang on the wall of the old Orkney house.

Returning to malt, not every house had a vat big enough to steep the grain, but if there happened to be a stream nearby, especially one that had a deep pool in it, this provided an ideal alternative. At Nabban in Firth (near Bridgend) there was one such pool. It was called Matman. On the southeast coast of St. Catherine's Bay, Stronsay, there was a deep pool called Matpow. 'Man' seems to mean 'deep' pool in some language or other, perhaps pre-Celtic? These deep holes were often found in marshy places. Take for example, Deasman in Innertoon, Stromness. 'Deas' is represented by Norse *dý* which is almost always written in the plural form 'Dees', so 'Deasman' is a deep hole in this locality. In the singular form 'Daman' is found in Mirbister in Harray. In Rousay, there is a place on the Sourin Burn called 'Man o Finyie'. 'Finyie' is Norse *fen* marsh. In Netherbrough in Harray, a deep pool in the burn (stream) there is called the Pow o Oman where the 'O' of Oman represents Norse *á* stream. At the edge of the Loch of Hundland, there is a well known as The Well o Oman. This name should not be confused with the Orkney surname Omand which has never been recorded in this area. On the Netherbrough Burn, there is a deep pool called 'The Forses o Mananeban', i.e., the 'rapids' of Mananeban. Manclett in Walls stood originally in a marshy area but today there is no evidence of a deep pool there.

Quoy

It means 'enclosure' — which in Orkney can be a very small area, approximately 3 x 3 metres, or it can be a large area encompassing half a parish. Its origin lies in Norse *kví* pen and in its Icelandic home was usually associated with milking sheep. There are many problems with this name which lie in its orthography. Since there is no initial 'kv' in Scots, 'qu' was adopted instead, hence the form 'quoy', but there was further confusion with the adoption of a 'qu' form, since 'qu' can itself be pronounced 'wh'. Take this example: there was a quarry in Birsay, Northside, which produced flat roofing slates. When I came to Birsay, I was told by a local man that the slates on my roof had come from the 'Whys o the Hill'. I could not understand this at first until I realised that 'Whys' was another form of 'Quoys'.

'Quoy' often appears in the form 'Queena' or 'Cuean'. This is because it has the definite article 'the' attached to it, and the definite article always comes at the end of the word. The plural of *kví* is *kví*ar, which appears in Orkney placenames as Quoyer or Quoire, and several are written 'Queer'. Perhaps the oddest form in which 'Quoy' appears is 'co' or 'cow'. See 'Hacco' as an example of this. Resting places (Norse *hvíld*) for coffin bearers — which must have been very small areas, were almost invariably called 'quoy', and took the ending 'co'. An especially good example of this is the stone which marked the meeting place of the parishes of Harray, Birsay and Sandwick, and also served as a resting place for a funeral party. Unfortunately, this stone was removed in road widening, but the name 'Whilco' is retained in the surrounding area to the east. When a group of new houses were built in the area, it was unfortunate that the spelling 'Quilco' was adopted.

References

Commissariot Record of Orkney and Shetland 1611–1684

Ordnance Survey Name Books, 1879–1880

Orkney Land Tax Roll 1653

Records of the Earldom of Orkney, 1299–1614

Rentals of the Ancient Earldom and Bishoprick of Orkney: Alexander Peterkin (Uthell Book)

Royal Commission on the Ancient Monuments of Scotland: Vol. II, Orkney

Bain, Alexander *An Etymological Dictionary of the Gaelic Language*

Ben, Joe *Descriptio Insularum Orchadiarum*

Bichan, Mary, Spence, Sheila, *Harray Orkney's Inland Parish*

Cleasby, Vigfusson and Craigie *An Icelandic-English Dictionary*

Clouston, J. S. *Proceedings of the Orkney Antiquarian Society*

Firth, John *Reminiscences of an Orkney Parish*

Guðmundsson, Finnbogi *Orkneyinga Saga*

Jakobsen, Jakob *The Placenames of Shetland*

Lamb, Gregor *Naggles o Pipittem, the Placenames of Sanday*

Lamb, Gregor *Orcadiana, Portraits of the Past*

Lamb, Gregor *Testimony of the Orkneyingar*

Lamb, Gregor *The Placenames of South Ronaldsay and Burray*

Maclennan, Malcolm *Gaelic Dictionary*

Macleod, Banks *British Calendar Customs, Orkney and Shetland*

Marwick, Ernest *The Folklore of Orkney and Shetland*

Marwick, Hugh *Orkney Farm Names*

Marwick, Hugh *The Placenames of Birsay*

Marwick, Hugh *The Placenames of Rousay*

Proulx, Annie *Fen, Bog and Swamp*

Sandness, Berit *From Starafjall to Starling Hill*

Torp, Alf *Nynorsk Etymologisk Ordbook*

About the Author

Gregor Lamb was born on a farm cottage at Binscarth, Firth, attending Firth School and Stromness Academy. He was a double Honours Graduate, in Geography at the University of Edinburgh and Education at the University of Aberdeen. After teaching in England and Scotland, and lecturing in education at teacher training colleges, Gregor returned to Orkney in 1974 as Headmaster of Stenness School.

Gregor has always been fascinated by Orkney's heritage and has published many books, from language studies to wartime aviation. This book is the result of research done during the Covid-19 lockdown, culminating in the most comprehensive study of Orkney's placenames to date.

www.ingramcontent.com/pod-product-compliance
Lightning Source LLC
Chambersburg PA
CBHW041303110526
44590CB00028B/4230